PRAISE FOR *BASELESS*

"A luminous meditation on the power of secrets and mysteries. Baker shows us the ways in which a government shielded by a bodyguard of lies threatens the foundations of democracy." —Tim Weiner, Pulitzer Prize–winning author of *Legacy of Ashes* and *The Folly and the Glory*

"The book follows a circadian rhythm of file requests, denials, archive visits, and attempts at dot-connecting, punctuated by dog walks and Baker's puttering around his Maine home. That structure gives the book a sweetly personal feel; no book about FOIA may be more accessible to a layperson." —Mark Athitakis, *The Washington Post*

"Engaging, bracing, and moving . . . Ultimately, what is so compelling about *Baseless* is not the prosecutorial brief. It's watching Baker, a thoughtful, sensitive, and vividly expressive soul, grapple with the pathological secrecy of his own government and with the heinousness of what he suspects it has done." —Daniel Immerwahr, *The New Republic*

"Staggeringly good . . . *Baseless* includes many tangents, all of them worthwhile." —David Swanson, *Counterpunch*

"Baker isn't just writing about cold war history and transparency. He's also implicitly posing a set of intertwined questions about life and art: How are we to conceptualize the coexistence of the secrecy-shrouded horrors of modern war with all of our world's little delights? Can writing help us feel our way toward some answers? . . . Every time Baker swerves from government-funded, classification-shrouded dreams of mass infection to his dogs, he creates a visceral reminder of what should be obvious: that all these phenomena exist in the same world. Our world. This modest-sounding payoff is actually quite startling in practice; again and again, reading *Baseless*, it hit me like a little electric jolt. This is about more than pointing toward wrongs: there's a suggestion, too, that we often file these wrongs—and our longstanding uncertainty about them—in the incorrect psycho-cultural boxes, where they become impossible to truly process." —Peter C. Baker, *New York Review of Books*

"A double thriller of sorts, artfully weaving together two distinct stories . . . Baker is an engaging writer, and *Baseless* is a gripping book." —Michael Sherry, *The American Scholar*

"The synchronicity is extraordinary, almost chilling: Nicholson Baker's gripping diary of his endless attempts to ferret out facts relating to the Pentagon's top-secret biological weapons programs is published while the whole world is suddenly upended and aghast amid a lethal biological attack of an apparently natural origin. I say *apparently natural* for as every page of this book is peppered with tales of bizarre weapons—infected feathers, for God's sake! plague-saturated voles!—you come away doubting everything the U.S. government ever says. And yet, through it all, Baker tells us with a meticulous diarist's calm about his dogs and the Maine countryside and the birdsong, and you feel, in the end, everything will be all right, and germ-free." —Simon Winchester, author of
The Man Who Loved China and
The Professor and the Madman

"One of America's most brilliantly creative writers navigates the mirrored labyrinth of government secrecy with a combination of astonishment and rage. Along the way, he discovers an array of long-hidden terrors while balancing the joys of daily life against the dread that envelops all who confront the reality of covert power." —Stephen Kinzer, author of
*Poisoner in Chief: Sidney Gottlieb and
the CIA Search for Mind Control*

"The leading villains in Baker's saga, which he aptly describes as 'a sort of case study, or diary, or daily meditation, on the pathology of government secrecy,' are the Air Force, Army, and CIA, and his disclosures are rarely banal but rather consistently provocative and disturbing. Using both direct and circumstantial evidence, the author suggests that illegal weapons have been used against North Korea and perhaps against so-called enemy forces in other nations. Readers should be impressed by Baker's persistence, and most will end up charmed, however obliquely, by his obsessions." —*Kirkus Reviews*

"Gripping . . . This flowing account reveals the dark side of wartime strategies clouded by denials of FOIA requests. It will fascinate Cold War–era historians and readers concerned about access to government information."

—*Library Journal*

"Written with bemused fascination and occasional outrage . . . this lucid yet freewheeling narrative unearths much queasy detail about biological weapons and their promoters. The result is a colorful, engrossing recreation of a sinister history—and a convincing case for opening government archives to public scrutiny." —*Publishers Weekly*

PENGUIN BOOKS

BASELESS

Nicholson Baker is the author of ten novels and six works of nonfiction, including *The Anthologist*, *The Mezzanine*, and *Human Smoke*. He has won a National Book Critics Circle Award, a Hermann Hesse Prize, a Guggenheim fellowship, and a Katherine Anne Porter Award from the American Academy of Arts and Letters. He lives in Maine with his wife, Margaret Brentano.

Baseless

My Search for Secrets
in the Ruins of the
Freedom of Information Act

NICHOLSON BAKER

Penguin Books

PENGUIN BOOKS
An imprint of Penguin Random House LLC
penguinrandomhouse.com

First published in the United States of America by Penguin Press,
an imprint of Penguin Random House LLC, 2020
Published in Penguin Books 2021

ISBN 9780735215764 (paperback)

THE LIBRARY OF CONGRESS HAS CATALOGED THE HARDCOVER EDITION AS FOLLOWS

Names: Baker, Nicholson, author.
Title: Baseless : my search for secrets in the ruins of the Freedom
of Information Act / Nicholson Baker.
Other titles: My search for secrets in the ruins of the Freedom of Information Act
Description: New York : Penguin Press, 2020. |
Includes bibliographical references and index.
Identifiers: LCCN 2019043384 (print) | LCCN 2019043385 (ebook) |
ISBN 9780735215757 ; (hardcover) | ISBN 9780735215771 ; (ebook)
Subjects: LCSH: Biological weapons—United States—History. |
Biological warfare—Research—United States. | Intelligence service—United States—
History. | United States. Freedom of Information Act. | Official secrets—United States.
| Government information—United States. | Cold War.
Classification: LCC UG447.8 .B28 2020 (print) | LCC UG447.8 (ebook) |
DDC 358/.3880973—dc23
LC record available at https://lccn.loc.gov/2019043384
LC ebook record available at https://lccn.loc.gov/2019043385

Printed in the United States of America
1st Printing

Book design by Daniel Lagin

Contents

Introduction

This book, which I began working on about ten years ago, grew out of a seemingly simple question. Did the United States use biological weapons during the early 1950s? Use them, I mean, not in laboratories in Frederick, Maryland, or in the deserts of Utah, but in foreign countries, on people whom the United States government viewed as enemies? I had a suspicion, back in 2009, that the answer was yes, but I wanted to know for sure.

So I did what one does when one wants to find out more about any episode of history: I read books and research papers, following their endnotes to available government documents, and I interviewed people. As I got in deeper, fascinated, sometimes horrified, I scrolled through Air Force microfilms, read oral histories, collected Chinese propaganda pamphlets, visited academic libraries that held manuscript collections, and spent weeks—no, actually months, all together—at the National Archives, the Truman Library, the Eisenhower Library, the Army Heritage and Education Center in Carlisle, Pennsylvania, and the Library of Congress. Because I carried around with me one unanswered question, all these repositories came alive. Newspaper collections spoke to me in a new way.

I loved the quest, at first—the endlessness of the quest, the infinitude of names and dates and plans and scientific research programs. One question broke open and led to another and another, and formerly dull-seeming tidbits of history glowed like fresh cherry tomatoes in the picnic salad of the twentieth century.

Eventually, in 2012, I made some requests under the Freedom of Information Act for Air Force documents that I knew existed but were inaccessible to regular people, people without a security clearance. And I waited. I got nothing. Really, nothing. I wrote a novel about a poet, a sex novel, a book of essays, and a book about being a substitute teacher. Presidents came and went. And still I waited. This was disheartening. I made more requests—from the CIA, the Air Force, and the Army. Still got nothing. I began to suspect that although I'd learned a fair amount by then about the Cold War—in fact, I knew some possibly startling things that nobody else knew—I might grow old and die without seeing extant memos and plans that were material to the basic question I was trying to answer.

I tried to write the book anyway. It grew and grew. I produced thousands of pages of notes and chronologies. The increasing prospect tired my wandering eyes, as Alexander Pope said of research: "Hills peep o'er hills, and Alps on Alps arise." You can spend a lifetime—some have—comparing and contrasting partially censored CIA plans for sabotage and subversion, or studying germ-warfare programs in Japan, in Britain, in Canada, and in the United States during the Second World War, which was the seedbed of many of the biomedical extravagancies of the Cold War. Wherever I started—say, in February 1952—there was always something before that moment that needed to be explained, and that something led to another perplexity that had preceded the one that I was trying to understand, so that I kept being pushed backward in time when I was trying to go forward. The boxes of documents crumpled; the book piles toppled; the Post-it notes that fringed them turned pale in the sun. What I knew was getting old.

Because I didn't want to go around forever with this mass of silently rotting knowledge in my head, I got the idea of writing a somewhat different, although related, book: one about life under the Freedom of Information Act, using my own unfinished quest for Cold War truth as a point of departure. After several false starts, in March 2019, I abandoned chronological succession and just wrote, every day, about what I knew, and didn't know, and what I needed to know, concerning a now remote but still crucially important stretch of American history. The result is a sort of case history, or diary, or daily meditation, on the pathology of government secrecy.

This is a book about waiting—waiting for responses from the Air Force and the Central Intelligence Agency and other places. It's about my own not entirely successful efforts to squeeze germs of truth from the sanitized documentary record of the U.S. government. It's about the exquisite pain of whited-out or blacked-out sentences and paragraphs—always the ones you want most to see—and the costs to national self-understanding of delayed disclosure. It's about the frustration of knowing that a document exists just steps away, on the other side of a wall in the National Archives, and yet you can't see it because it's supposedly so sensitive that its release would rend the flaggy fabric of national security. It's about the tick of time going by, as old secrets snicker in their file boxes. The seeming uselessness and toothlessness of the Freedom of Information Act. The "redactions"—that awful word. The blotted-out key phrase in a paragraph that turns it from something with meaning to something that means nothing. The back-and-forth of politely exasperated correspondence.

Since it's a diary, I've allowed into this book some of what traditional histories leave out: the writer's daily chairbound scene, the flummoxing overload of specificity, dreams, the weather, dogs, food. I've written about the work of some of the lawyers and journalists and assorted unsung heroes who have devoted their lives to hunting and gathering and forcing disclosures in governmental repositories. And I've included much of the germ-war story, too, because I can't not include it: America's disease-dispersing biobureaucracy is what I've been studying, on and off, for a decade, and by now I've reached certain conclusions, despite the incompleteness of the paper record. Every so often, as you'll see, I submit a new Freedom of Information Act request, or a new Mandatory Declassification Review request, and explain why it might be helpful to be able to read a certain document. Whether or not you agree with my account of what happened, I'm hoping that you will be shocked and revolted—and sometimes inspired—by some of the activities I describe in this book. I hope you'll read it and say, No, that's not acceptable. That can't be allowed to happen ever again.

Baseless was a long time coming, and I'm relieved to have finally gotten it done. Thank you, Ann Godoff, Sarah Hochman, David Rosenthal, and Melanie Jackson, for getting me to write it. Thank you, Casey Denis and Jane Cavolina, for overseeing publication. And thank you, Guggenheim Foundation, for giving me breathing room. The book is dedicated to my dear family, whom I love beyond treetops.

"FOIA." That vowelly word stands for a great law, the Freedom of Information Act, which Congressman John Moss finally got passed in 1966, after years of struggle. It deserves to be better understood—and strengthened. Or at least enforced. Secrecy is killing us.

March 9, 2019, Saturday

In 2012, when I was hopeful and curious and middle-aged and eager for Cold War truth, I sent a letter to the National Archives, requesting, under the provisions of the Freedom of Information Act, copies of twenty-one still-classified Air Force memos from the early 1950s. Some of the memos had to do with a Pentagon program that aimed to achieve "an Air Force-wide combat capability in biological and chemical warfare at the earliest possible date." This program, which began and ended during the Korean War, was given a code name: Project Baseless. It was assigned priority category I, as high as atomic weapons.

All twenty-one of these memos, numbered and cross-referenced, still exist, stored at the National Archives' big building in College Park, Maryland—but they are inaccessible to researchers like me. At some point a security officer removed them from their original brown or dark green Air Force file folders—where they'd been stored alongside thousands of other, often fascinating documents that are now declassified and available to the public—and locked them in a separate place in the College Park building, in a SCIF, or Sensitive Compartmented Information Facility, where only people with security clearances can go. In place of the actual documents, the security officer inserted pieces of stiff yellow cardboard that say "Security-Classified Information" and "ACCESS RESTRICTED."

After filing the FOIA request, I waited. A month later I got a letter from David Fort, a supervisory archives specialist at the National Archives' National Declassification Center. Fort said that my request letter had been received and that it now had a number, NW 37756. "Pursuant to 5 USC 552(a)(6)(B)(iii)(III), if you have requested information that is classified, it will be necessary to send copies of the documents to appropriate agencies for further review," Fort wrote. "We will notify you as soon as all review is complete."

After that came months of silence. A year went by. Then two. In May 2014, David Fort, now deputy director of the Freedom of Information division at the National Archives, wrote me an email. "Periodically our office contacts researchers with requests older than 18 months to see if they are still interested in us processing their requests," he said. "If I do not hear back from you in 35 business days I will assume you are no longer interested and we will close your request."

I wrote back that I was definitely still interested, and I asked Fort why it was taking so long. "Unfortunately," he replied, "because of the large number of cases we receive there is a large delay in being able to process requests."

In June 2016 I asked for another update. "We sent your documents out for a declassification review back in August 2014 and are still waiting for agencies to get back to us with determinations," Fort wrote. "As soon as that happens we can send you the documents."

ISN'T IT AGAINST THE LAW for government agencies to delay their responses to FOIA requests? Yes, it is: the mandated response time in the law is twenty days, not including Saturdays, Sundays, and holidays, and if one agency must consult with another agency before releasing a given document, the consultation must happen "with all practicable speed." And yet there is no speed. There is, on the contrary, a deliberate Pleistocenian ponderousness. Some responses, especially from intelligence agencies, come back after a ten-year wait. The National Archives has pending at least one FOIA request that is twenty-five years old. "Old enough to rent a car," said the National Security Archive, a group at George Washington University that works to get documents declassified.

So what should I do? Write more letters? Sue the Air Force? Sue the National Archives? Give up? Do these particular Pentagon memos even matter, when there are many thousands of declassified Korean War–era documents readily available to historians?

I did the simplest thing. I sent another email to David Fort. "Hi David—I hope all is well with you. I'm still hoping to see the twenty-one Air Force documents I requested in March 2012 (NW 37756). Seven years ago." I deleted the words "seven years ago." Then I typed them again. Seven *years* I've waited. I sent it.

For good measure, I also sent another email to David (who is a nice man) asking for information on a different request, a Mandatory Declassification Review that I'd submitted in March 2017. A Mandatory Declassification Review request, or MDR, is subject to different rules than a Freedom of Information Act request, and it can move along faster, or so I've heard. "Hi David—This MDR (# 57562, for two Air Force RG 341 documents from 1950) is now close to two years old. What should I do? Many thanks Nick B."

YESTERDAY MY WIFE, M., and I got two middle-aged, very small dachshunds from the Bangor Humane Society—possibly stepbrothers, one with long hair and one with short hair. They whimper and yowl and wag their tails so hard they make bonging sounds against the oven door. They're rescue dogs. M. saw them on the Humane Society website.

March 10, 2019, Sunday

The two dogs slept in our bedroom last night. The cat, Minerva, is getting used to them. It was so cold outside at six this morning that one of the dogs, Cedric, simply stopped walking in the middle of the street. He wouldn't move. I had to carry his shivering self home, while the other dog, whom we're thinking of calling Brindle, or Briney, or Bryn, trotted along next to me.

This afternoon, I heard back from David Fort. Kind of him to respond on a Sunday. He's in an awkward position, caught in the middle, with impatient inquirers like me on one side and huge, self-protective government agencies on the other. I interviewed him in the lobby of the National Archives Building in College Park two years ago. "What I tell researchers is we're in a bind," he said. "The National Archives has no legal authority to declassify records—with the exception of some State Department records if they're prior to 1950." Fort, who wears plaid shirts and is writing a book about the Battle of Bladensburg in the War of 1812, has reduced the backlog of open FOIA requests at the Archives. He tells his staff to be communicative with researchers. "There's a lot of frustration out there," he said. "All we can do is say we agree with you."

The Air Force is causing the holdup now, not the National Archives, but the National Archives, which has taken physical possession of the documents, is the point of contact. Fort said in his email that the Air Force is "the worst" at responding to declassification requests. In my experience, the Central Intelligence Agency is the worst. But neither of them are abiding by the law.

Let me explain why, out of the millions of pages of military records from the 1950s, these twenty-one withdrawn memos might matter. It's not only because any document that a government takes special pains to keep away from historians, using a yellow access-restricted card, is likely to be revealing in some way. It's also because these documents in particular may help answer one of the big unresolved questions of the Cold War: Did the United States covertly employ some of its available biological weaponry—bombs packed with fleas and mosquitoes and disease-dusted feathers, for instance—in locations in China and Korea?

THE PENTAGON INSTITUTED its secret crash program in germ-warfare readiness in the fall of 1950; six months later, in May 1951, North Korea's foreign minister, Pak Hon-yong (variously spelled Pak Hen En and Park Hun-young), made a formal complaint to the United Nations, announcing "a new monstrous crime of the American interventionists." During their rapid retreat from North Korea, Minister Pak alleged, U.S. troops had deliberately spread smallpox.

The American press barely noticed. "Foe Charges Use of Bacteria" was the May 9, 1951, headline of a tiny United Press wire service article, printed on an inner page of *The New York Times*, surrounded by ads for budget shoes from John Wanamaker, nylon robes from Gimbels, and Mother's Day hats from Bloomingdale's. "The Communist North Korean government demanded today that General of the Army Douglas MacArthur and Lieut. Gen. Matthew B. Ridgway be tried as war criminals for using 'bacteriological warfare' in the Korean War." That was all it said. The next day, a brief story in the *New York Herald Tribune*, republished in *The Washington Post*, began: "A charge that U.N. forces employed bacteriological warfare in North Korea, which caused 3500 smallpox cases between January and April, 10 percent fatal, was filed here today by the North Korean Communist Foreign Minister, Pak Hen En."

The charge was not lightly made, and it deserved more coverage. Minister Pak had sent a long cablegram to the United Nations, where he had no standing, because only the South Korean half of that artificially divided country was allowed to be a member of the General Assembly. What Pak said was that the Americans, with the help of the Japanese, had spread an epidemic disease—he called it smallpox—during their retreat late in 1950. "It has been established by medical experts that the American troops retreating from North Korea in December last year resorted to spreading smallpox infection amongst the population of the areas of North Korea temporarily occupied by them, trying by this means to spread a smallpox epidemic to the troops of the People's Army and Chinese volunteers," he said. Outbreaks of the epidemic had flared simultaneously in Pyongyang and several other provinces "seven or eight days after their liberation from the American occupation." By mid-April, Pak said, there were more than 3,500 smallpox cases, and 10 percent of patients were dying. "Areas which have not been occupied by the Americans have had no cases of smallpox," he said, and he charged that on General MacArthur's orders, the mass production of bacteriological agents had been carried out in Japan. "It has been reported in the press that MacArthur's staff spent 1,500,000 yen on the manufacture of the bacteriological weapon, having selected the Japanese government as intermediary in the placing of orders." This was a sign, Pak said, of the bankruptcy of the U.S. ruling circles' aggressive adventurist policy. The Americans believed that they would undermine the Korean people, but they had miscalculated. "Criminal methods of war do not intimidate the freedom-loving Korean people and will not save the American interventionists from inevitable defeat."

American authorities "flatly denied" the charges, according to the Associated Press, attributing the epidemic to an ineffective disease prevention program.

IN FEBRUARY 1952, Foreign Minister Pak charged that the Americans were at it again. "According to precise information of the command of the

Korean People's Army and the Chinese People's Volunteers," Pak said on the radio on February 22, 1952, "the American aggressive troops with effect from January 28 of this year have been systematically dropping a large number of infected insects from aircraft on to our troop positions on our rear, and these insects are spreading the bacteria of infectious diseases." The American imperialists were, according to Pak, "waging bacteriological warfare in our country on a wide scale," and they were doing so with the help of Japanese "myrmidons," whose crimes were known to the world.

The Associated Press briefly covered Pak's speech. "North Korea's foreign minister has accused United Nations forces of raining 'fleas, lice, bugs, ants, grasshoppers and spiders' onto North Korea," the article said, as reprinted in the *New York Herald Tribune* on February 23, 1952. "The Communist premier said former Japanese generals who were known to be specialists in germ warfare are assisting Americans in Korea." United Press covered the speech at greater length, saying that the North Koreans claimed that "deadly insects" were dropped on nine flights between January 28 and February 17. United Press identified the insects as "black flies, fleas, and bed bugs," which delighted an editor at the *Waterloo Daily Courier*, in Waterloo, Iowa (home of a large John Deere tractor factory), who put the story on the front page: "Reds Claim U.S. Planes Drop Bed Bugs." Some versions of the UP article carried an added paragraph: "The claim recalled Communist charges of more than a year ago that U.S. planes dropped potato bugs on Czechoslovakia to destroy crops." The insects were wrapped in paper bags or paper tubes, the Communists claimed.

From there the accusations grew in volume—gradually at first, but rising to an amazing steady onslaught, a "torrent of propaganda," as United Press called it. On February 25, 1952, Chinese prime minister Chou En-lai charged that President Truman had ordered the germ-warfare attacks. "Refusing to acknowledge their defeat, during the course of the talks the American imperialists are, on the one hand, making use of all kinds of shameful delaying tactics with the aim of preventing the success of the talks, and on the other, are conducting a cruel, inhuman bacteriological war," Chou said. The Americans were trying to extend and prolong the

Korean War, he said, and they sought to destroy the People's Republic. "In the name of the Chinese people, before the peoples of the whole world, I accuse the government of the United States of the criminal use of bacteriological weapons in violation of all principles of humanity."

 Initially *The New York Times* ignored this second round of charges, as if the editors had made a decision not to publicize such absurdities, but on February 25, 1952, the *Times* gave it a paragraph on page 2, reprinting an Associated Press version of the story: "The Peiping radio continued last night its new and violent accusations that the United States was using germ warfare in North Korea. Allied officers consider it possible that the Communists are plagued by epidemics and are trying to account for these to their own people." (Peiping is Beijing.)

On this same day, February 25, 1952, at a meeting of the Central Intelligence Agency, Frank Wisner, director of covert operations, gave a report to Allen Dulles and other department heads on the progress of an unspecified "deception matter." Two whited-out paragraphs follow shortly afterward. (CIA redactionists now mostly use white rectangles, rather than black rectangles, to withhold lines of text.) Also on this day, February 25, the Joint Chiefs of Staff approved the Joint Advanced Study Committee's recommendations on biological warfare. The committee recommended that the United States "be prepared to employ BW whenever it is militarily advantageous." "This action removed BW from its unfortunate association with the 'retaliation only' policy which governs CW," said a later memo. General Hoyt Vandenberg, chief of the Air Force, wrote an upbeat assessment of biowar prospects. "The research and development program is being expedited," he said, "and certain offensive capabilities are rapidly materializing."

On February 26, 1952, Kuo Mo Jo (Guo Moruo), a famous Chinese poet and political figure, president of the Chinese Academy of Sciences and the Chinese People's Committee for World Peace, issued a statement: "In violation of all principles of human morals, the predatory American troops in Korea are carrying out bacteriological warfare," Kuo said. "They have repeatedly scattered bacteria-infected insects in large quantities on the front line and in the rear of the Chinese and Korean people's troops. The vileness of this inhuman crime of the American invaders has shaken the entire Chinese people and provoked unprecedented indignation."

A spokesman for the Eighth Army in Seoul denied the germ-warfare charge the next day. "It is not true as far as this headquarters is concerned," the spokesman said. "We have at no time or in any place engaged in any such activities."

"Unofficially," reported the Associated Press, "Allied officers said Red charges indicated epidemics, perhaps the bubonic plague, were sweeping North Korea and the Communist propaganda machine was trying to blame it on the U.N. Command."

On February 28, Beijing's English-language broadcast led with five separate stories about bacterial warfare. "This is an abnormally heavy dose even for Peiping propaganda casts," said the Associated Press. One of the Beijing news stories recalled an incident in 1940, "when countless civilians in Chekiang province died of bubonic plague spread by the Japanese invaders."

On March 4, 1952, *The New York Times* published an article about Secretary of State Dean Acheson's repudiation of what he called "this nonsense about germ warfare in Korea." The headline was "ACHESON BELITTLES FOE'S GERM CHARGE." Acheson, patrician, big-eyebrowed, Groton and Yale educated, issued his statement: "I would like to state categorically and unequivocally that these charges are false," he said. He had, he added, proposed an impartial investigation into the allegations by the International Committee of the Red Cross; the Communists, fully aware of the falsity of their charges, had refused. "The inability of the Communists to care for the health of the people under their control seems to have resulted in a serious epidemic of plague," Acheson said. "The Communists, not willing to admit and bear the responsibility that is theirs, are willing to pin the blame on some fantastic plot by the United Nations forces." Acheson extended the State Department's "deepest sympathy" to those who were sick or suffering.

This provoked several apoplectic articles in *People's China*, an English-language magazine published in Beijing. A lead editorial asked: "Who will believe Acheson, that old apologist for the most abominable atrocities of napalm bombing, the wholesale razing of defenseless hamlets and murder of populations in Korea, when he brazenly claims that the United Nations forces have not used any sort of bacteriological warfare?" Paul Ta-kuang Lin, a Canadian-born associate of Chou En-lai who had studied at the University of Michigan and Harvard, wrote: "With the sneering cynicism so characteristic of the present leaders of American imperialism, Dean Acheson on March 4 denied the charges of bacteriological warfare and affected 'deepest sympathy' for the 'very sad situation' of Korean people, which he based on 'Communist inability to care for the health of the people under their control.' The people of the world know well by now what Acheson's denials are worth. They will throw the grim facts in Acheson's face and demand an accounting on the severest terms." The facts were incontrovertible, Lin said—there was the evidence of eyewitnesses, and of scientists. "The case against the American war criminals, however, is not based on such evidence alone," Lin continued. "It lies in the nature of American bacteriological warfare as an integral part of the long range policy and strategy of aggression by the Washington Government. When Acheson affects a shocked attitude as if he never heard of bacteriological warfare, he is flying in the face of facts which have long been a matter of record in the U.S. itself."

Month after month, the germ-war outcry continued, from news sources in North Korea, China, and Russia—claims that civilians were suffering from fevers in towns near the Yalu River, and that masses of feathers and clusters of out-of-season insects and dead voles were appearing in the snow after a single American plane had passed overhead. The allegations were countered by denials, back and forth, repeatedly, angrily. The Communists assembled a group of international lawyers ("jurists") to investigate the charges, and then they convened an International Scientific Commission—six scientists, one of whom was Joseph Needham of Cambridge University. And they publicized dozens of confessions by American POWs, who said they had received germ-warfare training, had flown bacterial bombing missions, and were sorry.

Either the Russians, the Chinese, and the North Koreans had planned and executed a gigantic coordinated hoax involving thousands of people, a "big lie"—as the American government said they had—or there was a core of truth to their claims.

Which is it? We may never have incontrovertible proof. But there are thousands of still-classified documents that could help us understand what happened.

ONE OF THE ACCESS-RESTRICTED DOCUMENTS I'd like to see—that I asked to see seven years ago and have a legal right to see—is a memo sent on August 15, 1951, from "Wilson" to "Grover." Its file designation is "471.6 BW Munitions." (BW is the abbreviation for biological warfare; the number 471.6 corresponds to bombs and torpedoes in the Defense Department's old decimal filing system.) Wilson is probably Roscoe C. Wilson, an Air Force general who'd been involved in the Manhattan Project during World War II and had commanded a bomber wing in Japan in 1945. In 1951, General Wilson was head of the Air Force's Office of Atomic Energy, or AFOAT, which held within it a team of about a dozen Pentagon planners and promulgators called AFOAT BW-CW, whose job was to advance the cause of biological and chemical weaponry. ("Accelerated, aggressive, if not drastic, action is indicated," one Air Force general wrote in December 1951.) This memo comes from their office files, now held at the National Archives.

Grover is Orrin Grover, a West Pointer and math whiz who was head of a different and more CIA-tinctured group at the Pentagon—the Air Force's Division of Psychological Warfare, which in addition to psychological warfare was concerned with "unconventional warfare and special operations." (The CIA and the Air Force worked closely together in the 1950s: Hoyt Vandenberg, the chain-smoking, movie star–handsome Air Force war hero, became, in 1946, the second director of central intelligence, even before there was a Central Intelligence Agency to direct; then, in 1948, he became secretary of the Air Force.) General Grover, who had a pencil mustache and looked a bit like David Niven, was a believer in "thought bombs"—i.e., propaganda leaflets and radio and other forms of aerially delivered psychological warfare—but as the files show he also took a special interest in the E-73 feather bomb, an adapted propaganda bomb in which disease spores were mixed with turkey or chicken feathers and stuffed into the bomb's compartments in place of leaflets.

Details of the design of the Air Force's E-73 feather bomb have been declassified since the 1990s, so that's probably not the reason this document is being held back, year after year, in the National Archives' SCIF. The document is withheld, possibly, because it describes some actual plan that involved the covert use of biological munitions in Russia, China, or North Korea. By 1951, the Central Intelligence Agency was a giant, far-flung, undersupervised aggregation of subversionists, paramilitary trainers, plague propagators, and nerve warriors, all operating under the bland cover of "intelligence gathering"—and one of their major targets was the Russian wheat crop.

Or perhaps the document is restricted because it refers to the work of the Japanese germ-warfare scientists of World War II—Ishii Shiro and the men of Unit 731—whose research had been, since 1947, exploited, applied, and extended by American disease-breeders and disseminationists at Camp Detrick, a large biological research unit in Frederick, Maryland, an hour from Washington, D.C., founded in 1942 and overseen by the Army's Chemical Corps. Camp Detrick was where the feather bomb was prototyped, with CIA money. Or—another guess—the document was withheld because it's about the testing of some other type of biobomb, perhaps one that holds insects. A 1950 annual report of the biological department of the Army's Chemical Corps says: "An investigation is being conducted in the Medical Division, Chemical Corps, with Biological Department support, to study the potential use of arthropods to transmit viral and bacterial agents of significance for biological warfare. The program during the past year has included development and assay of attractants for flies, and both field and library studies of Arctic mosquitoes." So the memo from Wilson to Grover could be about a potential bug bomb.

Or it could be about very little. It could just be that the security officer who filled out this yellow placeholder card on September 25, 1991—his or her initials are "DC"—decided that the memo held "sensitive information" and withheld it from history for reasons that we will never be able to divine when it is finally declassified. That happens, too.

March 11, 2019, Monday

I'm up early. There was a brief, puffy-flaked blizzard last night, and then the plows came grumbling. I tiptoed out of the room so as not to wake the dogs, who had burrowed into a tangle of blankets at the foot of the bed, but when I closed the door, with extreme care, the latch made a last tiny squeak, and immediately one of them was up, whimpering softly, and then the other was up, shaking himself so that his ears made slapping sounds, and then both of them were sniffing around, sneezing and tail wagging. I got back in bed. M. fell back asleep. As soon as we were both breathing steadily, the dogs arranged themselves on the blankets and began snoring.

I lay awake with my phone dimmed, thinking about anticrop warfare and reading some notes I'd made about the CIA in Cuba. The way to understand covert action, as practiced by the Central Intelligence Agency, is to realize that the same tricks and schemes are used over and over again. There is the same gradual escalation, the same planting of false news, the same bribery of politicians, the same huffy denials, the same urge to create social chaos that requires an imposition of martial law. The making of lists—lists of prominent people who are likely to welcome a new regime and lists of people to kill or imprison. Often in the early Cold War there's a fascination with the food supply, and with the sneakiness and deniability of biological weapons.

The Eisenhower administration went after Cuba in 1959, once the CIA had determined that Castro was drifting leftward and could not be swayed by offers of arms. Sugar was Cuba's money crop—so President Eisenhower drastically cut sugar imports. It was a "knife thrust in the chest," said Castro. That was the overt attack, covered on the front page of American newspapers. The covert anti-sugar program involved incendiary bombing and sabotage, and it also made the papers. Planes, flown at night, set fire to cane fields and blew up sugar refineries. *Revolución*, a Havana newspaper, claimed in January 1960 that an airplane of American origin had destroyed hundreds of tons of sugarcane in a single incendiary firebomb attack on the former Hershey mill near Havana. The State Department "vigorously" rejected the charge. "Any implication that the United States government is involved is an absurdity," said a spokesman.

In February 1960, two American fliers were killed on a cane-field-burning sortie, and the Cuban government said that this proved that the bombings had "the full complicity of U.S. authorities." In August 1960, Ray Treichler, one of the CIA's scientists, tainted a box of fifty of Castro's favorite brand of cigars with botulinum toxin. On December 21, 1960, during the last moments of the Eisenhower administration, Allen Dulles, head of the CIA, met with a group of executives in New York whose businesses in Cuba were imperiled—oilmen, heads of power and telephone companies, the president of Domino Sugar. The men wanted more hostile acts—more harm done to the sugar crop, more sabotage of sugar refineries, plus a disruption of electric power and a blockade of food and medical supplies. It was time to "get tough," the business leaders said—time to "take some direct action against Castro."

One CIA document (declassified in 1997, and then declassified all over again in 2012, but with more, not fewer, redactions than in the 1997 version) gives an accounting of American-sponsored acts of violence in Cuba between October 1960 and April 1961. "Approximately 300,000 tons of sugar cane destroyed in 800 separate fires" was one achievement. Also "150 other fires, including the burning of 42 tobacco warehouses, 2 paper plants, 1 sugar refinery, 2 dairies, 4 stores, 21 Communist homes," along with more than a hundred bombings, "including Communist Party offices, Havana power station, 2 stores, railroad terminal, bus terminal, militia barracks, railroad train." Six trains were derailed, and a commando raid put the oil refinery out of action "for a week." No war was declared, but Cuba was being terrorized by the United States.

And then came the Bay of Pigs—the high-water mark of American paramilitary lunacy, an attack, sanctioned by President Kennedy, on the Cuban coast, by fifteen hundred CIA-trained Cuban expatriates. Dead men in the water. Humiliation. Defeat. Denials by America's ambassador to the United Nations—"These charges are totally false, and I deny them categorically." The rage of the betrayed guerrillas. The rage of the president's brother, Attorney General Bobby Kennedy.

I spent all day reading about Cuba, amazed once again at the fierceness and persistence of the desire within the Kennedy administration to kill that island economy and its leader, using fire, bullets, germs, and poisons. In August 1961, after the Bay of Pigs, Che Guevara sought out Kennedy adviser Richard Goodwin at two in the morning at a cocktail party in Montevideo, Uruguay, at a regional conference, in order to present the possibility of a peace agreement, or at least a modus vivendi, between Cuba and the United States. Goodwin had been avoiding Che at the conference. Che said that if the United States was willing to work things out with Cuba, Cuba would curtail its alliance with Russia, pay reparations for nationalized property, and stop supporting leftist movements in other countries. "He then went on to say that he wanted to thank us very much for the invasion," Goodwin wrote. "It had been a great political victory for them—enabled them to consolidate—and transformed them from an aggrieved little country to an equal." Goodwin advised Kennedy to reject Che's offer and continue the program of covert violence, which is what Kennedy and brother Bobby did. The existence of this démarche from Cuba was kept secret until 1996, when Goodwin's memo was finally declassified.

LATE IN THE AFTERNOON, I sent a follow-up letter to the CIA about a memo sent by Frank Wisner in 1950. I'll tell you about it tomorrow.

March 12, 2019, Tuesday

It's a brilliant blue day and the Penobscot River is surging outside between snowbanks, over the cold invisible stones. I'm sitting at the kitchen table typing and listening to the refrigerator go. M. is at work. The dogs are under the table, asleep on green cushions. They're getting used to life with us. Just before we got them, a dentist hired by the Humane Society pulled out all their side teeth, which I guess were in bad shape, and a vet removed their testicles, so that now they had these sad empty shriveled pouches. They had a lot to adjust to all at once.

SIX DOLLARS IS WHAT IT COSTS to send a piece of certified mail these days, if you want a return receipt—and I do. The woman at the post office yesterday was extremely efficient, folding the label around the top edge of the envelope and tearing off the part that needs to be torn off. It's all pointless, I sometimes think, but I want the Freedom of Information Act to work the way it was meant to work, the way John Moss envisioned its working, so I go through the ritual of the follow-up letter. "You don't get anything unless you litigate," one lawyer, James Lesar, told me, depressingly. He's been in a declassification battle with the FBI that has lasted twenty years.

On June 20, 1950 (I think that's the rubber-stamped date—it's hard to read on my copy), Frank Wisner sent a memo to Marshall Chadwell. Wisner was then head of the CIA's new clandestine arm, the Office of Policy Coordination, or OPC. He was a sociable lawyer from the University of Virginia who'd worked for Allen Dulles in the Office of Strategic Services during the war, when his cryptonym was Typhoid. His wife, Polly, gave marvelous parties where Wisner told jokes in dialect and danced the crab walk, and everybody loved the two of them. Dulles had recommended him to State Department oracle George Kennan as the right man to head a new department of "political warfare" and other covert action. He'd joined the CIA payroll in 1948.

Marshall Chadwell was the head of the CIA's Office of Scientific Intelligence. During World War II, "Chad" Chadwell, a Harvard PhD in chemistry, had worked with Stanley Lovell and Vannevar Bush developing unconventional weapons and truth serums at the Office of Scientific Research and Development. One of his projects, code-named Aunt Jemima, was the mixing of the explosive RDX with flour so that it could be transported in sacks and, if necessary, baked into (toxic) muffins. After the war, Chadwell worked at the Rockefeller Foundation and then joined the staff at the Atomic Energy Commission. In March 1950, he was hired by the CIA. He was "notably mild-mannered and conciliatory," said an agency document.

Wisner's memo to Chadwell was three pages long. "OPC must, if it is effectively to carry out its mission, make use of the latest scientific and technological advances to modernize the field of clandestine unconventional warfare," Wisner wrote. "OPC is at present engaged in covert unconventional activity on a limited scale and is preparing for the following types of clandestine activity in the event of war."

Six blacked-out lines follow that sentence. It would be interesting to know what they say. They probably list activities like propaganda, economic warfare, sabotage, demolition, aid to anti-Communist guerrillas, and "subversion against hostile states"—those are some of the tasks that George Kennan assigned to Wisner in a 1948 document called NSC 10/2. There may also be a mention of novel interrogation methods, or even something about assassination or one of its euphemisms.

In his memo to Chadwell, Wisner went on to say that his group, the Office of Policy Coordination, was actively seeking new ideas and new devices. "We are particularly interested in the possibilities of BW, CW and RW"—that is, biological warfare, chemical warfare, and radiological warfare. The qualities Wisner was looking for in unconventional weaponry were: "(a) Relative ease of operation, maintenance, and transport. (b) Magnitude of effect. (c) Subtlety. (d) Difficulty of detection by the enemy. (e) Difficulty of development of countermeasures by the enemy."

More than thirty "types of activity" followed, all of them blacked out. "The list merely scratches the surface," Wisner said. I needed to read that list—the list of some of the nasty, ugly, wrong things this poor manic man had in mind to do in foreign countries in the 1950s, before he had a breakdown and electroshock treatments and eventually killed himself with his son's shotgun.

Oddly enough, this one 1950 memo from Wisner is maybe the rarest, most precious declassified document that I own. Which is strange, because I printed it straight off the internet almost twenty years ago, when I was working on a book about libraries, newspapers, and microfilm. Wisner's memo was one of thousands of CIA and military documents that Attorney General Janet Reno had gathered and gotten declassified, on the authority of President Clinton, in connection with an investigation into human radiation experiments—including plutonium injections that Eileen Welsome wrote about in a series of articles in the *Albuquerque Tribune* and in a brilliant 1999 book, *The Plutonium Files*. Welsome used the Freedom of Information Act, backed by an unstoppable lawyer for the *Albuquerque Tribune*, to extract and unredact documents from a reluctant Department of Energy. ("In most cases, the redactions were done to protect the DOE and the Atomic Energy Commission from embarrassment," Welsome told me. "And of course embarrassment is not protected by the Freedom of Information Act.")

The documents that Janet Reno's Advisory Panel on Human Radiation Experiments amassed were scanned as digital files in the 1990s and went onto a website called HREX, funded by the Department of Energy and maintained by the Argonne National Laboratory, near Chicago. I had a dial-up modem back then, so browsing was slow, but I made my way through a number of CIA documents on HREX and was amazed by what I found. Something told me I should print out some of them, in case they disappeared later. So I did—at low resolution, unfortunately, because a high-resolution TIFF file took a long time to download. I clipped the documents together and put them in a box, and the box went into a storage container.

The beautifully searchable, pioneering HREX database gradually went away after 9/11. A bare-bones copy of the website was saved by the Internet Archive, but not the individual documents. Possibly the paper copies are at the National Archives somewhere, but so far I haven't found them. Two people refer to this particular 1950 Wisner memo in books— John Kelly, former editor of *Counterspy*, in a chapter on radiation weapons published in *Abuse Your Illusions*, an anthology edited by Russ Kick; and Hank Albarelli, in his book on the death of germ-warfare scientist Frank Olson. In 2017, remembering the document and wanting to quote from it, I wrote a FOIA letter to the CIA asking to see it. I got no response. When we moved north in 2018, I found the box with the HREX printouts. And today, two years after my FOIA request, I sent off a letter to the CIA asking for it again, minus the redactions. This time I included a copy of the memo. "I haven't yet received a response from CIA to this FOIA request," I wrote the CIA. "Please let me know what's going on."

I wonder if I'll be able to read this document without blacked-out lines before I die.

March 13, 2019, Wednesday

M. came back from a walk up to Main Street with the two dogs. She had to carry Cedric part of the way home. It's another gorgeous day.

I filed my first Freedom of Information Act request about twenty years ago, on April 2, 1999, while I was working on the book about libraries, called *Double Fold*. My letter, addressed to the information and privacy coordinator of the Central Intelligence Agency, said, "Under the Freedom of Information Act, 5 U.S.C. subsection 552, I am requesting all information or records, including but not limited to Office of Strategic Services (OSS) information or records, on: Verner Warren Clapp, U.S. citizen, born June 3, 1901, employed by the Library of Congress circa 1923–1956, died June 15, 1972." Some weeks later a fat, securely taped envelope came in the mail. How amazing, I thought. Sent straight from the bowels of the CIA—and so *prompt*.

Parts of the Verner Clapp file were whited out, which was frustrating, but even so, I was interested to discover that Clapp, who'd been deputy librarian of Congress in the 1950s, had a top-secret clearance, and that he had monitored "CIA-financed Library of Congress activity."

Clapp left the Library of Congress in 1956, and with a grant of $10 million from the Ford Foundation, he founded a nonprofit in Washington, D.C., called the Council on Library Resources, which funded various microfilming projects and advanced text-compression machines. Here again I noticed something strangely Cold War–ish about Clapp's council: most of the people on the board of directors, and some of the grant recipients, too, had connections of one sort or another to military research or to the CIA. Using a now forgotten search engine called MetaCrawler, and also Namebase, a useful book-indexing and cross-referencing service run by longtime CIA watcher Daniel Brandt, I began looking up names. That's how this all began.

One of the board members of the Council on Library Resources was a scientist named Caryl Haskins. Haskins was president of the Carnegie Institution in Washington and author of *Of Ants and Men*, a book about ant and human behavior. He was a bald, studious-looking gentleman, a Harvard- and Yale-educated entomologist and radiation biologist who had induced genetic changes in mold spores and developed radar countermeasures during World War II. Haskins's name also turned up, I discovered, in Janet Reno's Human Radiation Experiments database. In 1951, so HREX documents revealed, Haskins was asked to help set up Project Artichoke, described by the CIA as "a special agency program established for the development and application of special techniques in CIA interrogations and in other CIA covert activities where control of an individual is desired." As part of the CIA's search for improved means of interrogation and more effective mind-control drugs, Haskins helped the Agency recruit a team of scientists and psychiatrists, including (I learned this from articles in the *Toronto Star* by reporter David Vienneau) a Montreal neurophysiologist named Hebb who blindfolded students in a sealed room for days in order to find out how they reacted to a diet of propaganda tapes combined with periods of total sensory deprivation. The students, Professor Hebb found, could be made to hallucinate and to believe in poltergeists; he paid them twenty dollars a day for their pains. Another HREX document that I'd happened to print out, a memo from

March 20, 1952, about the need for a "small testing facility within CIA for use in connection with Project Artichoke," was from Artichoke's project coordinator (name blacked out) to Frank Wisner, and to Wisner's boss, Allen Dulles, then the CIA's deputy director. Project Artichoke seems to have been—not to be too fancily psychological—an outward projection of Wisner's inner torment.

While I worked on the book about microfilm and newspapers, I kept wondering about Caryl Haskins—this enthusiastic fraternity brother (Phi Beta Kappa, Sigma Xi, Delta Sigma Rho, and Omicron Delta Kappa), recipient of more than a dozen honorary degrees, this learned ant scientist, who had a secret life as a CIA mind-control consultant. Another LexisNexis search led me to a piece by Ted Gup in *The Washington Post* about the Smithsonian Institution: Haskins had served on the Smithsonian's board during a period when it functioned as a cover organization for some exotic-bird research. One Smithsonian project, Operation Starbright, involved bird banding and bird tracking in the Pacific Ocean; Starbright seemed to be linked to a CIA project concerning the role of "avian vectors" in the spread of disease. Strange as it may seem, the CIA was interested in the fact that birds, dusted with disease spores, might be used to infect people, animals, or crops in an enemy country.

In 1982, Ted Gup filed a Freedom of Information Act request with the CIA for information on the Agency's avian-vector inquiry. Three years later, when he published his article, the CIA had still not responded except to say that his FOIA request was "awaiting processing."

More searching for "Haskins" and "Artichoke" and "CIA" eventually led me to a book by two Canadian historians, Stephen Endicott and Edward Hagerman. Their 1998 book, *The United States and Biological Warfare: Secrets from the Early Cold War and Korea*, mentioned something called the Haskins Committee. Was this the same Haskins? It was, it turned out. In 1949, Caryl Haskins had produced a secret report on the threat and the promise of biological agents. James Forrestal, the clinically paranoid secretary of defense, had asked for the report, but before Haskins and his colleagues had finished writing it, President Truman had fired

Forrestal, and then Forrestal killed himself by jumping from a hospital window.

The report, submitted to Louis Johnson, the new secretary of defense, in July 1949, took special note of biological sabotage: "Sabotage employment of biological weapons during periods of nominal peace is facilitated by the resemblance of the results of such sabotage to natural occurrences."

I wrote Dr. Haskins a letter, asking for an interview. His secretary politely refused, saying that 1951 was a long time ago. In 2001, Haskins died, at the age of ninety-three. His obituary in *The New York Times* included a quote from a 1939 interview he gave to the *New York World-Telegram*, regarding ants: "When they go to war they stab each other, spray poison and cut off each other's heads. They subjugate weak races and keep slaves. But they can be kind, too."

March 14, 2019, Thursday

Tremendous ear flapping from the dogs early this morning. Not enough sleeping. I lay awake reading the opening day of John Moss's congressional fact-finding session, November 7, 1955, about the people's right to know what their government was doing—the beginning of his ten-year slog to get a freedom-of-information law passed. James Reston of *The New York Times* testified in that first session, and so did columnist Joe Alsop, along with high officials from newspaper groups. "The public business is the public's business," said Harold L. Cross, who was freedom-of-information counsel for the American Society of Newspaper Editors. "The language of the First Amendment is broad enough to embrace, if indeed it does not require, the inclusion of a right of access to information without which the freedom to print could be fettered into futility." James Reston specifically warned about the CIA. "The news of the CIA and its operatives all over the world often confronts us with the most embarrassment that any reporter can be confronted with, the dilemma as to whether he is going to tell the truth or whether he is going to mislead the American people by putting out something put out by the Government which he knows not to be true. That whole area of the CIA, Mr. Chairman, I think, is a growing problem for the press, and I would think it would merit some attention by your committee."

The CIA itself, meanwhile, in November 1955, was busy plotting the assassination of President Sukarno in Indonesia, and helping United Nations ambassador Henry Cabot Lodge begin a new, vehement campaign to expose the "international Communist conspiracy." Frank Wisner's people at CIA were thinking about the varied uses of psychoactive drugs; they especially wanted a new a drug that would "promote illogical thinking and impulsiveness to the point where the recipient would be discredited in public." The Agency was guided by a fresh two-hundred-page study of psychological strategy, written by a panel that included the CIA's Paul Linebarger and a youthful prodigy named Henry Kissinger. (Kissinger was executive director of the Harvard International Seminar; Linebarger taught at the Johns Hopkins School of Advanced International Studies, and he wrote, some years later, under the pen name Cordwainer Smith, award-winning science fiction about a planet called Norstrilia, where live gigantic virus-infected sheep that produce a lucrative immortality drug, which sheep-strewn planet is protected by a laboratory full of mad mutated minks that drive away attacking spaceships by sending telepathic beams of psychotic rage and nerve warfare at them.) International diplomacy was a theatrical illusion, a cover story, the study—entitled "Psychological Aspects of United States Strategy"—said. "The world diplomatic front is a screen on which appears the apparent struggle between the Free World and the Communist camp," wrote Linebarger, Kissinger, and company. "Behind it the real struggle goes on in the sphere of weapons research, countermeasure capabilities, and the supreme problem of a technological breakthrough." The weapons research in which the CIA took an interest in November 1955 included work on fleas doped with plague, mosquitoes doped with yellow fever, and crop-killing funguses of wheat. All of it was messed up, and secret, secret, secret.

JAMES S. POPE—executive editor of the *Louisville Courier Journal* and former chair of the freedom-of-information committee of the American

Society of Newspaper Editors—was the first to speak at Congressman Moss's hearings, and he spoke stirringly. This was the first time, Pope told the committee, that a group of newsmen and congressmen had ever gotten together to discuss the basic right of the people to know what their government was up to. "If you really study the whole subject of secrecy in government," he said, "I think the effect on this country could be the biggest story of this year, or possibly of our time." Pope went on to say:

> I do not think many of us yet have realized the enormous implication of a battle in the middle of the 20th century for people to have access to information about the activities of their own public service. The fact that we have to fight for it at all is a sort of disgrace.

That's true—it's disgraceful. It's disgraceful that in 2019, people who want to write about momentous world events—changes of government, attempted assassinations, war plans—that were discussed at the highest levels of government in 1970, or 1960, or 1952, should have to pick through broken potsherds of redacted documents as if they were dealing with an ancient civilization. You can't have consent of the governed unless the governed know what they're consenting to.

If the American public had known that the CIA was behind the burning of all that sugarcane in Cuba, under the banner of "economic warfare," would they have allowed it? I'd like to think they would have said, Oh, please don't do that. Don't drop firebombs in the middle of the night. Don't blow up sugar refineries. And don't pretend to be who you aren't, and poke and meddle in the lives of countries you know very little about, and make kill lists of prominent leftists, as you did in Guatemala. Don't hire former Nazis and members of Hitler Youth, as you did in Germany, to harass and spy on and beat up people at Communist-affiliated peace marches.

If they'd known what some American bacteriologists were doing between 1943 and 1971, what would people have said? Probably many would have said, Don't breed diseases for heightened virulence by passing them through guinea pigs and monkeys. Don't find exotic maladies whose symptoms resemble other diseases in order to delay a diagnosis, so that people or animals will stay sicker longer. And don't, absolutely *do not*, breed diseases for resistance to antibiotics.

"Under project 465-20-001, insect strains resistant to insecticides are being developed," said the Biological Laboratories of the Chemical Corps in October 1952. "These represent a potentially more effective vehicle for the offensive use in BW of insect borne pathogens."

"Current work has been directed toward restoring or increasing virulence," said an annual report in October 1949 about anthrax research, "so that virulent strains may be produced which are selectively resistant to all drugs or any combination of drugs."

"More than 50 strains varying in pathogenicity from avirulent to highly virulent have been collected from various locations throughout the world," said the "Seventh Annual Report of the Chemical Corps Biological Laboratories" on July 1, 1953, in a section on tularemia, or rabbit fever. One purified strain, SCHU SD, tested on guinea pigs and monkeys, was based on cells originally isolated from a human ulcer. "The high virulence of this strain for man is substantiated by the high incidence of infection among vaccinated and nonvaccinated laboratory workers. Antibiotic resistant strains (e.g., resistant to 10 mg streptomycin) have been developed which, in preliminary study, retain the virulence of the parent strain."

Ted Gup, in his book on secrecy, quotes Samuel Johnson: "Where secrecy or mystery begins, vice or roguery is not far off."

BACK NOW TO CUBA. In 1961, the existence of Castro's government was intolerable to the roomful of men in John F. and Robert F. Kennedy's Special Group (Augmented). Castro's presence, so close to the American coast, drove the anti-Communists crazy. "The object in Cuba was not to put down an insurgency, but to develop one," said sabotage specialist Jack Hawkins to Taylor Branch and George Crile, in a piece in *Harper's Magazine* in 1975. "The work was done by the Agency. I remember them blowing up a refinery and making efforts to burn up sugar fields—things like that—but none of them was very successful. I don't know why they were doing it. What happens in these things is that the bureaucrats fall in love with their operations, and rational thought just flies out the window."

After the CIA's Bay of Pigs humiliation, Attorney General Robert Kennedy put a handsome paramilitarist, Edward Lansdale, in charge of Operation Mongoose. Mongoose was fiercer, darker, trickier than anything Eisenhower had approved. "My idea is to stir things up on island with espionage, sabotage, general disorder, run & operated by Cubans themselves with every group but Batistaites & Communists," Bobby Kennedy wrote in November 1961. "Do not know if we will be successful in overthrowing Castro but we have nothing to lose in my estimate."

Stir things up. General disorder. Sabotage. We have nothing to lose. This is the basic CIA model of covert international relations that the United States has been following since 1948: sponsor disorder in order to impose a new order. It has never worked, and it has led to decades of dictatorial repression and impoverishment, and hunger and torture and corruption. This has been said a hundred times, but it must be said again.

General Lansdale produced a long Cuba-planning document that circulated in January 1962. A copy went to President Kennedy. It included Operation Bounty, the dropping of leaflets that offered thousands of dollars for the deaths of Communist leaders, and a plan to interfere with the sugarcane harvest by making sugar workers sick with a nonfatal but incapacitating illness, to be spread by ticks, fleas, or mosquitoes:

> On a most discreet (strictly need-to-know) basis, Defense is asked to submit a plan by 2 February on what it can do to put a majority of workers out of action, unable to work in the cane fields and sugar mills, for a significant period during the remainder of this harvest. It is suggested that such planning consider non-lethal BW, insect-borne, introduced secretly to the target area by the Navy.

Mosquitoes were probably the insects Lansdale had in mind, perhaps carrying dengue fever or yellow fever: in 1960, the Chemical Corps published an "Entomological Warfare Target Analysis," which discussed the targeting of Soviet and Chinese cities with fever-doped *Aedes aegypti* mosquitoes, and they produced two feasibility studies, one for the dengue virus and one for yellow fever. (These feasibility studies exist only as titles in a database, and the target analysis is still heavily redacted.)

At a later Mongoose meeting, in September 1962, Marshall Carter, deputy director of central intelligence, warned there might be "disastrous results" from an attempt to infect sugar workers by means of disease-tainted insects, especially if word got out that the United States was behind it. But, Carter said, there was possibly a better way to reduce the cane yield in Cuba: "He mentioned specifically the possibility of producing crop failures by the introduction of biological agents which would appear to be of natural origin."

This particular sentence was redacted from documents for fifty-five years, until October 2017. So was Lansdale's phrase about "insect-borne" biological agents. The only reason we can read these words now is because of Oliver Stone's 1991 movie, *JFK*, about the Kennedy assassination. Although it contains distortions of the available record and fictionalized speeches, Stone's movie got Washington's attention, and made possible the passage of the JFK Records Act, which gave rise to a group called the Assassination Records Review Board. The ARRB brought thousands of hidden records into the light. Thousands more were held back until very recently, however. "There is a body of documents that the CIA is still protecting, which should be released," wrote two review board officials in an opinion piece in the *Boston Herald* in 2013. More of these sequestered pages were allowed to join the historical record in 2017. But the CIA and the FBI are, even now, keeping still other JFK documents and portions of documents in the dark, illegally.

"There was lots of sugar being sent out from Cuba," one CIA official recalled in *Harper's*, "and we were putting a lot of contaminants in it." One wants to ask the obvious question: Did the CIA, as part of its war against the Cuban economy, introduce disease into sugarcane fields? Not just toss around the idea, but actually do it? I don't know. I do know that in 1963, the Agency hired a "world-renowned plant pathologist"—his name has been blacked out—to make a study of "sugar cane crop vulnerabilities, on a world-wide basis." His advice and consultation on the subject of crop sabotage was in support of the CIA's requirement to "maintain an offensive biological agent capability." The plant pathologist was nervous about being exposed as a CIA contract worker: "He will not continue his efforts in our behalf unless we can protect his association with the Agency." The payment—in cash or cashier's check—was authorized by LSD scientist Sidney Gottlieb: it was part of the CIA's now famous MKULTRA program of biochemical and psychological experimentation.

Years later, in December 1979, Fidel Castro gave a big speech. The country was "sailing in a sea of difficulties," Castro said. Two of Cuba's biggest problems were agricultural, he said: the *roya* or rust of sugarcane, and the blue mold of tobacco. A year after that, in July 1981, Castro gave another speech, on the anniversary of the revolution, before a crowd of seventy-five thousand people. "In the last two years, four harmful plagues have hit our country," he said. These plagues were (1) African swine fever, (2) the roya of sugarcane, (3) the blue mold of tobacco, and (4) a new and more potent kind of dengue fever called hemorrhagic dengue, which had sickened 340,000 Cubans and killed 150 of them, many of whom were children. "We have deep suspicions that the plagues—especially the hemorrhagic dengue—could have been introduced into Cuba by the CIA," Castro said in his speech. Why was it so strange, he asked, to think that imperialism would use biological weapons against Cuba? "What can anyone expect from a government whose policy is known for its cynicism, its lies and its absolute lack of scruples?"

Castro's charges were "totally without foundation," said Dean Fischer, a State Department spokesman. The Cuban revolution was a failure, Fischer explained to reporters. "The Cuban government has always tried to blame the United States for its failures and its internal problems." Fischer announced that the Reagan administration, out of humanitarian concern, was sending Cuba three hundred metric tons of Abate, a pesticide that kills mosquito larvae.

Castro was even harsher in September 1981, when, in an angry speech to the World Interparliamentary Union, he again said that a hundred Cuban children had died of hemorrhagic dengue fever, and added a fifth plague to his list: acute hemorrhagic conjunctivitis, or pink eye. The CIA was now "relieved of all restrictions," Castro said. "Imperialism is using biological arms against our country. This is not a baseless charge." He tore into the Reagan government, although he never mentioned the new president by name. "I will never say that the U.S. people are fascist, nor their legislative institutions, nor their press nor their many creative social organizations, nor the considerable remainder of their noble democratic traditions and their commitment to freedom," he said. "But it is my deepest conviction that the group that constitutes the main nucleus of the current U.S. government is fascist":

> Its intransigent refusal to seek for and find an honorable coexistence among states is fascist. Its haughtiness, its conceit, its arms race, its quest for military support at all costs, its attachment to violence and domination, its methods of blackmail and terror, its shameless alliance with South Africa, its threatening language and its lies are fascist.

Republican senator Robert Stafford, head of the U.S. delegation, said that Castro's criticisms were "unfair and often untruthful, certainly impolite." Listening to the charges at the head table, Stafford said, was a unique and "very unpleasant" experience.

March 15, 2019, Friday

It's Sunshine Week in D.C. this week. I should probably be down there talking to people about government transparency, but I've already done some of that, and this year's not a big year for transparency, anyway. The best thing about Sunshine Week so far that I've come across is an article by Nate Jones on *The Washington Post*'s *Made by History* blog. Jones, who works at the National Security Archive at George Washington University, quotes former Lyndon Johnson press secretary Bill Moyers, who said that LBJ had to be dragged kicking and screaming to the signing ceremony of the Freedom of Information Act on July 4, 1966. President Johnson "hated the thought of journalists rummaging in government closets," Moyers recalled.

Jones assigns primary blame to the Justice Department for FOIA's enfeebled state. From the beginning, he says, the DOJ, which oversees FOIA compliance—and defends government agencies in FOIA lawsuits—has resisted the basic idea that the right to know is implied by the First Amendment. And it has often erred on the side of nondisclosure. In 1974, when Congress voted to strengthen freedom of information law, President

Ford's advisers Dick Cheney, Donald Rumsfeld, and Antonin Scalia—
who was then head of the Justice Department's Office of Legal Counsel—
argued in favor of a presidential veto. The veto was overruled.

I interviewed Jones in 2017 in the National Security Archive's offices,
which are on the top floor of GWU's Gelman library. In 2007, when he was
an undergraduate at Lewis and Clark College, Jones got interested in a 1983
NATO war game, Able Archer 83, that almost triggered a nuclear war. He
took a research trip to the Reagan Library in Simi Valley, California, where
he opened a box that had once held Able Archer documents. The folders
were now empty, their contents replaced by withdrawal slips. Jones asked a
Reagan Library archivist what the mechanism was for requesting these
classified documents. The archivist snickered and handed him a form. "Fill
this out and start waiting," he said.

"That got me kind of angry," Jones told me. Since then he's overseen
the filing of thousands of records requests at the National Security Archive,
and he's helped independent researchers with their FOIA struggles,
including Harvard's Matthew Meselson, who has been trying for years to
get documents relating to the "yellow rain" controversy declassified. (The
yellow powder was either the residue of chemical attacks by Russians in
the late 1970s against Hmong tribesmen in Laos, as Secretary of State
Alexander Haig charged in 1981; or it was bee feces; or it was pollen,
perhaps admixed with the chemical traces of American tear gas attacks.)
Jones fought for twelve years to get one revealing Able Archer document
released; the document finally arrived in 2016, on his birthday, although
10 percent of it was still redacted. I showed him my 2012 request for
twenty-one Air Force documents. "The Air Force is terrible," he said. How
was he able to stay positive about the declassification process, I asked,
when the gears turned so slowly? "I'm at the point where I've filed so many
FOIAs for so many years that every day I get packages of FOIAs coming
in," he said. "That's how I've made my peace with it." One FOIA requester
he particularly admires, he told me, is his colleague William Burr, editor
of *The Kissinger Transcripts* and other collections, who has a gift for getting
agencies to release documents.

_____

TODAY MY PLAN is to send off two or three letters to the CIA. I want to keep the rhythm going. I want them to get used to getting letters from me.

Yesterday night before bed I got curious about the tobacco disease that Castro had blamed on the CIA. I knew something about dengue and dengue's vector, the *Aedes aegypti* mosquito, and I knew a little about African swine fever, an exotic disease known in the 1940s and '50s as "wart hog disease," when germ-warfare planners mentioned it in planning documents. I'd read the 1977 *Newsday* article by Drew Fetherston and John Cummings about Cuba's sudden swine fever epidemic in 1971, which begins:

> With at least the tacit backing of CIA officials, operatives linked to anti-Castro terrorists introduced African swine fever virus into Cuba in 1971, an intelligence source said. Six weeks later, an outbreak of the disease forced the slaughter of 500,000 pigs to prevent a nationwide animal epidemic.

But I hadn't known that Cuba's tobacco crop had been hit with an epidemic of *mojo azul*, the blue mold of tobacco, scientific name *Peronospora tabacina*.

It was a sudden, severe epidemic. In 1978, before the blue mold crisis, Cuba produced 46,000 metric tons of tobacco. The 1980 crop was down to 5,000 metric tons. Cuba stopped tobacco exports and closed cigar factories. The blight attacked young tobacco leaves, said Cuba's minister of agriculture: "You touch them and they turn to powder." Cuban authorities called for a joint scientific investigation between Cuba and the United States, where tobacco farmers had suffered from blue mold outbreaks for years—but it didn't happen. A collaborative research program might be possible, said a State Department spokesman, if it were shown to be "in the interests of the United States." It wasn't.

And here's what I just found out. In 1963, Paul J. Wuest, a plant pathologist from Penn State, was hired by Fort Detrick's biological-warfare laboratories to study tobacco diseases. (Camp Detrick became Fort Detrick in 1956.) Wuest, who was an ardent mushroom grower at heart and worked at Fort Detrick for only a year, cultivated two varieties of blue mold disease in Detrick's greenhouses and studied how they acted on tobacco seedlings. "The young plants display a severe wilt as part of the dying syndrome," Wuest wrote. Other Detrick crop scientists studied whether chokeweed seeds could germinate among tobacco plants. While at Fort Detrick, Paul Wuest also wrote a big report, not for public release, entitled "Tobacco Growing and Economics of Tobacco in Selected Countries of the World," which revealed just where the most valuable tobacco was grown in Cuba (the plains of the Vuelta Abajo region), when and how seedlings were transplanted into the fields, and what temperatures favored the development of blue mold disease. "Optimum temperature range for infection is between 60.8 and 69.8 F," Wuest wrote.

WUEST'S NAME CAME UP thanks to a FOIA request for a list of technical reports submitted by Michael Morisy, cofounder of MuckRock, a small Cambridge, Massachusetts, nonprofit. In 2017, MuckRock won a gigantic victory over the CIA. With the help of a Washington, D.C., lawyer named Kel McClanahan, they compelled the CIA to put its CREST database of millions of declassified documents onto the internet. (CREST stands for CIA Records Search Tool.) You used to have to sit in a room at the National Archives Building in Maryland, on a plaid chair, at one of four terminals, under constant video surveillance, in order to search the millions of pages of the CIA's Freedom of Information releases for whatever it was you were curious about (Tibet, Albania, shellfish toxin, Berlin, U-2 flights, etc.)— now this enormous, jumbled boneyard, although weirdly hard to navigate and piano-rolled with redactions, is available to everyone, all over the world. It's a momentous development—perhaps the beginning of the crumbling of the edifice of CIA secrecy. I've looked at thousands of CREST documents in the past two years, some barely legible, some sharply scanned, some handwritten, some written in abbreviated cable-ese—they're almost always interesting in some way.

I RACED TO THE POST OFFICE to send off two Mandatory Declassification Review requests to the CIA. "Please remove the black cross-outs to the extent permitted by applicable law," I wrote. "Specifically, I would like to know the name of the 'world-renowned plant pathologist' that is referred to on page 3 of this document. The plant pathologist's name may be E. V. Abbott (Ernest Victor Abbott, born Ashland, Oregon, 1899–1980); I enclose a copy of his obituary as proof of death. If my guess is incorrect, and the document is about a different plant pathologist whose name you cannot reveal because he is still alive, I would like to know that fact."

The second document was from 1949. I'd found it on the CREST database: DOC_0001506872, "Foreign Activities in the Field of Biological Warfare." "Ten of its fourteen pages are completely whited out," I wrote, "and two other pages have big whited-out chunks. These hidden sections apparently cover biological warfare programs in other countries, including Japan, as of April 1949. Please engage in redaction reduction to the extent permitted by applicable law, so that I can use this document in my research."

March 16, 2019, Saturday

We watched *Hot Fuzz* last night and ate uncheesed pizza with risen crust made by M., and then walked the fast-trotting microdogs. The plowed drifts were melting upward into the air and the streetlights lit up the moving Isadora Duncan shapes of snow mist. Someone was doing night laundry in one of the houses by the river. The smell always makes me miss my son, who is now grown and living in Berkeley: when he was a teenager, he did his own laundry, and he had his own personal bottle of Tide because he loved the smell.

LOST THE DAY DOING RESEARCH—reading articles in rural newspapers about old epidemics. It's really remarkable how much you can learn from reading columns by veterinarians and farmers and doctors on the scanned microfilm of Newspapers.com. By four o'clock in the afternoon I was fact blasted and numb.

Edward Hagerman, one of the authors of *The United States and Biological Warfare*, died in 2016. He'd had Parkinson's disease, but I didn't know it. He was a military historian—a careful and kindly man, and a tireless FOIA requester. He liked archival work—aside from the densely endnoted biological-warfare book, which required years of research, he'd written *The American Civil War and the Origins of Modern Warfare*, for which he'd had to study muster rolls in the National Archives that nobody had looked at in many decades. He and coauthor Stephen Endicott both taught history at York University. In November 2008 I drove to Toronto to interview them.

Steve Endicott, who was fluent in Mandarin, had written a book about a 1931 strike of mine workers in Saskatchewan, and *Red Earth*, a study of a rural village in China during the years of the revolution. He'd also written a hefty biography of his father, the Reverend James G. Endicott, a former United Church missionary in China who'd been reviled in the Canadian and U.S. press for giving speeches in 1952 in which he claimed that the Communists were telling the truth: American airplanes had indeed dropped bombs full of insects and germs on North Korea and China. One of his speeches, on May 11, 1952, was at Maple Leaf Gardens in Toronto, before an audience of more than eight thousand people, as part of a three-day-long Canadian Peace Congress, where he described the American germ-warfare research program and the things he'd learned about the aerial biological attacks by talking to Chinese villagers and epidemic preventionists. At his speech, hecklers set off firecrackers in the aisles to disrupt the meeting.

In a 1952 pamphlet, "I Accuse," Steve's father gave a résumé of his charges. "As I listened to the testimony of honest old farmers," he said, "children whose bright, observant eyes had spotted tiny, unknown types of flies, and to medical workers of all kinds who had carried out expert culturing and analysis, I became convinced of the truth of the accusations."

> In the part of China where I investigated, the Americans had used a large leaflet propaganda bomb for the dissemination of insects, and a small porcelain-type bomb used for spreading germs. As one Chinese scientist explained to me (he had investigated the methods employed by the notorious Japanese bacteriological warfare Detachment 731),

the bacterial culture inside the bomb emitted a gas as the bacteria multiplied and at a certain point exploded the bomb.

I also investigated one of the propaganda leaflet bombs, around which a number of insects had been found when it fell on the snow-covered ground in the Mukden region. Actually, it had fallen on a newly dug grave, so that the fuse was still intact, as well as the little propeller which works the mechanism for opening the doors of the bomb.

Ned and his wife, Beverly, put me up for the night in their guest room. In the room were two horizontal file drawers that held the documents that Ned and Steve had used and quoted from in *The United States and Biological Warfare*, a book of painstaking archival sleuthage. (They kept two duplicate sets of documents.) "You might want to start with the Air Force files," Ned said when I asked if it would be all right to have a look. I said goodnight and stayed up until three in the morning reading memos and reports with "TOP SECRET" stamped on every page, including the Stevenson Report on biological warfare, which was submitted on June 30, 1950, just as the Korean War began, and wasn't fully declassified until 1996.

I interviewed Ned and Steve for a few more hours at Steve's house the next day. We talked about the feather bomb—the bomb developed by the CIA-funded Special Operations Division at Camp Detrick to hold feathers dusted with crop diseases and hog cholera. I thought, This is all so insane. Why was the U.S. government paying people to do this? Why did it take years of work by two Canadian historians to unearth research and development activities that should never have happened?

In 2013, I drove to Toronto again. This time Ned gave me his papers about germ warfare, the ones I'd looked through in his guest room, amounting to about twenty brown file boxes filled with old Air Force documents, old Dugway Proving Ground documents, Chemical Corps documents, interview transcripts, and FOIA request letters. He also gave me a pamphlet of his poems, inscribed "Love, Ned." Steve and his family took everyone out to a Chinese restaurant in Toronto and we sat at a round table and didn't talk about germ warfare.

The thing that really pained me was that Steve and Ned were wounded men. They'd taken such unbelievable abuse for publishing their book. The reviews, some of them, were truly savage. Years of work shrugged off, dismissed with the flick of a finger. Sheldon Harris, the reigning expert on Unit 731 and the American appropriation of Japan's germ-warfare research, denounced the book in the *Journal of American History*. "It is easy to dismiss this book as a black mark on the historical profession, and several scholars have done so," he said. "Sadly, this study is a prime example of shoddy scholarship masquerading as an objective examination of a controversial topic." (Never trust a reviewer who uses the word "shoddy.") Ed Regis, author of the informative and helpful though weirdly chipper book *Biology of Doom*, called Endicott and Hagerman's failures "appalling." "The evidence Endicott and Hagerman present for their extraordinarily dubious claim is notable only for its weakness," he wrote.

Actually, Ned and Steve were careful not to overstate their claim. Along with a massive dollop of previously unknown Cold War institutional history, their book offered a theory—not conclusively proven, as they conceded, but in their opinion supported by the available record. Their contention was that in 1952, and possibly also late in 1950, the United States had experimented with biological weapons in Korea and China. The authors write: "Though some documents have been shredded, others have been inadvertently lost or destroyed, and others are not expected to be opened in the foreseeable future, there is nevertheless a trail of documented circumstantial evidence that the CIA was closely involved in operation planning for the covert use of biological weapons during the Korean War, and that it had access to an extensive covert structure to implement these plans."

ONE OF THE MANY DOCUMENTS that Ned and Steve managed to get declassified, the "1951 Program Guidance Report," dated December 5, 1950, was a thirteen-page set of recommendations by the Committee on Biological Warfare of the Department of Defense's Research and Development Board

(RDB), chaired by MIT-trained weaponeer William Webster. Webster had worked with MIT's Vannevar Bush during World War II, overseeing the development of the atomic bomb; he had inherited the chairmanship of the Research and Development Board from MIT president Karl Compton, who had taken over from founder Vannevar Bush.

The document was passed around the Pentagon at a disastrous moment in the Korean War, when American divisions were in retreat from the Chinese border, after Mao's generals crossed the Yalu River into North Korea. "Our outnumbered soldiers are now hightailing it down the valleys of Korea," wrote newspaper essayist William L. White on December 4, 1950, "in the most humiliating spectacle the American flag has ever flapped over since the Battle of Bull Run!" A bigger war, with the Soviet Union, seemed imminent.

"The present international situation requires a re-evaluation of the BW program," the committee's report began. The United States was inadequately prepared. "The current situation demands an acceleration of BW research and development activities." The committee recommended intensified work on Q fever, rabbit fever, and plague, in addition to a number of animal and plant diseases, including hog cholera, wart hog disease, anthrax, and "virulent races of wheat, oat, barley and rye rusts." The committee was greatly troubled by delays in the development of biological dissemination devices. "Greater emphasis should be given to the development of continuous aerosol generators, novel devices, and ground contaminating methods for both overt and covert operations," they wrote. Balloons, gliders, and spray tanks all deserved further study and prototyping. "Special attention should be given to items such as the leaflet type bomb using feathers or other suitable materials as carriers of agents, particularly self-propagating anticrop agents."

The committee also suggested that the Department of Defense work more closely with "other government agencies" to improve disease weapons, and they called for the "investigation and evaluation of all potentially suitable methods or devices for covert or clandestine BW operations." They had special praise for the CIA's Special Operations Division of Camp

Detrick, creators of the E-73 feather bomb and other novelties. "The Committee commends the Special Operations Division at Camp Detrick for the originality, imagination and aggressiveness it has displayed in devising means and mechanisms for the covert dissemination of BW agents."

More civilian scientists were needed, as well—outside contracts and security clearances should be rapidly secured. In that way, "the knowledge of biological warfare of civilian scientists will be increased and better use will be made of their talents for BW research purposes."

This 1950 document was declassified, at Ned and Steve's request, in 1996.

WHILE THE COMMITTEE on Biological Warfare wrote this report, late in November 1950, a British soldier, in retreat in North Korea, noticed something unusual going on. It had to do with feathers.

About twenty miles south of Kunari, on a very cold day near the "waist" of Korea, a platoon sergeant from the British Middlesex Regiment marched with his men past a small village. The sergeant saw military police with white helmets standing guard; parked nearby were vehicles that looked like ambulances, but without Red Cross markings. As a courtesy, he went off the road to tell the MPs that his Middlesex platoon was the last of the friendlies—behind them were Chinese troops.

"I was told to clear off in no uncertain terms," the sergeant remembered. "It was extremely odd to be given this treatment when we were trying to give some advice."

The sergeant then noticed more puzzling goings-on. "As we were walking through the village I saw other chaps in fatigues who were very busy." They'd just arrived, it seemed. "I saw three or four of them with handfuls of feathers going into houses. They looked like fowl feathers." They were pulling the feathers out of containers, eighteen inches by eighteen inches by twenty-four inches, with snap fasteners—the kind that keep food warm. "They were running in and out spreading them. They were holding the feathers at a distance from their bodies, not in the normal way." The men wore gloves and parkas, but with no identifying insignia—and they had masks over their faces.

"It was all very fishy," the sergeant thought. "They were very surprised and unhappy to see us. It was obvious that something suspicious was going on, and that it was a clandestine affair."

A week later, the sergeant had another surprise. He was injected with a new, unspecified vaccine.

March 17, 2019, Sunday

People don't live forever—that's all there is to it. It's taken me all my life, but I'm starting to understand this truth.

TODAY I THOUGHT about something remarkable that happened in 1959. Beginning on July 1 that year, a group of people gathered on a road in Frederick, Maryland, near the entrance gate to Fort Detrick. They came every day. A placard said: "Vigil at Fort Detrick—an Appeal to Stop Preparation for Germ Warfare." A pamphlet said, "Biological warfare proposes to strike indiscriminately against babies, children, adults. It plans to kill animals and plants—man's source of food—on a massive scale. We are using talents and resources to plan famine, starvation, and disease. This is a negation of spiritual and moral values on which civilization depends." The vigil wasn't a gimmick, the pamphlet said. "We do it because our concern has led us here. Our vigil radiates the power of love, more powerful than atomic radiation."

The vigil, which may have been triggered by a disturbing article earlier that year in *Harper's Magazine* by retired biowar enthusiast Jacquard "Jack"

Rothschild, was sponsored by Quaker pacifists and members of the Fellowship of Reconciliation. ("Biological agents can attack a nation's food supply and greatly decrease its ability to make war," General Rothschild had written in *Harper's*. "The attack on the food supply is perhaps the most humane—the enemy could capitulate at the starvation point and food could be shipped in.") Lawrence Scott, the vigil's leader, was a Quaker peace activist, founder of the Committee for Nonviolent Action, a group that had tried to sail a thirty-foot protest boat, the *Golden Rule*, in range of a hydrogen-bomb test at Eniwetok Island in the Pacific in 1958. The protesters stood silently at Detrick's gate for a week, then a month, then two months. They wrote a letter to President Eisenhower: "We must turn back while there is yet time." By January 1960, they were making the papers. "The mute protest against germ warfare experiments at the Army base is carried out daily from dawn to dusk through sun, rain, wind and cold," the Associated Press reported. "The protestants come from all walks of life—teachers, physicians, scientists, ministers, students, laborers and housewives." A spinoff vigil began at the Army's chemical-warfare center in Edgewood, Maryland, in April 1960, with rallies in several cities. The Detrick vigilers ran a quarter-page ad in June 1960, quoting Marshall Stubbs, head of the Chemical Corps. "We have both in hand and in research, agents 10 to 50 times more toxic than were available a few years ago," Stubbs had told a congressional committee. "In addition to our work in the nerve gases we have new toxic substances which will attack other vulnerable systems of the body such as the eyes and the mind."

The protesters took particular issue with the notion, often repeated by chemical- and biological-warfare promoters, that germ weapons and war gases were more humane than traditional weapons because they didn't destroy property, and because some of them weren't fatal. "The argument that germ and gas weapons are 'more humane' is sugar coating for a very lethal pill," the vigilers said. "It is an attempt to overcome the moral revulsion which people have against poisoning and infecting other people like themselves." Sponsors of the vigil were well-known names in the peace movement: Henry Cadbury, Milton Mayer, Victor Paschkis, Richard Gregg—author of *The Power of Nonviolence*—and Clarence

Pickett, former head of the American Friends Service Committee, which had won a Nobel Peace Prize in 1947. At the bottom of the ad was a verse from the Bible about things done in secret: "And this is the condemnation, that light is come into the world, and men loved darkness rather than light, because their deeds were evil."

The Detrick Vigilantes, as the town of Frederick called them, kept on standing near the gate. They stood for a year, then a year and a half, then twenty-one months. On the last day, March 30, 1961, a hundred people stood in silence. It was one of the longest continuous war protests ever, one reporter said, and it may have led indirectly to later exposés: protests beginning in 1965 at the University of Pennsylvania of a lucrative germ-war research program called Project Spice Rack; critiques by Harvard professors Matthew Meselson, Jean Mayer, and Victor Sidel in 1966; writing by Elinor Langer in *Science* in 1967; and by Seymour Hersh in 1968, in his book *Chemical and Biological Warfare: America's Hidden Arsenal*, which devotes a page to the vigil. And those exposés led to President Nixon's announced renunciation of offensive biological warfare research in 1969, in his first year in office. The vigilers were part of that victory.

THERE WERE MAJOR SETBACKS during the Kennedy and Johnson administrations, however. On January 20, 1961, the day John Kennedy took the oath of office, Drew Pearson, a columnist with a wide readership, listed some things Kennedy might do to seize the world's imagination. We should forgo colonialism, Pearson said, and offer Khrushchev some of our grain supply "to help out his crop failures," and accept atom-bomb inspection in order to get a test treaty. Pearson's number one suggestion was this: "Renounce germ warfare and close Fort Detrick, the bacteriological laboratory at Frederick, Md. It has hurt us far more than any good we can ever gain."

The Kennedy administration didn't follow any of Pearson's suggestions. Robert McNamara, Kennedy's secretary of defense, tripled the germ-warfare research budget.

I SPENT THE AFTERNOON reading newspaper articles from 1959 and 1960. One article, from October 1959, was by a writer named Walter Schneir, who had interviewed people at Fort Detrick and written it up for *The Reporter*, a pricklishly liberal magazine. Schneir lists the types of infected insects that were, he said, "constantly available" at Detrick during the Marshall Stubbs era. "The inventory includes mosquitoes infected with yellow fever, malaria, and dengue; fleas infected with plague; ticks with tularemia, relapsing fever, and Colorado fever; houseflies with cholera, anthrax, and dysentery."

Also I came across a Wirephoto picture from January 1960 of Marshall Stubbs—bald and hollow-eyed—positioning a new, sleeker style of gas mask onto one of his secretaries. And I found an article that described a special secret show that Stubbs put on for congressmen in June 1960. He led members of the House Committee on Science and Astronautics to a special room, closed to reporters and members of the public, and did undisclosed psychochemical things to two dogs in order to "illustrate the effectiveness of some of the incapacitating chemicals being developed by the military for future use."

In the CIA's CREST database there was very little correspondence with Marshall Stubbs—just a thank-you letter to Stubbs from Charles P. Cabell, deputy director of central intelligence, after a visit to Dugway Proving Ground, the vast testing area in Utah, early in June 1960. "Colonel Armitage and his staff put on an excellent show for us with first-rate briefings and a field demonstration," Cabell wrote. "I am glad to note that members of the Chemical Corps Command and of this Agency remain in close touch on matters of mutual interest."

March 18, 2019, Monday

In Seymour Hersh's latest book, *Reporter*, which I read in bed in the wee hours this morning, I learned that Hersh and his wife named their son Matthew after Matthew Meselson, the Harvard biologist who, as a consultant for the Arms Control and Disarmament Agency, was probably the most influential opponent of biological warfare research. I was also interested to read that in 1967, Hersh's closely researched, fifteen-thousand-word, five-part article for the Associated Press on American chemical and biological weapons research was "shredded down" to a much shorter piece.

I found the piece on Newspapers.com. It was in a lot of newspapers—it took up half a page of the C section of the *Fort Lauderdale News*, for instance. It had been somewhat defanged in the editing, and shortened. What did Hersh do? He wrote a book on the subject, plus two pieces for *Ramparts* and a piece for *The New Republic*. The man was unstoppable. Hersh has always in the end gotten to say what he wants to say, because what he wants to say is interesting and shocking and (mostly) true, and people have an appetite for truth. He learned something important from I. F. Stone, he said: Read before you write. Hersh read the hearing transcripts and the research reports and he found out where the retired officers were and he interviewed some of them. And his book about chemical and biological research horrified people. "If there is one person who ought to read this book it is Mr. Richard Nixon," the *New Statesman* said, on the back of the paperback edition. Hersh quoted Jack Rothschild's proposal to seed the cold winds that flow down from Siberia past the China coast with anthrax or yellow fever, causing a reviewer in *The New York Times* to say that Rothschild was "generously contributing to the image of the United States as a nation gone berserk."

One of Hersh's articles, "Germ Warfare, for Alma Mater, God, and Country," is part of CIA's CREST database, I discovered recently. Somebody drew a line next to a particular paragraph in the CIA's copy, in which Hersh gives a slightly garbled account, retold to him by Kennedy insiders, of the CIA proposal to destroy Cuba's sugarcane crop. Hersh had heard that it was sugar beets they had wanted to infect, not sugarcane. The summary remarks by top Agency officers about Hersh's article are whited out from an accompanying document, a memo for the record summarizing a morning meeting on November 18, 1969, partly declassified in 2005. Two of nine paragraphs of the meeting minutes are also whited out— marked with 25X1, a redaction code of extreme vagueness. The 25X1 exception refers to a redaction that is required because the passage would reveal the identity of a human source, or "impair the effectiveness of an intelligence method currently in use, available for use, or under development." In other words, we are keeping this secret because we feel like it.

IT's ANOTHER ASTONISHINGLY BLUE DAY, with tree shadows on the white-painted doors of the garage. I pulled out one of Ned Hagerman's boxes this morning—the one that holds some of his many FOIA requests. When his request was refused, he filed an appeal. Years went by. There's an email, for instance, from David Fort, about Ned's request in 1996 for some documents from the late 1940s and early '50s from the Joint Chiefs of Staff. "Dear Mr. Hagerman," Fort wrote in 2012, "this is a response to your October 26, 1996 Freedom of Information Request case NND# 961147 for access to records in the custody of the National Archives and Records Administration." More than fifteen years had gone by between Ned's initial letter and Fort's reply. "Please contact this office if you are still interested in pursuing this FOIA or MDR request," it said. To which Ned wrote, "Thank you. Please proceed with the FOIA request."

One FOIA tussle Ned had was over an important, still partly classified history of the Air Force's biological-warfare program. It was written by Dorothy Miller of the Air Force's Historical Office, in Dayton, Ohio. It's called "History of Air Force Participation in Biological Warfare Program, 1944–1951." Dorothy Miller combed through hundreds of documents, some of them now inaccessible, wrote the hundred-page report, and had it typed in its final typescript form in September 1952, although it was probably distributed in draft form some months before that. Back then it was a top-secret document; now, after several downgradings, it mostly isn't.

In her history, Dorothy Miller is upbeat about the potential for biological weaponry. "By 1947," she writes, "military planners were beginning to reconsider, however cautiously, what the national objective in conducting a modern war should be. There was a growing consciousness that saturation bombing was not the key to real victory." America's recent enemies—Italy, Germany, and Japan, bombed and burned and ravaged as they were—were enemies no longer. Their rubble and poverty now constituted a "postwar problem," not a desired end. "The aim of any conflict is for one nation to impose its will upon another," Miller wrote. Moreover, saturation bombing, and even the novel force of the atomic bomb, wouldn't necessarily prevail against the new enemies, Russia and China, with their enormous armies in readiness. New types of "CEBAR" weapons—that is, chemical, biological, and radiological weapons—offered the possibility of conquering a nation without destroying it. Miller quoted General Donald Putt, then director of the Air Force's Research and Development Program: "Of the three munition phases of CEBAR," Putt said, "the USAF is most interested in the Biological (BW) agents."

Some pages later Miller itemized in more detail the advantages of a biological attack on humans, crops, and livestock: "The recognized capabilities of BW weapons include destruction of personnel without destruction of materiel; disabling of personnel with minimum loss of life; denial of an area by making it hazardous for a long time; reduction of yield of crops to disaster proportions; effective reduction of yield of all plants in a limited area; and destruction of the economic animal population over a large area." And there were other advantages to the waging of war by means of bacteria, viruses, and fungi. For one thing, it promised to be "comparatively cheap." Also, it offered "vast potentialities as a psychological weapon." Bioweaponry gave a country, she said, "almost an endless variety of ways to wage war." You could choose a disease that would kill outright, for example, or one that would merely sicken people temporarily, or one that would "cause death after a lingering illness." And there was the potential of mounting a dual attack, simultaneously biological and atomic: "Theoretically, by proper time fusing of the 4-pound biological bomb, a ring of BW contamination could be established completely around the areas affected by the blast, heat, and radiation of an atomic explosion," Miller said. "Demoralization would be complete."

Miller's report supplies many details about the research progress of the Air Force in that tense, mid–Korean War moment, when full-on war with the Soviet Union, and possibly with China, seemed inevitable. She describes the impossibility of international control of biological weapons, and the absence of any formal prohibition on their unilateral use. She itemizes, in bewildering detail, individual weapons that are in various stages of development in 1948, 1949, 1950, up through February 1951, the chosen endpoint of her study. (She wrote a part 2, covering later developments, in 1954.)

But what struck Ned Hagerman as strange, and struck Steve Endicott as strange—and what strikes me as strange—is that this document, written during a horrendous war that had killed tens of thousands of American soldiers (and millions of Korean civilians and hundreds of thousands of Chinese and Korean soldiers) makes almost no mention of Korea. One has to suspect that the paragraphs here and there that mention Korea—and China and Russia and wartime Japan—have been whited out. "In the absence of firm strategic guidance," Miller writes, "the USAF had to proceed unilaterally in formulating plans for using biological—" And then a third of a page is gone.

Naturally, Ned asked for the document to be released in full. After years and appeals and struggles and delays, it didn't happen. The document still has blanks. Two years ago, I wrote the Air Force asking for the redactions to be removed. I've heard nothing back.

What happened, I think, was that the redacteur whited out any paragraph in the document that connected events in the Far East with the Air Force's development program for biological warfare.

I could be completely wrong. The only way to prove me wrong is by declassifying the entire document.

March 19, 2019, Tuesday

The dogs are sleeping on the pillows under the table now, but soon I'll be giving them breakfast. Briney is halfway through a monthlong treatment for Lyme disease that the vet put him on before we adopted him. I have to tuck away an antibiotic pill in his food. Where we used to live, in southern Maine, practically everyone—and everyone's dog—had been through at least one bout of tick-borne Lyme disease. There were bull's-eye rashes all over the place. M. was treated for Lyme disease three times, twice with secondary infections, once with a severe allergic reaction to the antibiotic. It is the scourge of New England, and it's not, I think, a natural scourge. The Lyme epidemic is an unintended artifact of long-ago germ-warfare research.

If you look at a map of Lyme disease you'll notice that it didn't spread naturally. It has two separate foci of infection: one in Lyme, Connecticut, spreading out from there over the coastal Northeast, and one in Wisconsin. The Lyme, Connecticut, focalism was examined in a magnificently researched book by Michael Carroll, *Lab 257*. Carroll thinks that the ticks came from the Plum Island large-animal disease laboratory, at the eastern end of Long Island—which was a CIA-funded and Army-funded center

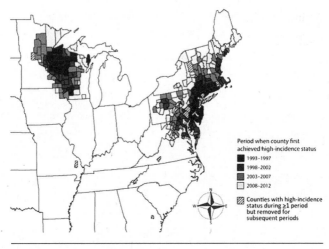

Period when county first
achieved high-incidence status
■ 1993-1997
■ 1998-2002
▩ 2003-2007
☐ 2008-2012

▨ Counties with high-incidence
status during ≥1 period
but removed for
subsequent periods

The two primary foci of Lyme tick disease.

Kiersten J. Kugeler, Grace M. Farley, Joseph D. Forrester, and Paul S. Mead, "Geographic Distribution
and Expansion of Human Lyme Disease, United States," *Emerging Infectious Diseases* 21, no. 8, August
2015, wwwnc.cdc.gov/eid/article/21/8/14-1878_article.

of research into tick-borne livestock diseases, both common and exotic. At
Plum Island, scientists—including one former Nazi scientist allowed into
the United States under Frank Wisner's Operation Paperclip—gathered
insects from all over and reared them in quantity and fed them with tainted
blood and kept track of which ones worked best to make farm animals
sick. Because the Plum Island lab in some eras was lax about biosafety,
Carroll suggests, disease-laden ticks found their way to Plum Island's
birds and deer. The deer swam from Plum Island across the bay to Lyme,
Connecticut, and kids there started coming down with fevers, swollen
joints, and mood disorders.

The other focus point, in northern Wisconsin, is more of a mystery. It
may have been the original source of a naturally evolved disease—the first
case of Lyme in the United States appeared not in Lyme but in Wisconsin,
in January 1969, at least according to one paper—or it may have something
to do with the fact that the University of Wisconsin was a hub of germ-
warfare research and expertise during World War II and through the
1950s. Exotic insects from faraway places and samples of disease variants
were being mailed all over the country during the Cold War—all over the

world, in fact; the original marriage of deer ticks with spirochetes could have happened anywhere.

What's troubling, or at least puzzling, about the Lyme-tick story is that Willy Burgdorfer, the Swiss-born scientist who in 1982 discovered the causative agent of the disease and gave it its scientific name, *Borrelia burgdorferi*, was himself a germ warrior. Burgdorfer worked at the Rocky Mountain Laboratory in Hamilton, Montana, which had a research contract with Camp Detrick. The aim was to turn ticks into drones of animal and human disease and find efficient ways to rear them in large numbers. Burgdorfer himself obviously loved ticks—big ones or tiny ones, soft ("argasid") or hard ("ixodid"). And he loved dissecting them— "thousands and thousands and thousands" of them, he told his oral historian, using Swiss-made watchmaker's forceps and eye-surgery scalpels in order to get at the tiny spirochetes of relapsing fever or rickettsia or Lyme disease that squirmed within. "Whatever I did ticks were involved," he said. Among entomologists he was known as the "tick surgeon."

One of Burgdorfer's published projects at the Rocky Mountain Lab— which had a tick museum and tick-rearing pens set in water-filled safety pans to prevent escape—was the development of a means of infecting soft ticks with Q fever, tularemia, leptospirosis, and Western equine encephalitis, all diseases of interest to germ-war weaponeers. In a paper for *The Journal of Infectious Diseases*, Burgdorfer and his Rocky Mountain colleague Edward Pickens describe cutting away the top of an incubating chicken egg using a dental saw, placing the ticks inside, and taping the top of the egg back in place. (The article begins: "The technique of feeding blood-sucking arthropods on chicken embryos has been used for the transmission of microbial diseases.") After eight to twelve hours, the trapped ticks would be found to have fed on the blood of the unhatched chicken. And if the egg had been previously infected with a disease, the ticks would then become vectors.

Another of Burgdorfer's experiments involved the feeding and inoculation of *Ixodes*—ticks with hard shells. He immobilized wood ticks, *Dermacentor andersoni*, in a miniature berm made of plasticine, and then successfully fed them two diseases, leptospirosis and rabies, from a capillary tube.

Burgdorfer's real defense-related research wasn't published, however. ("And why was that?" asked the oral historian. "It was classified," answered Burgdorfer.) Even so, a summary of Rocky Mountain activity in an annual report offers clues: "Passage of BW agents through various arthropods offers an opportunity to increase the virulence of the agents or to alter certain of their characteristics," said the annual report of the Chemical Corps Biological Laboratories in 1953. "This has been studied under contract at the USPHS Rocky Mountain Laboratory in Montana. Tularemia, Q fever, and plague have been passed through appropriate vectors and the resulting strains are being compared with the original strains supplied by the Biological Laboratories. Q fever rickettsiae multiplied so rapidly in the tick *Dermacentor andersoni* that the majority of the test ticks died." The ticks carried the disease but also made it worse. The digestive tracts of ticks were test tubes.

I just noticed that there's a new book out about Willy Burgdorfer and Lyme disease, called *Bitten*, to be published in May. In it, according to the advertising copy, Willy Burgdorfer reveals that "he had developed bug-borne bioweapons during the Cold War, and believed that the Lyme epidemic was started by a military experiment gone wrong." The author, Kris Newby, promises to uncover "darker truths about Willy." Good.

YOU MAY WONDER WHAT Q FEVER IS. It first attracted notice in 1935 in Queensland, Australia, where cowboys and slaughterhouse workers in Brisbane—especially meat inspectors in the "tank and bone house"—fell ill with a mysterious flu, possibly transmitted by bandicoot ticks, which then bit cattle. Its causative agent, named *Rickettsia burneti* after F. M. Burnet, one of the scientists who isolated it in 1937, was so mysterious, so hard to differentiate from other kinds of influenza, that he and his colleagues named it query fever. That's one version of where the name came from. The other version is that people first called it Queensland fever and then somebody shortened it to Q fever out of a wish to avoid naming a disease after an Australian state. "It is suggested that inhalation of tick faeces is the likely mode of entry of *Rickettsia burneti*," wrote a Brisbane epidemiologist in 1944.

Hundreds of British and American troops came down with Q fever in Italy in 1943. In Bulgaria it was called the Balkan grippe.

In the United States, at the Rocky Mountain Laboratory, a researcher in 1935 injected ground-up ticks that he'd gathered at Nine Mile, Montana, into guinea pigs and determined that the animals were suffering not from Rocky Mountain spotted fever, but from a new illness, which made them feverish and enlarged their spleens. Dr. Rolla E. Dyer, director of the Division of Infectious Disease of the National Institute of Health in Bethesda, visited the Rocky Mountain Lab in 1937 and examined some infected guinea pigs with interest. He promptly fell ill with what came to be called Nine Mile fever—which was later determined to be the very same sickness as Q fever.

Three years on, in May 1940, Dr. Charles Armstrong—another scientist at the National Institute of Health, known for having found ways to modify the polio virus so that it would infect mice and monkeys—took sick. Q fever again. More than a dozen people who worked in the NIH's laboratory building, Building 5, also became ill, and one, Asa Marcey, a sixty-year-old lab assistant, died. After that, Dr. Armstrong took a break from Q fever for a while in order to pursue other research. Late in May 1942, he flew from Washington to the Rocky Mountain Laboratory, where he soon checked himself into a hospital. This time he'd come down with a severe case of tularemia. He was laid up for months.

Then, after the war, in February 1946, Dr. Armstrong began a new series of Q fever investigations. Twenty-two people fell ill this time, all of them employed in NIH Building 5. "We started working on Q fever again a few weeks ago," Dr. Armstrong told a reporter for the Associated Press, "and it got away from us again, just as it did before." An elevator operator was near death. Armstrong suspected airborne transmission. "This outbreak is most unfortunate," Armstrong said, "but we are going to glean all possible scientific information from it." Eventually forty-seven people got sick. Two guinea pig populations, one housed on the first floor, one in the attic, became infected spontaneously.

A month later, forty people caught Q fever in Amarillo, Texas, in stockyards and meatpacking plants. Two died. Five meat inspectors in Chicago got sick, along with thirty-five sheep slaughterers at the Swift & Co. plant.

In 1947, the NIH built a state-of-the-art infectious-disease research building in Bethesda, Building 7, with a superheated-grid air-sterilization system, hoping to avoid more epidemics or fatalities. (In addition to the two Q fever epidemics, one researcher had died of scrub typhus and another of tularemia, both in 1944.) But the air-sterilization system didn't work; shortly after Building 7 opened, five research workers, along with a visitor who'd stood in the lobby and a couple who rented a basement room to one of the scientists (and washed his sheets and towels), all came down with Q fever. It turned out there were unfixable leaks in the building's plumbing that allowed inside air to circulate throughout every floor.

In 1950, a seventy-eight-year-old tailor in England fell into a coma and died. An autopsy was performed. The man's spleen and right testicle were found to be enlarged. The posthumous diagnosis was Q fever. "All who took part in the necropsy became infected, probably by inhalation."

So that's Q fever, one of a number of fractious fevers that the Committee on Biological Warfare of the Research and Development Board thought deserved intensified research and weaponization. Q fever tests at Dugway Proving Ground in Utah began in 1951. In July 1955, a group of thirty Seventh-day Adventists—all volunteers—were sprayed with Q fever germs at Dugway. "I really have never been any sicker than that," said one Project Whitecoat patient. In 1958, after further large-scale live tests, the jackrabbit population at Dugway was found to be carriers of Q fever. Native desert mice and deer were also infected.

An Army ecologist, Keith Smart, studied the elevated incidence of Q fever in Dugway's wildlife. There was "no adverse causative impact," he claimed.

March 20, 2019, Wednesday

I woke up around 5:00 A.M. from an unusually complicated dream in which I was at a hospital—a decrepit, half-abandoned hospital. I was supposed to find out something about some secret experiments that were happening there, but patients were lining up who had various illnesses and needed care. Then I was holding two rolled-up portable marimba scales, and someone was telling me that what I needed to do with them was to make something called a "birefringent autocollimator" by merging the two scales, one of which was harmonic minor and one of which was some mode in a different key. I thought I should avoid merging the two scales, since it wasn't going to lead to good music, but he was insistent. Before I could get the mallets out and play the gene-spliced keyboard I woke up.

I lay awake thinking of some of the animal experiments, and human experiments, I'd read about. Many wholly unnecessary things were done to guinea pigs—and monkeys. I remembered reading one document at the National Archives in June 2012—not the most awful, but it stuck in my head. I'd been trying to find some records of the Air Force's Psychological Warfare Division, but I hadn't had much luck—yellow "access restricted" cards replaced whole folders in one box. I went back to the biological-warfare

office records of AFOAT, the Air Force Office of Atomic Energy. I'd
already been through these twice, but each time I recognized more names
and understood things better. There were memos about anticrop agents,
chemical agents, types of bombs, meetings with generals and civilian
scientists—and then I came to a memo, now fully declassified, formerly
top secret, that described a nighttime bombing test at Dugway Proving
Ground in Utah. The test, which took place early in September 1952 and
was observed by Colonel Joseph J. Clark, who worked in the Offensive
BW Section of AFOAT BW-CW, was of the M-33 biological bomb,
which created a fog of *Brucella* organisms over a test grid.

On the test grid, which was surrounded by lights so that the bomber
pilot could see it, were a number of prefab houses: forty-nine of them.
There were also slit trenches and sampling stations. To be distributed
among the houses and the trenches and the sampling stations were more
than three thousand guinea pigs. At three o'clock in the afternoon, the
guinea-pig workers began at Baker Laboratory. (Baker Laboratory may
have been named after a person named Baker, but I don't think so. I think
it just stood for "Baker William," the letter code that military people
sometimes used for biological warfare.)

The boxing operation took hours. "It consisted of placing 3,230 guinea
pigs in individual boxes with only their heads sticking out through a hole
in one end of the box," the memo said. "These boxes prevent excessive
contamination of the animal's fur, thus eliminating, as far as possible, the
infections passed from one animal to another after the aerosol cloud has
passed." The guinea pigs were all boxed by 7:30 P.M. and were driven to
the test grid in refrigerated vans. Six crews distributed the boxed pigs
and the petri dishes at sampling stations. Everyone withdrew to safe
places. The bomber arrived overhead at 1:20 A.M. and dropped four M-33
clusters—each containing 108 four-pound submunitions filled with liquid
disease. Then he circled around and dropped three more cluster bombs.
Circled again and dropped two clusters.

After waiting an hour for the germ cloud to disperse, crews in
protective suits fanned out to collect the guinea pigs, the petri dishes, and
a few dud bombs. By five in the morning the animals were back in Baker

Laboratory. At this point a team of statisticians from Project Big Ben, a bioweapons analysis group at the University of Pennsylvania, arrived at the lab.

"The results of this test appear to be satisfactory from a munitions functioning standpoint," the memo concluded. "However, data on animal infection will not be available until autopsy is completed after a 21 to 30 day incubation period." The next test was scheduled for September 18.

When I first found that memo at the National Archives in June 2012, I found my way back to my Super 8 motel room in College Park thinking about those three thousand guinea pigs in little boxes out in the middle of a huge desert in the dark of a September night. At some point there is a lot of noise, as four-pound bombs burst open and fall around them. And then a cold sort of moist mist. They breathe the mist. They have no choice. Then they go back to their cages in the lab and live for another two or three weeks. Some of them get brucellosis, or undulant fever, which is a very unpleasant disease, but usually not fatal. All of the guinea pigs die, though, because scientists kill them so that they can look at their lungs and internal organs.

What a pointless horror. Honestly. Think about it. Three thousand guinea pigs with their heads poking out of little boxes in the middle of the night.

At the University of California, Berkeley, a teacher and bacteriologist, Albert Krueger, oversaw the Naval Biological Laboratory, which had an outpost on the island of Alameda, near Oakland. (Fulfilling the requirement that certain infectious research be carried out offshore.) Beginning in 1943, Krueger's team worked on experimental aerosol weapons using *pestis* as their active agent: plague. In 1951, *The New York Times* described one of Albert Krueger's experiments: "The experimental animals are encased in rows of cubicles with just their heads sticking out. The atomizer sprays a germ-laden mist past the animals' noses." If the droplets of mist are sufficiently small, the animal—a guinea pig or a monkey—becomes a victim.

Krueger's colleague across the San Francisco Bay, Karl F. Meyer, a Swiss-born veterinary doctor, ran plague experiments at the Hooper

Foundation for Medical Research, housed then in a beautiful building on Parnassus Avenue. Meyer, known to associates as "K.F.," paired a monkey that he'd infected with plague together with a healthy monkey, separated by a barrier, to find out whether the infection would spread aerially or not. "Usually the control died," he said in his oral history, "but we never knew whether he got it by inhalation or by direct contact, saliva being slopped over. So we developed that separating cage." It turned out, as Meyer discovered in what he called a "classical set of experiments," that the monkeys caught plague from each other by swallowing "large mucous particles" and not by breathing in tiny aerosolized infected droplets. "We never could produce in monkeys a pneumonic plague chain which I was looking for," he said.

During the war and just after, in 1944, 1945, and 1946, Meyer, hired by the Office of Scientific Research and Development to develop a dependable plague vaccine, injected bacteria into hundreds of inmates at San Quentin prison, after the prison's warden, Clinton Duffy, put out a call for "human guinea pigs." It was covered in newspapers at the time. "Some prisoners were hospitalized with high fevers," an Associated Press article noted in May 1945.

"This was a prison group which didn't squawk too much, during the wartime," Dr. Meyer said in his oral history. "Therefore, I tested some preparations which were very, very toxic, *very* toxic."

March 21, 2019, Thursday

The sun came out in the middle of the afternoon, and I wrote two letters to the CIA's information and privacy coordinator. It's time to ask for more of what is hiding behind the white-outs. Redaction is a form of psychological warfare directed against historians and journalists.

In one letter I asked for redaction removal in three pages of minutes of a director's meeting that took place on September 12, 1951. It's not a momentous meeting, I don't think. But actually I don't know. The third paragraph reads: "Mr. Dulles stated that he had a memorandum respecting the ▭ operation and handed such memorandum to Mr. Becker for the DCI." One short word cut and the sentence becomes meaningless. Dulles handed a memo to Becker to give to the director of central intelligence. What was the memo about? What operation was it? "Please reinstate the word," I said in my letter. "If you believe you cannot reinstate the word, please explain why."

The paragraph after that was whited out. Then the second page of the minutes was entirely blanked. The penultimate paragraph: again blanked. This everyday document qualifies as something that the CIA has released to the public, in keeping with its expressed policy of openness, but in fact they've kept half of it to themselves for sixty-eight years. "Please unblank," I said.

I also asked them to release all of CIA document RDP79M00983A001500040003-6, partly declassified in 2005. This was a twenty-three-page clump of items from 1977 about MKNAOMI, the CIA's biological-weapons research and development effort, begun as a joint effort in 1948 or 1949 with the Special Operations Division at Camp Detrick. It starts with a cover memo: "Note for ▭. From ▭. Re: Release of MKNAOMI material." There's a handwritten note: "This is what we know about how material went public. I am told there <u>may</u> have been a FOIA query." Signed, ▭. Then comes a page with a black diagonal bar across it that says "Next 15 Page(s) in Document Exempt"— meaning exempt from required FOIA disclosure. In those pages, according to the cover memo, are two subdocuments: a "Summary Report on CIA Investigation on MKNAOMI" and a "Contingency Plan for Stockpile of Biological Warfare Agents."

There follow three pages photocopied from the *Congressional Record* for November 4, 1975, in which Representative Edward Koch, future mayor of New York, engages in a correspondence with CIA director William Colby. Representative Koch says he is shocked and angered after reading in an article in *The New York Times* that the CIA in the 1960s undertook "an experiment using New York City's subways in which they flooded the subway system with a 'harmless simulant of a disease-carrying gas.'" Colby replies that the CIA "at no time" experimented with simulants in the subway, "nor did this Agency request that such an experiment be carried out." Koch is mollified. "With all the criticism, well warranted in my judgment, of the CIA, it is nice to report that one of the charges against it is unfounded." The last page of RDP79M00983A001500040003-6, too sensitive for public scrutiny, has another black diagonal bar across it. All in all, eighteen of twenty-three pages are held back.

What's nutty—and not that uncommon—is that two of the withheld component documents of RDP79M00983A001500040003-6, the Summary Report and the Contingency Plan, were already at least partially declassified. The contingency plan was published in full in 1976, with no redactions anywhere, as part of the Church Committee's hearings on intelligence activities, and is widely held in libraries. The Summary Report was also released, with large redactions, by the National Archives, but not until 2018, one of thousands of long-withheld texts that have surfaced as a result of the JFK Records Act. The redactions are supposed to be re-reviewed by 2021.

The CIA's Summary Report on MKNAOMI activity, written in 1975, is a helpful document. "From its outset the project was characterized by a compartmentation that was extreme even by CIA standards," the summary said. "Because of the sensitivity of the activity, queries by operations officers as to the availability of materials and delivery systems of the type being developed at Fort Detrick were automatically turned away by TSD" (that is, by the CIA's Technical Services Division, which was part of the Directorate of Plans, or Clandestine Service) "unless initial approval for contact had been given by the Deputy Director for Plans." The deputy director of plans from 1951 to 1958 was Frank Wisner. Few written records were kept, the paper says:

> Discussions with those involved in the project indicate that hand launchers with darts loaded with dog incapacitant may have been delivered for use in S.E. Asia. They also indicate that some of the material or crop spoilants may have been employed. While no direct connections to assassination planning have been found, there are disturbing similarities between the agents being investigated at Fort Detrick and some of the reported schemes for incapacitating or assassinating Castro.

A long blanked-out paragraph follows this passage.

Colby was mistaken in his denial of the CIA's involvement in the New York City subway germ-simulant test. "A study on the vulnerability of subway systems to covert attack and development of a method to carry out such attack was conducted," wrote the chief of the Biological Branch of the Technical Services Division in October 1967. "The study provided a threat model and information on uses of dissemination and methods of delivery which could be used offensively." The CIA's intelligence side collected a fair amount of information about the Moscow subway system, including how many ventilation chambers it had in each station and how deep they were. In February 1966, the Office of Research and Reports produced an analysis of new subway construction in Budapest, Warsaw, Moscow, Leningrad, and Kiev, and of how Soviet bloc subways might function as civil-defense shelters.

What I imagine some war planners were thinking was this: If everyone is forced down into subway stations while nuclear bombs go off overhead, wouldn't that be an opportunity to make them very sick?

The year 1975 was the beginning of FOIA's golden age. "Applications under the Freedom of Information Act are slowly beginning to dislodge documents from the Central Intelligence Agency, and tidbits from the agency's secret files are floating all over Washington," wrote Nicholas Horrock in *The New York Times* in May 1975. "An amendment to the Freedom of Information Act that went into effect in February has vastly increased the number of documents that are being declassified." The CIA had fifty people processing FOIA letters then—sixteen hundred requests had come in since the beginning of the year. Some whispered sense of the full Mr. Hydeian depravity of what CIA clandestinists had been doing in the dark for a quarter of a century was beginning to get out. In September 1975, a UPI photo of an unsmiling Senator Frank Church holding one of the CIA's assassination weapons, a nearly silent, painless dart gun called a "nondiscirnable microbioinoculator," appeared on the front page of *The New York Times*. The headline below was: "COLBY DESCRIBES C.I.A. POISON WORK." In public hearings, Senator Church questioned CIA director Colby about the dart or fléchette gun, which was meant to deliver a fast-acting toxin that "would not appear in the autopsy." "As a murder instrument, that is about as efficient as you can get, is it not?" asked Senator Church.

"It is a weapon," Colby solemnly replied, "a very serious weapon."

President Ford announced that in light of the revelations he would be giving thought to revamping the CIA. "Among plans being considered," according to the Associated Press, "are stripping the agency of its covert operations."

Michael Harrington, in Congress, said, "What has caused such widespread alarm, and what Mr. Colby has refused to deal with frontally, is the Agency's straying from legitimate information gathering to engage in direct manipulation of governments and institutions, often by the most violent of means." There was a difference between gathering intelligence, Harrington said, and pushing people around. "Of such strong-arm tactics Mr. Colby only says that 'little of this nature' is done any more, an assurance that must come as cold comfort to the widow of Salvador Allende and to other recent victims of CIA skulduggery."

March 22, 2019, Friday

M. was in the kitchen toasting some bread. It was six o'clock in the morning. I was sitting on the bed in the dark, typing, when Cedric came over and set his long nose down on my keyboard. He made wheezing, moaning sounds, very human sounds, as if he wanted to tell me something autobiographical. I held my hand for a long time on his small, warm head. Every dog has a novel in him. Then he curled up nearby on the covers and went to sleep.

The rain began in the midmorning and came down all day—cold rain. I ate some boiled potatoes for breakfast and thought about the word "aerosol." As a kid I loved the word—so light and vowelly, so smilingly scientific. I memorized, and could perform, the ad for Right Guard aerosol deodorant, where the man opens the medicine cabinet in his apartment and encounters his garrulous neighbor in a T-shirt: Hi, Guy!

But now I have a different feeling. Aerosols are about mass killing. First about the killing of insects. An inventor, Lyle Goodhue, at the Department of Agriculture in Beltsville, Maryland, had an idea of making an extremely fine bug-killing mist using pressurized freon mixed with pesticide. His supervisor, Frank Campbell, a medical entomologist, signed the paper describing the invention, and later Campbell and Goodhue worked on bug bombs during the war. "Aerosol Bombs Blitz Insect Armies" was a newspaper headline in April 1944. "Hundreds of thousands of men in our armed forces are probably giving thanks this very minute to the scientists who developed the aerosol 'bomb,'" the article said. "The aerosol fog is much finer than the sprays we have known. That's the magic of its work."

Frank Campbell went on to become the CIA's in-house entomologist in 1948, and Lyle Goodhue joined Airosol, a Kansas company that made bug bombs for home use. "As easy as turning on a light switch, a twist of the wrist releases a fine spray that penetrates every crack and corner," said an ad for the Airosol home atomizer in 1946. "Airosol DDT Insecticide is guaranteed to be the same DDT-Aerosol formula used by the U.S. Army in the amazingly successful insect control projects during the war." The bombs sold for $2.95.

Also during the war, a different sort of aerosol was talked about, but only in secret. "In May 1943 the Munitions Branch at Camp Detrick began the development of one or more munitions for dispersing liquid suspensions of 'N' or 'X' as clouds capable of causing infection by the respiratory route," wrote Herbert Tanner, a Detrick engineer. "The initial munitions program included an investigation of the immediately available M69 and M74 bombs for aerosol dispersion of 'N' or 'X,' either in liquid or semi-dry form." (N is the code for anthrax, X botulinum toxin, a potent, shelf-stable poison made from the bacteria that causes botulism.) Herbert Tanner went on to work at the Special Operations Division at Detrick after the war; he was, in fact, one of the Detrick germ warriors to be dosed surreptitiously with LSD by Sidney Gottlieb, during a now famous CIA experiment and/or party in a cabin on Deep Creek Lake. (Scientist Frank Olson, who later jumped out a window—or was helped to jump out a window—of the Statler Hotel in New York, was another guest.)

The M-69 submunition was a hexagonal six-pound firebomb: filled with napalm and clustered in a five-hundred-pound bomb, this horror killed untold thousands of people and destroyed many Japanese cities. The M-69 fell and exploded in a way that started terrible firestorms, but it was not well suited for creating the ultrafine aerosolized droplets of anthrax and botulin that could pass through a victim's mouth and throat and lodge deep in the lung.

In 1943, on the advice of British bomb designers, the Detrick engineers, in haste, began working with a different firebomb, the British Mark I bomb, Type F. It, too, was hexagonal, a pipe bomb, about twenty-one inches long and an inch and a half thick, but it was lighter and held less germ solution—it weighed four pounds. British scientists calculated that 106 of the Mark I Type F bombs, clustered together and dropped at high altitude from an airplane, would, so Tanner summarized, "produce a cloud of 'N' affording 50% risk of death for man to at least a distance of one mile and over an area of 500,000 square yards."

Impressed, the Army drew up contracts for the mass production of the bomb, renamed the SPD Mark I bomb. (SPD stands for Special Projects Division, which is what people in the know called Camp Detrick.) But when Tanner and his bacteriologist colleague Harold Batchelor, an aerosol specialist with a degree from the University of Wisconsin, began running tests at Horn Island, off the Mississippi coast near Pascagoula, using some extremely toxic botulinum poison, they were disappointed at how few guinea pigs they killed.

The men knew they had a potent agent: Detrick's scientists had chosen the most toxic strain of Type A of the botulism bacillus—on the belief, writes Rexmond Cochrane (in a 1947 history declassified in 1975), that "the Germans and Japanese would devote their greatest attention to preparing a defense against Type B, with which they were more familiar by reason of its greater incidence in their countries." Strain #57 of Type A of *Clostridium botulinum* killed all exposed test mice in seventeen hours, which was unusually fast: lab workers propagated it in "cultures of beef heart infusion broth containing chopped meat," and then moved it to a different medium, made of casein, pepticase, and corn steep liquor. They also sometimes tried adding powdered milk to the brew. When it was time to harvest the toxin, they used acids and centrifugation to force the flocculant mass to the bottom of the reactor vessels. "The thick mud that was formed was itself adequately concentrated for use in munitions," Cochrane writes.

But when Tanner and Batchelor filled their British-style four-pound bombs with this slurry and used them in tests on Horn Island, the results were not encouraging. "Guinea pigs used in tests with one, two and four bombs were killed by the contamination of their coats with the toxin," Cochrane said. "No toxin could be detected in their lungs." The toxin hadn't aerosolized, in other words, it had just splashed on the ground or on the animals. "It was substantially shown that the 4-pound Mark I British bomb filled with 12.5 percent toxin slurry would probably not be a lethally efficient weapon."

Tanner and Batchelor's Horn Island tests were the first American field tests of toxic biological agents. They'd hoped to create an aerosol cloud of guinea pig and human death, but the drops weren't small enough. "The supposition that liquids can be 'shattered' by a high explosive into fine particles, analogous to a brittle solid, is," Tanner wrote, "unsound."

There was, as well, another set of experiments performed on Horn Island. Around September 1944, four Canadian germ men came down to study the possibility of using houseflies and fruit flies to spread salmonella infections and shigella dysentery, using simulant organisms, as part of something called the Joint Insect Vector Project, carried out under the supervision of the U.S. Navy. "Almost 2,500,000 adult flies were reared at Horn Island for the studies," according to Cochrane's history. "Female adults were fed on evaporated or powdered milk for egg production and the eggs grown in lots of 10 to 15 thousand in a larval medium of yeast and ground alfalfa meal." The Canadian scientists were serious fly breeders: late in the war, at the Suffield Experimental Station in Alberta, they designed a test in which they dropped cluster bombs on an experimental tent encampment. Each tent held food—fruit or rice porridge or canned salmon—and each bomb held a hundred thousand or more disease-bearing flies.

Herbert Tanner's report of munitions development at Camp Detrick, written just after World War II and declassified in 1979—which I found at the bottom of one of Ned Hagerman's brown storage boxes—ends with a résumé of lessons learned and some thoughts for the future. The ideal biological-warfare rocket, Tanner said, would arrive at the target, "level-out, zig-zag along the ground, and dispense BW agent." He envisioned biological grenades: "Water holes used by snipers could be infected with grenades containing an appropriate BW agent." Biological weapons would make good military barriers, too, being "invisible, silent, persistent, deadly, and simultaneously effective against infantry, motorized troops, and armored equipment. Troops might penetrate a BW agent barrier temporarily, but not for long." If the target was a large farming region, "it may be possible to utilize high level winds and natural clouds to convey crop-destroying agents, especially those which are self-propagating." Robot planes filled with biological agents might be "very useful at times." Tanner even foresaw the possibility of subway sabotage: "A small glass vial containing micronized BW agent could be dropped from a subway train; following trains would soon spread the aerosol throughout the subway system." Biological warfare was in its infancy, Tanner believed. It was aimed at urban populations, massed troops, and other very large groups. "For this reason it is destined to grow in importance."

The experiments on Horn Island had not worked out, but Tanner and Batchelor had an alternative in mind, a place to test aerosolized disease on live animals and people on a large scale. Not an offshore island, with all its risks and inconveniences, but a huge, airtight metal sphere on stilts, right in Frederick, Maryland. It was to be called the Eight-ball.

March 23, 2019, Saturday

Potatoes boiling in the dark at five in the morning. The whisper-whistling of the steam escaping from around the glass lid. The steam rising, lit by the light under the microwave. Microdroplets of escaping water vapor. M. and both dogs asleep. Trusting the world with their unconsciousness.

Secrecy attracts people who like to get away with things. Everyone knows this. Wars attract people who like to get away with things. Secrecy enables war's infinite series of atrocities, some small, some huge.

President Franklin Roosevelt's biological warriors were obsessed with stealth. "The matter must be handled with great secrecy as well as great vigor," wrote Secretary of War Henry Stimson to Roosevelt in 1942. "Stringent security measures were taken not only to prevent the enemy from obtaining information as to our efforts and results, but also to keep the public and the armed forces from becoming concerned over the possibility of biological warfare," wrote Rexmond Cochrane. "Frederick, Maryland, a pleasant little town of 16,000, was a satisfactory home for a secret project," said Sidney Shalett, in a 1946 article for *Collier's*. "The town minded its own business in an admirable way." The editor of Frederick's local paper, the *News*, told Shalett, "We thought they'd been making colored smoke for airplanes." No fuss was made when Detrick staffers were hospitalized with odd diseases—glanders, tularemia, cutaneous anthrax, parrot fever, etc. At its peak in 1945, 3,900 people worked at Detrick, and yet not a whisper about what they were doing appeared in the press during the war.

At the center of Detrick were the scientists, and some of them were cold human beings with eccentric tastes. Herbert Tanner's boss, Dr. Oram Woolpert, head of the Munitions Division, was one of Detrick's founders. In the 1930s, at the University of Chicago's Department of Hygiene and Bacteriology, Woolpert, who had a BA from Harvard and a medical degree from Rush Medical College, injected diseases into unborn guinea pig fetuses while the mother guinea pig was alive and anesthetized. He did this because the guinea pig fetus was, as he said in a paper published in 1936 in *The American Journal of Pathology*, a "test tube animal." The diseases he injected included tuberculosis, diphtheria, and infantile paralysis. "Fetuses from about 30 to 40 days of age were inoculated by needle puncture through the maternal uterine wall and fetal membranes," he wrote. Sometimes, with older fetuses, he injected a concentrated, purified solution of polio virus directly into their brains: "We found it possible also to inoculate older fetuses intracerebrally by needle puncture through the intact maternal abdominal wall."

He did these things not a few times, but repeatedly, methodically— one might say compulsively. "Usually the mothers were sacrificed at section but in many cases the operations were completed surgically, the mothers were re-bred and used again, some of them repeatedly, in similar experimentation."

Woolpert was party to many wartime animal experiments at Detrick. "Various species of animals were exposed to anthrax alone or with co-agents, by subcutaneous hypodermic inoculation, cutaneous application, respiratorally in the cloud chambers, and per rectum and per vagina by enema and douching," Rexmond Cochrane's history reports. Woolpert infected monkeys with two diseases at the same time to see how that worked out—not well for the monkeys—and he and his colleague John Schwab withheld nutritional elements from monkeys' food and then infected them "intranasally" with diseases, discovering that this, too, led to increased mortality. Tularemia, or rabbit fever, was thought to be promising as a "casualty agent against troops," so Detrick's lab workers misted monkeys with it. "All challenged animals developed subcutaneous induration and edema near the umbilicus, a usual tularemia phenomenon, with the skin becoming hemorrhagic, necrotic, or ulcerative," Cochrane reports. The monkey's spleens and livers had swollen, too, the scientists learned when they killed them and cut them up. Twenty-six lab workers at Detrick fell ill with tularemia. Some were given antibiotics right away, and some got antibiotics after five or six weeks. Recovery of the ones who got delayed antibiotics took five to fourteen months. Everyone had "residual fatigue."

Dr. Woolpert was fascinated by, and seemingly inspired by, the Japanese germ scientists of Unit 731. He told another colleague, Murray Sanders, about the Japanese wartime research. "We think they've killed a lot of people, Murray," Woolpert said. "We think that they've been poisoning wells and reservoirs."

Ishii Shiro and his covivisectionists had dusted birds with anthrax spores and used feathers as a transmission medium; in 1949 Oram Woolpert's Special Operations Division followed suit, using not anthrax, but the spores of two fungal crop diseases, wheat stem rust and rye stem rust. "The first test, conducted at Camp Detrick, consisted of dusting birds with cereal rust spores (*Puccinia graminis avenae*, Race 8) and releasing them for 1 ½ to 24 hours in cages covering approximately 100 square feet of seedling Vicland oats," wrote Geoffrey Norman, Detrick's top crop-disease specialist. The results were good: "a heavy rust infection resulted." The second test required ten homing pigeons (and, presumably, the expertise of Dr. Paul Fluck, a bird bander who was consulting for the Special Operations Division); the pigeons were dusted with disease spores and released a hundred miles away from their home barn. Not all of the pigeons came back, but four of the returnees were parked for a few hours in a cage near some oat seedlings. And then, over a period of nineteen days, the war scientists plucked a few feathers at a time from the pigeons and inspected them to see whether they still held fungal spores. They did.

For the third test, the Special Operations Division planted four small plots of oats on an "isolated island" in the Virgin Islands. "Four groups of pigeons, trained to return to their respective plots, were dusted with rust spores and liberated from an airplane." Success again: "Heavy infection resulted in all plots." But using birds to kill oats wasn't easy: "The problems involved in collecting, stock piling, and processing birds would tend to limit the use of this method," Norman wrote.

Then came the feather bomb, built using leftover leaflet bombs, with CIA money.

March 24, 2019, Sunday

At 5:22 this morning I got back in bed to find both dogs asleep, tucked around M. I adjusted their positions so they wouldn't pin down the blankets and got in. If they want to sleep with us let them sleep with us. They seem to love us, which is flattering. And we love them. No question. It's love. Love and sleeplessness. Not since we had tiny babies have I felt this feeling of scooping up a small, warm sleeping creature and gently moving it, him, her to a different place on the bed.

I kept thinking today of the list Rexmond Cochrane gives of all the animals killed in the pursuit of germ weaponry at Camp Detrick during World War II: 2 roosters, 5 pigs, 11 cats, 25 ferrets, 30 sheep, 34 dogs, 48 canaries, 75 "wistar rats" (white rats), 98 brown mice, 166 monkeys, 225 frogs, 399 cotton rats, 4,578 hamsters, 5,222 rabbits, 16,178 rats, 32,339 guinea pigs, and 598,604 white mice. The killing increased during the Cold War. In 1951, Dr. Cornelius P. Rhoads, wartime head of the medical branch of the Army's Chemical Warfare Service, told attendees at a conference that there was a severe shortage of animals, especially dogs and cats, for use in experiments, "to determine the effects not only of the weapons the enemy might throw at us, but of the weapons we may try to use on them." Dr. Harry Blair, of the University of Rochester's radiation-injury project, said he was sending agents out on scouting missions, paying $35.00 for each dog and $3.50 for each cat. Dr. Howard J. Curtis, of Brookhaven National Laboratory, said it was terrible that dogs were being gassed at animal shelters when they could be experimented on. "If you asked a man whether he wanted to be gassed, or used for an experiment with a 50 per cent chance of recovery, there is little doubt which he'd choose," Dr. Curtis said. "Why not give animals the same chance?"

WE DROVE TO A FARM SUPPLY STORE in the morning to buy dog food. Kids with braces from the 4-H Club were raising money by selling pancakes and maple syrup. It was a day of massive thaw, and the sky was a different kind of blue, a spring pale blue. All the dried salt and grit had been rained from the roads—there were glittering rivers of snowmelt circling Bangor's potholes. Even the yellow dividing line looked cleaner.

Another American Cold War laboratory that consumed experimental animals in large numbers was the U.S. Army's 406th Medical General Laboratory, headquartered in the Mitsubishi Building in Tokyo. I first learned about the 406th Laboratory in Stephen Endicott and Ned Hagerman's book. "By 1949 and through the Korean War period," Endicott and Hagerman write, "the activities of Unit 406 required huge quantities of small animals—twenty thousand white mice monthly, guinea pigs, even frogs—for the testing and manufacture of biologicals. Some of these animals were supplied by former associates of General Ishii."

A guiding hand behind the establishing of the 406th was Brigadier General James Simmons, one of the early visionaries of the American biological warfare program. Simmons was an army doctor and laboratory scientist who believed that "through health we can defeat the evil threat of Communism." In 1933 he shipped rabbits, cebus monkeys (the kind of monkeys organ-grinders used to own), and *Aedes aegypti* yellow-fever mosquitoes from the Army Medical School to St. Louis, where a new form of equine encephalomyelitis, or sleeping sickness, had just mysteriously appeared. Simmons wanted to see if he could "transmit sleeping sickness from human victims to animals through the medium of mosquitoes," reported the Associated Press. "The monkeys dozed preparatory to approaching martyrdom, and the mosquitoes buzzed menacingly."

The mosquitoes, which were allowed to feed on the arms of sick people, were descended from a particular colony shipped from the Philippines in 1925; Simmons and his future germ-warfare colleague Raymond Kelser—a veterinary scientist who believed that "the livestock population, as a target, would offer advantages over the human element"— had developed a theory that these particular 1925 Philippine mosquitoes might be responsible for the recent spread of equine encephalomyelitis to laboratory guinea pigs and horses in the United States.

Simmons and Kelser were two of a number of twentieth-century war scientists who, in their eagerness to study and breed and distribute to dozens of unsafe laboratories samples of outré diseases and insect carriers, unwittingly helped epidemics to spread. Rabbit fever, Q fever, bird flu, Lyme disease, wheat stem rust, African swine fever, and hog cholera all look, to my nonscientist's eye, like unnatural epidemics that owe their outbreaks to the laboratory. Some mischance with a pipette, a leaky centrifuge, a humid wind from the south, some dirty medical laundry, a hole in the mosquito gauze—and suddenly people are in the hospital with fevers, or crops are withering.

MY GRANDFATHER, ROGER BAKER, was a pathologist—a specialist in fungal diseases. I grew up hearing about mucormycosis and cryptococcosis at the dinner table. In fact it was when I was flipping around in Endicott and Hagerman's book in the University of New Hampshire library somewhere around the year 2000, and I spotted one of my grandfather's diseases in a list, that I thought I should really learn more about the germ-drunk phase of American history. Among the diseases investigated at Camp Detrick, Endicott and Hagerman said, were plague, anthrax, brucellosis, tularemia, glanders, brown spot of rice, rice blast, and psittacosis. Plus another one: coccidioidomycosis. That one I recognized. My grandfather Baker— author of two pathology textbooks and editor of *Human Infection with*

Fungi, Actinomycetes, and Algae, a giant tome that practically killed my grandmother, who handled the correspondence with contributors—had talked to me about coccidioidomycosis, or valley fever. It was a nasty and difficult-to-diagnose (and difficult-to-spell) malady—an "opportunistic fungus"—that farmworkers could contract by breathing in the dry dust of tiny, long-dormant cells. These fungal cells come alive in the moistness of the human lung and form spherules, and you begin coughing blood. If the disease isn't treated, it can spread everywhere, in skin lesions, in the joints, and in the brain's lining. And then you die. When I was a teenager I'd read and sometimes helped my grandfather proofread his papers on "acutely fatal mycoses," complete with horrifying, stomach-clenching photographs of dying or recently dead people with lesions and infarcts. This was the very last picture that was taken of this living person, I thought, and he or she looks so miserably sick, so not wanting to be photographed for medical research. It was hard to believe that government scientists at Camp Detrick had seriously contemplated the dusting of human beings with a cloud of dried coccidioidomycosis organisms. And yet they had.

THE QUESTION OF COURSE OCCURRED TO ME: Had Roger D. Baker himself received defense funding for his own scientific work? Well, not really— except for once. In 1944, while teaching anatomy and pathology at Duke Medical School, he'd published a small paper in *The Archives of Surgery* entitled "Untoward Effects of Various Substances Recommended for Burns or Wounds." The paper described experiments that he had performed on rats, under contract with the Office of Scientific Research and Development. (The OSRD was a federal agency that, during World War II, under the guidance of MIT's Vannevar Bush and Harvard's James Conant—with administrative help from Caryl Haskins—developed germ weapons, radar, napalm, Agent Orange, the proximity fuze, and the atomic bomb, along with many other long-shadowed instrumentalities of war.) My grandfather had etherized rats and partly skinned them alive so as to simulate a human wound or a burn, and then he had dabbed at these exposed and vulnerable patches of raw underflesh with various trauma-care emollients. After a day or two he killed the rats and dissected them. This was a repellent and, in my opinion, unnecessary line of investigation. But it wasn't as bad as shooting darts dipped in botulinum toxin at goats to see how long it took them to die, or inventing napalm. Vannevar Bush, MIT's godfather of germ warfare, reportedly woke up screaming sometimes, thinking of all the Japanese people he'd burned to death by recommending a new substance, napalm, to Henry "Hap" Arnold, head of the Army Air Forces.

But my grandfather's work on coccidioidomycosis and other fungal diseases fed into and benefited from an academic establishment that was enriched, and led astray, by war-related research. Microbiologist Norman F. Conant, my grandfather's close colleague at Duke Medical School, with whom he'd authored a textbook on mycology, had a research contract with Fort Detrick in the 1950s and '60s. Thousands of bacteriologists and medical mycologists and lab technicians and biochemists and pathologists and entomologists were drawn into confidential financial arrangements with Detrick and the Air Force and the Navy and the CIA, all through the '40s and '50s and into the '60s. Major universities, most notably the University of Pennsylvania and Johns Hopkins and U.C. Berkeley, but including my hometown University of Rochester, became more or less dependent on military biomunificence and were debased by it. At Stanford University, a team of chemists worked on aerosol clouds. Professor Louis H. Schwarte of Iowa State, a veterinarian, studied the efficacy of infecting hogs with cholera using feathers. During World War II, at Harvard Medical School in Boston, a team of pathologists (one from the University of Wisconsin, one from the University of Connecticut, one from Harvard) convened at Huntington Memorial Hospital to study and compare and propagate highly virulent strains of Newcastle disease and fowl plague (now called bird flu), and at Stanford's medical school, Stanley Lovell evaluated the military worth of coccidioidomycosis spores. Gordon M. Fair—wire-rimmed dean of Harvard's Graduate School of Engineering, head of the Harvard Faculty Club, and master of Dunster House—was also chairman of a Pentagon "Panel on BW Dissemination," in which role, in 1952, he visited Camp Detrick and Dugway Proving Ground, discussed the need for "hot agent" tests on Plum Island, and took in reports on the improved ballistics of the feather bomb.

"He traveled widely," said a eulogist of Gordon Fair, "to lend his competent aid in alleviating the lot of men, women, and children in almost every part of the disease-ridden and hungry universe."

STANFORD UNIVERSITY OWES A LOT to the Chemical Corps. The Stanford Aerosol Laboratory, headed by chemistry professors Philip Leighton and William Perkins, had nine separate military contracts and was "continuously engaged in the Chemical Corps research and development program from 1946 to 1961," according to a report published in February 1963. Professors Perkins and Leighton spent much of their professional lives modeling how clouds of disease, as simulated by fluorescent particles, would filter through cityscapes and mountain ranges and verdant forest canopies.

In September 1953, as part of Operation Airflow, Perkins and an ad hoc committee chaired by the surgeon general of the United States went to Dugway Proving Ground in Utah to determine whether it would be safe to use Agent N, anthrax, in open-air tests there. The committee's carefully hedged findings, presented to Utah's state health commissioner (Dr. George Spendlove) but not revealed publicly, were that it would be safe to test subcomponents of an anthrax cluster bomb at Dugway as long as nobody was within thirty miles of the test, and as long as the wind was just right: "Provided tests with N are conducted within the range of conditions obtained in the tests examined, and the source strength does not exceed five E61 bombs filled N slurry of count 5×10^{10} organisms per liter (or the equivalent), a human respiratory dose of 30 N organisms is unlikely to be exceeded at distances of 30 miles or greater." And, the committee said, "it is possible to schedule N field tests so that cloud travel is not toward inhabited areas which are at distances less than 30 miles." I found this report in 2012 at the National Archives; it was declassified sometime in the 1990s, forty years after it was written.

In 1958, Professor Perkins (I think it was Perkins, but it may have been one of his associates) went to Dugway again to study the airflows created by a new type of disease sprayer, mounted on an F-100A jet. The sprayer, made by North American Aviation, had a special nozzle that could spray very small particles, five microns in size or smaller. Five of six trials, which happened at night, used a simulant, and one sprayed Q fever on guinea pigs. "The flight trials proved the feasibility of spray attacks, and showed that an area 10 miles or better could be covered downwind," according to an end-of-year report by the Chemical Corps. "Results indicated that if human beings had been in the area, 99 percent of them would have been infected." This led to a calculation of the sprayer's "remarkable" efficacy: "On a night when the wind was blowing at ten miles per hour, three large aircraft, each carrying 4,000 gallons of liquid BW agent, could spray an area of 150,000 square miles, causing more than half the people in the area to become ill."

In 1969, when Seymour Hersh's book was out and students at Stanford were upset over the university's military contracts, a reporter for the *Stanford Daily*, Michael Sweeney, called up Professor Perkins on a Sunday and asked him whether his research had to do with offensive biological warfare. "No," Perkins said, "it doesn't involve biological warfare at all. I don't know where you ever got that." It was a study of "atmospheric diffusion from the standpoint of air pollution," Perkins said. "I don't even know how to begin doing biological warfare stuff."

March 25, 2019, Monday

Today is that particular kind of shiny before-spring day that I love. The ground is desolate—it's brown and poisoned by too much road salt—but it's definitely visible, on a fifty-fifty basis with the snow. There's been so much meltage in the past few days that sometimes, from certain directions, there's almost no snow at all, only discrete gray piles hiding off in the distance behind trees. And over it all is a huge Bangor sky that doesn't have a single thing in it, not a gull, not a goose, not a cloud, not an airplane. Just a big clangingly, smilingly, enigmatically empty Maine sky.

I thought of what happened in September 1950 in San Francisco. Something invisible, an aerosol, came from the sky. No one saw it happen, but, so the newspapers said, an odd, hot-weather foulness hung over the city. "Citizens blamed everything from sewer gas, burning garbage and garlic, to tired cigars and the cooking of Brussels sprouts for the odor," wrote the International News Service. The *Oakland Tribune* listed "a combination of refinery, garbage, cooking and Bay mud flat odors." These made for "a pungent concentration that caused even the oldest San Franciscano to admit: 'San Francisco smells.'"

What was happening just then, in secret, was that scientists of covert warfare from Camp Detrick, along with Berkeley's Albert Krueger and Captain Cecil Coggins of Naval Intelligence, had converged on San Francisco in order to investigate the "offensive possibilities of attacking a seaport city with a BW aerosol." From a Navy ship cruising two miles offshore, Krueger and Coggins fogged San Francisco and the East Bay with organisms that simulated disease, to see if they turned up at sampling stations around the city. The experimenters made six pretend attacks over a one-week period, pumping spores of *Bacilli globigii* (a stand-in for anthrax), *Serratia marcescens* (a stand-in for tularemia and other ills), and zinc cadmium sulfide particles out of "readily available commercial spray nozzles" into the air. Every pair of lungs in the Bay Area participated in this experiment, unknowingly. On shipboard, the spray nozzles, eight of them, manufactured by the BETE Fog Nozzle Company of Greenfield, Massachusetts, were attached to a standard-issue Army decontaminating apparatus, M3A1, now adapted to become a contaminating apparatus. "The bacterial suspensions were agitated in the tank of this apparatus to insure uniform mixing." Sometimes the nozzles clogged, but mostly the contaminator did its job well.

Serratia marcescens, an organism chosen because it formed distinctive red colonies in petri dishes, wasn't entirely innocuous—some San Franciscans contracted a rare kind of infection from it, and at least one, Edward Nevin, died. When Nevin's family sued decades later, Oram Woolpert, Fort Detrick's retired director of research, claimed that the simulants were harmless—he said that when his own staff handled *Serratia marcescens*, nobody got sick. But he knew differently. A safety report from Camp Detrick from October 1949 reads: "Inhalation of *Serratia marcescens* and *Bacillus globigii* has caused sufficient respiratory symptoms in several persons so that it has been necessary to issue a regulation requiring the wearing of protective equipment." Detrick staffers got protective gear, the city of San Francisco got nothing.

The sampling effort was comprehensive—petri dishes were set out all over San Francisco, and in the East Bay from Richmond to San Leandro.

The samplers worked under the direction of Joseph J. Stubbs, of Detrick's Special Operations Division, and Stubbs was aided by his close friend Frank Olson. It was one of Olson's first CIA-sponsored projects—Dr. John Schwab, head of Special Operations, had invited Olson to join the team earlier that month. The atmospheric disseminationists from Stanford were also involved, tracking how clouds of zinc cadmium particles moved over the bay. "Dr. W. A. Perkins and associates of the Department of Chemistry, Stanford University, who under contract with the Chemical Corps, Department of the Army, are currently engaged in studies of aerosol travel, cooperated and participated to the fullest extent in every phase of this work, and were responsible for gathering much of the meteorological data," said the report.

When, twenty-six years after it happened, word of these tests got out in the press—with help, oddly, from the Church of Scientology—Edward Nevin's grandson, a lawyer, sued the government for $11 million. The government said that the sudden, unprecedented appearance of a cluster of *Serratia marcescens* infections, never seen before or after, occurring just after the Army-Navy-CIA nozzle-fogging, was entirely coincidental. The judge, hostile to Nevin, agreed. An appeal failed. The Supreme Court refused to hear the case.

At one point during the trial, General William Creasy, Detrick's pugnacious former commandant, who testified in uniform, lost his temper and challenged Nevin to a fistfight in the hall. Creasy told the court that if he'd had it to do all over again, he would still have authorized the test without telling the city it was happening. "I could only conduct such a test without informing the citizens it was being conducted," he said. "I could not have hoped to prevent panic in the uninformed world in which we live in telling them that we were going to spread non-pathogenic organisms over their community."

In 1988, Leonard Cole published a very good book, *Clouds of Secrecy*, about this case and other germ experiments over American cities. When he wrote it, the Camp Detrick document, "Special Report No. 142: Biological Warfare Trials at San Francisco, California, 20–27 September 1950," had redacted sections. "Although blocked out in several places by the army's censor, the report offers, through its charts, diagrams, maps, and narrative, a striking view of the San Francisco germ warfare test," Cole wrote. The copy that I have, from the National Security Archive, has no redactions. I've read every word. There is nothing in this report that should have been kept secret for more than thirty years. The only reason it was kept secret is that it is clear evidence of governmental insanity.

March 26, 2019, Tuesday

I'm going to Washington on Wednesday to be on a panel at the National Archives. A new movie about Joseph Pulitzer, publisher of the *New York World*, is being shown there; I'm interviewed in the movie, so I'm on the panel. Also I get to see my daughter and her new husband, who live in Washington.

I left today, a day early, in order to get some research time in at the Library of Congress and the National Archives. At 4:25 A.M. I whispered goodbye to M. The dogs moved to the place on the bed where I'd been sleeping and made themselves into small motionless warm circular shapes like chocolate cakes.

I drove past the Curtain Shop and Denny's and the Comfort Inn. There was nobody else on the road. All the parking lots were empty and the traffic lights were set to flashing yellow. The world felt surreal and postapocalyptic, but with real potholes. At the Washington airport, with some time to kill, I inhaled a bit of couscous and had a coughing fit while rereading some more of Leonard Cole's *Clouds of Secrecy*.

Cole mentions many other open-air tests, one of which happened in Minneapolis. In 1952, the Ralph M. Parsons Company (an oil-refinery engineering firm that had done a good deal of work for Detrick), working with "Stanford scientists"—probably chemists William Perkins and/or Philip Leighton—sent plumes of zinc cadmium particles into the city's air from aerosol generators mounted on trucks and installed on rooftops. Camp Detrick had come up with a cover story, a fairly good one, printed in newspapers: General Creasy said that the Army had hired the Ralph M. Parsons Company to perform a series of twenty to thirty "smoke screen" tests, in order to learn more about how clouds of simulated smoke behave in different kinds of weather. The tests were necessary, General Creasy said, untruthfully, in order to determine whether smoke screens would be useful in hiding a city during an atomic attack. Creasy claimed that there would be no nuisance or inconvenience to Minnesotans. It was all just civil defense.

Actually, the Minneapolis foggings were part of an ambitious series of experiments meant to find out how clouds of anthrax and other airborne diseases would behave over Russian cities. Zinc cadmium sulfide dust was the simulant for anthrax, useful because it was fluorescent under ultraviolet light, and Minneapolis was the simulant for Kiev, in Soviet Russia. The Ralph M. Parsons Company opened an office on Third Avenue in Minneapolis to carry out the testing program. Ten full-time staffers and sixty-five part-timers, mostly students from the University of Minnesota, logged the data and worked the blowers. Mysterious small gray boxes, "ticking and purring," appeared around the city, some sitting in snow piles outside people's houses. "I am not at liberty to say what these boxes are," said a police spokesman, "but they are nothing for citizens to get alarmed about."

A reporter for the *Minneapolis Star Tribune*, Sterling Soderlind, looked closely at one of the gray boxes. "A small metal nozzle extends from the side," he wrote. It seemed to be sucking air in. A Ralph M. Parsons employee arrived. "They need changing every three hours," the Parsons man explained; he wouldn't let Soderlind peek inside.

The boxes were air-sampling machines. One of the objectives of the Minneapolis study was to gather data on "the penetrations of the aerosol cloud into residences at various distances from the aerosol dispenser." At the Clinton School, on East 28th Street, an elementary school and kindergarten, scientists charted the degree of aerosol penetration floor by floor. They were up on the Clinton School's roof with their fogging machines. The mayor had given his permission for all of it: Creasy had told him the fake smoke-screen civil-defense story.

In St. Louis, simulant city for Leningrad, Creasy again sold his cover story to newsmen, who reported that the government was studying "methods of blotting out cities through the use of smoke screens." Some of the cadmium dust would be released from balloons floating over the city, the newspaper said. The scientists chose a "densely populated slum district," according to an Army report; with the help of a police escort, they blew cadmium dust over the Pruitt-Igoe housing project. Years later, one of the Pruitt-Igoe residents, Doris Spates, wondered if the government's dust clouds explained why her father had died suddenly in 1955, and why she had cervical cancer, and why four of her eleven brothers and sisters had died young of cancer.

Cadmium is a poison—known, in 1952, in the scientific literature, to be a poison. It's not something you want delivered as infinitesimally tiny sulfide dust particles into your lungs. "They were wearing masks and operating what looked like a big fog machine," a Minneapolis resident recalled. "It was blowing all over, and there was a residue left on the cars." The people of Minneapolis and St. Louis, the very aged and the newborn, hale or sick, were given no masks; they breathed the cadmium particles for months.

I RENTED A CAR at the airport and drove to the Library of Congress, near the Capitol Building, where I spent the morning looking through some declassified letters in the General Henry Arnold Papers. No redactions here. The letters described a plan—one of several—to starve Japan into a state of unconditional surrender toward the end of World War II. On May 29, 1945, Brigadier General Victor Bertrandias, who'd lived in Japan before the war and had, as a salesman for Douglas Aircraft Company, sold American warplanes to the Japanese air force, sent a letter to Hap Arnold, head of the Army Air Forces, suggesting that the United States could achieve a quick aerial "knockout" of Japan by poisoning the rice crop and bombing fishing boats and schools of fish. Bertrandias calculated that ten missions employing 600 low-flying B-25 bombers, each carrying 550 gallons of a solution of ammonium thiocyanate crystals—a plant poison already under consideration as a means of "killing or damaging food crops established for support of isolated Jap garrisons in the Pacific"—could poison more than four million acres of rice, or 57 percent of the rice crop near "six great metropolitan centers—Tokyo, Yokohama, Osaka, Nagoya, Kyoto, and Kobe." If war gas was authorized, then mustard gas would work as well as or better than ammonium thiocyanate at killing the rice plants.

Meanwhile, Bertrandias went on, "the best fishing waters, as determined by ichthyologists who are familiar with the seasonal movements of large schools of fishes, could be bombed from low altitudes by B-25s." He listed the kinds of fish to be destroyed: sardines, tuna, sea bream, yellowtail, cuttlefish, mackerel, prawns, shrimp, trout, and herring. Small fishing boats would also be attacked by B-25s. "Destruction of these two main sources of food, even for a short period of time, should reduce the Japs in the home islands to near-starvation and bring them to accept our terms of unconditional surrender," Bertrandias believed. He included maps of Japan with target overlays showing the positions of rice-growing lowlands. "I shall be very happy to furnish any additional information or data which you feel might be of value in developing this idea to its fullest destructive potentialities. Very truly yours, V. E. Bertrandias, Major General, U.S.A." General Arnold made a brief marginal note: "To Target Analysis Committee for their action. H.H.A." One of Arnold's officers wrote Bertrandias to thank him for his suggestion. "The plan which you propose is an interesting one and has been proposed with a number of variations by other people and agencies," wrote John A. "Sammy" Samford, director of the Joint Target Group and future director of the National Security Agency. "Your presentation, however, is very complete and adds materially to our reference data." Bertrandias's plan had a basic weakness, however, Samford felt compelled to observe: it "required too high a degree of success before any appreciable effects are achieved." Even so, Samford very much appreciated Bertrandias's effort. "We are particularly interested in your suggestions with respect to one particular place and are hopeful that on your next visit here you will find time to see us again."

I looked up from the letter at the Manuscript Reading Room of the Library of Congress. All was quiet and scholarly. A staff person was wheeling a cart full of manuscript boxes to a researcher. The wobbling wheels made a low, chuckling sound. A microfilm machine whirred. I looked back down at the folder and took a picture of a page. Everything in it had been declassified in 1975. There was another letter from General Arnold in it, dated May 30, 1945. "Consideration is being given to the use of gas in the war against Japan," Arnold wrote to General Joseph Stilwell, who'd requested it. "The Army Air Forces together with the Chemical Warfare Service are continuing to study both the strategic and tactical employment of gas by air." This was after the burning of Tokyo and other cities.

I WENT OUT TO THE LOBBY and got a drink of water at the drinking fountain, which was unchanged from the first time I did serious research in the Manuscript Reading Room, in 2002. Back then I was researching something that happened at the library—something that the Air Force did to the library. Beginning in February 1948, the Air Force (and the CIA, via the Air Force) secretly hired the Library of Congress to find bombing targets in the Soviet Union. The job of the Air Research Unit— as outlined in a letter from the Air Force's director of intelligence, flying ace General George McDonald, to Luther Evans, the librarian of Congress—was to make maps and annotated overlays of industrial concentrations, population distributions, and transportation systems. They were to perform "combustibility and firebreak analyses," and investigate "the probable psychological, sociological, and political vulnerability of specific urban areas to strategic air attack." They would also make digests of published material, such as newspapers and magazines, in a form that was "suitable for incorporation into the Strategic Vulnerability

Branch's Bombing Encyclopedia." All this information was to be combined into a comprehensive report covering "each selected urban area." As a start, the library would need to hire, right away, sixteen photo interpreters, three draftsmen, nine analysts (including a well-paid psychologist and a slightly less well-paid sociologist), fifteen abstractors and translators, plus miscellaneous indexers, typists, file clerks, research assistants, and messengers. It was the library's job, in other words, to figure out what parts of Moscow, or Kiev, or Leningrad, to bomb, and what that city's reaction would be if the United States bombed it. And it all had to be secret. The Air Force would provide security clearances. "It will be necessary that control of all USAF classified information used in this program be retained by the USAF and that it not become a part of the records of the Library of Congress."

For a while it was called Project Treasure Island—because they were finding bits of informational treasure, places to bomb, in "open sources"— in articles in glossy Soviet magazines about new factories, in want ads, in random snapshots taken by travelers. This Cold War military arm of the library, kept entirely secret from the public, expanded and split into two separate divisions, occupying two floors of the Annex, a big deco-style building, a block from the main building, built in the 1930s to hold millions of books and magazines and newspapers. The Air Research Section produced "bombing objective studies" and was staffed by people with security clearances. They relied heavily on intelligence documents— captured German Luftwaffe photographs of Russian cities, for instance, and Project Wringer interviews of repatriated Nazi soldiers whom the Soviets had used as forced laborers on construction projects.

The Air Information Section employed émigrés from Eastern Europe, Soviet Russia, and China, who translated and abstracted from open sources. Most of these staffers, being foreign-born, lacked security clearances. Seymour Lubetzky, one of the Library of Congress's master catalogers, was released from his normal duties to set up the Air Information Section. "The materials to be exploited," Lubetzky wrote, "include books, pamphlets, periodicals and newspapers issued in or by Russia and her satellite countries." They were to begin with current publications and then work as far back as 1928, the year of Stalin's first Five-Year Plan—on the alert for items that were "important for strategic vulnerability requirements." There were guards at the doors and locks on the safes. The library hired and trained dozens of photo interpreters for the Air Research Division. I interviewed Dorothy Depenbrock, who reputedly trained the best photo interpreters. I interviewed several photo interpreters, too—or "target analysts," as they were called. Depenbrock never told her husband what she was doing. "We were working on a high," she said.

In November 1948, the library delivered to General Charles Cabell, head of Air Force Intelligence, its first "Urban Area Analysis." "The project was completed in an outstanding manner," Cabell wrote librarian Evans, "and it is one of the most useful intelligence contributions since World War II." The reports to come would be, Cabell said, "a major factor in accomplishing the mission of the Directorate of Intelligence." Evans replied that he was greatly pleased by the general's most thoughtful and generous letter. "Please be assured," Evans wrote, "that it is our devoted purpose to perform the most useful work possible for your organization."

In May 2002, I called up Dino Brugioni, former CIA photo-interpretation expert, and I asked him what he knew about the Air Research Division at the library. The Air Force had targeted seventy Russian cities for destruction, Brugioni explained; Air Research's job was to gain information about each area in order to, as he put it, "create a target chart for the Strategic Air Command to bomb the place." The idea was to "take out the whole city," he said. The target chart was the centerpiece of the target folder, which was big, like a newspaper; the Strategic Air Command would, using the library's charts as guides, glue metal shapes onto plexiglass sheets in ways that simulated the tin-roofed radar-reflectivity signatures of the seventy enemy cities they meant to destroy. To practice his mission, a bombardier, housed in a shed on a lumber truck, would "fly" slowly over this plexiglass simulacrum of a target complex; when he got a radar fix on his assigned pattern, he pretended to release his bombs.

Air Research and Air Information expanded rapidly; and Burton

Adkinson, the map librarian, who had helped set up the Air Force program, began to have doubts by early 1950. Adkinson had learned that the Strategic Vulnerability Branch was due to be renamed the Air Targets Division, a designation that didn't leave much to the imagination. And the Air Force now wanted Air Research to hire forty more analysts in order to "increase the rate of production." Where were these new people going to sit? The library's Navy-funded project, called the Technical Information Division, had grown, and space in the Annex, built to hold the nation's published, copyright-deposited output, was getting tight. Air Information/ Treasure Island used the library's collections constantly, so it made some sense to keep that group where it was, Adkinson believed; but perhaps Air Research—its employees, its stereoscopes, its captured photo files—should now find quarters elsewhere. He told General Moore of the Air Force that Air Research's activities were "not really part of the Library program, even if broadly interpreted." As far as he could tell, the only reason that the library was doing this kind of work for the Air Force was that the Air Force had a ceiling on the number of civilians it could employ.

Then in June 1950 came the Korean War. Suddenly it was a military emergency. Librarian Luther Evans, a squinty Texan with a temper who loved "air power" (pronounced "air parr"), toured the Annex and made a decision to crush down the paper collections. History lost, war planning won. The Air Research targeteers would stay at the library. "Present plans call for converting additional library space to the use of the Air Force projects," Evans wrote General Cabell. Air Research got 68 percent more floor area. "At this troubled time," Evans said, "I should like to reaffirm the Library's pride and pleasure in its ability to be of service to your organization." In March 1951, Verner Clapp noted in his diary that he had visited the Annex, deck 7, north, with Luther Evans and Frederick Wagman. "Agreed: To dispose of stuff from Dupl. Coll. by weeding good stuff, advertising the remainder & pulping if no bids are recd," he wrote.

From that moment on, the Library of Congress was in a more or less continual space crisis. "Library of Congress, at 153, Suffers Acute Growing Pains" was the headline in *The Washington Post* in 1953, but the growth in the collections could have been accommodated without strain had the library not undergone a rapid, undisclosed militarization. The financial paragraphs of the 1952 Annual Report noted a "shift during the last few years of emphasis in the Library's program from regular to defense-supporting activities." Nineteen people worked in the library's Manuscripts Division that year, while 112 people worked in the Air Information Division, and 121 worked in the Air Research Division—plus another 156 people in the Technical Information Division paid for by the Navy.

The Korean War was the beginning of the end for the library's huge and irreplaceable wood-pulp newspaper collections: in trying to figure out how best to bomb our enemies, we bombed ourselves.

But the Air Force money was good. A ledger sheet in one of the files records a transfer of $1,223,000 "to continue the confidential projects in the Library of Congress in the Air Research and Air Information Divisions for the fiscal year 1953." One former employee, Paula Strain, told me she first worked as a messenger, picking up maps and charts from the CIA, the Army Map Service, and the Pentagon. Strain remembered the time she was asked to pick up a check from the Air Force for over a million dollars; she sat on it on the drive home to make sure it wouldn't blow away.

Strain eventually moved up to targeting work herself. She looked for bridges, railroad marshalling yards—"things you drop bombs on," she said. If there were no photographs, she relied on Project Wringer reports. There were tricks, too—if a number of sources mentioned a bad smell in a certain place, that was a clue that there might be a petrochemical plant nearby. At one point, Strain was assigned to find targets in Wuhan, in China. Years later, she said, she visited China and was pleased to discover that a certain steel mill was just where she'd said it was. In retirement, she wrote a historical guide to the Maryland section of the Appalachian Trail. "I'm glad we didn't bomb," she said.

THIS CAME BACK TO ME as I sat in the Library of Congress's manuscripts room, where I'd spent many hours in 2003 and 2004 reading about the creeping growth of a spy culture at the library. I closed the folder from the Henry Arnold Papers and pushed my cart up to the desk and thanked the nice people who worked there. My car was parked, as it happened, on the street just beyond the Adams Building, which is the name the library has given to the Annex. I looked up at the fifth floor, where, for more than two decades, many people had worked very hard to find exactly how to destroy foreign countries. "We would have bombed a lot of Buddhist temples," one former staff member said. "They looked a lot like machine gun emplacements."

The division still exists, very much reduced: it's now called the Federal Research Division, and it produces research studies on contract for government agencies. But the library is just a library now. What's missing is all the priceless printed stuff they microfilmed and tossed out to make room for the Cold War.

I TOOK PICTURES of the bronze decorations set into the doorway of the Adams Building, where so many military secrets had been hatched. The hieratic figures were of mythical gods: Ogma, Itzama, Ts'ang Chieh, Hermes, Tahmurath, Sequoyah, and Quetzalcoatl. And Odin, god of poetry and war. Then I got in my Korean-made Kia rental and drove to interview nuclear historian William Burr, one of the FOIA masters at George Washington University's National Security Archive. We sat in the archive's big conference room, which was filled with boxes from the John Marks collection of MKULTRA mind-control documents.

Marks is the author of *The Search for the "Manchurian Candidate,"* a classic book of CIA history—truly an amazing work of sleuthing and synthesis. "This book has grown out of the 16,000 pages of documents that the CIA released to me under the Freedom of Information Act," Marks wrote. "Without these documents, the best investigative reporting in the world could not have produced a book, and the secrets of CIA mind-control work would have remained buried forever, as the men who knew them had always intended." A redactionist had gone through, crossing things out with a crayon, he told an interviewer (Dominic Streatfeild, author of *Brainwash*). "I have to admit that I scraped some of the crayon off with my finger to see what was underneath."

I asked Bill Burr for a success story, and he told me about inheriting a 2006 Mandatory Declassification Review request to the Air Force from Michael Dobbs, a journalist who was working on a book about the Cuban Missile Crisis. Dobbs waited for several years for records, and then he published his book, *One Minute to Midnight*, in 2008. He then transferred his Mandatory Review Request to Bill Burr—declassification requests are transferable!—at the National Security Archive. Finally, in October 2014, the Air Force released to Burr a nuclear targeting study from 1956 that included a computer printout of several hundred pages from Curtis Lemay's Strategic Air Command. (A targeting study created with the help of the Library of Congress.) The printout, although heavily redacted, listed more than twelve hundred Soviet bloc cities slated for "systematic destruction," including Bucharest, Budapest, Dresden, East Berlin, Hanoi, Harbin, Nanking, Prague, Pyongyang, Riga, and Shanghai. Every city was assigned a priority number and a certain number of "designated ground zeros," where individual atom bombs would land. Moscow and Leningrad were priority 1 and 2, and within Moscow were 179 designated ground zeros, one of which was Red Square; Beijing was priority 13, with 23 designated ground zeros. Each target was accompanied by its corresponding number in the Bombing Encyclopedia. The National Security Archive said that these documents presented "the most comprehensive and detailed list of nuclear targets and target systems that has ever been declassified."

Another document that Burr recently got released, he told me, was a 1964 paper from General Maxwell Taylor, chairman of the Joint Chiefs of Staff under Presidents Kennedy and Johnson. The paper discussed nuclear attack options that specifically targeted urban populations—using "population loss as the primary yardstick for effectiveness," as General Taylor put it—so as to "destroy the USSR and Russia as viable societies." The word "viable," which appears three times, caught Burr's eye: "If 30 percent of the urban population and 50 percent of the industrial capacity are the goal," one passage said, "the execution of Attack Option V in SIOP 64 would destroy such a level of the Chinese urban population and industrial capacity that China would no longer be a viable nation."

Burr impressed me: this patient, undemonstrative man, who had chosen to spend some of his life piecing together the long-suppressed specifics, the actual language, of American war plans. Paraphrase and summary wasn't enough. I told him that I sometimes thought that redaction was a form of psychological warfare directed against historians, a way of wearing people down and making them go away.

"That's what it amounts to," said Burr. "But part of it is budgets. There aren't enough people doing the reviews." The State Department is pretty good, he said. Burr is still waiting for responses from the Department of Defense to some appeals that he made in the 1990s.

March 27, 2019, Wednesday

My Airbnb was in an odd little housing development with many gentle speed bumps and winter-bleached lawns. At the National Archives, outside of Washington in College Park, Maryland, they took away my outdated ID and made a new ID with a new picture. I've watched myself get older in these ID cards from the National Archives and the Library of Congress.

You have to divest yourself of everything in a locker downstairs in order to enter the charmed space of the Archives II Building and get on an elevator to the reading room, which is a huge modern research atrium with space for several hundred people. One side of the room is a tall glass wall that looks out on nothing but trees. The furniture is light gray and each desk has a comfortable office chair and a light. If you want to photograph declassified documents you must take your box up to a desk where they give you a piece of paper with the declassification number handwritten on it—something like NND917105—and you slip a piece of red paper in a sheath of plastic hanging from the light at your desk to show that you are photographing documents that are truly declassified and not ones that for some reason should have been withheld from you but were given to you by mistake.

At some times of day the sun pours in. In a room on an inside wall are floor-to-ceiling shelves full of three-ring binders—these are finding aids, some old, some new, for various branches of government. Without them researchers have no way of filling out the call slips to get the boxes that hold whatever they're looking for.

I thought I'd try to find the series of Human Radiation Experiments, or HREX, documents that had been on the web twenty years ago—the records that held the memo from Frank Wisner to Marshall Chadwell asking for ideas on how to make covert use of biological, chemical, and radiological novelties. The staffer who helped me moaned when I said I was looking for the records of the Advisory Committee on Human Radiation Experiments. "It's up there; I know where it is," he said, "and it's in no order. There used to be a finding aid, but somebody took it. I told them not to throw out the index, but they did." Even so, he came up with a digital spreadsheet that listed every box of HREX records and, in a separate column, its source. Some of the sources said "DOJ" (Department of Justice) or "ACHRE" (Advisory Commission on Human Radiation Experiments), and some were CIA. I told him I was looking for some CIA documents from 1950. He wrote down the box numbers and was gone for fifteen minutes. He came back smiling. "I found them," he said. "You should have no problem." Together we filled out a call slip and I signed it. The clunk of the time stamper meant my call slip was official. The slip went into a little wooden receptacle with everyone else's. Someone would pull those boxes in the next hour or so. Each scheduled retrieval period was called a "pull," in fact—there were four or five pulls throughout the day.

While I waited, I looked through a binder listing State Department records and found some things under "Psychological and Political Warfare 1947–1952." According to one of the *Foreign Relations of the United States* volumes, which are beautifully edited volumes of correspondence published by the State Department, this series of documents had to do with something called "the Packet," an accounting of all of Frank Wisner's big projects at the CIA's Office of Policy Coordination. In the CREST database I'd come across several references to the Packet—and I'd asked John Prados, another sleuther at the National Security Archive, about it. The Packet, which was three hundred pages long, seemed to be the Family Jewels of the early CIA. (The "Family Jewels" was the name CIA people gave to a bundle of photocopied CIA projects of dubious legality assembled by director William Colby in the 1970s, at a moment when various misdeeds were leaking out; by the time they were finally released in 2007, with many gaping redactions, John Prados and others at the National Security Archive had been waiting for a response to their FOIA request for fifteen years. "Given all the illegal activities actually listed in this document, the hidden sections are all the more disturbing," wrote Amy Zegart, in *The New York Times*'s Washington blog.)

THE IDEA OF THE PACKET arose late in November 1951. It seems to have been CIA director Bedell Smith's idea. Roscoe Hillenkoetter, his predecessor, left the CIA in October 1950. He left partly because his heart wasn't in it and he wasn't getting good press—he was blamed for failing to warn everyone about North Korea's attack in June 1950. But he left also because he and the increasingly powerful Frank Wisner didn't get along. Hillenkoetter didn't like what was going on at the Office of Policy Coordination. He wasn't a great fan of psychological warfare, he told an in-house CIA historian a few years later, and he sometimes thought that the Office of Policy Coordination should not be part of the CIA—it should be housed in the Pentagon, because it was "essentially a military operation." Other times Hillenkoetter said that there was a need for something like the OPC but that it had been "badly organized." He would have set it up differently, he said. "Its establishment was the result of a directive sparked by the State Department with most lukewarm support from the Defense Department and opposed by C.I.A.," he told the interviewer, Arthur Darling.

Think of that for a moment. *The director of the CIA was opposed to the CIA's own clandestine service.* Hillenkoetter believed that the primary role of the Central Intelligence Agency was intelligence, not psychological or political warfare—it should function as "the president's personal information service," he said, "although very definitely not limited to his use alone."

When Hillenkoetter resigned, Harry Truman put Bedell Smith in charge. Smith was a rage-prone, cleft-chinned Army Intelligence insider recovering from an ulcer operation. He'd met and personally crossed swords with Stalin, having worked as ambassador to the Soviet Union—and he was also a talented administrator: he'd been Eisenhower's deputy in wartime Europe. Hillenkoetter's parting advice to Smith was that he should get control of the Office of Policy Coordination. "Either obtain complete control of OPC or disassociate it completely from CIA."

Bedell "Beetle" Smith failed. He tried to learn as much as he could about Wisner's projects, but he didn't trust Wisner to tell him everything. The Office of Policy Coordination, fueled by money and mania, was already out of control. There were too many projects, too many covert operators in too many countries accountable to nobody. Wisner was hiring crypto-Nazis and former Hitlerjugend in Europe to infiltrate the Soviet zone of Germany, for one thing. General Smith tried for a year to work with Wisner and get some control over what OPC was doing, but he couldn't—Wisner was able to fillet the speckled trout of disclosed truth very cleverly, employing his best corporate-lawyerly skills, and make it seem as if he were keeping Smith in the loop when he wasn't. He used his close links to the State Department to withhold knowledge from the CIA, and his close links to the CIA to withhold knowledge from the State Department, and because he had the ear of influential people at *The New York Times* and *The Washington Post*, along with Joe Alsop, the columnist, and because he and Polly Wisner gave great cocktail parties, he had a fair amount of power in Washington. The secrecy of what he was doing gave him an aura of mystery. The word "intelligence" helped, even when what he was doing was extremely dumb. Wisner was, in fact, a bumbler. A manic bumbler can be very dangerous, and Wisner had actual assassins working for him, fixers in the final sense. Allen Dulles, smoking his pipe, egged him on, planning the moment when Bedell Smith would shuffle over to the State Department and he, Dulles, would take over the CIA and give black ops their freedom. Secrecy is the refuge of the incompetent—so said the Moss Committee on Freedom of Information.

In order to get more control over Wisner's rumored, half-disclosed covert projects, Bedell Smith and some of Harry Truman's people came up with the idea of another layer of oversight. It was called the Psychological Strategy Board, and President Truman asked Gordon Gray, a wealthy Reynolds Tobacco heir—and law-firm colleague of Frank Wisner—to run it. Smith announced in a director's meeting, "We should prepare a comprehensive summary of OPC programs and individual major projects for submission to the Psychological Strategy Board at an early date." Wisner should do the summary, Smith said, with the help of ⬚ and Kilbourne Johnston, Wisner's deputy, an authority on biological weapons. The summary should include the project's name and code name, its objective, a brief description, its current status and its accomplishments to date, its cost so far and future projected costs, and an estimate of personnel requirements. "The Director suggested that there be only four of these booklets prepared, one being retained permanently by CIA and the other three to be submitted to and returned by the other members of the PSB."

Frank Wisner was not happy about the Packet. Putting all that operational detail down on paper was not his style. He and his associates, tough guy Hans Tofte and lawyer Tracy Barnes, proceeded with extreme slowness to pretend to gather up information about OPC's projects. Wisner wanted, I think, to wrap up some of the disasters so that he wouldn't have to include them in the Packet. He viewed the Packet as "an acute security problem"—so he said in a meeting in June 1952, under a paragraph of something Allen Dulles said that is fully whited out. "Thirteen people on the PSB have read our black book." The Packet was a threat to his autonomy—it held things that he was trying to keep from Bedell Smith, from the president, and from the Policy Planning Staff of the State Department.

In its volume on the growth of the intelligence establishment, published in 2008, the State Department has a helpful footnote: "The 'Packet' has not been found, but several documents dealing with Department of State consideration of it are in National Archives, RG 59, S/P Files: Lot 64 D 563, Political and Psychological Warfare."

Which is why I was asking for the RG 59, S/P Files: Lot 64 D 563. But what I should be doing, of course, is filing a FOIA request for the Packet itself. You don't have a chance if you don't try.

I WENT DOWN TO THE LOWER LEVEL and got some lunch in the National Archives cafeteria. Something that Bill Burr said yesterday struck me as very true. He said the budget of the archives, adjusted for inflation, is the same now as it was in 1980. Or did he say 1990? Anyway, a long time ago. The National Archives is supposed to handle the mighty Niagara of recorded material from all branches of government with a budget that has stayed flat for decades, while the budgets of most other agencies have gone up. More people in the Pentagon and the Department of Homeland Security and the CIA and on and on are writing more emails and pushing more paper, and the archives must deal with it all somehow. There's a gigantic warehouse of unprocessed records in Suitland, Maryland. Let's take our confused country's past seriously and give the National Archives enough money to perform its function.

So. Here are two—no, three—simple things that Congress could do to allow historians to have more actual knowledge to chew on, and thereby improve the subtlety and complexity of our understanding of the twentieth century—our understanding of where we went wrong and where we went right. First, double the budget of the National Archives. Second, give the National Declassification Center, which is a quasi-independent group within the National Archives, unilateral power to declassify all documents older than thirty years without sending them back to the originating agencies for further decades of slow review and redaction. Third, automatically declassify any document that is more than fifty years old— no exceptions. No exceptions.

The CIA and the Air Force spend a ludicrous amount of time whiting out paragraphs on very old historical documents about long-ago plans for long-ago wars. It's just a way of slowing down revelations about shriveled horrors until they are so lost in the past that their power to shock is muffled by soft winding sheets of time. The CIA and the Air Force are waiting for people like Bill Burr to die. They may not know it yet, but they're waiting for me to die.

Another thing Bill Burr said that struck me. He said that he'd heard that the CIA might be going to a pass-fail system of declassification. The declassifiers would stop redacting and simply not release a document if there was something in any part of it that they believed was exempt. That would be a disaster. The CIA can't be allowed to do that. At least if they release a document that has, say, two readable pages and fifteen pages that are withheld with the words "Page(s) denied," researchers know that the document exists.

But everything over fifty years must be freed for scrutiny. Right now. The Agency is now hiding what's left of its (vandalized) records with sustained legal vigor—because if everything the CIA did from, say, 1948 to 1968, even leaving out the insanities under Nixon and Carter and Reagan and the Bushes, et al., were fully revealed all at once, there might be a political supernova of toxic horrified shrapnel that would force the Agency to shut down in disgrace, and all those thousands of employees would have to find other work. Or, probably, people would just carry on doing what they're doing.

We might want to rename the Agency, as well. If we named it the PWE, say—the Political Warfare Executive—then CIA records might come to seem further away and more historical, as OSS records now do.

SENATOR DANIEL MOYNIHAN, thirty years ago, had a related idea. Break the CIA in two, he said. The intelligence function—the writing of learned research reports about the political situation in various countries—should go to the State Department, which had been doing it all along anyway, and the operational, paramilitary, counterinsurgency side should go to the Department of Defense. Except that Moynihan was wrong about relocating the paramilitary side. Just get rid of it. Covert lying and targeted killing and bribery and drones and all of it—and the hiring and training of indigenous thugs—whether it is done by the CIA or by Army Rangers or by Blackwater contractors, always, without exception, leads to disaster. That's what the immediate declassification of all CIA documents fifty years old or older would confirm. The CIA is failing to comply with the Freedom of Information Act, and hoarding its secrets forever, because the hoarding of secrets allows it to survive. The Agency narrowly missed being shut down in the 1970s, when the Church Committee pulled the drapes back and showed some of the squirming horror, but it was able to escape dissolution.

AT THE NATIONAL ARCHIVES, in order to determine whether the boxes you've requested have arrived, you look at a binder, open on a swiveling pedestal, for your name. I looked, pretending to be nonchalant, and there my name was! I signed the pink sheet and one of the staffers rolled out a cart with three large gray boxes on it. The boxes were from record group 220, entry A1/42100-H, stack 650, row 44, compartment 19, shelf 6. Their declassification number was NN3-220-46-002.

Sunlight filled the room, which was fairly crowded. By early afternoon everyone was settled in, turning pages, reading things that had never been published, sometimes making little low whistles of amazement. I could hear someone's desktop scanner going.

Each of my boxes was heavy. The normal archival box, called a Hollinger box, can hold roughly a thousand pages, although in practice they are more loosely packed and the folders take up room. These human radiation boxes were maybe three times the size. I began going through them. In less than half an hour I found the precious Frank Wisner document. It was still hard to read the date, but I think it was June 20, 1950. For about twenty-five years, that photocopied document has sat in that folder. I felt a thrill looking at it. Even though I'd printed exactly the same scanned facsimile of the page on my own office printer more than fifteen years earlier, with the same redactions, this was printed out at a higher resolution. It was a relief to find it, because it meant that when I cited this paper I didn't have to cite something that had no source except a box in my office.

Whoever had done the redacting was very old school. He or she seems to have used some kind of brush, like a Wite-Out brush except dipped in black ink. Very abstract expressive. Wisner had the document typed, so

these later blackouts were the most human thing about it. At the bottom
of the page someone had stamped:

THIS DOCUMENT IS
A SOURCE REFERENCE IN
A HISTORICAL PAPER
_____

DO NOT DESTROY

I took some pictures and looked a little further in the folder—and there
was the October 2, 1951, memo by Caryl Haskins describing the Artichoke
meetings he'd had with experts about enhanced interrogation techniques.
"As you know," Haskins writes, "I visualized that we might form an
advisory committee for this work consisting of approximately six people,
and the six who were considered were ⌐――――――――¬ and myself."
There was a list of proposed subprojects having to do with "Interrogation
Techniques and Their Relative Effectiveness"—all blacked out. This
redacteur used a different implement—it looks like some kind of black oil
crayon. Haskins ended by saying, "This seems to be about as far as the
Committee can go until further information on Agency requirements
becomes available."

Neither Haskins's name nor his initials appeared on the October 2,
1951, memo, but another memo a few pages on said, "In a memorandum
to Dr. Chadwell dated 2 October 1951, Dr. Haskins indicated that the
Panel had contributed about as much as it could for the present," etc. That's
how I knew who the sender and recipient were, despite the redactions.

IN THE EVENING I went to the showing of *Joseph Pulitzer: Voice of the People*,
a movie by Oren Rudavsky. The movie made me cry a little bit, in the dark.
Halfway through it, there's a nice quote from Pulitzer himself: "There is
not a crime which does not live by secrecy," Pulitzer said. "Get these things
out into the open, describe them, attack them, and sooner or later, public
opinion will sweep them away."

March 28, 2019, Thursday

Well, today was as blue as anything I've seen in our nation's capital, and I spent the morning, again, at the National Archives. I got a baked good from the cafeteria and thought about the CIA's feather bomb. It's such a strange idea—to fill a bomb with feathers. As if you're having a pillow fight with your enemy.

The people who tested the feather bomb worked at Camp Detrick for the Crops Division and the Special Operations Division. A British-born biochemist, A. Geoffrey Norman, was head of Detrick's Crops Division. During the war, Norman and a scientist from the University of Chicago, Ezra Kraus, had tested many defoliators and crop killers, the most efficacious of which was VKA, or vegetable killer acid. ("No other growth regulating compound proved superior to VKA," wrote Rexmond Cochrane in his end-of-war report.) VKA was a plant hormone, 2,4-D (full name, 2,4-Dichlorophenoxyacetic acid), one of the components of a mixture that some years later came to be called Agent Orange. In trials at Beaumont, Texas, and Terre Haute, Indiana, with the help of plant pathologists Charles Minarik and Edgar Tullis from the United States Department of Agriculture, Norman treated test plots with VKA mixed with diesel fuel, tributyl phosphate, and other substances, and worked out how best to deliver it to rice, wheat, and other staple crops from B-25 bombers fitted with 550-gallon tanks. When the war ended, Norman, Minarik, Tullis, and others continued their work on plant poisons, sharing their research with the British government (who later used defoliants in Malaya), and then, after the CIA established the Special Operations Division at Detrick, they began Project 4-04-14-004, "use of feathers to dispense agent." After the experiments with spore-laden homing pigeons, they gave up on living birds and just used turkey feathers, inspired by one of Ishii's wartime feather bombs.

Norman's report, Special Report No. 138, staple bound, with a tan cover, published on December 15, 1950—at a moment in the Korean War when large numbers of American men, and Chinese men, and Korean men, were freezing and dying in the mountains—was called "Feathers as Carriers of Biological Warfare Agents: I. Cereal Rust Spores." It was approved by Oram Woolpert, MD, who was by then director of Camp Detrick's Biological Department, with his signature on the title page. The tests of the feather bomb were carried out in the open air, in Upstate New York, near Watertown, on fields of oats planted on an Army base then called Pine Camp—now called Camp Drum. "The purpose of the feather test described in this report was to determine if feathers dusted with cereal rust spores and released from aircraft in an M16A1 cluster adapter (used for leaflets and fragmentation bombs) will permit the transference of spores to cereal plants so that rust infection may ensue," said the report. Even though it was a bomb, the weapon was still stealthy, still plausibly deniable: if you dropped leaflet bombs and feather bombs in the same area, nobody would notice the feathers in the fields, maybe, and you could always say that you were just distributing printed anti-Communist tracts.

The turkey feathers were mixed in a mixing drum with spores of *Puccinia graminis avenae*, Race 8, packed in bombs, and dropped on oat fields at Pine Camp. "Two weeks after the release of the munition, stem rust was found in all of the lots located nearest the impact area," the scientists reported. "It is concluded that feathers dusted with 10 per cent by weight of cereal rust spores and released from a modified M16A1 cluster adapter at 1300 to 1800 feet above ground will carry sufficient numbers of spores to initiate a cereal rust epidemic." The Pine Camp tests were possibly called "Project Purple"—so one document indicates; maybe other withheld documents will confirm that name.

There were seventy thousand World War II leaflet cluster bombs on hand, and all they needed was a slight modification in order to handle feathers—or indeed any other sort of bundled particulate matter. The Russian army was huge, but if there was no wheat at home, a collapse from within was inevitable. In April 1951, some of the military men who had supervised the feather-bomb tests received special Army commendation ribbons from General Anthony McAuliffe, head of the Chemical Corps; each of the men had "performed meritorious service in that he planned, carried out, evaluated and helped prepare reports on certain scientific experiments of a classified nature of great value to the United States." Their picture appeared in the newspaper—without any mention of what meritorious service they'd performed.

Once the E-73 feather bomb was a reality, shown to have performed well on fields of oats in New York, the Air Force and the CIA began figuring out how best to use it to ruin Soviet agriculture. The plan came to be called Project Steelyard—perhaps this was an allusion to the counterweighted steelyard scales that farmers traditionally used to measure how much heavy things (like bags of grain) weighed. On February 20, 1951, an Air Force memo to the Army called for "400 lbs of wheat rust (TX) and 1600 lbs of stem rust of rye to be used against the winter wheat and rye crop of the USSR," with more to come in February 1952. The Army accepted the order but said that the rye-disease delivery would have to wait until March 1952. The Air Force also asked for five thousand E-73 cluster bombs, a number that included a thousand clusters for testing and "plans now being formulated." In September 1951, a cable went from Air Force headquarters to Air Materiel Command, in Dayton, Ohio, with overseas shipping instructions for "biological warfare munitions":

Request immediate action to be taken by your HQ to arrange shipment to Lakenheath, U.K. of 400 adapters, M16A1 (modification C) with delivery to USAF Commanding Officer, Lakenheath as soon after 1 Oct 51 as possible. Shipping instructions are: (1) Each adapter must be enclosed in a box, and designation on each box and all shipping instructions such as bills of lading will be marked "Hardware." (2) There will be no markings or other indication on boxes or bombs to indicate purpose. (3) Fuzes and fills for adapters will not, repeat not be included in shipment. Adapters have been modified at Edgewood Arsenal.

Someone has written "DESTROY" in pencil below the text of this cable.

Colonel James E. Totten, head of the Biological and Chemical Warfare Division of the Air Force's Office of Atomic Energy, described the wheat-destruction plan in a lecture in November 1951 to officers at the Air War College, in Montgomery, Alabama. "The presently limited anticrop capability for employment of plant pathogenic agents against the cereal crops wheat, rye and barley in USSR has been incorporated in war plans and operational details have been developed for readying date of March 1952," Colonel Totten said. The plans were not limited to the Soviet Union, and they included poisons as well as diseases, according to a handout Totten distributed at his lecture. "Work is proceeding on anticrop operations in the Asiatic Theater," the document said. "Plans for complete anticrop operations, including employment of chemical spray (2,4-D ester) in both USSR and China will be prepared on completion of the current tests at Avon Park AFB, Florida which should establish operational feasibility."

A factory for vegetative agents, code-named NOODLE, was being built at Pine Bluff Arsenal in Arkansas, according to a Department of Defense progress report prepared in December 1951 by Earl Stevenson of Arthur D. Little and CIA chemist Willis Gibbons. "The anti-crop program is aimed at the bread basket of the Soviet Union," the report said. "Unfilled bombs for these agents have been produced and delivered to overseas bases. This year, increasingly significant quantities of anti-wheat and anti-rye agents have been harvested." (This report also described tests at Dugway Proving Ground in Utah with Q fever, undulant fever, rabbit fever, and parrot fever, and the building of a sarin nerve gas plant code-named GIBBETT in Muscle Shoals, Alabama.)

In October 1952, Orrin Grover, head of the Air Force's Psychological Warfare Division—a division directed to "supervise covert operations in the scope of unconventional BW and CW operations and programs"—wrote in a memo that the need for more bombs and spores had increased: "Additional BW requirements for the cluster adapter have arisen," he said. "Present plans include establishment of alternate launching sites for wheat and rye missions, and an additional anti-crop operational plan is being formulated. Furthermore, 200 cluster adapters have been released for anti-crop and anti-animal field test purposes and the test program envisaged for the next year will require the expenditure of still additional clusters." One alternate launching site was Wheelus Air Base, in Libya, temporary home of the CIA's 580th Air Resupply and Communications Wing.

Also in 1952, the CIA's Office of Research and Reports began work on a detailed study of feather-bombable targets, with charts and maps, dryly entitled "The Pattern of Land Use in Relation to Target Grains in the USSR and the Probable Spread of Stem Rust on Cereal Grains." A draft was circulated in October 1952, and the final report appeared early in 1953, ready for the projected total war with Russia, now rescheduled for 1954. The report divided European Russia into three regions, based on what was grown there. Region I was winter wheat and barley. Region II was spring wheat. Region III was winter rye and oats. The CIA's crop strategists made certain simplifying assumptions: "If the attack is to be made with use of E-73 feather bombs which are carrying spores of rusts that will attack wheat, rye, barley, and oats separately or in combination, it is not necessary to consider separately the target potentialities of the area seeded to each grain." They also knew how much damage each successful feather bombing would do, based on the tests in upstate New York: "The Pine Camp test of the currently available BW crop munition achieved primary infection over an area of 25 miles." Then the infection would spread. "Research now complete indicates that 'heavy' damage in excess of

100 square miles can be expected from each focus of stem-rust infection that is established under favorable conditions."

It's remotely possible, though perhaps eternally unprovable, that some of the anticrop field tests that Orrin Grover referred to actually happened over fields in Soviet-bloc countries. Romania and Hungary were hardest hit. "Hungary, once the granary of Central Europe, reports a wheat crop 40 percent below expectations," the Associated Press said in July 1953. "Refugees said thousands of families in Hungary recently were without substantial food for days." Hungarian cattle were dying, too, owing to a shortage of fodder combined with an epidemic of foot-and-mouth disease.

Let's declassify all the documents about CIA operations in Eastern Europe. Really, all of them.

AT 11:30 A.M. I went out to my car in the National Archives parking lot and talked to Christopher Lydon by phone for his radio show, *Open Source*. I rambled, because I'm caught up in the early 1950s.

What is so clear to me, going through my hundreds of pages of notes from various declassified documents, is how wars introduce a red shift in human cruelty. It happens in battle, but also among civilians. Normally gentle people become somewhat cruel in wartime, and somewhat cruel people become monsters. You can see it in weapons development. Before a war, there's a lot of earnest talk of defensive research, but once the war begins, the fury builds and the idea of defense is replaced by the idea of killing as many human beings as possible. If you can't kill human beings, you kill experimental animals. Or you blow up miniature fake towns in the desert.

Here's an example. Before the Korean War, the Air Force and the Chemical Corps were experimenting with bombs filled with *Brucella suis* germs. Brucellosis, a disease found in Maltese goats—a herd of which were brought by the Department of Agriculture to Maryland in 1905— and also in pigs and cattle, is a serious affliction in human beings, but more than 90 percent of people who get it survive. By early 1952, after a year and a half of misery and defeat in Korea, the Air Force and the Pentagon were unhappy with brucellosis and wanted a "killer agent." Colonel Totten and his Air Force colleagues had a conference in the Pentagon with Captain Coggins of the U.S. Navy. The first item of business was *Pasteurella pestis*, or plague. "Captain Coggins stated that the Navy desired pasteurella pestis in quantity immediately." The Navy had 125 people "highly trained with pestis" at the biological laboratory in Alameda, and had plans for a plague pilot plant, for which the Research and Development Board had approved $10 million. "The Navy has an approved project known as 'monkey man,'" Coggins said, "which would involve a series of tests with live or hot agents, the first half of such tests utilizing monkeys as the subjects, and the second half utilizing human volunteers, probably from San Quentin." A marginal note indicated that the Navy had earmarked $50,000 for the project.

The "monkey man" idea was shelved, however, as I learned from another document from March 6, 1952. Major Glenn E. Davis, one of the Air Force's weapons evaluators, had talked to Albert Krueger at his office in Berkeley. Of "monkey man" he wrote: "Continuation of this project to include studies on man has been stopped by the Navy Bureau of Medicine for fear that legal steps could be taken in the event of death of volunteer test subjects." Only monkeys would die.

But the plague development schedule could still be met, Krueger told Davis. "He is willing to provide everything in his power to assist, if necessary," Davis wrote, "but he cannot provide personnel on a long-term basis."

Major Davis went on to ask Krueger what he thought of coccid-ioidomycosis, one of my grandfather's diseases. Krueger didn't think much of it: it lasted well in storage, but it had "no significant lethality." It sickened, but it didn't often kill. Plague was Krueger's interest—plague along with "irradiated animal studies." If an animal was blasted with radiation, as a survivor of an atomic attack might be, the animal was, so Krueger had found in his experiments, more likely to get sick from an introduced disease. "The relationship between sub-lethal dosages of radiation and onslaught of disease is extremely important to operational use of BW," Krueger explained. The Navy Bureau of Medicine would look into the defensive aspects of this topic, Davis wrote; Krueger's lab at Berkeley "would then collaborate on offensive aspects." Monkeys would be irradiated, and then sprayed with germs, and then they would die.

These interservice plague meetings took place in the early months of 1952—which was just when the North Koreans said that the Americans were dropping plague on them. The war had gone on too long: bloody-mindedness was in the air. Harry Truman wrote a long, fierce note to himself about what needed to happen. It was time to "get the Chinamen out of Korea," Truman wrote, on January 27, 1952. He envisioned an ultimatum, to expire after ten days, telling Moscow that the United States would destroy every military base in Manchuria unless the Chinese withdrew. "If there is further interference," he added, "we shall eliminate any port or cities necessary to accomplish our peaceful purpose." This meant all-out war, Truman angrily scribbled. "It means that Moscow, St. Petersburg, Mukden, Vladivostok, Peking, Shanghai, Port Arthur, Dainea, Odessa, Stalingrad and every manufacturing plant in China and the Soviet Union will be eliminated. This is the final chance for the Soviet Government to decide whether it desires to survive or not."

DINNER WITH MY DEAR DAUGHTER and son-in-law in their apartment at Foggy Bottom. They're newlyweds, and have very touchingly and kindly arranged and framed things that M. and I have given them. I padded around their apartment admiring their new life together.

March 29, 2019, Friday

I was eating a Nature Valley Granola Bar for breakfast in my car when a man came down the road pushing a fat-faced, smart-eyed baby in a stroller. He turned out to be the man who owned the Airbnb. Can I get you something to drink? he asked, with a Russian accent. Tea? I said thanks but I had some coffee.

I'm old enough that I can remember how great it was when suddenly Russians appeared in our country after perestroika. All those decades of insane suspicion. Most people in foreign countries are reasonably kind, fairly generous. Most people want to get along with other people.

Suddenly, when Gorbachev got off the plane in Washington, there were huge sighs of relief and relaxings of shoulder tension. Russia—it's just a country. It's not a casserole of enemies. The Kremlin is just the name of a big building. Communism isn't an infection that must be fought with other, real infections.

It's in the corridors of power that the deep crazy suspicions and enmities live. Dean Rusk, James Angleton, Frank Wisner, Allen Dulles, Paul Nitze, James Forrestal, Dean Acheson, Richard Helms, Henry Kissinger, Robert McNamara, McGeorge Bundy, Cord Meyer, George

Kennan. These are not normal people. They should not be allowed near a diplomatic pouch or a negotiating table. They should not have the ear of the president. They are people who make things worse.

Think of Guatemala. Think of how proud Frank Wisner was of what he did there, installing a new government, as if a new government were a new dishwasher. Like some of the germ scientists, Wisner was a giddy, danger-loving tinkerer. If I do this, will it blow up? Will it get out of control? Will it distract me from my deep sadness? Wisner was experimenting on human societies, to see whether, by creating chaos and fear and economic uncertainty—in a country like East Germany, say, or Albania, or Guatemala—he could inject new foreign material intracerebrally, into the neural fabric of their governance. "Albania," Wisner wrote in November 1951, "because of its very limited defense capabilities, its small size and its isolation from the Soviet block, is an ideal laboratory for experimentation on OPC techniques and for the development of new concepts of clandestine operations such as the propaganda supply drop." Albania was an experimental animal. ("Our 'allies' wanted to make use of Albania as a guinea pig, without caring about human losses," said one survivor, Abas Ermenji.)

Even before the Korean War, there were powerful people in Washington who were brooding over Guatemala. Jacobo Arbenz, who was leftist and popular, was running for president, and he might win. Senator Alexander Wiley asked Senator Theodore F. Green to convene a special session, soon, on Guatemala. "It seems to me that Guatemala is going to be a source of Red infection throughout Central America," Senator Wiley wrote, "and the sooner we help sterilize that source, the better." That was in May 1950.

In August 1950, Wisner's Office of Policy Coordination made plans to place someone under cover at the Instituto de Antropología in Guatemala. The undercover agent, Arthur E. Baldry, would recommend "suitable indigenous Guatemalan personnel for use as principal agents in connection with political and psychological warfare projects." The idea was to make it look as if the agitation was internal and domestic, when actually it was the United States jabbing a stick into a small foreign country's business. "In view of the rapid growth of Communist activity in Guatemala and the probability that Guatemala may become the central point for the dissemination of anti-US propaganda in Central America and the Caribbean islands, it is considered necessary and appropriate to commence counter-propaganda in the area," said the project sheet, now declassified and in the CREST database. "In order to carry out a psychological warfare program which will appear to be indigenous in its origin, native elements must be found to execute OPC actions. The risk of detection of a U.S. interest behind the propaganda will be lessened through proper selection of indigenous agents."

Soon the United Fruit Company, which owned practically everything in Guatemala—the railroads, the plantations, the port facilities—got involved. Someone whose name is whited out on a CREST document (declassified with redactions in 2003)—probably Tommy "the Cork" Corcoran, lobbyist for United Fruit Company—met in CIA offices with Allen Dulles and others, in order to deliver the message that the fruit company was greatly concerned and "wished to offer the use of their facilities and personnel to assist CIA in any program which we may contemplate for combating the growth of Communism in Guatemala." They were "willing to go to any lengths to assist the Government," the representative said. "Mr. Dulles talked to ⬚ briefly and assured him that we were very much interested in his proposal and that he would ask Col. J. C. King to contact him in the near future."

Eventually planning intensified and got a code name, PBFORTUNE. In January 1952, a cable went out from the Office of Policy Coordination to ⬚: "HQ desires firm list top flight communists whom new government would desire to eliminate immediately in event of successful anti-communist coup." There follows a whited-out list of names.

In August 1952, a weapons shipment to Guatemalan coup plotters was okayed by CIA director Bedell Smith: 140 light machine guns, 1,000 rifles, 1,500 machine pistols, 30 antitank rifles, 2,500 blast grenades, and lots of ammunition. On September 18, a memo went from ⬚ to ⬚, "Subject: Guatemalan Communist Personnel to be disposed of during Military Operations of Calligeris." (Calligeris was the cryptonym for Carlos Castillo Armas, the CIA's chosen replacement for Arbenz.) The list of 132 names is divided into two categories: "Category I—persons to be disposed of through Executive action," and "Category II—persons to be disposed of through imprisonment or exile." The list had been personally reviewed and revised by Castillo Armas.

And then the State Department (rightly) called everything off.

BUT THAT WASN'T THE END OF IT. Wisner's Office of Policy Coordination waited—and then started building again, stealthily at first, with a plan of economic warfare aimed at the coffee crop. "In order to support the current political objective of harassing the power of the pro-communist government of Guatemala, a project is planned to injure the internal economy of the country," reads a typewriter draft of a planning document from March 1953. It could be Frank Wisner's typewriter—Wisner was closely involved in Guatemala planning and he was a believer in the unsigned, undated, and unletterheaded document—but there's no way to be sure. "It is proposed," the coup planner typed, "to develop a plan that would either temporarily, or permanently, curtail Guatemala's export market for coffee, and thereby reduce its income and its foreign exchange." It was called Operation Fiber. "The objective of the FIBER program is to attain a means of sufficiently damaging the economy of Guatemala and/or the Guatemalan Government to bring about the collapse of the pro-Communist government in that country."

What followed was a list of ways for the United States to make things go wrong in the Guatemalan coffee world. These included denial of shipping, denial of fuel, sabotage of docks, rail sabotage, staged boycotts by American longshoremen, false rumors of imminent currency devaluation, and sabotage of the actual coffee beans. Several ways to sabotage coffee beans were proposed: (1) "wetting down while in storage at dockside warehouses," (2) "inducing moisture in ships' holds," and (3) "sabotage of coffee trees by inducing hemileia rust (disease) which kills trees over a period of time." (Someone by hand later inserted "or spreading rumors of" before "hemileia rust," to soften this sentence.) That led to a complicated psychological warfare proposal: "PW project (black) to ostensibly discover plans of Communists to introduce hemileia rust in crops of countries other than Guatemala." The "discovery" of a (fictitious) Communist plot to spread coffee rust around Latin America could also, the document continues, serve as cover for the CIA's actual spreading of coffee rust disease, by casting suspicion that the disease was "introduced in Guatemala as retaliation by the other Central American states"—wheels within wheels. A final proposal was to introduce a particular non-native pest, the black bug of coffee, into Guatemala's dockside coffee stocks or on ships.

The black bug that Frank Wisner, or one of his crew, was thinking about was the coffee borer, *Hypothenemus hampei*, an insect that nibbles a small hole in a coffee bean and lays its eggs inside. If a saboteur scattered even a few of these nonnative bugs over bags of coffee, or in the coffee bags, someone else—an American coffee buyer perhaps—would see them and worry that the whole shipment had been infected.

There's another Fiber document in the CREST database—written in the cryptonymic code of CIA planners of that era and dated May 15, 1953—about the psychological warfare plan that should follow the stopping of coffee shipments:

> When FIBER shipments are stopped, propaganda should be sent all SGRANGER nations calling attention to this supreme bungle on the part of BGGYPSY advisers to the WSBURNT government.

Translated, this means:

> When coffee shipments are stopped, propaganda should be sent to all Latin American nations calling attention to this supreme bungle on the part of Soviet advisers to the Guatemalan government.

Another way of discrediting the Arbenz regime, in other words. The letter ends: "Thus can Headquarters continue its campaign against the

BGGYPSYS in WSBURNT and, at the same time, provide a peg for actions of all types involving objectives similar to those of Operation FIBER even if FIBER is not initiated."

The CIA's research office produced two studies that were obliquely in support of Operation Fiber. Coffee was vulnerable to "humid conditions," said one study from May 1953, produced at the request of J. C. King. "Ship sabotage of Guatemalan coffee could, therefore, be accomplished by interfering with the air circulation, or breaking steam pipes that would cause humid conditions, or by opening portholes during storms that would cause partial flooding of the cargo." Price rigging might be another way of destabilizing the government, the study said: the CIA could buy a great deal of Guatemalan coffee and then dump it on the market all at once, forcing the wholesale coffee price (and coffee workers' wages) down to an unnaturally low level. "Political repercussions might follow."

A second CIA study, dated September 23, 1953, exists only as a title: "'Black Bug' in Coffee Shipments."

Any ten-year-old would be able to tell you why releasing coffee-boring bugs and coffee-withering funguses within a poor, heavily coffee-dependent nation was the wrong thing to do. But at the CIA, the OPC's plotters of rollback mulled over these biological options for months. Coffee rust and the black coffee berry borer are both now an ongoing problem in Guatemala—also in Cuba and other Latin American countries. Whether Wisner's covert warriors had anything to do with the spread of these crop troubles we may never know.

What we do know is that many at CIA headquarters were opposed to a CIA-instigated coup in Guatemala. "The operation as laid on was disapproved by many analysts and desk officers in CIA and Department of State," said a draft historical paper written shortly after the successful coup, which was code-named PBSUCCESS. "Those who held this opinion generally believed in the overall objective, i.e. elimination of Communist influence in Guatemala, but were convinced that the method chosen to accomplish the objective would at best return only partial and short-term advantages in exchange for grave long-term risks."

We also know that Guatemala never recovered from PBSUCCESS.

In 1984, Philip Roettinger, a former CIA case officer and Marine Corps colonel who was involved in the 1954 coup, wrote a penitent op-ed piece for the *Los Angeles Times.* "I now consider my involvement in the overthrow of Arbenz a terrible mistake," Roettinger wrote. "When I authorized Castillo Armas, then in a Tegucigalpa safehouse, to return to Guatemala and assume the presidency that we had prepared for him, I had no idea of the consequences of the CIA's meddling. Our 'success' led to 31 years of repressive military rule and the deaths of more than 100,000 Guatemalans. Furthermore, the overthrow of the Arbenz government destroyed vital social and economic reforms, including land distribution, social security and trade-union rights."

The CIA's man, Castillo Armas, ruled for only two years. Then he was assassinated by a right-wing rival. Decades of havoc and terror squads followed. "Guatemala has suffered a spectacular form of violence," said René de León Schlotter in 1976, "spectacular not only for having lasted through the past two decades, but also for its intensity—the high number of victims and the cruelty of the methods used." Much of the violence came from the extreme right, Schlotter said. "Allow me to reaffirm that the responsibility of the United States, although indirect, is very real and serious."

AT THE NATIONAL ARCHIVES I ran into Bill Burr near the elevators. He was just leaving for the day, bringing his computer over to the guard's desk to open it, as everyone must, so that he could prove that he wasn't walking out with some memo. We shook hands. He said he hadn't had much luck finding things that morning.

Nowadays you sometimes have to show the underside of your laptop to the guards, too. Maybe somebody once tried to sneak out with a document taped there, or hidden under a false bottom. It's mostly still a system in which the original documents, in all their crinkly colorful rusty-paper-clipped variety, are offered to everyone, which is kind of a miracle— a miracle with risks, because documents can disappear.

One set of thefts happened in 2003, when former Clinton White

House national security adviser Sandy Berger worked his way through supersecret counterterrorist planning documents contained in National Security Council files and "SMOFs," or Staff Member Office Files—"a large number of original and unique documents"—stealing some number of emails, faxes, drafts, notes, and discussion papers along the way. There is no way to know what exactly he walked out with during his four visits, or whether his intent was to hide embarrassments in the files from the 9/11 Commission, at which he was due to testify. Berger was a trusted high-level person, an international lawyer, who arrived wearing a voluminous overcoat. He was given special treatment, allowed (at least until the staff got suspicious) to work in the private office of senior archivist Nancy Kegan Smith. He engineered moments of privacy by saying he had to make important phone calls or by asking for a Diet Coke. At times he appeared "agitated." A staff member from the archives, unnamed, wrote an email about one of Berger's thefts:

> Okay, I know this is odd. He walked out the door in front of me and into the hallway. The door closed. Shortly after it closed, I proceeded to go get him a Diet Coke. When I opened the door and started down the hall, he was stooped over right outside the doorway. He was fiddling with something white which looked to be a piece of paper or multiple pieces of paper. It appeared to be rolled around his ankle and underneath his pant leg, with a portion of paper sticking out underneath.

The staff member walked past him, on his way to get him the Coke he'd asked for. They didn't make eye contact. "I can't be 100 percent sure of what I saw," he wrote, "because it happened so quickly. But there was clearly something there more than his pants and socks."

Berger made oddly frequent trips to the bathroom, stealing, it turned out, several different copies of the same report. The report, written by Richard Clarke, recommended a number of ways to improve American antiterror programs. At one point Berger hid some of his thefts under a construction trailer on Ninth Street, near the main archives building. Although he lied adroitly to archives officials about what he'd done, he was eventually caught. "I inadvertently took a few documents from the

Archives," he told the press. Inadvertently? In your pant leg? Republicans were trying to assassinate his character, Berger's spokesman said, when he had been "a tireless defender of his country."

Should Richard Clarke's recommendations for antiterror programs, or indeed any of the documents that Sandy Berger looked through, have been locked away in a SCIF, per CIA-mandated procedures, and designated as SAP (Special Access Program) materials, a higher classification than top secret? The answer is no. Especially after 9/11, the answer is no. They were records from a recent presidency, and those records would shed light on governmental policies directed at terrorists and suspected terrorists. The level of secrecy was unnecessary and fetishistic. After 9/11, the records should all have been freely available for everyone to read, unredacted except for phone numbers, email addresses, and the names of people who might unfairly be suspected of some heinous act. House Speaker Tom DeLay was being absurd when he described Berger's theft from the archives as being a "gravely, gravely serious" security breach.

Even so, Berger obviously should not have been stealing historical documents. He was, it seems, trying to spruce up the record of the Clinton administration by removing things that might look bad in the light of later events. That was the harmful act. Theft of documents from an archive in order to mislead the public was the crime. Betraying "national security" was not.

Berger was charged with a misdemeanor and forced to serve a hundred hours of community service. His security clearance was taken away—temporarily. He left the law and became a corporate consultant, helping companies find new markets in foreign countries. Eventually Berger's consulting firm, Stonebridge International, merged with former secretary of state Madeleine Albright's consulting firm, and became Albright Stonebridge Group.

IN THE ARCHIVES' READING ROOM, the smiley attendant rolled out a cart full of several boxes of State Department files. The first box I opened had the fat file I was looking for, "Political and Psychological Warfare

1947–1950." But before I looked through it I saw another folder, which held a set of State Department memos and papers having to do with the decision to take away the passports of people who said things that were critical of the United States. I took some pictures of the passport correspondence, and then I opened the psychological warfare folder. Immediately I realized that I was holding in my hands the very inceptional moment, the big bang, of covert action. George Kennan's crucial memo was there, in draft form, in the original typescript, from April 1948, grandly entitled "The Inauguration of Organized Political Warfare." No redactions—not even the small cuts that were in the version printed in the State Department's *Foreign Relations of the United States* volume from 1993 about the beginnings of the CIA, entitled *Emergence of the Intelligence Establishment*.

Kennan's "The Inauguration" is a worrying document because it was written with the knowledge of what had happened in Italy a few months earlier, when CIA agents with bags of cash had bribed politicians and newspapers and spread false news and rumors in order to sway the Italian elections. Kennan fully approved of the corrupting of the Italian political universe, it seemed; he just wanted it now to be put on a firmer institutional basis. He says, for instance (with a formerly redacted clause in bold): "We cannot afford in the future, in perhaps more serious political crises, **to scramble into impromptu covert operations as we did at the time of the Italian elections."**

Kennan envisioned the formation of Liberation Committees, led by prominent Soviet refugees, who could thereby stay in the public realm, "with access to printing presses and telephones." That was mainly an overt effort, with some covert guidance. But secrecy, as a primal force, as an ideal atmosphere for effective political action, was what really interested him. He modeled his vision on British and Soviet practices—on Churchill and Stalin. They knew how to set events in motion without showing their hand. What the United States needed to create, he thought, was a program of "remote and deeply concealed official control of clandestine operations so that governmental responsibility cannot be shown." The money would come from the U.S. government, but it would pass through private

American organizations, laundered of its official federal taint, in order to flower as a spontaneous expression of American ideals—and it would support "indigenous anti-Communist elements" and "underground activities" in Communist-controlled countries, but covertly, using what Kennan called "private intermediaries."

Toward the end of his paper he makes the big, broad declaration that set it all going:

> It would seem that the time is now fully ripe for the creation of a covert political warfare operations directorate within the Government. If we are to engage in such operations, they must be under unified direction. One man must be boss.

The man Kennan wanted, and got, was Frank Wisner. Kennan didn't know Wisner personally, he said—it was Allen Dulles who pushed his protégé forward. Kennan wanted to call the new directorate the Office of Special Projects. But Wisner, who understood the useful invisibility of blandness, called it something more forgettable: the Office of Policy Coordination. Kennan's notion—not a good notion—was to find a single person and give him the freedom to do whatever he needed to do in secret, with minimal paperwork, using a lot of money, and breaking any rule of international law or diplomatic usage he wanted to.

The draft became an official State Department Policy Planning Staff memo on May 4, 1948. Then the gears began to turn at Truman's National Security Council. Suddenly they had a bailiwick of their own. A wondrous, almost legalistic document, called NSC 10/2, landed on the desks of the president's inner circle. It included the notion of governmental deniability. The duty to lie, the patriotic, presidential obligation to lie, was built into Kennan's world of political warfare from the very beginning.

NSC 10/2 began as if it were a piece of sweeping legislation, or a declaration of independence: "The National Security Council, taking cognizance of the vicious covert activities of the USSR, its satellite countries and Communist groups to discredit and defeat the aims and activities of the United States and other Western powers, has determined that, in the interests of world peace and US national security, the overt foreign activities of the US Government must be supplemented by covert operations." And then came the list of all the covert things that were allowable under this new dispensation—the sabotage, the economic warfare, the "assistance to underground resistance movements," and all the rest of it—all born secret and meant to stay secret: "so planned and executed that any US Government responsibility for them is not evident to unauthorized persons and that if uncovered the US Government can plausibly disclaim any responsibility for them." "Plausibly disclaim" is the almost comical circumlocution in place of the simpler word: "lie." Later "disclaim" was sharpened to "deny," and the doctrine of plausible deniability became a sacred phrase. It's not that one must reluctantly sometimes dissemble in order to hide an occasional ungainly bit of diplomatic wheeling and dealing—no, denial is mandatory and permanent. The deception, the cover story, is basic to the whole activity. Nothing must be as it is. Everything is cover for something else. A tiny handful of unelected desk warriors, middle-aged men and their sworn-to-secrecy female secretaries, were entitled to know about devious, manipulative, violent operations that might affect—did affect—millions of families all over the planet.

This was a form of treehouse, boy's-club, prep-school ugliness that oozed out of the overheated brains of men overtrained as lawyers, full of their own sense of a kind of power beyond military power. A power of legitimized illegalism. A power to wage political war via cablegram in a suit and tie, and drop hints to newspaper columnists over cocktails in a Georgetown living room that same night.

Some of the correspondence in these early files is still "Access Restricted"—for example, a memo of August 17, 1948, from Kennan to Wisner is absent, and passages from attachments to correspondence in late April 1948 from George Kennan to Undersecretary of State (and future Secretary of Defense) Robert Lovett were blanked sometime after 1988. It's clear, however, that Lovett was solidly behind the new political-warfare proposal, and that he thought the plan had "a certain urgency." Lovett wrote Defense secretary James Forrestal to say that the Office of Policy

Coordination was going to need the "wholehearted cooperation of the military authorities in Germany." Forrestal met with Frank Wisner, and Wisner told him about some of the things he wanted to do. Forrestal then wrote Lovett: "I wish to assure you of my wholehearted agreement with you in regard to the importance of political warfare and the desirability of obtaining the full cooperation of the United States military authorities in Germany with respect to those measures, mentioned in your letter, which will support the political warfare program," Forrestal wrote. Forrestal had run Wisner's ideas past Army officials, who were in "complete agreement." The program of Communist rollback and subversion, the hiring of refugees and rightist thugs and former Nazis, was launched.

I came across one letter in the file from Kennan to Wisner, dated January 6, 1949. "Mr. Wisner: I have examined carefully the volume entitled 'OPC Projects Fiscal 1949–1950,'" Kennan wrote. "In my opinion, this presentation contains the minimum of what is required from the foreign policy standpoint in the way of covert operations during the coming year." Kennan said that the Policy Planning Staff might actually have to add a few more operations to the list. "As the international situation develops, every day makes more evident the importance of the role which will have to be played by covert operations if our national interests are to be adequately protected."

Kennan kept pushing, goading Wisner to do things. More operations, more countries, more secrets. On October 25, 1949, Kennan produced a paper on the need for immediate covert propaganda operations in China. The overt propaganda program should be restrained, emphasizing "the traditional good will of the American people for the Chinese people," he said. The clandestine propaganda operation, on the other hand, should be big. It should speak with many voices, sometimes contradictory voices, all of which would, however, seek to "drive a wedge between the Chinese and Stalinism." The propaganda outlets should be directed remotely, "through a series of particularly remote cut-outs" (i.e., front organizations, seemingly independent of the United States government), and allowed to work on their own. "Some of these mouthpieces will inevitably go bad on us or get off the track," Kennan wrote. "That is the risk which any imaginative and aggressive covert organization must take." Only by being bold and taking risks, Kennan said, could we hope to counter Soviet imperialism.

And then, decades later, it seems that Kennan had a very different view. "The political warfare initiative was the greatest mistake I ever made," he said.

Vannevar Bush and George Kennan were both brilliant, confident men, proud of being tough-minded as well as erudite, and vain about their ability to turn a phrase. Both loved being near the center of power. Vannevar Bush was the maître d' of biological warfare, and George Kennan was the metaphysician of political warfare. Frank Wisner got an earful from both of them and gave what they told him his own maniacal twist. We're still suffering from what the three of them set in motion in 1948, with Harry Truman's blessing.

I LANDED LATE at Bangor airport. Got home after midnight and crept into bed with warm M. and the dogs, feeling I'd escaped from the crucible of the Cold War. But I hadn't.

March 30, 2019, Saturday

A State Department official had the idea of giving a skateboard to Castro as a kind gesture. Others in the State Department said no. Giving a skateboard to Castro would be very ill-timed, they felt, and would send all the wrong signals.

When I woke up I realized that my dream was based on something I'd seen yesterday at the National Archives. In the State Department file about the infancy of Wisner's Office of Policy Coordination is a proposal based on an article by Wallace Carroll in *Collier's*. The proposal, called Operation Flat Top, was an overt psychological warfare project—it envisioned "the sending to European ports an aircraft carrier on which would be constructed a miniature replica of a typical American town to exemplify the 'American Way of Life.'" Wallace Carroll was consulting for the CIA. The idea was to give people a sense of the perfect wonderment of an American Main Street, but perched on top of a giant motorized instrument of war, an aircraft carrier. Some people at the State Department thought it was a bad idea and some thought it was a good idea. In the end it didn't happen.

I photographed only some of the Flat Top correspondence because there was so much to read. Often it's the thing you don't photograph that stays in your head.

Other things I noticed in the files: some of the supersecret documents had a front page of wide diagonal red stripes to indicate that only privileged people with a need to know could read them. And I came across a memo from Paul Nitze, Kennan's hard-liner theorist, who wrote a thoughtful memo about the meaning of the phrase "psychological operations." Did "psychological operations" merely mean "activities designed to influence the attitudes, actions and capabilities of foreign peoples"? Or was it a code word for everything—a "cover name to describe those activities of the United States in peace and in war through which all elements of national power are systematically brought to bear on other nations"? Or was it both? Frank Wisner clearly thought it was both.

In the morning I asked M. what she was thinking about. "Large, huge thoughts and little tiny ones," she said. "The usual."

IN THE AFTERNOON I read about one of the bombs described in the "Seventh Annual Report of the Chemical Corps Biological Laboratories," published July 1, 1953, with a picture on the cover of a propeller bomber spraying some kind of aerosol from its undercarriage. "The E-93 bomb," said the report, "is a miniature munition for disseminating dry agent-fill, approximately 3 in. long by ¾ in. diameter." It was designed by the Ralph M. Parsons Company, the same engineering firm that helped build the giant test sphere, the Eight-ball, at Detrick—where experimental animals and Seventh-day Adventists breathed in Q fever and other aerosols. The body of the E-93 bomb was a standard carbon-dioxide cartridge—the kind of cartridge people used to use to make soda water, or to inflate flotation vests in airplanes—onto which was attached a tail assembly. The bomb had undergone wind-tunnel testing. (The Ralph M. Parsons Company had also helped Camp Detrick and the Navy's Bureau of Ordnance develop and test the 300-pound E-4 biological mine, which is not to be confused with the 1,400-pound, ten-foot-long, submarine-launched biological torpedo mine, the XB-14B. The E-4 was a stealthy weapon, designed to be towed into place by an underwater demolition team: "Upon release it will sink to the bottom in depths not over 75 feet, remain there for a predetermined time, then surface and disseminate its fill, and will finally sink again." The XB-14B torpedo mine deployed twelve above-water fog nozzles arranged in a "wagon wheel" configuration; in 1953, in Operation Whitehorse, this weapon blew clouds of simulant organisms on Floridians near Panama City, where the navy operated a Mine Countermeasures Station. In 1954, in Operation Moby Dick, an XB-14B mine fogged the California coast.)

I'd first come across a mention of the E-93 miniature munition in 2009, working my way through the Air Force's AFOAT BW-CW files. I found it in a training lecture by Major James E. Fasolas, an Air Force weapons expert. The goal in a BW weapon was to make a big aerosol cloud with a lot of little bombs, Major Fasolas explained to his students on July 17, 1952. "It is better to generate the cloud only a few feet from the desired target—namely a man—so that the agent would not have to travel a great distance to reach it. We hope to accomplish this by setting up a large number of small clouds over the entire target, the larger the number of small clouds the better." Six miniature E-93 bombs would cluster in a four-inch sphere made of ribbed plastic. "Our ultimate hope is in the spherical shaped munition which I just showed you," Fasolas said. "These spheres when dropped form a random distribution pattern on the ground; by fluting the outer surface we can get very wide area coverage. It has been calculated from test drops that one B-29 load of 5,000 spheres can cover 14 square miles with an effective coverage. You can see why we like the sphere."

According to a marginal note, Major Fasolas worked for MATS, the Air Force's Military Air Transport Service, which was a big but low-profile service arm where the CIA tucked away some of its projects. MATS ran the balloon-bomb squadron, part of one of the CIA's Air Resupply and Communications wings, tasked with "air support of Unconventional Warfare Operations." The history of Air Resupply is sketchy, but it had something to do with leaflets and crop-disease balloons and a place called Mountain Home, Idaho. "The Military Air Transport (MATS) has been assigned the responsibility of establishing training and initial supply of field units to carry out the necessary operational missions utilizing balloon delivery techniques," a memo said.

I once spent a day looking into James "Joe" Fasolas's life. He earned a degree in organic chemistry in 1943 from Virginia Polytechnic, where he was president of the Cadet Corps. His father made turbines at the Westinghouse plant near Philadelphia. In 1949, Fasolas and his wife moved into Apartment C of the new Watkins Acres Apartments in Frederick, Maryland. In April 1952—just when the Communists were charging that the Americans were spreading plague and other diseases— he was listed as a potential attendee at a two-day interservice symposium on plague at the Department of Defense, along with Albert Krueger, Captain Coggins of the Navy, and William A. M. Burden, a wealthy art collector and mass-destructionist.

In 1956, Major Fasolas studied at the Air University. He won a Distinguished Flying Cross in Vietnam. In 1969, he began making stained-glass windows. In retirement in Fort Walton Beach, Florida, he taught art glass and made a window in his house that was written up in the local paper as "a beautiful 85-piece glass creation in cool blues, aquamarines, golds, and greens." Fasolas loved the color red. "He always uses some red in everything he makes," the article said.

You have to remember that everybody is a human being, made of many colors of glass.

COLONEL JAMES TOTTEN, who pushed as hard as anyone at the Air Force to develop bioweapons and extol their efficiencies, spent his old age carving wooden canes, collecting Oriental rugs, and raising flowers. "Because of his knowledge of orientals he was in demand as appraiser, lecturer and judge," wrote his eulogist. "In his quest for things beautiful and aesthetic, Jim became a horticulturist, growing beautiful flowers and plants in his landscaped garden." He was thoughtful of other people, and had a sly sense of humor, the eulogist said. "We who served with him loved and admired him and we know we are better men because he passed our way."

In retirement, Edgar Tullis, in charge of rice-disease development at Fort Detrick, also grew flowers. "As an amateur breeder of day lilies he developed many beautiful varieties," according to an obituary in *Phytopathology*. "As a grower of camellias and a judge of camellia shows, he was a highly respected member of that group of plant fanciers."

March 31, 2019, Sunday

Today I thought about Charles Senseney's sports coat and what you can find out by reading the newspaper. Senseney, who developed the M-1 dart gun and worked for the Special Operations Division at Detrick, was one of the men who had carried out the CIA's subway aerosol experiment in New York. In 1975, the Senate Select Committee on Intelligence called Senseney to testify. "He wore a plaid sports coat and a white tie as he offered his expert opinion as to what a couple of anthrax-laden light bulbs could accomplish in the subway," the *New York Daily News* wrote in 1998. "Put New York out of commission," Senseney said. Without that plaid jacket and white tie, Senseney's testimony is just words on a page. With it, he's a person.

On September 18, 1975, at ten o'clock in the morning, the Senate Committee to Study Governmental Operations with Respect to Intelligence Activities met in the Russell office building, room 318, to hear testimony from Charles Senseney, Edward Schantz, and Robert Andrews. Senator Frank Church called the meeting to order and asked Professor Schantz to swear that his testimony would be the whole truth and nothing but the truth. Schantz said, I do.

Schantz was a professor at the University of Wisconsin and an expert on shellfish toxin, which is what the hearing was about: "the puzzlement of the poisons," as Senator Church put it. Several kinds of poison, including cobra venom, had turned up in a CIA storage safe. They were supposed to have been destroyed, on Nixon's orders.

I only know a few things about Schantz, mostly found in newspaper articles. He'd grown up on a Wisconsin dairy farm and had worked for Carnation milk before becoming a war scientist. He was an authority on brucellosis as well as shellfish toxin. Once, in 1951, eleven dairy cows from adjoining farms suddenly died after grazing near the fence at Camp Detrick. It turned out that Detrick employees had been spraying near the fence. Edward Schantz studied the remains of one of the dead cows and confirmed that the death was caused by an arsenic-based weed killer.

Schantz told the committee that when he worked for the Special Operations Division at Detrick he'd purified about twenty grams of clam poison from clams gathered in California and Alaska—enough shellfish toxin to kill ten thousand people. The poison was coated on darts produced for the CIA by the Special Operations Division. Senator Church asked Schantz how long the poison remained poisonous. Schantz said he'd tested it recently, and it was "every bit as potent as the day I prepared it." He thought it might last a hundred years.

After Schantz testified, the committee called Mr. Senseney. They asked him about the darts and the shellfish poison—and then, for a time, they got interested in something else. Senator Gary Hart of Colorado asked: "Are you familiar with a so-called vulnerability study or experiment on the New York subway system?"

"I participated in that," said Senseney. "I rode a subway and sampled the air." That got a laugh.

Senator Hart asked how the experiment worked.

"Well," said Senseney, "there was one person who was the operator— if you want to call it an operator—who rode a certain train, and walking between trains, dropped what looked like an ordinary light bulb which contained a biological agent." The next train through the station stirred the agent up in the air, Senseney said. "It went quite well through the entire subway, because we started down around 14th Street and sampled up as far as 58th Street, and there was quite a bit of aerosol all along the way."

Hart said, "Just from one light bulb?"

Senseney said, "From one light bulb."

Senator Walter Mondale asked Senseney about the shellfish toxin. It should have been destroyed when President Nixon ordered all toxic agents destroyed, shouldn't it? What did Mr. Senseney know about the delivery of the shellfish poison produced by the Special Operations Division to the CIA?

"I would look at it this way," said Senseney. "We were prepared to actually destroy everything. However, much of the material that was stored in SO Division was being stored for another agency. It did not belong to the Department of Defense."

Senator Mondale said, "It belonged to the CIA?"

"That is correct," said Senseney.

I wish I knew more about Charles Senseney. He was married to Anna Mae Burke Senseney for sixty-one years. He went to Harvard University. He lived much of his life in Damascus, Maryland. He loved baseball. He wore a white tie. He died on June 1, 2007.

One more thing I know, also from a local paper. Charles Senseney was one of Dudley Glick's six casket bearers, as reported in the Frederick *News*. In December 1964, the chief of the Special Operations Division, Dudley Glick, who was also an authority on purified shellfish poison, died suddenly at Fairfax Hospital in Virginia. *The Baltimore Sun* said it was an "apparent heart attack." Years later, someone wrote a letter to *The Frederick News-Post* saying in passing that Glick was a biological research and development victim: Glick Place, a street in Frederick, was named in Dudley Glick's honor, and Willard Place was named after Joel Willard, a Detrick electrician who died of anthrax inhalation.

So when Senseney performed the light-bulb experiment, he'd already carried the coffin of one of his colleagues who'd died in the line of duty.

THE FREDERICK *NEWS* offers other moments of linkage. On March 27, 1951, Frank Olson and Oram Woolpert were two of the six casket bearers at the funeral of Walter Irving Nevius. Nevius had managed the anthrax pilot plant in Vigo County, Indiana; he died at age sixty "after a long illness." On April 10, 1953, Frank Olson and Joseph J. Stubbs were guests of honor at a Camp Detrick tenth-anniversary party. "Both Dr. Olson and Dr. Stubbs came to Frederick in 1943 when Camp Detrick was in its infancy," the *News* reported. "Other guests at the party were Mrs. Stubbs, Mrs. Olson, Dr. and Mrs. John L. Schwab, Dr. and Mrs. Herbert G. Tanner, Lt. Col. and Mrs. Vincent Ruwet, and John C. Malinowski." According to a Camp Detrick document, John Malinowski worked on something blacked out in 1951, and he was with Frank Olson at Sidney Gottlieb's LSD experiment in 1953—although he wasn't drugged because he didn't drink. Malinowski also worked on the "Pennsylvania Turnpike Test" in 1961, and he had tickets to the World Series in 1964, and in 1966 he met Jack Dempsey at Dempsey's restaurant, walked the Freedom Trail in Boston, and drove a Plymouth Commando Fury.

John McNulty, who fogged San Francisco with *Serratia marcescens*, was a casket bearer on December 4, 1953, at Frank Olson's well-attended funeral, along with John L. Schwab and Norman Cournoyer, both research colleagues and friends of Olson's.

Cournoyer, in a 2002 movie made about Olson's death, refused to confirm that biological weapons were used in the Korean War. "I don't want to say it," he said. "But, there were people who had biological weapons and they used them. I won't say anything more than that. They used them." In an interview with *The Baltimore Sun*, Cournoyer told reporter Scott Shane that he believed that Frank Olson was murdered. "Frank was a talker," he said. "He wasn't sure we should be in germ warfare, at the end." Cournoyer said, "If the question is, did Frank Olson commit suicide, my answer is absolutely, positively not."

Scott Shane quotes from the CIA's "A Study of Assassination," found in the training files for the Guatemala coup and declassified in 1995, now available not on CREST but on the National Security Archive's website: "The most efficient accident, in simple assassination, is a fall of 75 feet or more onto a hard surface," says the manual. "Elevator shafts, stair wells, unscreened windows and bridges will serve. Bridge falls into water are not reliable." The document describes the act itself, but with a mysterious whited-out redaction: "The act may be executed by sudden, vigorous ⬚⬚⬚ of the ankles, tipping the subject over the edge."

AT A LITTLE AFTER 5:00 P.M., when we walked the dogs, the sun sent a side blast of light down the street. The river is a choppy matte-gray color, and noisier now because of all the melting.

April 1, 2019, Monday

April fools. I sat in the car by the river for several hours and thought about the firebombing of cities, and about a man I'd interviewed by phone in 2002. He didn't want his name used, so I'll call him Luke. Luke worked for the International Organizations division at the Library of Congress in the early 1960s. The job of the division was to compile a comprehensive list of all the upcoming conferences of all the world's scientific and cultural nongovernmental organizations. Putting together the World List of Future International Meetings was tedious work, Luke said, but the salary was good; of the dozen or so people in the department, all but two were paid, indirectly, by the CIA.

Luke told me that he hadn't slept very well after I'd first called him to set up an interview. "We were sworn to silence," he said. "We would check the periodicals for meetings, and then we would contact the organizations by letter and ask to be put on their mailing list for their future editions. This sort of spirals along as you go into one field—say agriculture, Asian agriculture." The list of future meetings, which was unclassified, would go to the CIA, and the CIA would figure out whom to send where in order to make contacts and gather intelligence.

The Soviets were aware of what was going on. "Striving to pry out secrets from scientists of various countries," *Izvestia* charged in May 1966 (as translated by *The New York Times*), "the C.I.A. organizes special operational groups to participate in international conferences and meetings." The spying had begun in 1958, the paper explained, after the United States and Russia agreed on a cultural exchange program. "As the number of Americans going to the Soviet Union grew year by year, the C.I.A. increased the number of its agents among them." *Izvestia* said it would refrain for the time being from publishing the names of scientist-agents who had helped the CIA, but they should know that "Soviet laws provide harsh punishment against espionage."

THERE WERE MANY CIA-sponsored efforts at the Library of Congress over the years—training programs for Agency employees, indexing and abstracting work, microfilming work, technical translations. The pastor of the Russian Orthodox Church of St. Nicholas, on Massachusetts Avenue in Washington, Father Paul Lutov, was sent to Europe by the Tolstoy Foundation, a CIA front, to gather and bring home anti-Communist refugees who then got well-paid jobs at the library working on bomb targeting or translating or indexing. Paul Lutov himself worked at the Air Research Division into the 1960s. Lutov's Church of St. Nicholas suddenly had a lot of money to build an imposing new cathedral and war memorial shrine honoring the victims of World War I and the Bolshevik Revolution. One of the Church of St. Nicholas's most active parishioners was Boris Pash, reputed arranger of assassinations at the CIA. Years ago I asked the late James McCargar, who was Frank Wisner's colleague in Romania, whether the CIA had helped pay for the construction of the Russian Orthodox church. "No," said McCargar. "And if they had I wouldn't tell you."

Another early CIA venture at the library was the Mid-European Law Project, funded by Allen Dulles's faux charity, the National Committee for a Free Europe. DeWitt Poole, one of its founders, wrote in November 1950 that the Free Europe committee's goal was to "take up the individual

Bolshevik rulers and their quislings and tear them apart, exposing their motivations, laying bare their private lives, pointing at their meannesses, pillorying their evil deeds, holding them up to ridicule and contumely." To do this, they needed horror stories from the subject states of Eastern Europe, and they got them from scholarly refugees spirited out of the Soviet orbit and employed by the Library of Congress with Free Europe funds. Twelve expatriate Mid-European scholars labored to write books on the "means and measures by which the legal systems of normally democratic peoples are being debased into instruments of totalitarian dictatorship"—that's how one of the library's annual reports phrased it. Congress and "other government agencies" used the services of these lawyers; their work was digested and fed back into the propagandizing of CIA's Radio Liberation and Radio Free Europe. Some Mid-European titles were *Church and State Behind the Iron Curtain*, *Legal Sources and Bibliography of Czechoslovakia*, *Forced Labor and Confinement without Trial in Bulgaria*, and *Forced Labor and Confinement without Trial in Poland*, all published for the Free Europe committee by Praeger, which, it was revealed later, brought out many CIA-subsidized books. The CIA had created a feedback loop of paranoia and counterproductive provocation.

KAZYS SKIRPA, the former Lithuanian ambassador to Nazi Germany, came to work at the Library of Congress in 1949. He remained on the library staff for sixteen years, pounding the floor with his cane when he wanted to emphasize a point. To some, Skirpa was a hero of the anti-Soviet struggle—a street in Kaunas, Lithuania, was named in his honor some years ago; to others he was the founder of a collaborationist group called the Lithuanian Activist Front, which put out a flyer that said "The Time Has Come to Settle Accounts with the Jews," before the killings began in 1941.

I asked Luke if he knew about the people working in the Annex of the library, at the Air Research Division and the Air Information Division. Did he know they were doing bomb targeting? He didn't know that, he said. He saw them on coffee breaks and wondered what they were up to.

There was a "Polish Mafia," he said. He was quite curious about them because they were paid so much. "There used to be a bunch of guys that would sit in the back of the Thomas Jefferson reading room," he told me. "In those days you could smoke in there. I'm sure you would have found these same guys sitting around a Waffen SS table."

TOWARD THE END OF 1951, Major General John A. "Sammy" Samford, the new director of Air Force Intelligence, wrote Luther Evans asking him to hire more staff in Air Research in order to speed up the urban-area analysis and "accelerate our techniques of bomb damage assessment." (General Cabell had by this time stepped up to the Joint Chiefs of Staff, on his way to becoming Allen Dulles's deputy at the CIA; he was let go by President Kennedy in 1962, a casualty of the Bay of Pigs.) One employee looked at cities in various countries—Czechoslovakia and Hungary were two he mentioned—in order to figure out which areas were residential and which industrial, and what the heights of various industrial buildings were. "We tried to determine what these buildings were made out of," he told me, "so that somebody else could run stuff through computers and determine what kinds of bombs it would take to level these things."

In 1953, the year that the Air Force bombed North Korea's hydroelectric dams, drowning villages and flooding rice fields, library employee Joseph Podoski, a senior analyst in the Air Information Division, made a close study of the dams of Eastern Europe. One of his travel reports describes a trip he made to New York in search of hard-to-find materials. At the New York Public Library, Podoski looked through a Polish transportation magazine but unfortunately found "very little on dams." He did, however, come across a brochure about the Imatra Power Station in Finland—a large hydroelectric plant only a few miles from the Soviet city of Svetogorsk—that had some good photos. And at the Engineering Societies Library, he had real luck: he located some prewar issues of a Warsaw journal called *Przeglad Mechaniczny* (*Mechanical Revue*) that had "excellent material and photographs on some Polish dams."

It has to be said: in the 1950s, the Library of Congress secretly became a military intelligence agency. As the defense-funded programs grew, security became all-important. "Your attention is again called to the danger of discussing your work in the Coffee Shop and in the AID area," said a 1951 security memo to all Air Research staff. (AID stood for Air Information Division, where the abstractors without security clearances worked.) Top-secret documents were to be stored in the vault—and to enter the vault you had to go to one of eight designated vault persons who signed out a key from the main office. Rough drafts, negatives, carbons, and worn typewriter ribbons went into burn baskets; if you worked overtime, after the burn-basket emptier had come through, you had to lock up your classified trash in a combination-lock safe for the night. The first time you violated regulations you got a warning in your file; the second time, a one-week suspension; the third time, you were recommended for dismissal. Because the library harbored so much secret activity, the administrators who got ahead tended to be Cold War hard-liners with security clearances.

A REPORT CALLED "Fire Spread in Urban Areas," the product of several years of concentrated work beginning in 1952, was one of the Air Research Division's most comprehensive bomb-damage investigations. According to the project proposal from the Air Force to Luther Evans, some incendiary attacks on urban areas had been "highly successful," and some less so; analysis had shown that the damage could vary by as much as 7:1 per unit weight of bombs. "The study would evolve upon the premise that numerous, scattered fires, whether initiated by any source such as an atomic bomb or by large numbers of small incendiary bombs, are potentially a primary means of extensive urban area damage by merging and spreading, and ultimately developing into a general conflagration."

The library took the commission. "It is a distinct pleasure to be of service to the Directorate of Intelligence," Evans wrote in reply.

To do the fire research, the library's Air Research Division hired an engineer named John Wolverton, who'd assessed the efficacy of Japanese bombing raids for the postwar "Strategic Bombing Survey." Wolverton took charge of a group of structural engineers and stereoscope experts. They amassed background reading material, some of it public—such as an account of the fire after the 1906 San Francisco earthquake—and some of it classified. They studied George Ingle Finch's *Fire Spread in Area Attack and the Stick Shape and Density*, for example, and a British analysis of the vulnerability of Italian buildings to incendiary and high-explosive bombs, and Tanabe Heigaku's *Investigation for the Probability of City Great Fire*. Wolverton's team began by reviewing the before-and-after pictures of fifty-two Japanese cities, twenty-two German cities, and two Italian cities, all of them damaged by British or American firebombs in World War II. Most they eliminated, because the cities had burned on several occasions: in a metropolis like Tokyo or Berlin it was, they found, "impossible to determine the fire area that resulted from a single attack."

After much study, the researchers narrowed their comparative work to eleven places: the blasted remnants of Hiroshima and Nagasaki, and the burned regions of Kure, Sakai, Turin, Genoa, Darmstadt, Kassel, two townships of Wuppertal, and Hamburg. These cities had left "fire perimeters" and "burn lines" that were clearly discernible in poststrike photographs.

The researchers traced the shapes of burned blocks and buildings on acetate; they estimated heights and fire loads; they measured air gaps and street widths; they noted tree lines (the foliage of trees soaked up heat and sometimes kept a fire from creeping farther outward, they saw); and they calculated burned versus unburned percentages, trying out several mathematical models of flame propagation. One complexity they noted was that Japanese and German buildings burned differently. A light-frame Japanese structure would burn for fifteen minutes and then cool, whereas a multistory German building, filled as it was with "heavy woodwork and furnishings," would burn for hours, and its masonry walls would store and radiate heat, setting buildings on either side on fire. For this and other reasons, the library researchers found that "the curves developed for German cities would not be consistent with those prepared for the Japanese cities."

There was no mention of people in the urban fire spread study—only of building materials, housing densities, and "radiating bodies"—meaning outside walls. There was talk of the "pillaring" of heated air, of the "great inrush of air across the entire perimeter of the burning area," which, in the case of Hamburg, "possibly exceeded 100 miles per hour." While Wolverton's fire researchers worked at the library, the United States continued its firebombing of Korea halfway around the world.

In 2002, I emailed the Library of Congress for a copy of "Fire Spread in Urban Areas." The head of the Federal Research Division said that it was classified confidential, but he gave me the exact accession number. I filed a Freedom of Information Act request. Three years later the report, published in 1955, arrived in the mail. Back then I thought three years was a long time. Now I know it's normal.

April 2, 2019, Tuesday

Today every grass blade was shining when M. and I walked the dogs around the block in our flannel pajamas, with our coats on. At the kitchen table we talked about how we can't eat pork. "Once you've seen pig's faces and seen pig's souls you can't eat pork," M. said.

I READ A CIA MEMO on CREST this morning about mistakes in sanitizing documents. In Google I found it by typing

"sanitizing" site:cia.gov

I got about a hundred hits. (You can't search for a word like "sanitizing" using CREST's own search bar—you'll get a quarter of a million hits for "sanitized"). The first one was from August 1975, about how to sanitize documents before handing them over to a House or Senate committee. Here's how: You make two Xerox copies of the document. On one copy you put a red line through things you want to redact, referring to the sanitization guidelines, and write in the suggested paraphrase above. Then, using the second copy, a clerk puts correction tape over the places you've redlined and types in the new words or phrases. "Then you take the taped copy and run it through the Xerox again to ensure that the taped material cannot be read."

Another CIA memo from May 1986, declassified with redactions in 2012, discussed the problem of sanitized documents in which "portions intended for redaction can be clearly read after copying." Problems arose, said ⬛, CIA's information and privacy coordinator, "from the color of the marking pen, the dryness of the pen, or the type of copier utilized." Even though ⬛ and a case officer personally reviewed every sanitized document, ⬛ said, there was a possibility that sensitive information could slip through.

> Because I have long been concerned that technical means or computer-enhancement techniques might permit someone to restore "blacked out" information, we have formally requested OTS to review our present redaction process and our requirements and to recommend a procedure which would make the redaction process more certain.

Someone named Jack, on a cover note, handwrote: "Ben—A chronically recurring problem. It is most appropriate that Lee attempt to do something about it." Which confirms that the whited-out name in the document is Lee Strickland, the CIA's information and privacy coordinator in 1986. Why would it be necessary to hide his name?

Steven Aftergood, who writes the *Secrecy News* blog for the Federation of American Scientists, published this nice tribute when Lee Strickland died in 2007:

> We first encountered him perhaps 15 years ago when he was the head of the CIA Freedom of Information office, where he used to reliably deny our FOIA requests. Over the years he seemed to enlarge his horizons and to admit the possibility of contrasting views. He taught his students at the University of Maryland that information policy could be exciting as well as important. And he was a nice guy.

Strickland's big public moment came in 1997, when he—in response to a FOIA lawsuit filed by Aftergood and the Federation of American Scientists—released a figure for the CIA's total budget appropriation: $26.6 billion. It was the first time since the founding of the CIA that any budget figure was made public. "This move was opposed both by the House and the Senate," Aftergood wrote at the time, "and could only be accomplished through a lawsuit." Aftergood and Kate Martin, a lawyer at the Center for National Security Studies, argued in the lawsuit that under Clinton's Executive Order 12958 and clause (b)(1) of the Freedom of Information Act, information may be withheld only if its release "reasonably could be expected to result in damage to the national security." Therefore the CIA's failure to release the budget information was a violation of the Freedom of Information Act.

In conceding, however, the CIA offered only one overall budget number. "We will continue to protect from disclosure any and all subsidiary information concerning the intelligence budget," wrote George Tenet in a terse statement, "whether the information concerns particular intelligence agencies or particular intelligence programs." In 1999, Tenet ended even that brief moment of openness and stopped giving out any budget numbers at all.

In 2002, Aftergood filed another lawsuit, asking for the CIA to disclose intelligence budget figures for the years 1947 and 1948. "CIA's sustained refusal to disclose the 1947 and 1948 intelligence budget totals is a violation of the Freedom of Information Act," Aftergood wrote, "because the requested historical information has no bearing on national security today. Nor does it implicate intelligence sources and methods." Aftergood lost.

In 2005, a top CIA official, Mary Margaret Graham, made a slip of the tongue and revealed that year's intelligence budget at a conference in San Antonio, Texas, to an audience that included a reporter from *U.S. News and World Report*. The news made *The New York Times*. "It is ironic," Aftergood told the *Times*. "We sued the C.I.A. four times for this kind of information and lost. You can't get it through legal channels."

THERE'S SO MUCH we may never know. But thanks to another FOIA user, Tom Knudson, we know about Operation Green, a series of experiments in the early 1950s that aimed at infecting pigs with hog cholera, using feathers. Knudson, a Pulitzer Prize–winning reporter, first wrote about Operation Green in 1982. He's a man who, I gather, hates pointless animal experiments, and hates animal traps. When he was a young reporter at the *Des Moines Tribune*, he got wind of some testing at Eglin Air Force Base in Florida and some field trials carried out at Iowa State "of a highly confidential nature."

He sent out several FOIA requests for records relating to Operation Green and hog cholera and got back an unhelpful response from Norman Covert, Fort Detrick's freedom of information officer. "No such records have been located at Fort Detrick," Covert said. "Most of the files on biological warfare were either destroyed or transferred to other records holding areas when the program was disestablished in 1971." The Air Force had no records, either; an information staffer said that they'd had nothing to do with the tests. But the library at Dugway Proving Ground had a copy of the actual report, entitled "Field Evaluation Study of Desiccated Agent on Carrier for an Antianimal Biological Warfare Munition (Operation Green)," published on March 12, 1952, by Camp Detrick, approved and signed by Leroy D. Fothergill, M.D., acting director of the Biological Laboratories—and Rotarian, Episcopalian, immunologist, discoverer of equine encephalitis in the brains of children, graduate of the University of Nevada and Harvard Medical School.

When Knudson moved on from Des Moines, he left his research files at the Iowa State University Library for future inquirers, and a kind librarian there sent me scans of the material on hog cholera, which included Knudson's notes and transcriptions. I loved seeing how hard Knudson had worked—how quickly he had worked—to master a complicated story. In the final report for Operation Green, submitted on November 1, 1953, Knudson noticed something about "unusual" viruses, and the mention of an attempt to "alter the nature of the virus so as to develop a highly pathogenic type of virus having a specific affinity for the central nervous system." MKULTRA for pigs, more or less.

THERE WERE NO REDACTIONS or sanitizations in the Operation Green report—what a privilege to be able to read what's actually there. It had originally been classified top secret, and then it was reclassified as confidential in 1963, and then it was fully declassified in 1970. Evidently nobody had asked to see it until Knudson did in 1982.

The experiments had several phases. First, Louis Schwarte, professor of veterinary science at Iowa State, freeze-dried (or "lyophilized") pig blood containing hog cholera germs and instilled the powdered disease into the nostrils of healthy pigs, who got very sick several days later. Schwarte also exploded balloons filled with cholera powder in a small pig-populated enclosure. These pigs, too, got very sick. That was step one.

Step two was to harvest blood from fifty-six infected pigs, freeze-dry it, grind it up in a ball mill, and send eleven pounds of it in small steel vessels to Camp Detrick. Step three was to mix the dried blood with feathers, pack it into paper containers, and ship the containers under refrigeration to Eglin in Florida. Each container was made of kraft paper and was about thirteen inches in diameter and seven inches high, with a rip cord—roughly the size of a birthday cake.

Step four was to load the disease into the bomb—which was an E-73 modified leaflet cluster bomb, just like the bomb that was used in the crop-killing experiments in Upstate New York. Four paper cakes went into each bomb, and just before the plane took off, someone pulled the four rip cords, tearing the paper in order to release the disease-powdered feathers inside.

Step five, which happened on July 14, 1951, was to fly a B-26 airplane over thirty-one hog pens and drop the experimental bombs, which opened fifteen hundred feet above the ground, releasing a cloud of turkey feathers and blood dust—the release looked like white smoke. Each pen held five pigs and had a single human observer standing by to record the behavior of the animals when they encountered the feathers. The smell of dried blood in the air interested the pigs. "A short time after the burst and before the feathers actually began to land, or in several cases in pens where no feathers had landed, the pigs suddenly rose in a group and trotted energetically about the pen apparently searching for something," the report said. After some days the animals got very sick and lay prostrate around their water tanks—there are several pictures of dying pigs included in the report—whereupon they were taken to be electrocuted and autopsied. Dr. Schwarte and two other veterinarians autopsied all the pigs, "with the exception of two which died in the pen and had been cannibalized." All told, Schwarte killed more than 1,200 pigs in his search for a better way to kill pigs, according to Tom Knudson's notes (along with 750 guinea pigs, 2,000 mice, and 700 rabbits). Congressman Robert Sykes of Florida, a germ-war enthusiast, visited Operation Green and watched one of the practice bomb drops. Strange to think that E. B. White was writing *Charlotte's Web*, about Wilbur the pig, around the time that these pig-bomb trials were going on.

In October 2016, I wrote Knudson to ask him if he had any thoughts on the utility of the Freedom of Information Act in journalism. "FOIA successes have become harder to come by over the years," Knudson answered. "Agencies seem to be craftier at coming up with ways not to release things. But I still use it."

DID THE CIA USE HOG CHOLERA in its shadow war against Communism? Yes, I think so. Not in China in 1952 but in East Germany in 1953 and 1954. A campaign of sabotage spread through East Germany at that time, according to the United States Information Agency. There were incidents of damaged railroad signals and tracks, which led to train accidents— hundreds of passengers were killed or injured, and 198 rail workers were arrested. Other targets of sabotage were dockyards, coal mines, factories, and farm animals—cattle and pigs. The sabotage evidently flowed from a plan by the Psychological Strategy Board to "covertly stimulate strikes, demonstrations, economic and industrial sabotage, and other revolutionary acts short of mass rebellion, aimed at putting pressure on the Communist authority for specific reforms, discrediting such authority, and provoking open Soviet intervention."

Thousands of East German pigs began dying in a hog-cholera epidemic that began after the CIA-abetted, "largely spontaneous" Berlin riots of 1953. (Soviet foreign minister Molotov charged that on June 17, 1953, "mercenaries and criminal elements from the American sector of Berlin" had set fire to food stores and other shops, triggering the East Berlin riots, and he angrily rejected an offer from President Eisenhower of $15 million worth of food.) The number of sick pigs went from 119 in 1951 to more than 70,000 in the first three months of 1954, according to the Associated Press, citing an East German news agency report. "Nine persons had been tried and imprisoned on charges of spreading animal epidemics," the Communist news agency reported, and an East German supply minister, Karl Hamann, was sentenced to ten years on charges of "sabotaging food deliveries."

The CIA's intelligence arm followed the hog-cholera epidemic closely. It was a "not inconsiderable problem in East Germany," said an information report cabled to Washington in May 1954. "During the third quarter of 1953, 40,337 hogs had to be slaughtered prematurely as an emergency measure." Another CIA intelligence report, from December 1954, said, "During the last six months, hog cholera has continued to spread throughout the DDR with the result that over 200 East German veterinarians have been arrested and accused of sabotage."

James Conant, who left the presidency of Harvard in order to become high commissioner of West Germany in 1953, wrote to Secretary of State John Foster Dulles that offering food to the East Germans was "smart propaganda." He added, in a handwritten note, "I assume that our objective in the East Zone is to keep the pot simmering but not to bring it to a boil!"

I SAT BY THE PENOBSCOT RIVER, remembering reading the scene in *The Lord of the Rings* when Gandalf uses magic to turn the river waves into white horses and drown the Black Riders. The river is really churning now.

Vannevar Bush believed in unconventional weapons. Hog cholera weapons. Fowl plague weapons. Invisible weapons. Magic weapons.

Dr. Bush, whose father was a Universalist minister, looked a bit like Ichabod Crane, said a *New York Times* profile in 1944. "His face is gaunt, his blue eyes are keen, and an obstinate lock of coarse straight hair shoots forward over a comparatively low forehead." He was at that time spending $3 million a week developing new ways to die.

"This is a war of science," Bush said. "Our weapons must be the last word."

Bush took the first step toward the creation of a germ-war program in September 1940, more than a year before Pearl Harbor. "The subject of so-called bacteriological warfare has been brought to my attention," he wrote to a colleague. "I would assume that there would be included a consideration of offensive and defensive measures in the field of human, animal and plant diseases."

Bush's friend Frank Jewett, president of the National Academy of Sciences, embraced the idea and formed a committee, the WBC—a scrambled abbreviation of Biological Warfare Committee. Edwin Fred, a bacteriologist and dean of the Graduate School of the University of Wisconsin, became chairman in 1942, and his friend Ira Baldwin, a baldish, soft-faced, ministerial-looking plant pathologist, took over as Detrick's first scientific director. Fred and Baldwin had written a book together about the bacteria that grow in leguminous root nodules. Now they were refining illnesses with an enemy in mind. And from there, in the space of three years, we ended up with four thousand people brewing anthrax, crystallized botulism, and other potions at Camp Detrick.

After the war, Dr. Bush kept going—kept pushing for germ weapons— as head of the Joint Research and Development Board of the Defense Department, a group devoted to the "development or improvement of weapons, methods of warfare or counter-measures." Bush's board was an umbrella organization that watched over a number of committees— including one for chemical warfare and one for biological warfare. The BW committee was chaired by Ira Baldwin, who was by then president of the American Society for Microbiology and dean of the University of

Wisconsin's Department of Bacteriology. In August 1947, Baldwin submitted a report to Vannevar Bush on "The Technical Aspects of Biological Warfare." It began with a conclusion: "Biological warfare has potentialities sufficiently great to demand a strengthened program of research and development." Now was the time to start hiring and reopening closed pilot plants, Baldwin thought. To revive the program, "between five hundred and six hundred technically trained people would be required," the report said. With that level of staffing, botulinum toxin, brucella bacteria, and anthrax spores would be ready for production or large-scale testing within two years; the agents for tularemia, melioidosis, and plague would take perhaps five years. But more field-testing would be needed under wartime conditions.

An ideal disease weapon, the report said, would be easily produced and would have "moderate persistence": it would last long enough to dependably sicken its victims, but not so long that it would "incapacitate the attacked nation for years after the conflict ends." And it would have a low risk of "retroactivity"—it wouldn't lay low the people who had chosen to employ it.

Baldwin's committee put human diseases at the top of their list, and called for research into the "improvement of virulence and infectivity of agents." Next came crop diseases, including potato blight and the stem rust of wheat. Rice blast, *Piricularia oryzae*, was singled out by the committee for its crop-destroying potency: "The quantity of Piricularia spores necessary for a destructive infection is measured in terms of ounces of spores per acre of crop." Animal diseases came third in order of priority; these included rinderpest, foot-and-mouth disease, hog cholera, warthog disease, and fowl plague.

Baldwin's report went to Vannevar Bush and Defense Secretary Forrestal. But progress was slow. "I suggest that the subject of biological warfare appropriately might be introduced at the National Security Council," Forrestal wrote President Truman in March 1948, "as soon as Dr. Bush advises me that sufficient progress has been made on an objective estimation of the military value of biological warfare."

IN MAY 1948, President Truman awarded Vannevar Bush and Harvard's James Conant Medals of Merit and Bronze Oak Leaf Clusters. But somewhere along the way Bush mysteriously fell out of favor with the president. "For quite a while I was close to him and helped him all I could," Bush wrote later. "But then it all stopped. I always thought, perhaps without reason, that I became inconvenient to Truman's palace guard and got poisoned." One of Bush's last acts as part of the Truman administration, before he resigned from the Research and Development Board in October 1948, was to forward another report from Ira Baldwin to the secretary of defense. This one, entitled "Special BW Operations," was about "subversive or covert actions involving the use of biological agents." These had certain advantages, according to Baldwin's committee. They were difficult to detect and "versatile." Germs could kill, starve, or create "profound psychological disturbances," they said.

On a full-page, sideways chart, many potential covert methods and weapons were listed, including the infecting of water supplies, darts, and small arms ammunition; the contaminating of stamps and chewing gum and tobacco; and "crop destruction by weed seeds." A number of diseases—including stem rust, fowl plague, and hog cholera—were carried over from previous reports, but some were new: glanders, vesicular exanthema of swine (which resembled hog cholera and therefore would delay a diagnosis, according to a Detrick antianimal scientist), and, down at the bottom of the page, "parasitism by insect pests, as potato beetles." All these options would, of course, have "adverse psychological effects." The committee recommended the development of new offensive biological agents, ones that would be "suitable for special operations but not necessarily suitable for large-scale military operations." They weren't sure, though, about the feasibility of using "air masses for the dissemination of BW agents into foreign countries"; more study was needed there.

Wait—potato beetles? Colorado beetles? In 1950, the East Germans and the Czechs charged that American planes were dropping large numbers of potato beetles on their potato fields—and they were laughed at when they protested. Yet here the beetles were, listed on a late 1948 chart of potential covert weapons. There was an asterisked note: "Would probably not show considerable effect until after several seasons."

Having quietly made the best case he could for germ warfare, overt and covert, Vannevar Bush resigned. He wrote a book, *Modern Arms and Free Men*, which is sprinkled with hints about biological weapons, and he took an unpaid position on the board of directors of Merck, the pharmaceutical company.

I SHOWED MY MOTHER-IN-LAW, Carroll, a picture I'd taken of a sculpture at the front entrance of the National Archives Building. On the base of the sculpture it said "Eternal Vigilance Is the Price of Liberty." Carroll asked what that meant, and I realized I wasn't quite sure. I said that I guessed it meant that to keep a nation free you need to be able to observe what its government actually does. The National Archives made that possible by saving governmental records. "If you were able to see everything that a government does . . ." I trailed off.

"You would turn and run," said my mother-in-law.

April 3, 2019, Wednesday

B ig slow aggregated flakes of snow coming down in the morning—like Queen Anne's lace, M. said.

WHEN THE DOCUMENTARY record is suppressed, full of holes, punctured by secrets kept, all historians have to work with is discrete moments or data points. One moment is the story told by the platoon officer in the Middlesex Regiment about feather-flinging masked American military policemen in an abandoned North Korean town. The story is found in an extraordinary book with an interesting history of its own: *Unit 731*, by Peter Williams and David Wallace, both BBC newsmen and documentarians. In *Unit 731*, published in 1989, in a section called "Korean War," the story of the British soldier's inexplicable experience is linked to Ishii's use of infected feathers and his notion of "tactical BW retreats." A tactical BW retreat is when you withdraw your forces from an area and leave diseases behind for the enemy to encounter. The disease that Williams and Wallace mention is Songo fever, now known as Korean hemorrhagic fever.

Note that in the American edition of Williams and Wallace's book, published by the Free Press, the part about the Korean War is cut out. You can only read it in the British edition, published by Hodder & Stoughton.

Songo fever first came to the attention of Japanese germ warriors in 1939, when occupation soldiers in China got sick with a new and terrible illness in a Manchurian town that the Chinese called Sunwa and the Japanese called Songo. A second epidemic broke out in 1942, and Kitano Masaji, one of Ishii Shiro's colleagues, began a search for what caused it. Songo fever began with a high fever and a violent headache, and then you began to bleed. You bled from the nose and from the eyes, and your internal organs bled. Everything that could bleed, bled. Sometimes your kidneys failed. The death rate from Songo fever, initially, was about 30 percent.

Kitano's hypothesis was that the disease was spread via a tiny ticklike mite, a "laelaps mite," that lived on a kind of field mouse, or vole. "We made an emulsion with 203 ground-up North Manchuria mites and salt water, and injected it into the thigh of an ape hypodermically," Kitano wrote in a scientific paper published in 1944. "This first ape became feverish with a temperature of 39.4 degrees Celsius on the 19th day after injection and moderately infected. Then we took blood of this feverish ape and injected it into the second ape, which became feverish and produced protein in its urine." Kitano's discovery of this "strange and unusual disease" spread by ticks made headlines in *Asahi*, the Japanese newspaper: "ANOTHER VICTORY SHOUT FOR MILITARY MEDICINE."

Kitano's "apes" were, in fact, great apes—human beings. One of Kitano's colleagues said later, "I had to participate in the experiments of Kitano and the military doctors that were already in progress, namely, injecting people, spies; this was the result of orders and simply had to be obeyed."

IMMEDIATELY AFTER THE WAR, members of Unit 731 were interviewed by Karl Compton, president of MIT, who felt they were "holding back," and then by epidemiologist Murray Sanders, who was told that the Japanese army had only engaged in defensive research. Arvo Thompson, a Camp Detrick veterinarian, located Ishii and got from him blueprints of biological bombs. In May 1947, Charles Willoughby, General Douglas MacArthur's head of intelligence in Tokyo, who was in charge of the interrogation program and its records, said that Ishii and his colleagues might be induced to reveal what had really gone on in the germ laboratories by a promise of immunity from war crimes prosecution. Alden Waitt, head of the Chemical Corps, got a cable from MacArthur's office in Tokyo sent May 6, 1947: "Ishii states that if guaranteed immunity from 'war crimes' in documentary form for himself, superiors and subordinates, he can describe program in detail." Much fresh knowledge of Baker William, that is, biological warfare, would accrue:

> Ishii claims to have extensive theoretical high-level knowledge including strategic and tactical use of Baker William on defense and offense, backed by some research on best Baker William agents to employ by geographical areas of Far East, and the use of Baker William in cold climates.

When someone at the State Department introduced a doubt about the wisdom of promising immunity to Ishii's team—since they had, in fact, violated the rules of land warfare in their experiments on prisoners—General Waitt called Willoughby in Tokyo to say that the inquiry into Japanese biological research was already yielding important data. "I consider it vital that we get the information and that secrecy (which would be impossible if war crimes trials were held) be maintained," he said. In the end, the United States made a deal with Ishii and his men and kept quiet about it. The Joint Chiefs of Staff's view prevailed: "The utmost secrecy is essential in order to protect the interests of the United States and to guard against embarrassment."

Norbert Fell, MIT class of 1923, who'd worked at a mine in the Mojave Desert and at Buick Motor Company as an executive, and had patented a hay-fever drug for Parke, Davis, was the first emissary from Camp Detrick to offer the Japanese scientists immunity from prosecution. In exchange, he got a load of information, including "approximately 8,000 slides representing pathological sections derived from more than 200 human cases of disease caused by various B.W. agents"—slides that had

been hidden in temples and buried in the mountains of southern Japan—
as well as a report on crop-disease research, a lecture given to spies and
saboteurs (translated into English for use at Camp Detrick), and more
specifics about the experiments on "Manchurian coolies," who were "used
as subjects during field trials of bacteria disseminated by bombs and
sprays." The human subjects, wrote Fell, "were used in exactly the same
manner as other experimental animals."

What Fell sent back was exceedingly interesting, but it seemed there
might still be more. Charles Willoughby (a German-born, monocle-
wearing white supremacist, referred to by his colleagues as "Baron von
Willoughby") offered the scientists a range of modest financial inducements:
"direct payments, payments in kind (food, miscellaneous gift items,
entertainment), hotel bills, board (in areas of search for buried evidence,
etc)." The money seemed to cement their trust.

In November 1947, two Detrick scientists, Edwin Hill and Joseph
Victor, made the long trip to Tokyo to probe the memories of as many of
the germ men as possible. They had several talks with Kitano and his
coworker Kasahara Shiro about Songo fever. "Both men were extremely
cooperative and gave information freely," wrote Hill and Victor in their
detailed Songo fever summary. "Slight hesitancy appeared before admitting
details of human experiments. However, assurance that we knew the
results and the number of such experiments overcame reluctance to talk
about it." Kitano and Kasahara told the Detrick emissaries that when they
first encountered the disease in Songo, they injected a sick soldier's blood
into two monkeys. "One monkey had fever on the 5th day. The second had
no response. During the period of fever, 5 cc of blood from the first monkey
was injected into a 3rd monkey with negative results." Then two rabbits
were injected with the patient's blood. "One developed inflammation with
edema and redness of the scrotum as well as orchitis showing interstitial
edema and slight histiocytic infiltration. This animal was sacrificed on the
7th day—the other two had no reaction."

The human Songo experiments began after the war intensified, in
November 1942. The men reported that "203 mites picked from field
mice in that area were emulsified in 2 cc saline and injected s.c."—i.e.,

subcutaneously—"in one man with positive results." Then the blood from fevered men was injected into horses, and the horse blood was injected into other horses, "with positive results in one of two cases."

Kitano and Kasahara also described their investigation into tick-borne encephalitis, which they'd discovered in a group of Manchurian lumberjacks, half of whom had died. They injected a suspension of one dead man's brain into two monkeys, who both got sick. One monkey recovered, and one developed paralysis and was "sacrificed" and dissected. Kitano revealed to Hill and Victor one of his methods of mass-producing typhus vaccine using the brains of Manchurian ground squirrels. "A 10% emulsion of infected squirrel brain" was injected into the body cavity of an uninfected squirrel, which was then kept alive in a state of semihibernation at low temperature and fed very little. "At its height of infection, peritoneal cavity is opened under anesthetics of chloroform or ether. The peritoneum is carefully scratched and washed with 0.2% formalised physiological saline."

Hill and Victor were busy for weeks, interviewing and writing up interviews with brainsick germ warriors. Genji Sakuyama said he infected guinea pigs with typhus and then injected their emulsified brains into people, who sickened and died. He also worked on tick-borne encephalitis and Songo fever. Dr. Takahashi told them about an octagonal chamber where human subjects inhaled aerosolized diseases sprayed from flit-guns. Dr. Hukimasa Yagasawa told them about his research with stinking smut of wheat, chosen because it caused damage to wheat crops in Manchuria and Siberia. "It was believed that western Oregon and Nebraska because of their climate would be suitable targets for this disease," Hill and Victor wrote. "For test purposes, a large number of varieties of American wheat were planted and experimentally infected with the agent." Yagasawa also mentioned rice blast as an effective plant pathogen: "As a matter of fact," Yagasawa said to his interrogators, "the Japanese were very much afraid that this particular disease might have been used against them."

Dr. Tabei Kanau said he injected a man with shigella dysentery. Three days later the man got diarrhea, and on the fourth day he hanged himself. Tabei also fed prisoners a solution of sugar water and paratyphoid. The disease was very contagious, he discovered when he placed one sick patient in a room with three uninfected ones. In an effort to find the most virulent strain of typhoid fever—V, VW, or W—Tabei fed thirty-six Manchurians tainted milk and sugar water. Tabei then heightened the virulence of the most lethal strain, VW, by passing it through three men in succession. In a vaccine experiment, Tabei found that none of the three vaccines available was able to immunize against VW. "Deaths occurred in 2 cases and 3 committed suicide."

On December 12, 1947, Edwin Hill and Joseph Victor completed their accumulation. "No question of immunity from war crimes prosecution was ever raised during these interviews," Dr. Hill wrote. (It wasn't necessary; that had been settled already.) Charles Willoughby had offered his "wholehearted cooperation." In addition to informational interviews, the Detrick scientists had gathered a substantial collection of pathological specimens, including slides and bits and pieces of material from 246 plague victims, 135 cholera victims, 101 Songo fever victims, 36 anthrax victims, 16 mustard gas victims, and 30 suicides. "Such information could not be obtained in our own laboratories because of scruples attached to human experimentation." The collection of pathological specimens, they added, was the only material evidence that these experiments on humans had taken place. "It is hoped that individuals who voluntarily contributed this information will be spared embarrassment because of it and that every effort will be taken to prevent this information from falling into other hands."

Hill and Victor sent their report on to Alden Waitt, head of the Chemical Corps, and Detrick scientists began digesting its forbidden riches. At the same time, the Soviet government announced that Kitano, Ishii, and others were wanted men—war criminals.

General Willoughby claimed he didn't know where they were.

April 4, 2019, Thursday

I went out before six with Cedric and was shocked by the blue glow in the air. It had snowed a thin layer over everything in the night. At the end of the street, the sky was orange over the gray of the river. I looked back at the house and saw a street light, orange, reflected in one of our upstairs windows. I took a picture of it and went inside.

ON OCTOBER 9, 1951, Major Glenn E. Davis, one of the officers who'd won an award for meritorious service for his work on the feather bomb, gave a lecture to officers at the Air War College at Maxwell Air Force Base in Alabama. The lecture has been declassified. I saw it mentioned in a footnote and asked for a copy from the Air Force Historical Research Agency, also at Maxwell Air Force Base. They sent it right away. Thank you, Historical Research Agency!

Project Baseless was at its peak in the fall of 1951, and the Air Force needed more officers who understood unconventional weapons. A cable went out from the Air Force's Biological and Chemical Warfare Division to seven major Air Force commands, including Curtis LeMay's Strategic

Air Command in Offutt, Nebraska. "In keeping with BASELESS, an expedited training program is being proposed to provide a nucleus of trained personnel for major air commands and for a field agency which will be responsible for operational suitability testing of biological and chemical warfare munitions and disseminating devices," said the cable. "Anticipate course will provide basic indoctrinational training of officers, otherwise qualified, to serve as staff planners in pursuing BASELESS."

In keeping with Baseless, Major Davis talked to Air Force officers about "protoplasm and poison." "If protoplasm and poison can assist in winning wars they then become profoundly interesting to the militarists," Davis said. "Admittedly we are face to face with a numerically superior power. This undoubtedly has engendered keen interest in so called mass anti-personnel weapons."

Davis goes on to do something I'd not seen before in all the Air Force documents I'd paged through at the National Archives. He lists the biological agents the Air Force is interested in, and then he calculates their approximate cost per pound.

Plague was top priority, Davis said. It was "acute, severe, prostrating, high fever, chills." And its cost: twenty-five cents per pound.

Brucella melitensis, or undulant fever, also cost a quarter a pound. So did glanders. Davis said that work on glanders had been suspended for a while, "but has now been revived under contract with Naval Biological Laboratory." (Glanders, normally a disease of horses, causes swollen lymph nodes and, in males, a swollen scrotum; it was studied on and off at Detrick as a possible human agent, where half a dozen people were infected, including a male typist in 1953.) Parrot fever (an exotic disease, sometimes fatal, first spread in the twenties by imported tropical birds) and Q fever were more expensive—they cost three dollars per pound. And anthrax cost twenty dollars a pound to produce. Botulinum toxin, being highly concentrated, was the most expensive weapon: it cost four hundred and twenty dollars per pound to make.

Davis also talked about crop disease. Wheat and oat stem rust was "highly epidemic," and there was "no practical treatment." But it was tricky to produce: "Must be grown on fields of grain under conditions that do not allow for infection of local crops." That made it expensive: ten dollars per pound. Rice blast disease was also epidemic, and it cost forty dollars per pound. Hog cholera cost four dollars per pound. Davis listed promising targets for biological attacks: troops, tanks, island strongholds, airfields, industrial areas, urban areas, animal populations, and food crops.

"Another intriguing thought about BW," said Davis, "is its use in conjunction with other weapons, particularly atomic or radiological weapons. The confusion and disruption following an incendiary, HE, or atomic attack would be an incubator for disease agents. The burden placed on medical and sanitary facilities would probably be intolerable." (HE stands for "high explosive.") He described Krueger's research at Berkeley and at the Naval Biological Laboratory, which, he said, "demonstrated that a sub-lethal dose of radiation causes a test animal to be abnormally susceptible to disease, in fact, may even succumb to ordinary vaccinations."

Three years after Davis gave his lecture at the Air War College, he died in an accident at Andrews Air Force Base. He was on the runway, waiting to take off, when his ejection seat hurled him through the canopy of his airplane. He had a wife and a month-old daughter. His friends from Camp Detrick sent condolence cards. Davis is buried in Arlington Cemetery.

April 8, 2019, Monday

Yesterday we got back from several days in Rochester, where we celebrated my dear dad's birthday—he is eighty-five and looks about sixty-five.

IN BED, I THUMBED THROUGH lots of old photographs on my phone. Daughter, son, wife, father, mother, stepmother, mother-in-law, brother-in-law, sister-in-law, sister, sister's partner, daughter, son, wife, wife, wife, son, daughter. Wife. I was smiling in the dark.

Then every so often I'd come across a screen capture I'd made of a document or an old newspaper article. A mysterious Q fever epidemic hits eighty men in Italy in 1950. A tainted hog-cholera vaccine kills thousands of midwestern pigs in 1949. ("HEAVY HOG LOSS PROBED" was the headline in *The New York Times*.) The biowar blowback epoch of American history has injected itself into my life, the photo-stream record of my life. Meals eaten, bowls of bean soup sipped, group selfies, airports where we've picked up loved ones—and then suddenly a clump of a thousand snapshotted Air

Force documents from the National Archives in which men talk about how much progress is being made titrating diseased bits of glop, injecting them into animals, freeze-drying the purulent exudate, and dropping it from airplanes.

THE AIR FORCE'S three most influential proponents of infectious warfare were Nathan Twining, William Burden, and Jimmy Doolittle. Very different men, physically different, different in background and in interests—but all three of them united in a belief that weaponized disease was the way to win the war with the Communists.

General Nathan Twining was a solemn, sad-eyed mass murderer who liked to fish. He's now remembered as the Air Force officer who, in September 1947, wrote a memo saying that UFOs—or "flying disks," as they were called back then—were real objects. "The phenomenon reported is something real and not visionary or fictitious," Twining wrote. Exactly: the "disks" were real and identifiable. They were large, shiny polyethylene balloons made by General Mills. The company had several ingenious balloon engineers on staff, and it had classified contracts with the Air Force, the Navy, and the CIA. The balloons bobbed and glowed at sunset on the horizon, carrying secret payloads of scientific equipment. Some balloons held propaganda leaflets, some tested the upper limits of the atmosphere, some carried microphones and listened for nuclear detonations, some held surveillance cameras, and some dispensed crop diseases. All the balloons came from an American cereal company in Minnesota; none came from a faraway planet.

During the war, in 1943, after an emergency landing in the Pacific Ocean, General Twining and his crew floated for six days on lashed-together life rafts; Twining shot an albatross and ate the fish out of its stomach. In 1944, in Italy, he ordered the Fifteenth Air Force to drop a thousand tons of bombs on the Benedictine abbey of Monte Cassino. In August 1945, he signed the order for the atomic mission against Hiroshima.

When the North Korean army attacked the South Korean army in

June 1950, and the United States intervened in the Korean civil war, Twining turned his attention to Soviet Russia. Late in August 1950, he gave a speech at the annual convention of the Air Force Association. "Russia's fingers are in the fire in Korea," he said. "They will lose. We must meet and defeat them in the main event."

Two months later, on October 10, 1950, as Chinese troops gathered at the Yalu River, readying themselves for a counterattack, President Harry Truman promoted Twining to deputy chief of staff of the United States Air Force under Hoyt Vandenberg. A war was coming, Twining believed, a big war, against limitless armies. The only way to win against the hordes was with a new class of weapons.

On October 20, 1950, Twining issued a top-secret order to all of his deputies in the Air Force. "The Joint Chiefs of Staff have agreed," he wrote, "that action should be initiated at once to make the United States capable of employing toxic chemical and biological agents and of defending against enemy use of these agents." Twining ordered his deputy chief of staff for operations, Thomas D. "Tommy" White, to "Integrate the Air Force capabilities and requirements for Biological and Chemical Warfare into existing and future War Plans." And also to "Develop appropriate tactics and techniques for aerial delivery."

This general order, and refinements thereto, came to be known as the Twining Directive—code name Baseless. In December 1951, the name was thought to have been compromised: Project Baseless was officially changed to Project Respondent, a word with a more retaliatory connotation. In October 1953, shortly after the end of the Korean War, the Twining Directive was rescinded. "Eventually," Dorothy Miller wrote in part 2 of her history (it, too, has blanked-out places), "there was to be general agreement that the Twining directive was ill timed. It had been conceived in an emotional atmosphere that did not engender a calm appraisal of the potential of biological warfare." Twining went on to be chief of staff of the Air Force under President Eisenhower, and then chairman of the Joint Chiefs of Staff. He was a great believer in fallout shelters.

General Jimmy Doolittle, the number two germ-war booster, is famous for leading a mad firebombing raid on Japan in 1942. Doolittle's

Raiders were the first American heroes of World War II—they were all over the papers because they'd taken off from an aircraft carrier and tried to set fire to Tokyo. Their raid was unsuccessful—several of Doolittle's planes were shot down, and the fires they set were quickly put out—and the act was a gift to the hard-line Japanese militarists, who could now say truthfully that Tokyo was fighting for its existence: that the Americans wanted to do everything they could to destroy civilian life in Japan's capital city, out of revenge for Pearl Harbor, an attack on a military base.

"General Doolittle, without doubt, will go down in history as the most revered air hero of the 20th Century," according to the University of Texas Library's page on Jimmy Doolittle in a now removed introduction to its James Doolittle collection of papers. "His high standards of truth at any price and strict code of ethics inspired thousands of people in every walk of life."

What is not so well known about Doolittle is that he was a big fan of germ weapons. On August 10, 1951, an Air Force memo says, "General Doolittle has expressed his desire to have a briefing on recent developments in the Biological Warfare field. In compliance with General Doolittle's desires, two briefings for General Officers, will be held on 16 August 1951." A week later, Doolittle and various top officers received a full presentation on the Air Force's germ-readiness program—anticrop, antianimal, and antihuman. The top people were there—including Air Force chief Hoyt Vandenberg, Vice Chief Nathan Twining, the budget director, the surgeon general of the Air Force, and knowledgeable scientists from Camp Detrick. They heard about the "Air Base Contamination Study at Carswell AFB" (known as Project Silver) and anticrop tests at Eglin Air Force Base in Florida. Detrick's Dr. Geoffrey Norman showed a film about the feather bomb trials at Pine Camp in Upstate New York.

Doolittle, a graduate of MIT, an amateur boxer, and a friend of Frank Wisner's, became the Air Force's consultant in biological warfare in 1952, and he helped to reorganize the Air Force's research and development staff into something called the Air Research and Development Command, located in Baltimore, Maryland, close to Johns Hopkins, Edgewood Arsenal, and Camp Detrick. In charge of the research and development group, Doolittle put his protégé and former chief of staff, Earle "Pat" Partridge, another proponent of biological warfare, who'd just finished a tour commanding the Fifth Air Force in its firebombing of North Korea.

On April 17, 1952—after the North Koreans and Chinese had made their second set of formal germ-warfare accusations against the United States—Doolittle spoke at a symposium on biological and chemical weapons in the Pentagon. "From everything I've heard today," Doolittle said,

> despite the sometimes note of pessimism, it appears to me that the considerable problems inherent in the selection, development, production, and use, of a suitable BW agent, are in no way insuperable. On the contrary, I'm satisfied that this competent group of people here, together with other interested agencies—working together—all-out—with adequate support, can and will promptly solve the problems necessary to give us an operational BW agent, with it the substantial increase in our offensive capacity, and hence, substantially increase national security.

Then Doolittle did something interesting—he talked about the Communists' germ-war charges. "The recent accusations in Korea, I'm satisfied," he said, "are an effort to find out what our position is, what our plans are, and just what we intend to do. I'm satisfied that it's an attempt to get us to commit ourselves to talk. We could have said such things as 'We couldn't possibly have done it, because we don't have a BW capacity,' which would have been a very valuable piece of information for the Russians to get. We could also have said, stupidly, that we will never use BW first. It would be an important piece of information for them to get." Next Doolittle quickly dealt with the "moral aspects" of biological warfare. "In my estimation, we have just one moral obligation—and that moral obligation is for us to develop at the earliest possible moment that agent which will *kill* enemy personnel most quickly and most cheaply. And I speak of cheaply in connection with our national resources, and content that our most valuable national resource is our own young people. Thank you."

In 1954, in a report on how to reform the psychological-warfare and paramilitary side of the CIA, Jimmy Doolittle famously said that anything goes, any sort of underhandedness, when you are opposed by a police state as evil as Russia. "It is now clear that we are facing an implacable enemy whose avowed objective is world domination by whatever means and at whatever cost," Doolittle wrote. "There are no rules in such a game. Hitherto acceptable norms of human conduct do not apply. If the United States is to survive, long-standing American concepts of 'fair play' must be reconsidered." The U.S. government must develop new and ruthless ways to "subvert, sabotage, and destroy our enemies," he believed. There are two versions of this report in the CREST database, both redacted—one has blacked-out paragraphs and pages, and one has whited-out paragraphs and pages.

Doolittle became vice president of Standard Oil Company, served on the boards of various other corporations, celebrated reunions with his Doolittle's Raiders cronies, and was feted for his heroism year after year. He died in 1993 at the age of ninety-six.

It hurts to think that this man is held up as a hero. He's an awful man. Truly. An urban terrorist firebomber, an advocate of covert illegal subversion, and a would-be spreader of disease.

IT'S A REAL BLIZZARD NOW. Local schools are closed. I'm still at the kitchen table, still thinking about things that happened more than sixty years ago. Some sixty-year-old facts are considered not secret and some are considered supersecret, so secret that they affect the current security of the United States.

William Armistead Moale Burden was the third and least well known of the Air Force's in-house germ-war advocates. Burden, Harvard class of '27, heir to the Vanderbilt fortune, loved air power, the hydrogen bomb, and modern art. In the thirties he headed an aviation trust and served on the boards of directors of mining companies, and during the war he was assistant secretary of commerce for air. Then he went back to managing his investments as an aviation analyst and mining-company official in New York. When the Korean War began to go badly, Thomas Finletter, secretary of the Air Force, a corporate lawyer and friend, asked Burden to become his special assistant for research and development at the Pentagon. Burden, who was in photographs a pouchy, owlish man, and was by his own account a discriminating wine connoisseur as well as a collector of great paintings, had an office next to Finletter and several capable assistants, and he began doing what he could to accelerate production of the hydrogen bomb. "This was an immensely interesting period," Burden said in his oral history, "because the development of the hydrogen bomb, in which I played an important part, took place during this period." Burden takes credit for convincing President Truman to go ahead with the H-bomb, over Robert Oppenheimer's objections: "I was able to enlist the backing of Secretary Finletter, and through him, the President, and won out on this issue," he said.

The Greenhouse series of bomb tests happened in 1951 and 1952, under Elwood "Pete" Quesada, who set up a doomed test village on a fragile Pacific atoll and exposed a large population of dogs, pigs, and mice to thermonuclear burns and detonations. In Burden's autobiography, *Peggy and I: A Life Too Busy for a Dull Moment*, he reproduces a color photograph of the first hydrogen fusion explosion at Eniwetok on November 1, 1952— an orange glow on the horizon. Then Burden moves on to a new chapter describing his work as head fund-raiser for the Eisenhower campaign and his leadership of the Museum of Modern Art, where he and MOMA warmly embraced the anti-Soviet-realist abstractions of Pollock, Motherwell, Rothko, and others of the New York School.

Burden doesn't mention another weapons system that especially excited his interest in 1951. Although his Air Force office files are still mostly classified, beautifully typed little notes signed "W.A.M. Burden" keep popping up in the records of the Air Force's BW-CW Division. Burden asks for informational BW briefings. He takes tours of Camp Detrick and Edgewood Arsenal. He sets up a Detrick visit for his boss, Secretary Finletter, who, Burden says, is interested in agents and munitions, and who is planning to discuss biological and chemical warfare matters when he's in Europe, meeting with the British prime minister, Winston Churchill, and General Eisenhower, commander of NATO. Burden makes suggestions, politely but forcefully. He is opposed to any sort of "retaliation only" restriction on the use of biological weapons: "What is being done about the policy of using BW for other than retaliatory purposes?" he asks in November 1951. "What action has to be taken by the Chief of Staff, the Secretary of the Air Force or the joint secretaries to achieve this?" Some of the Burden correspondence is still classified—for instance, a memo with enclosure "re Offense Defense Plans" from October 8, 1951. The next day a memo reports an "informal conversation between Mr. Burden and Captain Coggins of the Navy, in which Captain Coggins proposed, among other things, that a Joint Task Force of an ad hoc nature of the three services be established to assist in accelerating the BW-CW program."

In a memo from October 29, 1951, Burden set down his thoughts on how to speed up progress on biologicals. First off, the services needed a new test center for "hot tests," he said. "The present center at Dugway is unsatisfactory because of climatic limitations." It should be an offshore island, but not too remote, he thought. "Experience at Eniwetok proves that tests at far off locations are infinitely more expensive than in the continental U.S." Research and development funding should increase. "Every pressure should be exerted on Army Ordnance to speed up development." British biological munitions needed trials "as soon as possible." Plague was a top priority—the Navy's plague pilot plant in San Francisco must be restarted. "Everyone agrees that human tests are necessary and that they can be carried out without risk through using such an agent as tularemia for which a completely successful vaccine is available. Volunteers will not be difficult to recruit." And, Burden advises, General Doolittle should lend his prestige to the ongoing effort. "Might it be helpful to have General Doolittle, as an enthusiastic believer in BW, to participate?"

After the hydrogen bomb and MOMA, Burden, in the late 1950s, drew close to the CIA, run by another "lifelong friend," Allen Dulles. Burden served on the board of the Farfield Foundation, one of the CIA's covert conduits in its funding, and co-opting, of leftist writers, artists, and musicians—Mark Rothko owes much to the CIA and William Burden. And in the late 1950s, as an investor in (and onetime director of) American Metal Climax, a mining company with interests in the Congo—source of most of the world's available supply of uranium—Burden became fixated on the idea of getting rid of Patrice Lumumba, prime minister of the newly independent republic of the Congo, formerly the Belgian Congo. When Burden became ambassador to Belgium in 1959, he discussed assassination plans with Belgian government officials. "The Belgians were sort of toying with the idea of seeing to it that Lumumba was assassinated," Burden recalled in his oral history, held at Columbia University. "I went beyond my instructions and said, Well, I didn't think it would be a bad idea either, but I naturally never reported this to Washington—but Lumumba was assassinated. I think it was all to the good." Burden made several trips from Belgium to Washington to discuss Lumumba with Allen Dulles and President Eisenhower. "Lumumba was such a damn nuisance, it was perfectly obvious that the way to get rid of him was through political assassination," Burden said, "and this is something which the United States has not been willing to engage in, much to our damage, as we see in the present situation in Vietnam. The death of one or two people in North Vietnam might shorten the war by a year or more, and is certainly thoroughly justified, in my opinion, by history and everything else."

President Eisenhower came to agree with Burden about Lumumba, it seems. On August 18, 1960, in a National Security Council meeting, Robert H. Johnson, a note-taking NSC staff member, heard Eisenhower say "something—I can no longer recall the words—that came across to me as an order for the assassination of Lumumba." There followed, according to Johnson, an interval of stunned silence. Dulles cabled the Congo station to say that Lumumba's removal was "an urgent and prime objective." In September, the CIA's deputy director, Richard Bissell, told Sidney Gottlieb to pack a syringe, pick an infection from the agency's germ-war cupboard—which, he said, held brucellosis, tuberculosis, anthrax, smallpox, and Venezuelan equine encephalitis—and travel to the Congo. Lumumba managed to avoid being infected, however, and the Agency said it had nothing to do with CIA asset Joseph Mobutu's men who, in the end, committed the murder. The Belgians dismembered Lumumba's corpse and dissolved it in acid.

Robert Johnson's recollections, made in 1975 during the Church Committee's inquiry, were kept secret until 2000.

April 9, 2019, Tuesday

Last night M. made a dal of yellow lentils and ginger and our son sent us a song he'd recorded. M. and I listened to it several times and danced around the kitchen table.

Cedric, the smaller of our two rescue dogs, does not at all like the snow. He tries to limp on all four paws, which is impossible. I think the road salt makes the coldness penetrate his paw pads. I held him while Briney sniffed around the space where M.'s car had been. Back indoors.

TWO PEOPLE I didn't write about yesterday: General Earle E. "Pat" Partridge, Jimmy Doolittle's former chief of staff, and General Partridge's special agent, Donald Nichols. Partridge's bombers gradually destroyed all of North Korea and much of South Korea, while Partridge wrote sweet letters to his wife, Katy, in Tokyo and sent her presents from the South Korean government. (The Rhee government gave her, for instance, "four solid gold buttons about half an inch in diameter" with engraved designs.) "In spite of the fact that it is freezing weather here, the Koreans still manage to grow chrysanthemums, which are truly lovely," Partridge wrote her in November 1950.

Doolittle wrote General Partridge a letter in the frozen days of December 1950, when the war looked bleakest. "You, and your boys, have done magnificently," Doolittle wrote. "All America and the free world can well thank God that Pat Partridge has been filling Pat Partridge's shoes in Korea." The next day, General George Stratemeyer, Pat Partridge's superior officer, wrote a cable to Partridge: "Reference any covert activities on the part of personnel operating under you, it is desired that you clear same with Colonel Dickey, who in turn, it is desired, will keep me advised thru G-2, General Willoughby. It is my desire that we go all out in cooperation with G-2, USAK, G-2, FEC, and CIA." (Colonel Dickey may be C. A. Dickey, commander of the 442nd Counterintelligence Corps, which had a "positive clandestine intelligence mission" in Korea, according to the CIA's in-house historical journal, *Studies in Intelligence*—much of which is now searchable, though sometimes redacted, as part of the CREST database.)

The firebombing of Korea wasn't enough for Pat Partridge. He also wanted to destroy North Korea's rice supplies. In his microfilmed diary, which I got (unredacted) from the Air Force Historical Research Agency, Partridge observes, on March 3, 1951, that a certain Dr. Cohen, a bomb-damage statistician, is visiting. (I think Partridge is talking about A. Clifford Cohen, a mathematician from the University of Georgia, who spent some months with the Fifth Air Force in 1951.) "I took advantage of his presence to pitch him a problem regarding the destruction of rice supplies," Partridge writes. The North Korean rice supply was stacked in straw bags, visible from the air. "It seems to me that there should be some way of insuring that this can be made inedible:

> Presently, we are attacking it with Napalm in an effort to burn up the stacks themselves. We are not sure that this method is effective and I asked that Operational Analysts study the problem. In passing, I mentioned that there are now available in the States many chemicals which might be utilized for spraying rice crops to discourage the growth of the rice while still in the paddies. He mentioned the use of

2,4-D weed killer as an example of the type chemical now coming available. We have no idea how much would be required per square mile nor whether there is any chemical which would do the trick. His investigation would be strictly exploratory.

Early in March 1951, Partridge had a series of vaccinations: "Typhus and smallpox are endemic in this area, so this morning I took both typhus and smallpox inoculations," he wrote. "I also took a flu shot, just in case. That leaves me only typhoid and cholera yet to go." One wonders whether he'd heard something about a new disease that had just appeared among American troops—Songo fever.

Also in March 1951, General Stratemeyer was surprised to hear from Don Zimmerman, his former chief of plans and policy, who now worked for a scientific group at the Joint Chiefs of Staff called the Joint Advanced Study Committee. Zimmerman wrote him that Air Force headquarters at the Pentagon wanted a request to come from Stratemeyer's Far East Air Force "for the use of chemicals and biologicals in the Korean War." The Air Force was, in other words, hoping that Stratemeyer would ask for supplies of chemical and biological weapons and for permission to use them. Stratemeyer does not record in his diary what his reply was.

GENERAL PARTRIDGE WAS WORKING by this time very closely with an eccentric, mentally unstable spy and fixer, Donald Nichols, who had the ear of President Syngman Rhee and help from Rhee's brutish police force to get things done. Nichols claimed the Air Force gave him a license to murder, and he supervised, or at least observed, tortures and atrocities in South Korea in which hundreds of suspected Communist sympathizers were executed and buried in mass graves.

At Earle Partridge's request, Nichols, who had cabinets full of cash from the Rhee government, was put in charge of something called Special Activities Unit #1, which name was later changed to Detachment 2, 6004th Air Intelligence Service Squadron—Air Force people just called it "NICK." NICK became a special-ops team of fifty Air Force people and nine hundred Korean agents. What all they did is not fully known, but Nichols received many medals, including the Distinguished Service Cross for recovering parts of a Russian fighter plane from North Korea.

After the war, Nichols adopted three children, including one of his Seoul houseboys, and, sacked by the Air Force, received a diagnosis of schizophrenia and a series of shattering electroshock treatments at a hospital at Eglin Air Force Base. Partridge anxiously wrote Nichols's doctors that his former assassin and spymaster, traumatized by the war, deserved "maximum permanent medical retirement." In the 1960s, Nichols was tried and acquitted for indecent assault upon a boy, who said Nichols had shown him pictures of naked women. "He put his mouth to my personals," the boy said, "and I came to a climax and then he quit and gave me two dollars and I went home."

Nichols still had money—bricks of cash hidden in the freezer—and he moved to Mexico with cash and candy bars and wrote his memoirs, for which Pat Partridge wrote the foreword. Partridge said that Donald Nichols was "the most amazing and unusual man among all those with whom I was associated," who carried out a "long series of extraordinary exploits that called for imagination, for a high order of organizational capability, for maximum operational skill under the most difficult circumstances and for personal courage far beyond the normal call of duty." In an oral history, Partridge said Nichols "finally went crazy, really, literally."

All these details are taken from Blaine Harden's beautifully researched biography of Nichols, *King of Spies.* "The primary source of written material for this book was Nichols's military service record, which I requested from the air force under the Freedom of Information Act," Harden writes. He was less successful in getting a different set of Air Force records from the National Archives: hundreds of intelligence reports written by Nichols. "Archivists could give me only near-empty boxes of file folders, each of which contained a single sheet of blue paper labeled 'access restricted,'" Harden wrote. "So far, my efforts to obtain bulk or individual declassification of these historically important documents have failed." The records were removed from their folders in 2011.

Obviously somebody is hiding something. Perhaps some of the reports have to do with Syngman Rhee's prewar police-state atrocities, as described by Nichols. "I've witnessed many executions," he writes in his autobiography, "and to the last second they're fighting for their Communist way of life." Or, really, who knows what the documents are about? That a known piece of paper is actively being suppressed is a valuable piece of information—often the only thing it is able to tell the world while its suppression is in effect.

Toward the end of his autobiography, Nichols writes: "Many other concepts are floating around in the vacuum above my shoulders and aft my nose, but at this point in time, security will keep many of the known secrets of Korea. I would never be tempted to breach security." It's at least possible that Nichols and his crew had a hand in, or knew about, small-scale, covert uses of war gases and biological weapons in Korea—the ones that the Communists described in minute detail.

PARTRIDGE WAS AN AIR FORCE GENERAL; most of what he did was overt. Donald Nichols was also in the Air Force, but most of what he did was covert. Project Baseless, the overt Air Force program of biowar research, development, and training—the effort on the part of Jimmy Doolittle and William Burden and Nathan Twining and James Totten (and do not forget Robert Lovett, secretary of defense) to achieve a large-scale, Air Force–wide "practical capability" in biological weapons at the earliest possible date, to be used against Russia and China in a total war—is, in a way, a blind, a smoke screen, a foil, for the looser and smaller-scale experiments in unconventional weaponry, including feathers and insects and modified leaflet bombs, that the Communists were (I believe legitimately) complaining about—and sometimes exaggerating.

Some of the filmed footage the Chinese produced, in making a case for their germ charges, looks staged—staged in a way that is similar to the slightly-after-the-fact re-creations in the wartime documentaries produced by John Ford, John Huston, and William Wyler. That it was staged and reenacted doesn't mean the events didn't happen, just that it was difficult to get a film crew there in time to record something that took place in a remote village several days earlier.

I called Blaine Harden to thank him for writing his book, and he told me an interesting story. He was able to get the complete and unredacted 191-page Air Force dossier on Donald Nichols, which included details of electroshock therapy, because he got to know the retired Special Forces man who was doing the declassifying. This man read through the file and was so appalled, said Harden, by what the Air Force had done to Nichols that he gave it to Harden without anything held back. Harden had no luck, though, with the intelligence reports removed in 2011 and replaced with "Access Restricted" cards. The withdrawn documents, he gathered, may have had something to do with sources and methods, or, possibly, with weapons of mass destruction. That's all he could find out. He gave up on trying to get them released and finished the book with what he had.

HANS TOFTE, a dashing, multilingual Dane, recipient of a Legion of Merit for his wartime service in the OSS, was another covert operator in Korea. In July 1950, just after the war began, Frank Wisner hired Tofte to run black operations out of Japan. "Basically I was told to choose a site and build an operations base outside Tokyo, big enough to handle one thousand people, with our own communications," Tofte recalled later. He chose a location south of Tokyo, now the site of the Atsugi naval air base.

Tofte made up his own rules and forged his own documents and quickly built a paramilitary empire, called JTAG, for Joint Technical Advisory Group. "We never asked for military orders in Japan or Korea," said Tofte to historian Joseph Goulden, "but wrote our own to look like the official papers without which nobody could move." His men were trained as saboteurs, guerrilla warriors, and escape-and-evasion specialists. There was a special "chemical section" at Yokosuka where a group of Japanese war scientists—allied with something called the Noborito Research Institute—worked. "We ignored the embargo on bringing indigenous personnel in and out of Japan and moved hundreds of guerrillas and agents in and out of our own training and staging camps both in the war zone and throughout occupied Japan."

Goulden interviewed Tofte for his big book about the Korean War. One day, reading it, a word jumped out at me: "belt." Tofte says that he created a belt, a saturated belt, in fact, of guerrilla warriors across Korea, "a 'belt' across the peninsula to be saturated with trained guerrillas as guides, working from fixed inland positions that would be given pilots as part of their combat briefings."

And then, in January 1951, Tofte got very sick. He lay in a coma in Tokyo, suffering, he said, from "intestinal fever and malaria." He told his wife he would be in the hospital for a few more weeks. By the end of March, Tofte was back home in Mason City, Iowa, talking to reporters about the war. He didn't say he worked for the CIA, just that he worked at MacArthur's headquarters in Tokyo. Americans must never forget, Tofte said, that the Russians were working overtime toward the destruction of the U.S.A. The American people should "get ready for the big showdown just as surely and urgently as we got ready after Pearl Harbor."

Tofte was fully recovered from his illness, he said. Soon he would be back in Japan, managing more missions.

I wonder whether Tofte had survived a case of Songo fever. Maybe he'd been commanding a group of feather-flinging commandos, saturating the belt? Not inconceivable.

"Although Tofte spoke freely of Korean operations in many interviews, because of security strictures he would give scant details of CIA activities in China and the USSR," Goulden wrote. "Despite the passage of three decades the CIA refused my Freedom of Information Act requests for access to the voluminous reports Tofte filed during his tenure in Korea." Tofte told Goulden that his accumulated monthly reports were "the size of a Manhattan phone book."

Tofte worked as Frank Wisner's personal aide, and helped with the Guatemala coup and other Latin American missions, but he fell out with the CIA and was fired in 1966. He was critical of director Richard Helms, and he charged the Agency with staging a "silly cloak and dagger raid" on his house in Georgetown, on 35th Street. According to Tofte, CIA agents confiscated some classified papers from his third-floor office and took his wife's jewels, "including a 130-carat half-moon sapphire, a very rare thing, that usually sits in the turban of a maharajah of India." Among the papers, Tofte said, was his own analysis of the blunders in Vietnam, the Dominican Republic, and the Bay of Pigs, and a letter from Richard Helms asking Tofte to remain in the Agency for life. "The CIA has operated in a manner beyond the law of the land," he said. Tofte sued Helms and the CIA for $25,000; Helms later admitted to a congressman that the warrantless search was a mistake.

In 1978, when the CIA was under attack, Tofte wrote a letter to *The New York Times*: "Without the C.I.A.'s covert action, America would not be where it is today," he said. "The American public owes it a debt of gratitude."

April 10, 2019, Wednesday

The iPhone has a bug, or maybe it's a feature, that causes it to rotate every photo you take of a document (pointing the camera straight down at the paper, which is positioned flat on a table) so that it is upside down. To read the photograph of the document, you must either physically turn the iPhone, which never ends well, or tap several places to rotate it via software. The rotate symbol, with a little arrow, makes it turn by 45 degrees each time. The places on the phone where you must touch are on three corners of the screen. So there's a small challenge involved in reading what's in the picture. Sometimes that's helpful, because you notice things—place names, people's names, marginalia—when you're forced to go through the photos one by one, spinning them around.

There's one image I keep coming across. It's a photo I took of a color print of a turkey feather. The print was pasted into one of the sixty original copies of "Feathers as Carriers of Biological Warfare Agents," the 1950 Camp Detrick report on the feather bomb. The close-up photograph shows how much fine dust of disease a feather can hold, almost unnoticeably, secretly, in its interlocking barbed tines. "The feathers used for this test were washed, fluffed, white turkey plumage of a uniform size (average 3 ½ in.

long by 1 ¾ in. wide; 5300 per pound)," the report says. "Such feathers will hold loosely up to 80 per cent by weight of rust spores. After violent shaking approximately 10 per cent by weight of spores are retained."

Feathers were one of Ishii's methods of dissemination. In the fall of 1950, just as the sixty recipients of "Feathers as Carriers" paged through the report and saw the charts and the photos, that soldier from the Middlesex Regiment ran into a group of masked men tossing handfuls of feathers in a Korean village during the American retreat.

HERE IT IS APRIL and the world is white and the plows are scraping and the road salt is being flung out in arcs. I made some coffee and poured it into a thermos and then for several minutes afterward the coffee machine made distant exploding sounds, as if an artillery battle were happening several miles away, as its heater vaporized a few last drops of water.

This Air Force word "capability" interests me. It comes up over and over. "Development of the feather bomb had made possible an immediate Air Force capability against cereal crops," wrote Dorothy Miller in 1951. "The fact that the armed forces, particularly the USAF, are attempting to attain a combat capability in the employment of BW-CW, is considered highly classified," says another 1951 document. "Another comment of General Bullene that was a little startling was his statement that the Navy has a greater capability in BW at this time than the Air Force."

And then on May 31, 1952, comes a crucial entry in the microfilmed copy of Air Force general Otto Weyland's war diary, at the moment when General Mark Clark took over from Matthew Ridgway as head of United Nations forces in Korea. The passage from Weyland's diary is, as I remember, the very last frame of microfilm on that reel. It says that General Clark met with General Partridge, General Doolittle, and General Everest:

> General Clark reviewed his troubles on Xoji-do, Panmunjom, with
> President Rhee, and the possibilities of Chinese attacks. He discussed
> BW and CWS and stated that the JCS had told him of good available
> capabilities. I warned him that our ability for the favorable delivery of

chemical munitions in this theater was practically zero and with rather limited back-up capabilities in the U.S. General Doolittle who has been working as a consultant on BW stated that there were no practical capabilities in this field at this time.

So Jimmy Doolittle, in-house consultant for the Air Force on biological weapons, says there are no practical capabilities, while the Joint Chiefs of Staff, which included heads of the Navy, the Marine Corps, the Army, and the Air Force, say there were good available capabilities. How can there be such a divergence of opinion among men privy to the highest military secrets?

Conrad Crane, an Army historian, found Doolittle's phrase, "no practical capabilities," in Otto Weyland's diary and used it as the title of a paper in 2002. In it he does his very best to make a case for American innocence in the germ-war controversy. In "'No Practical Capabilities': American Biological and Chemical Warfare Programs During the Korean War," Crane, a tall man I saw once in 2008 at the Army Heritage and Education Center in Carlisle, Pennsylvania, paraphrases the diary entry:

> Spurred by an intense enemy propaganda campaign trumpeting germ warfare accusations and by queries from the Department of the Army about requirements to attain the ability to employ chemical weapons, General Mark Clark, commander of United Nations Forces in Korea and U.S. Far East Command, requested in mid-1952 that he be given some retaliatory capability against enemy chemical or biological warfare.

"Somehow," Crane goes on, "the Army inquiries led Clark to believe that the Joint Chiefs of Staff had 'good available capabilities' in biological and chemical warfare, but when he briefed that to a visiting Doolittle, Vandenberg's biological warfare consultant responded that 'there were no practical capabilities in the field at this time.'"

Actually, both statements could be true. There could be no overt capabilities—an ability to employ a given weapon on an industrial scale—and plenty of quick-and-dirty covert capabilities, which could happen here and there. Ishii's use of feathers to spread anthrax was a covert capability. The use of feathers by the Special Operations Division to spread crop disease, for which awards and felicitations were passed out to various Detrick employees, was, according to the Research and Development Board, a means of "covert dissemination." Feathers were covert—and feathers were one of the things that the North Koreans and the Chinese said they'd found in 1952 after American artillery shells exploded and after aircraft flew overhead. "On March 5 the enemy artillery bombarded our positions on the western front," said Chinese prime minister Chou En-lai on the radio. "A salvo of shells was fired from which, on exploding, feathers flew which, as it turned out, were infected with bacteria." "Bacilli anthrax were found on feathers dropped by American aircraft," said a Chinese pamphlet entitled "Stop U.S. Germ Warfare!" The pamphlet continued: "This is fatal to draught animals such as oxen, donkeys and mules and infectious to human beings. The specimens tested were taken from among feathers dropped on March 11 by American aircraft over Peichingtzu village, Peichingtzu district, Antung City."

Ticks, fleas, mosquitoes, and other insects can also serve as covert vectors, and the Chinese and North Koreans claimed they'd seen these, too. Detrick's Special Operations Division, Dorothy Miller's history reminds us, was founded to work on "covert or sabotage operations." A National Security Council paper from January 1950 has this: "BW weapons are uniquely suited for use in sabotage. Minute amounts of active materials are sufficient to produce considerable damage. The effects of sabotage may be delayed, often for days, since diseases do not manifest themselves immediately."

Another 1951 Pentagon document, produced by the Joint Advanced Study Committee, says, "With the exception of limited covert and anticrop capabilities, the United States possesses no offensive capability in the field of biological warfare." Well? A limited covert capability is not no capability. The committee goes on to say:

> Probably one of the most attractive and profitable uses to which BW could be placed is in the field of covert operations. The ability of special agents or guerrilla forces operating behind enemy lines to place small

quantities of BW agents accurately where they could be most effective
offers tremendous possibilities. Covert use has a further advantage in
that distinction between this type of BW and naturally occurring
outbreaks is most difficult, and therefore might be used with crippling
results well in advance of the initiation of hostilities.

In March 1951, an unnamed lecturer at the Air War College itemized some
of the more unusual means of delivering biological agents. "Some of the
other delivery ways that have been tried," he said, "are impregnated small
bore ammunition, canister base ejection bombs, land mines, aerial darts, free
balloons, animal and insect carriers and sabotage." Hanson Baldwin, *The
New York Times*'s military editor, got wind of these ideas, and he wrote, in
October 1951: "Biological warfare is half in, half out of the laboratory, but
it is primarily a weapon for saboteurs, a weapon of opportunity—not a
'main line of defense.'"

All this is what leads me to conclude that the vastly expensive, A1-
priority Air Force biological-weapons-development program eventually
came to function as cover for what was a small-scale, plausibly deniable,
CIA-managed, opportunistic effort, an offshoot or subset or ancestor of
MKNAOMI and MKULTRA, about which we have little so far on paper,
but about which we have immense detail, very peculiar detail—perhaps too
peculiar to be invented—from the Communists. As Jimmy Doolittle rightly
said, there were no "practical capabilities in the field"—meaning that there
were no teams of trained Air Force germ handlers, no stockpiles of mass-
produced weaponry, no large refrigerated lockers to hold perishable agents.
But what the Chinese were publicizing was something smaller than this.
They showed pictures of a single leaflet/feather bomb, from a single plane,
and said they'd found nonlocal insects crawling around nearby. They said
they'd found fragments of some kind of ceramic bomb. They found feathers.
They described other oddly shaped munitions, including a cardboard cylinder
with a parachute that sounds a bit like a bomb I saw a picture of in the
Chemical Corps files in the National Archives. Why would they make such
improbabilities up, and stick to them with such persistence, unless they
believed them? They were not surrealist poets, they were leaders in the midst

of a terrible war. "Big lies" have big empty voids in them, vaguenesses, whereas the charges that kept coming from China had ever finer detail. More microscopic images, more scientists with tweezers, more eyewitness accounts. What they describe are items that roughly correspond with various laboratory prototypes and weapons still in the testing phase, not "standardized" mass-manufacturable items readily available to fighter-bomber squadrons in large quantities. The Communists were, I think, describing a small, covert testing program—actually probably several covert tests.

They did fabricate evidence, though. The Russians, the North Koreans, and the Chinese all, at times, lied about what they'd found in the snow. That's just a fact. "Two false regions of infection were simulated for the purpose of accusing the Americans of using bacteriological weapons in Korea and China," wrote Lavrentii P. Beria, Russia's secret-police chief, in April 1953, just after Stalin died. But I think the simulations and the lies had more to do with whether the insects (and voles and spiders and grasshoppers and even clams) were infected with diseases than with the aerial arrival of the insects themselves.

THE AMERICANS DENIED EVERYTHING. Denied and denied and denied. The CIA orchestrated the countercampaign, with help from the State Department. At a director's meeting on March 11, 1952, Frank Wisner said his people had "stirred up some life in the BW counterattack and had used the Director's suggestions in this matter." Wisner, at the meeting, said that the Communist charges might be cover for a breakdown in the peace negotiations, or they might signal a resumption of full-scale war in Korea. Bedell Smith said that the United States had to fight back. "We should organize in order to take immediate counteraction to any and all Russian propaganda," he said, according to the meeting minutes. "We had nothing to lose by 'using the bigger lie.'"

On March 13, 1952, Bedell Smith asked Wisner to "produce two or three sentences on the BW matter" that could go into someone's upcoming speech—perhaps a speech to be given by one of the delegates at the United

Nations, but there's no way to know because the name is whited out. On March 19, 1952, in another director's meeting, Smith said that it wasn't yet the time to "fire our big gun" on the germ-warfare matter—by which he meant issuing a "statement on BW by the President." This, too, is followed by a blanked paragraph.

Bernard Malik, Russian delegate to the United Nations, was pressing the germ-warfare charges hard. At a March 14, 1952, meeting of the U.N.'s Disarmament Commission, Malik said that the United States was using germ warfare for the purpose of "mass extermination of civilian populations" and called for a condemnation by the U.N. and a prohibition on biological weapons. American delegate Benjamin V. Cohen made an angry denial: the charges were "false, unwarranted and uncorroborated." Would the Disarmament Commission, Malik asked, be willing to take up the question of a ban on atomic weapons and germ warfare? Cohen said he was not interested in taking up the matter just yet—a worldwide study, a "census," of armaments must happen first. "No responsible government can agree to cut its own defenses without knowing where such cuts will leave it in relation to the armed forces of other countries." Malik said that was just a stalling tactic. The British delegate, Gladwyn Jebb, sitting with Bernard Malik at his right elbow and Benjamin Cohen at his left elbow, said that seeing as how there were wars in progress in Korea, Malaya, and Indochina, the time was not "propitious" for disarmament negotiations. North Korea and Communist China were not heard from—both countries were barred from membership in the United Nations.

Benjamin Cohen called a press conference the next day, a Saturday, to attack Malik. "We don't intend to let him get away with these dishonest, absurd and monstrous falsehoods," he said.

On March 16, 1952, a Sunday, *The New York Times*, in an editorial, said that Bernard Malik had reached a "new low of falsehood and fantasy even for him" by repeating the Chinese and North Korean germ charges. It was a "parade of nonsense," the *Times* said, a "manufactured nightmare." On March 18, 1952, a columnist for *The Philadelphia Inquirer*, Ivan H. Peterman, wrote: "As the Roman tyrant Nero demonstrated, the more flamboyant the lie, the more its attraction to dupes and stupids." Peterman wondered if the "germ warfare lie" was meant to divert attention from something else. "It's just possible the Russkies are going to release some of their own over-supply of germs."

A Soviet poet of some fame, Samuil Marshak, produced a bit of light verse about insect warfare, called "The New Song of the Flea," published March 20, 1952. Here are some stanzas:

> It's housed in a fine laboratory,
> It's fed on government food,
> Professors and scientists all
> Look to the flea's own good.

> Lodged in a house of glass,
> Living alone is he;
> And Shiro Ishii himself
> Calls on the President's flea.

> The flea detachment rises
> Into the upper air,
> Bound for a foreign country—
> For a country over there.

> The villains of other ages
> Are known to history,
> But vilest of all is the spreader
> Of the plague-infected flea.

Marshak's poem was one of hundreds of press clippings and radio transcripts amassed by the State Department in 1952 as evidence of the Soviet Union's "Hate America Campaign." *The Saturday Evening Post,* whose editors were friendly with the CIA, published an article about the Hate America Campaign in their August 9, 1952, issue, which had a Norman Rockwellesque painting of boys in a treehouse on the cover. (The treehouse bore a sign that said "No Girls Allowed," and the boys were using a pulley to haul their dog up in a box.) "The effect of the fraudulent germ-warfare scare upon the Asiatic world was electric," wrote Betty Milton Gaskill in the *Post*. "It will go down in history as one of the most monstrous hoaxes ever perpetrated." The harm done to American interests was incalculable, she believed. "Such a screaming propaganda build-up is, of course, the traditional way in which totalitarian states prepare their people for their own aggression." The Hate America Campaign was "an all-out struggle for the mastery of men's minds," Gaskill contended; the Soviet Union was spending vast sums in an effort to degrade and discredit our democracy with "fantastic lies." What we were doing now, she said, was like fighting artillery with a BB gun. To counter the calumnies, America needed to fund a "propaganda program of our own comprehensive enough to meet the Russian challenge."

There was no such thing as a Hate America Campaign, the Soviets claimed, on August 1, 1952, in an English-language magazine called *News*; there never had been a Hate America Campaign. Russia hoped for an improvement in its relations with the United States. "Neither at the present time nor at any time in the past have there been insurmountable differences between the two countries," the editorial said. American policy makers were "whipping up propaganda hostile to the Soviet Union."

ONE BIG AND SUPPOSEDLY DEVASTATING refutational moment came on April 3, 1952, when *The New York Times*, on page 1, published an article by A. M. Rosenthal headlined

REDS' PHOTOGRAPHS
ON GERM WARFARE
EXPOSED AS FAKES

———

Experts Who Studied Pictures
Printed in Peiping Paper
Say Charge is False

———

EVIDENCE IS CONCLUSIVE

———

Germs Shown Are Harmless,
Insects Not Carriers and
Bomb Is for Leaflets

Rosenthal's lead was very strong: "Photographs published by the Chinese Communists as 'proof' of the use of germ warfare by the United States were exposed today as complete frauds," he wrote, and he went on to itemize the fraudulence point by point, with the help of experts. The pictures of "deadly bugs" were actually of harmless insects, according to the chief curator of insects and spiders at the American Museum of Natural History. One picture, he said, showed a tiny insect called a springtail, hugely magnified and "incapable of carrying disease." The photos of microscopic organisms were either "utterly innocuous bacteria or meaningless blotches," according to René Dubos, "internationally eminent bacteriologist attached to the Rockefeller Institute." And finally, most tellingly, the alleged germ bomb was a fake. "The photograph of a 'germ bomb' supposedly dropped by the United States was a picture of a nonexplosive bomb used to distribute propaganda leaflets, which for physical reasons is not adaptable even theoretically to carrying germs," Rosenthal reported. The *Times* reproduced, courtesy of the Army, a photo of a propaganda bomb filled with wrapped circular packets of leaflets, with this caption:

> A fully loaded United States M1621 cluster adapter bomb, which holds 22,500 psychological warfare leaflets, is shown at the Far East Command printing plant in Yokohama. According to the army, this is the bomb shown in Pictures 7, 8 and 9 in the Red paper as a germ bomb.

"The four compartments which contained the leaflets can be clearly seen," said an army spokesman. "Normally the hinged cover will be opened by a time fuse while the bomb is in the air. The wind will then whip open the cover and spread the leaflets over a wide area." (All the photographs were republished in *Life* magazine, in a two-page spread about the "big germ-warfare lie.")

The Army spokesman probably wasn't being intentionally misleading.

It's more likely that he was unaware that the Special Operations Division's feather bomb existed. Not only was the leaflet bomb "theoretically" adaptable to the delivery of germs, the adaptation had already happened and had been field-tested on crops and pigs. René Dubos wasn't being misleading, either, when he jeeringly dismissed one picture as "some junk colored by dye," and another as "monumentally insignificant." But why was Dubos so fierce and sneery—so quick to dismiss a scientific possibility on the basis of a photograph in a Chinese newspaper?

During World War II, when Dubos was on the faculty of Harvard Medical School, he had consulted for the War Department on Project Y, an effort to mass-produce the shigella bacteria that cause dysentery, and he had provided technical information to Karl Meyer's plague workers in California. Was Dubos so fierce, I wonder, because he knew firsthand the magnitude and ambitiousness of the American offensive germ-war effort? How hard they'd all worked during the war to manufacture disease? And how much vileness the Americans had incontrovertibly appropriated after the war from the Japanese? Did it exasperate him to know that the Communist charges could actually be—at least partly—true?

MATTHEW RIDGWAY, Supreme Commander of the United Nations forces in Korea, who wore a live grenade pinned to his chest, offered the most forceful denials. On March 11, 1952, the Associated Press reported his attack on the Communists' "known falsehoods": "'There is not one scintilla of truth in the communist assertions—repeat, not one scintilla of truth,' Ridgway shouted." The Communists were just covering up their own epidemics, he said.

On March 24, 1952, Ridgway said the charges were "disturbing." The germ-warfare business was "completely in accord with the deliberate and repeated employment of falsehoods of Soviet leaders," he said. "It is all a part of the big lie. The result is more hatred and more animosity and less chance of getting the world situation straightened out."

General Mark Clark took over from Ridgway as commander of United Nations forces on May 12, 1952. He said, "The baseless charges concerning germ warfare have been refuted by my predecessor and I can state unequivocally that the United Nations has at no time engaged in any such illegal type of warfare."

On May 23, 1952, Ridgway, returned from Korea, addressed a joint session of Congress. The Communist allegations of germ and gas warfare were, he said, "false in their entirety."

> In the whole black record of false propaganda, these charges should stand out as a monumental warning to the American people and to the free world—a warning as menacing and as urgent as a forest fire bearing down upon a wooden village. The extent to which Communist leaders world wide have gone in fabricating, disseminating and persistently pursuing these false charges should impress upon the brains of those who yet fail or refuse to see the purpose of communism, the deadly danger with which it confronts us and the free world.

Harry Truman's public denial—the firing of Bedell Smith's "big gun"— came several days later, in a talk in the White House Rose Garden: "The Kremlin bombards the world with cries of peace—peace," the president said. "And the Kremlin brings on war—war, at every point that she possibly can. The Kremlin cries that we have used germ warfare. There isn't a word of truth in that. We have never broken the Geneva convention in our operations in Korea. And they know that. They know it well. But they keep on passing out the lies that have no foundation in fact whatever."

April 11, 2019, Thursday

I keep thinking of a phrase I saw in a CIA document: "flat, indignant denial." I came across it in a meeting memo from the Eisenhower era, after the Korean War, declassified and published by the CIA in 1999 in a collection of documents about the intelligence war in Berlin. There's a lot of material in the collection about the Berlin Tunnel, which was dug by the CIA in 1954 from West Berlin into East Berlin in order to install wiretaps on the telephone and telegraphic cables serving the headquarters of the Soviet Army.

One document describes a conference in Allen Dulles's office in November 1954, with Frank Wisner and Berlin chief William Harvey and others, in which the men weighed security precautions and contingency plans relating to the tunnel—which was clearly a bold and ambitious (and also foolhardy and provocative) undertaking. One precaution they'd taken was to give the tunnel a strong steel door set in cement slabs, with a bar and an alarm system. Another was to mine the tunnel with C-3 plastic explosive packed in garden hose "threaded behind the liner plate in sufficient quantities that when exploded it will collapse the tunnel without causing a major explosion."

Should Harvard's James Conant, high commissioner for Germany, be informed of the tunnel? No, Allen Dulles decided, Conant should be kept in the dark. "After considerable discussion and careful reconsideration it was the DCI's decision that Conant should not be briefed," the memo records. The group also took up the question of what to do if the East Germans discovered the tunnel and lodged a complaint. "In the event of discovery and any possible protest," Dulles and his colleagues agreed, "the official American reaction is to be flat indignant denial ascribing any such protest to a baseless enemy provocation."

There it is. Not just plausible denial. Plausible *indignant* denial. Since Conant wasn't briefed about the tunnel, he could claim that the charge was a baseless provocation. When, in fact, it was completely true.

ONE OF THE U.S. GOVERNMENT'S more shameless denials happened in 1950, several months before the Korean War began. In December 1949, the Russians held a trial in Khabarovsk, a city in eastern Siberia near the Chinese border. Twelve Japanese germ men, held captive by the Soviets, were charged with war crimes.

One medical officer, Nishi Toshihide, chief of Branch 673 of Unit 731 of the Kwantung Army, testified that he had been stationed in the town of Sunyu, near the Russian border, where he bred fleas, guinea pigs, rats, mice, and voles, sending them on to Harbin, headquarters of Unit 731, for use in experiments.

In January 1945, Nishi told an interrogator, he had supervised an experiment in which ten Chinese war prisoners were tied to stakes and fatally wounded with bomb shrapnel. They wore helmets, and their upper bodies were shielded; their lower bodies were naked. "The bomb was exploded by means of an electric switch and the shrapnel, bearing gas-gangrene germs, scattered all over the spot where the experimentees were bound. All the experimentees were wounded in the legs or buttocks, and seven days later they died in great torment."

Karasawa Tomio, a doctor, was chief of the production section of Unit 731. He was asked by the Russian prosecutor if he pled guilty to the charge brought before him. He answered that he fully pled guilty to "devising the most perfect methods of producing bacteria on a mass scale" and employing these bacteria as instruments of bacteriological warfare. "While producing huge quantities of bacteria, I, as a bacteriologist physician, knew that they were intended for the purpose of exterminating human beings," Karasawa told his interrogator. "Nevertheless, at that time, I was of the opinion that this was justified by my sense of duty as an officer of the Japanese Army and therefore did all in my power successfully to carry out my duties as defined in the orders of my superiors."

Every month, according to Karasawa, the unit he commanded was able to manufacture hundreds of pounds of plague, anthrax, typhoid, paratyphoid A, cholera, and dysentery. Chinese prisoners were injected with various types of disease and then observed. These experimental subjects were called *maruta*, "logs," he said. In field trials, prisoners were tied to stakes, and anthrax bombs were exploded near where they stood.

"I was a participant in these criminal activities and committed a crime against humanity, for which I must pay the penalty," Karasawa said.

Another defendant, Segoshi Kenichi, a pharmacist and laboratory assistant, described the Ishii bomb, made of ceramic and filled with plague-infected fleas. "Since the bodies of these bombs were ceramic and thin-walled," Segoshi explained, "a very small quantity of explosive was needed to explode them, consequently the explosion was of low power, and this saved the fleas from destruction."

The outraged Russians mounted a propaganda campaign, demanding that the Japanese emperor be tried for bacteriological crimes and accusing the Americans of "deliberately protecting" Ishii, Kitano, and other Japanese scientists, indeed of elevating some of them to high positions in the medical establishment, and of generally turning Japan into their Far Eastern military base—all of which was true. MacArthur's occupation government offered bold denials. "It is repeated here," reported *The New York Times* on February 4, 1950 (with perhaps a faint hint of disbelief), "that the Allied command in more than four years of occupation has been unable to find any evidence that the Japanese plotted germ warfare and it is asserted that surviving Japanese Army commanders were unable to give any evidence that there was a bacteriological department in the Japanese armed forces."

Suddenly, early in 1951, Songo fever appeared in Korea, where it had never been, in a series of isolated infections in the narrow midsection of the country, dividing North Korea from South Korea. A belt of infection.

TODAY, WHILE I WAS PARKED in a parking lot, typing out the details of horrendous long-ago experiments, a couple had a huge shouting argument near my car. The man said, "You're pissed because you didn't know your own Social Security number. You're stupid." The woman threw her purse on the asphalt and said, "I don't give a shit!" They both got in a white car and drove away.

In the sky was a long, low, slowly evaporating white cloud. A beautiful cloud.

April 12, 2019, Friday

The Russians published a 535-page book, dark blue with gold-colored letters on the front and on the spine, about the Khabarovsk trials. The title is *Materials on the Trial of Former Servicemen of the Japanese Army Charged with Manufacturing and Employing Bacteriological Weapons*. I bought my copy in 2008 from Oxfam Broomhill, via AbeBooks, for $23.81: "Binding a little loose, corners bumped, page edges a little dusty, but in generally sound condition, with clean, bright, unmarked contents." All true. It was one of the first books I bought when I decided to learn more about the biowar universe that Steve Endicott and Ned Hagerman had written about. But when the book came in the mail, I didn't read it. Sometimes you eagerly order a book, and then when it comes you put it in a pile and pay no attention.

Now I can't stop reading it. How can these awful things have happened in our beautiful world?

On December 26, 1949, Nishi Toshihide, a physician, formerly of the medical service, testified in Khabarovsk that when he joined Unit 731 in 1943, the chief was Major General Kitano. Later, General Ishii took over. Ishii ordered the mass production of fleas, Nishi said. The prosecutor asked

Nishi about some sweets prepared by Colonel Oota. "Colonel Oota said the chocolates contained the bacteria of anthrax," Nishi replied. "The chocolates were intended for sabotage actions."

Nishi also knew about the frostbite experiments. Prisoners, warmly dressed but bare-armed, were taken outside when it was twenty below zero. A fan blew air over their arms. "This was done until their frozen arms, when struck with a short stick, emitted a sound resembling that which a board gives out when it is struck." Then they were brought inside. "These researches were being conducted with a view to future war with the U.S.S.R."

Do you repent of your deeds? the prosecutor asked.

"I consider that the experiments on the people confined in Detachment 731's prison were inhuman," Nishi replied. "I also realize that the rats and fleas bred by my branch were the cause of great evil."

The next day, December 27, 1949, Kajitsuka Ryuji, a doctor, testified in Khabarovsk about his part in the germ experiments. Kajitsuka, who was head of medical administration in the Kwantung Army, said that Ishii had returned from a trip to Europe in 1931 believing that Japan had to prepare for bacteriological warfare. All the other powerful countries were preparing for it.

"Ishii said that plague epidemics arose easily under natural conditions, but that it was not easy to induce them artificially," Kajitsuka said—hence the necessity for human experimentation. Ishii said that there were various ways to spread diseases, including sabotage, artillery shells, and bombs. Metal germ bombs, when they exploded, became hot and killed bacteria, which was why Ishii developed a germ bomb made of porcelain, Kajitsuka explained. If you wanted to spray germs, you must spray from a low altitude or the germs will die—unless you used fleas. "It was therefore decided to use plague-infected fleas." Kajitsuka himself worked on Songo fever, and on vaccines for typhus, plague, and cholera.

Much of the work at Unit 731, he conceded, was incompatible with the aims of medicine and of science. "That I myself was connected with this work and shared in it," he said, "I consider complicity in villainy, and I repent of it."

In the evening session that day, the prosecutor questioned three men who had worked at Detachment 100, which was a center for the training of saboteurs, and also for the mass production of diseases of wheat, cattle, and horses. Defendant Hirazakura, a veterinarian, bought a number of cows; in the event of war with Russia, the cows, infected with disease, would be released into herds in North Khingan Province.

Defendant Mitomo, who had volunteered for duty at Detachment 100 to be with his friends, contaminated rivers and reservoirs with glanders and anthrax, and fed prisoners porridge mixed with lethal doses of heroin. Mitomo injected one drug-weakened Russian with cyanide, dissected him, and then buried him near the cattle pit. There was a murmur of indignation in the courtroom. Not in the cattle pit, Mitomo clarified; in a different pit.

Defendant Takahashi said, "Detachment 100 could produce in the course of the year: 1,000 kilograms of anthrax germs, 500 kilograms of glanders germs, 100 kilograms of red rust germs." Takahashi now believed that what he had done was wrong, he said. "I repent particularly the fact that under my direction young Japanese committed such atrocities."

THAT SAME DAY, December 27, 1949, a spokesman at MacArthur's headquarters in Tokyo told reporters that there were no known cases in which Japanese germ-warfare scientists experimented on American prisoners of war, or indeed on prisoners of any nationality.

"Headquarters added that the Japanese did some experimentation with animals," reported the Associated Press, "but there was no evidence that they had ever used human beings."

THE DETRICK SCIENTISTS read this book about the Khabarovsk trial carefully, I suspect. They studied the reports by Fell and Hill and Victor. And then they tried to improve on what the Japanese had planned to do to the Russians. Kill the wheat, kill the pigs, kill the chickens, kill the cattle, sicken the population. It was the only way to win the war, they believed. Big science would make up for a smaller army. The Department of Defense was, said Secretary of Defense Louis Johnson on Saint Patrick's Day in 1950, "developing brand new unprecedented devices that challenge the existence of all known weapons." The hydrogen bomb was just one of these novelties, he said: "I assure you that we are equally alert to the possibilities inherent in the biological and chemical fields, as well as the radiological." Scientific research was necessary, Johnson said, because the United States was outmanned in troop strength by Russia. "What we lack in numbers," he said, "we must therefore make up in superiority of weapons."

What the men of Camp Detrick did, denying it and hiding it all the while, was to study the worst things that Japanese biological science had ever done—would ever do—and then copy it.

I READ SOME OF SHELDON HARRIS's *Factories of Death*, about Unit 731 and the American cover-up, at the Kia car dealership while waiting for a new tire. I had a stack of books on a chair in the waiting room, while an old *Mary Tyler Moore* episode played on the screen. The titles of the books in my stack were:

The Biology of Doom
The United States and Biological Warfare
Factories of Death
A Higher Form of Killing

I turned them so that their spines faced toward the back of the chair. It seemed rude to have that unhappy library in the dealership's waiting room, while people chortled to an old, innocent sitcom.

April 13, 2019, Saturday

It's 3:52 P.M. in the afternoon and there's a huge humid smell in the air. If I were a bulb in the ground, this is the day I would begin growing. I spent the morning thinking about crop failures, hunger plans, and voles, and then I thought about Albania, and in the afternoon got to thinking about two journalists, John Powell and David Wise. David Wise died, it turns out, back in October. I'd wanted to talk to him.

There were several early books that broke open the CIA's hermetic seal, but *The Invisible Government*, by Wise and Thomas Ross, published in 1964, was at the top. It had a huge effect, partly because it was serialized in several big newspapers and excerpted in *Look* magazine. "There are two governments in the United States today" is how it began. "One is visible. The other is invisible." At the heart of the invisible government was the CIA. One reviewer, John Berry, wrote: "Wise and Ross trace the development of this potential Frankenstein's monster from its conception during the Truman administration to its present state of seemingly unbridled power." The *Pittsburgh Courier*'s reviewer said: "This book is an education."

I'd actually looked up David Wise last year and gotten his phone number but hadn't called. And then he died of pancreatic cancer. *The New*

York Times obituary was full of good touches. It told how CIA people had threatened to buy all copies of *The Invisible Government*, and the editor at Random House said they'd just print more.

Some years later Wise filed a FOIA request for records relating to the publication of *The Invisible Government*, and he got back a document in which someone at CIA recommended a media campaign, employing Agency assets to plant unfavorable reviews and thereby "lessen the book's impact." One hostile review was by syndicated columnist Jenkin Lloyd Jones, editor and publisher of *The Tulsa Tribune*. "The discrediting and dissolution of the CIA are high on the Communist agenda," Jones wrote. "It is sad we live in a world where national survival requires the maintenance of a large intelligence agency. It is unfortunate that we must occasionally depart from our traditions and try, by covert means, to influence the political fortunes of another nation." Allen Dulles wrote Jones in 1958 that he'd read one of Jones's "most interesting" editorials, and he enclosed two of his own speeches—Dulles's letter is now in the CREST database.

THE IDEA OF BUYING all the copies of a book reminded me of something in *Bitter Fruit*, an early and still-absorbing account of the Guatemala coup by Stephen Schlesinger and Stephen Kinzer. In a chapter called "The Aftermath," the authors talk about a leftist named Pellecer, who fled Guatemala after the coup. In Mexico, Pellecer changed his political beliefs and began producing anti-Communist tracts, which were published with CIA money. "Best deal I ever had," the publisher said. "The CIA pays for the printing, and then they buy all the copies."

The preface to *Bitter Fruit*, which appeared in 1982, thanks "the congressional authors of the Freedom of Information Act (FOIA), who provided us with an indispensable tool to review the inner workings of United States foreign policy." Using FOIA, Schlesinger and Kinzer obtained a trove of documentation from the State Department. The CIA gave them little, however. They sued the CIA, with the help of the American Civil Liberties Union—and lost. They wrote the book anyway. Two decades later, thousands of pages about the Guatemala coup were

released, with no harm to national security. Today, the CIA's Guatemala/
PBSUCCESS files still await full declassification and redaction removal.

IN 1951, a fever, never before seen in Korea, began killing American
servicemen. It appeared in isolated spots or foci strung like beads across
the narrow midsection of Korea. It wasn't hemorrhagic smallpox, which is
a bacterial infection; it was hemorrhagic fever—Songo fever, a virus with
similar symptoms. (In hemorrhagic smallpox your face turns black before
you die; in hemorrhagic fever your face turns purple.) The Far East
Command set up a Hemorrhagic Fever Center, the 8228th Mobile Army
Surgical Hospital, in the midst of the epidemic, and they enlisted the help
of Kitano Masaji and his germ-warfare colleagues to help them understand
what was going on.

Let's think about this. The very disease that Kitano had isolated,
identified, purified, and made more virulent—the disease that he and his
helpers had repeatedly injected into monkeys, horses, and human beings—
was now at large in a band across Korea, several years after the United
States government had secured Kitano's cooperation.

"The majority of the cases occurred north of the 38th parallel in the
Yonchon-Chorwon-Kumhwa section of the front and the remainder in a
belt along the 38th parallel," wrote Carleton Gajdusek, an epidemiologist.
"All evidence points toward infection from a common localized source
over a brief period." Another study, by Dr. Joseph E. Smadel, said: "The
epidemic area extends as a belt across the peninsula with the southern
border at the level of Seoul and the known northern border at the present
main line of resistance. Within this general area the disease is seeded in
sharply defined foci in rural areas." Smadel, who worked at Walter Reed
Army Medical Center in Washington (where my grandfather worked late
in his career—he took me there once and showed me a slide of a rabbit's
heart), had been in touch with Songo scientist Kitano Masaji with questions
about the disease; he cited Kitano's paper, the one that relies on injections
of "apes."

The new disease, although known to American Army doctors for months, didn't find its way into newspapers until November 1951. The United Press, on November 8, said: "United Nations troops in Korea are being attacked by a strange, Oriental virus caused by a mite bite." In 1939, when the virus was first encountered, it was called Songo fever, said a Marine Corps doctor, Walter M. Bartlett, but now it was known as "epidemic hemorrhagic fever." The chief Far East Command surgeon in Tokyo, Brigadier General William E. Shambora, confirmed the existence of the disease. "Dr. Bartlett said that the disease is killing one out of five or six of its victims, and that there are no drugs that will stop it."

The Associated Press's article of the same day began: "A mysterious new disease, apparently brought to the battle lines by Chinese Communist troops, has infected an undisclosed number of United Nations soldiers in Korea." According to the AP, a North Korean informant had told doctors in September that the disease existed in Chinese troops. The disease, he said, "often resulted in death within 24 hours."

The next day, in another Associated Press article, Brigadier General Shambora explained that the Japanese called it Songo fever "after the name of the river near Harbin where they first discovered it." The Japanese also called it Kokka disease, he said. There had been 196 diagnosed cases and 25 deaths among Americans. The disease had existed among American troops as early as March 1951. This AP dispatch was delayed and censored by military authorities and published anyway: "The censor declined to pass previously published quotations from North Koreans that the disease sometimes caused death within 24 hours and that the death rate appeared to be about 15%."

Songo, or epidemic hemorrhagic fever, was not, absolutely not, germ warfare, the Associated Press said. "There was no suggestion in any dispatches that the disease among Allied troops might involve bacteriological warfare in any way. Apparently it was contracted from sick prisoners or refugees."

A British doctor, R. Andrew, published an account of forty hemorrhagic fever patients he cared for in the British Commonwealth General Hospital in Kure, Japan. Most patients recalled the field mouse or vole, he wrote, that was somehow associated with the disease, although the etiology was obscure. Some voles were "tame enough to take food from the men's hands," Dr. Andrew reported. "One patient found one in his bedding a month before his disease began; he developed severe haemorrhages during the course of his illness and died."

In addition to bleeding and high fever, there were other symptoms—blurred vision, severe backache, uncontrollable hiccups, chronic vomiting, memory loss, and delirium, "with a tendency to wander at night, to spit, shout, or swear in garbled fashion." Andrews tells the story of the man who found a field vole in his bedding. Soon after he left Korea for Japan, he became feverish, with increasing mental confusion. He developed a "gross hemorrhage into the infundibular stalk" of the brain. He began vomiting blood. His cause of death: "epidemic hemorrhagic fever with widespread hemorrhages and terminal inhalation of vomit."

IN DECEMBER 2008, I interviewed a former Marine, Tom Kennedy, at his apartment in Manhattan. Kennedy, who won a Purple Heart after removing wounded men under mortar fire in 1953, came down with a bad fever soon after the fighting stopped in Korea, and couldn't move from his sleeping bag. He thought he had malaria, which was fairly common among soldiers. "A helicopter came out to our little outpost," he told me, "and they put me on a stretcher and flew me over hills that I had been walking on for so many months." The helicopter landed at a special MASH unit, where there were three Quonset huts. "The first Quonset hut, you're probably going to die. The second Quonset hut, you had a fifty-fifty chance. The third Quonset hut, you're probably going to walk away." The doctors put Kennedy in the first Quonset hut, and he spent some days there, burning up. "They looked at me like they were looking at a corpse," he said. "There was no cure, but they gave us a lot of water. It was an awful place, because people were screaming and dying." Then they moved him to the second Quonset hut, and finally to the third. He was told that he'd had a new disease, hemorrhagic fever, that was carried by a tick on a rat. He was discharged with no mention on his record of his monthlong convalescence.

Because the United States forces couldn't prevail on the battlefield,

Kennedy believed, they sought help from Japanese germ scientists and tried to kill a lot of enemy soldiers with disease. "There was no history of hemorrhagic fever in Korea until its use as a germ weapon," he wrote in an autobiographical note in 2015. "I was one of those American service members exposed to this secret crime against humanity."

Another soldier, a trombonist named Jack Elbon, woke up in a sweat one night in 1953. A doctor took a look at him and sent him to the 48th MASH unit, strapped to the outside of a helicopter. At the hospital, he spent the night next to a South Korean soldier, who said he just had the flu. "I should be back on the front lines," said the soldier. The next morning the Korean soldier stiffened, turned purple, and died.

A Japanese doctor visited Elbon and said he had hemorrhagic fever, which was similar to bubonic plague. The doctor asked if he'd seen any rats where he'd been in Munsan; the Chinese had infected rats, he said. "I haven't seen any rats," Elbon answered, "but I have been bitten by mosquitoes."

Elbon spent weeks in the hospital. Every night his fever spiked. His weight dropped from 160 to 125. He lived on a half a piece of toast, a cup of tea, and a cup of pear juice. "It seemed as though someone from that ward would die every night," he said. "I spent long days reliving my life from early childhood, from life during the Depression, to being a teenager during World War II. I even replayed football and basketball games in my mind." Finally his fever broke.

"You are one of the lucky ones," said a nurse, "you are going to live."

Elbon was shocked to discover that he'd been discharged with zero disability and the wrong diagnosis—infectious mononucleosis and jaundice. Back in West Virginia, he signed up for college, but he was weak, and he slept a lot. He couldn't practice the trombone because his embouchure was gone. "All hopes of playing professionally evaporated."

"I was one of the first victims of germ warfare," Elbon wrote on Koreanwar.org. But Elbon was a committed anti-Communist, and he believed—the Japanese doctor had told him so—that Communists were the source of his ordeal, not the Americans and the Japanese.

JOHN W. POWELL, a journalist who was in China during much of the Korean War—he was tried for sedition afterward for writing articles sympathetic to the Communist side—wrote, in 1980, "It is a subject for interesting speculation as to how an 'infection belt' of hemorrhagic fever suddenly stretched from one coast of Korea to the other along the 38th Parallel, while not appearing either in Manchuria or along the transport routes in North Korea leading to the parallel." In a short, disturbing book, *Unit 731: Testimony*, Hal Gold wrote, "The facts available appear to encourage the belief that the Americans, assisted by their former Japanese enemies, carried out against the North Koreans biological warfare attacks which ended up backfiring."

April 14, 2019, Sunday

In Quaker meeting I looked out the window at the still-empty trees and saw a bit of beech bark dangling and moving in the wind although the rest of the tree was still. There was light—honest, plain light—on everything. I thought of a time I climbed a maple tree and reached a point at which I knew I was too high. All the dappled boughs around me were moving, and I felt like an ant clinging to a grass-blade. And then, amazingly, I noticed an ant was up there with me. It was as high as I was. What was it doing up there? What was I doing up there?

M. and I had lunch in the sun, with the dogs tethered. Mostly they were good and didn't bark. M. raked some leaves from the brown grass in a pile and found tufts of green new growth underneath. She'd read an article on the Maine tick-control website that said that raking out dead leaves is a good thing—raking and mowing. There are definitely fewer ticks up here near Bangor than there were where we used to live.

DALE JENKINS WAS the U.S. government's Cold War mosquito man. He was chief of the entomology section at Fort Detrick from 1957 to 1962, which was probably the high point of anti-Soviet mosquito research in the United States. Jenkins's lab was able to produce half a million disease-infected mosquitoes a month. Which wasn't enough, apparently: in a summary report from January 1960, the Chemical Corps said it had proposed the construction of a full-scale plant that would have a monthly output of 130 million mosquitoes. "The advantages of arthropods," said the report, "are these: they inject the agent directly into the body, so that a mask is no protection to a soldier, and they will remain alive for some time, keeping areas constantly dangerous." The Detrick staff bred their mosquitoes on a diet of sugar syrup and blood; the females laid hundreds of thousands of eggs on moist paper towels. When the eggs hatched, the larvae were immersed in blood plasma taken from a rhesus monkey that had been injected with blood taken from a person in Trinidad who'd suffered from yellow fever in 1954.

Jenkins's chosen mosquito in 1960 was the king of crepuscular infectivity, *Aedes aegypti*, which he and his colleagues had been using to infect human volunteers, and had been releasing (uninfected) from airplanes and helicopters over Florida and Georgia all through the 1950s. (The operations had colorful names like Project Big Buzz and Project Big Itch.) Jenkins's chosen disease was yellow fever, a sometimes fatal disease for which there was no cure—although there was a vaccine. "Yellow fever has never occurred in some areas, including Asia, and therefore it is quite probable that the population of the U.S.S.R. would be quite susceptible to the disease," the summary report says. "It would be impossible for a nation such as the U.S.S.R. to quickly undertake a mass-immunization program to protect millions of people." A yellow fever mosquito attack would be difficult to detect and impossible to treat, according to the report, making this agent-vector combination an "extremely effective BW agent." Yellow fever mosquitoes, the report said, "could be disseminated in 2 ½-lb containers of the 750-lb cluster; 4.5-inch spherical bombs for aircraft dispensers; and 3.4-inch spherical bombs of the BW SERGEANT warhead."

Jenkins, a former Eagle Scout and a butterfly collector with an entomology degree from Ohio State, began his research career more than a decade earlier, at the Army Chemical Center in Edgewood, Maryland, where he became an authority on bloodsucking insects of all kinds—ticks, chiggers, fleas, and biting flies—but especially the voracious, cold-resistant, tree-breeding mosquitoes of Alaska and Canada, near the Arctic Circle, about which he and a colleague wrote a paper in 1946. At the Rocky Mountain Laboratory in Montana, he worked with Cornelius B. Philips on chiggers, the tiny ticklike mites that transmit scrub typhus, known in Japan as tsutsugamushi disease, scourge of American soldiers in the Far East. In Japan and Korea, voles, or meadow mice, harbored tiny ticklike mites, "trombiculid mites" (Jenkins and colleagues published a paper on their classification in *The Journal of Parasitology*), and the mites bit people, and the bitten people got tsutsugamushi disease, which can be fatal. Jenkins tried, unsuccessfully, to substitute North American chiggers for Far Eastern mites and North American white lab mice for Far Eastern meadow voles, placing the scrub-typhus-inoculated mice that he and Cornelius Philips immobilized into little "capsules." There's a picture of him in August 1948 with his sleeves rolled up, sitting across from Philips, tweezering diseased chiggers onto tiny encapsulated mice, which look like shotgun shells.

Jenkins took a particular interest in tracking the movements and range of mosquitoes: in 1949, he and a colleague, Charles Hassett, began releasing mosquitoes doped with radioactive phosphorus and tracking them with a Geiger counter. They published a paper about it in *Science*: "A method has been developed for producing readily detectable radioactive mosquitoes by rearing the yellow fever mosquito *Aedes aegypti* in beakers of distilled water containing radioactive material," Jenkins and Hassett wrote. They used an isotope of phosphorus, with a half-life of fourteen days. "The larvae were fed ground dog-biscuit, using the standard rearing techniques."

In 1950, Jenkins and Hassett spent time in subarctic Canada, in Churchill, Manitoba, near an American Air Force base, where they released three million radioactive mosquitoes. They recovered 141 of them. The other 2,999,859 wandered off.

A MYSTERIOUS EPIDEMIC, probably unrelated, struck several Eskimo villages above the Arctic Circle in 1949. The headline in *The Ottawa Journal* was "42 Stricken, 15 Dead in Arctic Plague of Deadly Influenza." Officials imposed a quarantine on forty thousand square miles of subarctic Canada. The fatality rate was 20 percent. There was a puzzling etiology—sometimes the disease was called plague, sometimes "killer flu," and sometimes the cause was tainted caribou meat. The disease was similar to polio, said one source, "which left some of its victims suffering from paralysis." *The New York Times* called it a polio epidemic. Or maybe it was influenza type A. Caucasians did not get sick.

Suspicions were aroused in the Soviet Union. There were large American air bases in the far north. Canada's Defense Research Northern Laboratory, which did cold-weather weapons testing, was in Fort Churchill. Dale Jenkins had been busy since 1946 studying cold-weather mosquitoes and biting flies near Fort Churchill. Maybe the Eskimos had been downwind of some kind of germ-warfare test? *Pravda* said, "As far back as the summer of 1949 reports penetrated into the Canadian press, according to which American tests of bacteriological warfare have been tried on Eskimos in the Canadian far north. As a result an epidemic of plague developed there." Kuo Mo Jo, the Chinese poet, in his huge speech against U.S. germ warfare on March 29, 1952, raised the charge again: "In the summer of 1949, the U.S. government carried out bacteriological experiments on Eskimos, causing an outbreak of bubonic plague among them. This is a fact universally known."

It seems just as likely that the poor Inuits had accidentally gotten sick from a disease to which they had no natural resistance.

LIKE THE JAPANESE biowar scientists, Jenkins became skilled at the mass rearing of insects in the laboratory. He wrote papers on how to grow vast quantities of chiggers by feeding them mosquito eggs, and how to induce egg-laying in female mosquitoes by gassing them with carbon dioxide.

Beginning in 1949, if not before, Jenkins's scientific career was mainly devoted to finding various ways to turn insects into weapons, just as the Japanese had. And yet in 1963, in a paper in *Military Medicine*, Jenkins claimed, remarkably, that there had been no research at all into insect-borne weapons during the Korean War. "In 1951 and 1952, the Communists loudly proclaimed in a false propaganda campaign that the United Nations, and specifically the United States, dropped fleas, grasshoppers, spiders, and other arthropods infected with agents of diseases that had been occurring in Communist troops in Korea and Tsingtao, China," Jenkins wrote. Then he said: "The United States had never investigated the potential of using arthropods for BW. In 1953, partly as a result of the false charges, a program was established to investigate this field to determine the defense requirements."

"This categorical statement," wrote Steve Endicott and Ned Hagerman in *The United States and Biological Warfare*, "is demonstrably not true." Steve and Ned cited a list of research projects from October 30, 1951, that included $160,000 for "arthropod dissemination." I've seen the phrase "arthropod dissemination" myself several times in the Korean War–era records of the Chemical Corps held in the National Archives. In fact, American interest in "EW," or entomological warfare, goes back to the early 1940s, at least: "Early in August 1943," wrote Rexmond Cochrane in his history of Camp Detrick, "two new problems were given to each of the four branches: the development of rice fungi as BW agents, and the study of certain arthropods as potential BW agents for the destruction of food crops." The "certain arthropods" in this case were most likely potato bugs, Colorado beetles: the French, the British, the Germans, and the Americans all investigated these black-and-orange-striped pests during World War II. In 1950, the Chemical Corps Biological Laboratories included a subsection in their annual report to the Research and Development Board on "Insect Dissemination of BW Agents." Scientists were, the report said, working with arctic mosquitoes and flies, and investigating the possibility of using insects to spread tularemia, or rabbit fever. "Studies on the growth and viability of selected pathogens, including the virus of equine encephalomyelitis, in mosquitoes are contemplated," the report went on. "The development, by selective breeding, of housefly strains resistant to various insecticides and environmental factors is continuing." Manifestly there was a lot going on with insects in the Chemical Corps in 1950, 1951, 1952, and 1953—the Korean War years.

So why was Dale Jenkins spreading misinformation? Perhaps he thought that there would never be anything like a Freedom of Information Act—that none of the Chemical Corps official reports to the Research and Development Board would become public. (Some are still unavailable, in fact. In March 2017, I asked the FOIA officer at Dugway Proving Ground for several annual reports of the Chemical Corps Biological Laboratories and, despite two follow-up emails, I've heard nothing back.) Perhaps, as with René Dubos, Jenkins simply didn't want the Communists' charges to be true.

ONE OF THE FIRST THINGS THAT HIT ME, back in 2008, was the word "voles." On a YouTube channel called Real Military Flix, I found one of the Chinese propaganda movies about alleged American bacteriological warfare, and I watched it. "On the morning of April the fifth, more than seven hundred ratlike voles, infected with plague, suddenly made their appearance in Kan-Nan district, after the intrusion of an American aircraft," the narrator says. "Most of the voles were dead. They carried plague bacilli, as proved by bacteriological tests." The movie camera pans from the native voles of northeast China, with long tails, to some specimens of Kan-Nan voles that fell from the sky. "Note the short tail," the narrator says. "This phenomenon is therefore completely unnatural."

Why, as part of their "big lie," would the Chinese assert something so improbable? If they were inventing germ-warfare charges out of whole cloth, would they really come up with a story of seven hundred air-dropped dead and dying voles?

Those voles may be a clue to the whole mystery. At the U.S. Army's 406th Medical General Laboratory in Tokyo—where researchers, including some former Unit 731 scientists, studied scrub typhus, or tsutsugamushi disease, among other illnesses—voles were part of laboratory life. For instance, in "Notes on Some Chiggers (Acarina: Trombiculidae) from

Southern Korea," E. W. Jameson and Seiichi Toshioka, working at the 406th laboratory from January to October 1952, tweezered a whole menagerie of mites off of *Apodemus agrarius*, the Korean meadow vole. Voles were of particular importance in 1951 and 1952 because they were part of an intense investigation into Korean hemorrhagic fever.

Voles were also bred in quantity by Unit 731 scientists during the Second World War, and they were specifically mentioned in January 1952 in an article in *Mainichi*, a Japanese weekly, by Sakaki Ryohei, a former Unit 731 officer. Plague was a good weapon, Sakaki wrote, except that "great care has to be taken in its manipulation." There were many ways of disseminating plague, the author went on. It could be mixed into shrapnel in shells, for instance. "It may also be dispersed by dropping rats and voles previously infected with the bacteria by injections using special methods such as parachute containers; or by dropping bacteria-laden fleas."

Then comes the Kan-Nan incident, on April 5, 1952. Joseph Needham, the British scientist and historian of science, one of the International Scientific Commission members who went to China to look into the Communist germ-warfare charges, wrote about the Kan-Nan incident in poised, deliberate prose, as part of a report of six hundred closely printed pages, maps of the "intrusions" of American planes, entomological bibliographies, many appendices, and a foldout wall chart of "Incidents in NE China and Korea" arranged in chronological order. In 2012, Raymond Lum, a librarian at Harvard's Yenching Library, let me study the original report of the commission in the perfect stillness of the library stacks one long afternoon, and then he had all of it beautifully photographed and uploaded to the Harvard Library website. More recently, Jeff Kaye, an independent researcher and blogger, posted a scanned and easily scrollable version on Document Cloud. It's a remarkably detailed document, worth taking a look at.

"On the morning of the 5th April 1952, the countryfolk of four villages from the town of Kan-Nan (Kan-Nan hsien), awoke to find themselves surrounded by large numbers of a rat-like animal," Needham and the commission reported. At about 11:30 the night before, Chinese air observers had seen an American F-82 night fighter fly overhead. "In the morning, the villagers found many of the voles dying or dead in their houses and courtyards, on their roofs, and even on their beds, while others were scattered around the outskirts of settlements." The inhabitants collected hundreds of these unseasonable and "regionally anomalous" creatures. A schoolboy found seven voles on the roof of his house. "Most were newly dead. Some had their heads broken, others had external lesions, others had their legs broken, and those that were caught alive moved about only with difficulty." Many had been carried around by cats. The commission estimated that because there were a great many cats in the area, some voles had been eaten—leading them to estimate that perhaps a thousand voles had fallen from the night sky.

The villagers, understandably, went into a state of emergency: they collected every vole they could find and burned it. One young man, T'sai Kuo Chin, found two voles under a cupboard—both sick and dying. He killed one and saved the other in a bottle. The villagers gathered up all cats and dogs and killed them and burned them, too. Only four voles were left from the original night. T'sai's bottled vole lived for a little while, then died.

That was the situation several days later when two plague preventionists, Chang Chieh-fan and Chi Shu-li, arrived on the scene. They examined the now decaying corpses of the voles, including the two found by T'sai. "One of the voles which died about one day before was autopsied and was examined bacteriologically. The other three had already putrefied and were used only for zoological identification." They found no fleas on any of the voles. They searched haystacks and hiding places to see if they could find any surviving voles that had escaped the original roundup, but they found none, only some mice and two sewer rats.

Officials quarantined the area, worried about plague. They treated everything with DDT and "lysol." To get rid of fleas they scorched rooms in houses by burning a layer of straw on the floor.

Nobody got plague. Nobody got sick of anything at all. Seven hundred voles had been dropped from a plane and there'd been not a single case of disease. The Chinese attributed the absence of disease to their prompt plague prevention efforts.

Two plague specialists autopsied the bottled vole. They found that the intestines were slightly putrefied. They ground up pieces of the putrefied intestine and injected them into a white rat, who died four days later. They autopsied the rat, who had a swollen spleen and a swollen liver. They cultured smears from these organs and discovered that coliform organisms grew— not surprising. "Among the coliform growths, there were two colonies resembling that of plague bacilli, partially overgrown by coliform bacteria." The scientists had no success in isolating the plaguelike colonies. They ground up some of the viscera of the second rat and injected it into another white rat, which also died four days later, with swollen lymph nodes. When they did smears they found that many colonies of coliform bacteria grew, including four "resembling that of P. pestis."

Some months later, in July, when the International Scientific Commission visited China, one of the commission's scientists, Dr. Zhukov-Verezhnikov, "personally carried out a post-mortem examination of a guinea-pig which, as passage animal, had been infected with the Kan-Nan strain and had died the same day." Needham and the commission concluded that (a) a large number of anomalous voles had fallen, and (b) the voles had been carrying plague. "In the opinion of the Commission," Needham and his colleagues report, "there remains no doubt that a large number of voles suffering from plague were delivered to the district of Kan-Nan during the night of the 4th/5th April, 1952, by the aircraft which the villagers heard. This was identified as an American F-82 double-fuselage night-fighter."

I think we have to stipulate that a whole lot of strange voles fell from the sky; (a) is indeed true. But were these voles carrying plague? All that the plague preventionists found, having autopsied one vole, were coliform bacteria and some partially obscured colonies that might possibly resemble plague. Then Dr. Zhukov-Verezhnikov shows up, injects a guinea pig with the experimental material saved months earlier, and easily finds evidence of plague bacteria. Presto. Not convincing.

I think that the Kan-Nan vole incident was part of a CIA deception operation that developed after the initial, mercifully brief covert germ operation was discovered and publicized by the Communists—and angrily denied by the Americans. It was meant to frighten people into thinking the voles carried plague. But the reason nobody got sick is that these voles were plague-free.

By April 1952, the secret germ-war operation was completely blown. There would have been no point in trying out more actual plague weapons on China. What actually fell on the four villages, in this case, were hundreds of sick laboratory voles, the survivors of various experiments in one of the pathology laboratories that CIA people had access to—perhaps the 406th Medical General Laboratory. They were in some way tossed from a plane—perhaps manually, the way some leaflets were tossed, since no bomb or other container was found. It was a cover and deception operation. The intent was to create fear and uncertainty and confusion and panic—and deniability. Throwing voles from a plane is not germ warfare. It's just a stupid thing to do. It was all a modified limited hangout. It resembled a known action called "Operation Red Frog"—in which CIA and military intelligence officers caught a hundred big Korean frogs, painted them red, and dropped them from a plane, in order to give the Communists "something to really bitch about." It was nerve warfare, not germ warfare.

LIKEWISE SPRINGTAILS AND WOLF SPIDERS. Springtails are tiny, jumpy, wingless, cold-resistant creatures, sometimes called snow fleas; Chinese authorities charged that masses of them appeared in "very peculiar" locations in China: on verandas and outside windowsills, for instance, and on the headgear and clothes of soldiers. Unlike ticks, mites, and mosquitoes, springtails don't bite and they don't carry disease: Needham and the Communist scientists were mystified by their use, since they weren't known vectors for infection, and the American scientists—for instance, the insect curator from the American Museum of Natural History consulted by *The New York Times*—were eyeball-rolling and dismissive. But it could simply be that springtails were dumped here and there on China because, like voles, they were handy and plentiful and weird and creepy. American medical entomologists were, as it happened, rearing springtails en masse in laboratories in Japan (they fed them with dried yeast pellets) in order to use the springtails' eggs as food for experimental colonies of scrub-typhus-infected chiggers. The springtails ate dried yeast and laid eggs, and the eggs fed the chiggers, and the chiggers sucked the blood of the voles, and in this way pathology progressed.

The eggs of wolf spiders, too, were used experimentally as "highly satisfactory" chigger food, and wolf spiders were also, according to the report of the International Scientific Commission, "found in large numbers on snow or on ice at a temperature below zero degrees Centigrade in Antung and K'uang-Tien, following the intrusions of American planes."

I think maybe the Americans were cleaning out their scrub-typhus labs, sprinkling whatever they were done with onto China.

April 15, 2019, Monday

The edges of old secrets are blurred and the middle is spongy and there are frangible bits of recorded truth spread around in the secrets like pieces of thin ceramic.

It's raining on tax day. I've been awake thinking about Japan's rice crop.

THIS WEEK I'M GOING TO DEVOTE to asking for more things from the government. I'm going to go to the post office and mail off some FOIA letters. That's my plan. I want to believe in this American government, and asking for things under the Freedom of Information Act is an expression of faith in the system. I want it to work.

UPSTAIRS, A PHRASE CAME TO ME: "the gorgeousness of everything." The gorgeous, precarious fabric of consciousness. The foolishly squandered but endlessly lavish preciousness of any life. If you are dissatisfied with the world, that means you believe that the world—in my case the North American world—can be improved.

We need to know what happened in Washington, D.C., in the 1950s. I can't help believing that if we know what happened we will do better in the future and that there's hope. Sometimes I have doubts. Sometimes I have doubts about the whole human experiment. We were too smart and figured out ways to group expendable young men together into armies, with swords and shields and then later with artillery and tanks and airplanes. And now drones. Russia has a drone now, naturally, to counter the CIA's fleets of drones. The recent overarmed era in the million-year history of our species has been difficult. And yet think of all the greatness of the twentieth century. The music, the magazines, the movies. *The Russians Are Coming*, for instance, with Alan Arkin—"We are, of course, Norwegians." Saul Steinberg, Tracy Chapman, Nabokov, Maeve Brennan. Aretha Franklin. The century of observation and improvisation. And the greatness of the twenty-first century, too. Rachel Aviv, for instance.

Upstairs I thought, What do I really want from a book? I want truth in every paragraph. I want surprises. I want a sense that everything is not hopeless. That we can do better. I want a sense that life is a complicated mixture of emotions and inconsistencies. Life is a sandwich. I want to include, or simulate, the pleasure of eating a sandwich.

When I woke up whenever it was—hours ago now, I guess—I reached out with my hand and found that Cedric had scooted up so that he was elongatedly sleeping between M. and me. My hand found his paw. I held his paw for a while and felt the braille of joy of his paw pads.

IN 2010, Julian Ryall wrote a piece in *The Telegraph*, "Did the United States Wage Germ Warfare in Korea?" Ryall went to North Korea and China and interviewed Professor Masataka Mori, who has spent his life studying Unit 731 and its Cold War echoes. And he talked to a man named Sim Dok Hwa, from the small village of Chongbori, near Pyongyang. "I was one of four boys in my family, but my three brothers died," Sim told Ryall. "My grandfather also died in the germ bomb attacks." The bomb that fell was unlike ones he'd seen. In the fields afterward they found many unusual flies—flies with long legs. A month later, people began getting sick. "It was a terrible thing for me to lose my family like that," Sim said. "I know that Americans are our enemy, but they should apologise."

A Pentagon spokesperson, Major Maureen Schumann, made a brief reply to a list of questions sent by Ryall: "The long-standing US position is that allegations of biological weapons use in the Korean War is 'the disinformation campaign that refuses to die.' Our position has not changed. The allegations have proven baseless time and time again."

IN THE AFTERNOON I submitted two Freedom of Information Act requests and sent in Form 4868 to the IRS for a tax-return extension. One of the FOIA requests is for the deleted words in a passage that has been bugging me for over a year. In the daily log of phone calls and conversations of CIA director Roscoe Hillenkoetter, there's a moment on May 2, 1950, in which Hillenkoetter answered a question posed by Frank Wisner about ⬜⬜. Hillenkoetter replied that the answer was "⬜⬜." "This has been tried and it works—is very efficacious." Such a tiny thing—but it seemed worth pressing the CIA's secret keepers to find out what Hillenkoetter was talking about. What is very efficacious? Pepto-Bismol, or waterboarding? Weed killer, or LSD? Either it's trivial, in which there is no legal justification for it to be whited out, or it's significant, in which case we'd like to know what it is.

The other request was for the release of a whited-out paragraph in a director's meeting from March 6, 1952. "The document is more than sixty years old and is of historical importance," I wrote. "What did Mr. Wisner say at this meeting?"

When I got home M. said that Notre Dame was burning.

April 16, 2019, Tuesday

I got up at 2:30 A.M. and the dogs woke up and followed me out to the kitchen. When I didn't turn on the lights and didn't feed them, they got bored and returned to the bedroom.

CRYPTONYMS. The CIA's cryptonym for Italy was KMULCER. CABOCHE-1 was the cryptonym for the National Alliance of Russian Solidarists, or NTS, a group of anti-Bolshevik, anti-Semitic extremists who collaborated with the Nazis during World War II. Operation CARCASS, according to memos from 1951 in the CREST database, aimed to train members of CABOCHE-1 to function as "penetration agents," so that they could go on missions in the USSR and create "covert resistance nets." CARCASS was a phase of a larger plan of penetration and subversion sometimes called Project AEROSOL, which was in turn allied with Project REDSOX. Operation SPAIN, also part of Project AEROSOL, sent Russian Solidarists into the Soviet zone of Germany, where they would engage in "dissemination of propaganda, encouragement of defection, organization of resistance, and gathering of intelligence." Some CARCASS,

REDSOX, and AEROSOL documents were declassified and released as a result of the Nazi War Crimes Disclosure Act of 1998—another of Bill Clinton's successful theme-based declassification projects.

Project BGFIEND, the Office of Policy Coordination's effort in KMWAAHOOLAND—that is, Albania—was approved in June 1949. "The Albanian project at this time was the major interest of OPC as a whole and was regarded as the most urgent and sensitive operation being planned at the time by the U.S.," according to a CIA history from 1954, declassified in 2007. It grew out of the CIA's operations against Communist guerrillas during the Greek civil war, and then it expanded, and became, per a 1951 status report also declassified in 2007, "a coordinated program of political, psychological, and economic warfare designed to render Albania useless to the Soviet Union as a base for operations." The goal was total rollback: "Its maximum objective was the overthrow of the Albanian regime." A CIA ship, the *Juanita*, disguised as a marine-biology research vessel, departed for the Mediterranean, aiming to make "black propaganda" radio broadcasts in Albanian—but the *Juanita* had a rough Atlantic crossing and was not put into operation.

BGFIEND involved the dropping of agents, supplies, and propaganda leaflets. Sometimes the leaflet drops were "deceptive," or "diversionary," meant to distract from the dropping of agents, who were supposed to make connections in KMWAAHOOLAND political or military circles. "Leaflets were dropped for cover purposes only," a memo to ⬜⬜⬜ from ⬜⬜⬜ reported on September 10, 1952. This mission included twenty-five thousand copies of a leaflet called "Government of Thieves."

At a BGFIEND base near Munich, Germany, Albanian paramilitarists were subjected to "intense guerrilla training" by CIA trainers. Once trained, they infiltrated—and were often imprisoned or killed. "The apparent ease with which security forces have been able to capture and ambush our teams suggests that we have overestimated our agents' survival capabilities," a CIA report said, with a passing note of regret.

In October 1951, Albanian radio announced the fate of thirteen spies and saboteurs who dropped into the countryside. "All these 13 spies and subversive agents were trained in a special course in an American espionage center in Munich," the Ministry of the Interior said, accurately. "All of them have been killed."

Over time, as with subsequent interventions, the CIA's missions became gradually more assassinational. The terminology becomes less ambiguous even as the cryptonyms proliferate. In February 1952, DYCLAVIER, one of many cryptonyms for Wisner's Office of Policy Coordination—DYCLUCK and DYCLIP are others—received a dispatch regarding BGFIEND operational plans: a mission to sabotage the power station at Vythukes was envisioned, along with one "Coup de Main liquidation mission."

But the real target for liquidation was the entire country of Albania, as Frank Wisner made clear in a memo of June 4, 1952, to his assistant director, Kilbourne Johnston. "From a purely cold-blooded point of view," Wisner wrote, "it might be better for us to concentrate all efforts to further disorganize and hamstring the tottering Albanian economy, thus leaving the Russians with the unhappy alternative of pouring in resources of their own or allowing the fate of a rotting and desperate Albania to appear before all the world as further evidence of what happens to countries and peoples within the Soviet orbit." You may or may not be able to change the regime, but you can definitely ruin the country's economy and leave it to rot.

KOREA, FORMOSA, JAPAN, East Germany, the Ukrainian resistance, Guatemala, infiltrations into China, Iran, France, Albania—all of it was happening at the same time, with a continuous further sporulation of projects and subprojects, and all the operations existed in a parallel universe of cryptonyms and "legends"—false identities. In Guatemala cables Wisner was WHITING, Tracy Barnes was PLAYDON, Guatemalan ambassador John Peurifoy was JMBLUG, Honduran ambassador Whiting Willauer was SKILLET, Richard Bissell was LYNADE, and Bedell Smith was STARKE. ODYOKE was the United States, WSHOOFS was Honduras, KUBARK was CIA, and ODACID was the Department of State. On April 10, 1954, Whiting sent an urgent cable to Skillet, at the request of Starke: "Skillet should not have any further direct contact with local authorities or other non Odyoke individuals with regard to any aspect of Success except pursuant to and within limits of authorization from HQS Odacid and Kubark. Starke very concerned with regard present extent official exposure and considers that this raises serious question desirability continuing operation as previously planned." Even so, the action against the elected leadership of WSBURNT continued.

I DON'T KNOW Kilbourne Johnston's CIA cryptonym, but his real name appears fairly often in the files of the Air Force's BW-CW Division—he seems to have worked for the CIA and the Air Force concurrently. He may be a central figure in the Korean War germ-warfare controversy, or then he may not. He was a war hero—a recipient of the Distinguished Service Cross for extraordinary heroism in World War II—a graduate of West Point, the gravelly-voiced son of Hugh "Iron Pants" Johnson, who ran the National Recovery Administration under Roosevelt. (At some point Kilbourne added a T to his last name.) Bedell Smith installed him under Wisner because Johnston had organizational talent, something Wisner lacked.

Johnston was one of the CIA's experts on unconventional warfare, especially biological and chemical warfare plans against the Soviet Union. He was the source of a CIA report in January 1952 on "the use of cereal rusts as biological warfare agents in the USSR." He was asked to give two-hour presentations at the Air War College on "Soviet Vulnerability to CW-BW," and at high-level indoctrination sessions at the Pentagon on antipersonnel and antianimal weapons, "with special attention to hog cholera."

And here's an odd coincidence. It may mean nothing, but Kilbourne Johnston was in the Far East in the early months of 1952, during the period when North Korean and Chinese villagers were in a panic over all those insects, spiders, and voles that they said were falling from airplanes.

The summary report that someone in Johnston's party wrote about the trip (name blanked), which Johnston made with Lyman Kirkpatrick, might make interesting reading, but it has nine pages denied in full and several long paragraphs whited out.

In May 1952, on his return from his round-the-world tour, Johnston became ill—seriously ill, it seems, because he was still sick in August. Soon afterward, he stopped being assistant director of policy coordination, and he faded from the CIA's available documentary record. He left the Agency and the Air Force, headed a lithography company, Silverlith, and then became a vice president at Champion Paper, in Hamilton, Ohio. He died in 1972 in Santa Cruz. His traveling companion, Lyman Kirkpatrick—future inspector general of the CIA—was also stricken on their trip. Kirkpatrick spent the rest of his life in a wheelchair.

I should ask the CIA to unredact the report that ⬚ wrote about his trip with Johnston and Kirkpatrick to the Far East. Presumably the travelers were briefed on a number of covert operations, including General Li Mi's army of CIA-supported nationalist Chinese troops in Burma. One Asian operation had to do with a penetration plan of some kind: On January 14, 1952, Allen Dulles, at a CIA director's meeting with Wisner and Bedell Smith present, said that "General Ridgway was in accord with our plan for penetration and that Mr. Kirkpatrick and Col. Johnston would be thoroughly briefed on this matter prior to their departure and would talk further with Gen. Ridgway when they saw him." No further details are given. On February 1, 1952, Wisner read aloud a cable he'd received from Kirkpatrick and Johnston at a meeting with Smith. Smith said that it appeared that they were "getting along in this area." What area were they getting along in? Will we ever know? What did Johnston think of the Communist charges of fleas, voles, and mosquitoes?

TODAY A LITTLE GREEN CARD came in the mail—proof of certified-mail delivery of one of my FOIA requests. The CIA had received my request letter on March 28. "L. Moody" signed for it. Progress, in a tiny way. Of course it would be nice if they had assigned me a number. Out of everything I've requested in the past two years, I've only gotten one acknowledgment. After about a year, they sent me an actual document, with big gaps. Later I discovered that the same document had been published in one of the State Department Foreign Relations volumes, years ago, with many fewer deletions.

April 17, 2019, Wednesday

Dreamed I was running for office on a vegetarian ticket, and somebody tricked me into eating some dubious meatballs, which out of politeness, while chewing, I complimented, whereupon my opponent said in a speech that I'd lied about being a vegetarian.

Garbage day today. I was going to go to the Bangor Public Library, because I've been a recluse in the past month and M. told me there's a new coffee shop at the Bangor Public. But when I was driving down Route 2, instead of continuing on to Bangor I turned in at the cemetery. It's one of the finest cemeteries anywhere—an Olmsted sort of design, with hills, but made earlier than Olmsted. There are many ups and downs and the headstones cast long shadows down the hills to which they cling. I found some shade and parked and looked over at a row of men—four men with leaf blowers blowing glittering leaves like tumbling ocean breakers down a slope. They had superpowered leaf blowers, but they were far enough away that it wasn't too loud and I could hear their motors go in and out of phase. So beautiful, the leaves' farewell. I drove closer and took a picture or two. There were actually five men having a wonderful time. Sometimes there were so many leaves in the air that they would completely surround and envelop one or two gravestones.

Life is short enough, and there is a piece of stone at the end of it: we don't need to hurry people in that direction any faster than their own bodies do. A war is just a way of populating graveyards with people who, almost all of them, would have much preferred to live longer—would have preferred another type of government job. The mistake is to convince young men of eighteen or twenty that their selfless, eager, almost puppyish desire to be admired is worth ending their lives for. It's not.

Do something heroic that doesn't get you and a bunch of other people, friends and enemies, killed. And don't pay attention to the old generals who want to coach you to attack and die. They lived, after all. Be a leaf tumbling and leaping around a gravestone. Don't be a gravestone.

I'VE BEEN TELLING YOU about a lot of unpleasant things in this book, and I'm sorry about that. But there's one huge victory that I haven't stressed enough—MuckRock's victory over the Central Intelligence Agency. The principals in the story are Jason Smathers, Emma Best, Michael Morisy, and Kel McClanahan.

It begins with a 2009 article in *Mother Jones* about the CREST database, those millions of pages of digitally scanned and declassified (though often redacted) documents that I've been quoting from practically every day—and that were then accessible to the public only at a cluster of four computer terminals at the National Archives. "Is the agency covering up what it has already uncovered?" asked Bruce Falconer at *Mother Jones*. Falconer sat at one of the terminals (near a sign that said "The CIA will gather and store information about your visit automatically") and looked up *Mother Jones* on CREST, where he found a copy of a piece in the magazine about the CIA's close ties with Bechtel Corporation, which was followed by a note to ⬚⬚⬚⬚ from ⬚⬚⬚⬚ that dismissed *Mother Jones* as a "locally produced scandal sheet published by a dissident group."

The CIA was reluctant to put CREST on the web, Falconer wrote, because the Agency didn't want to risk disclosing sources and methods.

"The fear is that foreign spies, utilizing the so-called 'mosaic principle,' could piece together fragments of information from a wide range of declassified sources to make deductions about ongoing intelligence operations," Falconer explained.

Jason Smathers took the next step. Smathers, big and bearded, is currently a minister in a church that he founded in Casa Grande, Arizona. A long time ago, when he was an IT engineer at AOL, he stole ninety-two million email addresses and sold them to spammers. "I know I've done something very wrong," he said to the judge; he spent a year in a federal prison at Camp Pensacola, where, he told me, he thought hard about the nature of ultimate truth and learned that it was possible to live without material things.

When Smathers got out of jail, he spent many days at a coffee shop doing freelance IT work. There he met a minister who saved his marriage and "shared the gospel" with him. Smathers, converted, went to Golden Gate Baptist Theological Seminary and became a pastor. Along the way, he submitted FOIA requests, hundreds of them, first on his own and then as a member of MuckRock. Some of his requests were fruitful: In 2010, he asked federal agencies for copies of their five oldest FOIA requests. After much prompting and years of waiting, various agencies, including the CIA, sent copies of letters from a long time ago that requested documents from an even longer time ago. Peter Kornbluh, for instance, who works at the National Security Archive, had been waiting for more than ten years for records from the CIA about the Chile Declassification Project, Smathers's FOIA request revealed. So that was a success.

But mostly the CIA found a way to deny him. Smathers, frustrated, came up with something he could ask for that he thought couldn't be rejected: "Complaints received by the CIA about its employee cafeteria(s)." Several months later—practically fiber-optic speed in the world of FOIA— he got actual copies of several emails. "As of late," someone wrote, of a whited-out cafeteria location, "there seems to be a shortage of almonds for the breakfast cereals, such as oatmeal, cream of wheat, etc." Employees at the CIA's Burger King restaurant weren't nice, someone said. The Subway restaurant made a submarine sandwich with stale bread, said someone else. "PLEASE PLEASE . . . do not serve us stale bread." Jon Stewart made a comedy segment out of it on TV.

Then, on July 1, 2011, Smathers wrote another FOIA request letter. "I hereby request the following records: The entire CREST database in electronic format. Do not send paper, I am requesting the computer database or electronic records which make up the records considered to be the CREST system." Smathers said he looked forward to receiving the CIA's response within twenty business days, "as the statute requires."

A month and a half later, he got a rejection: "We have determined that the requested material must be denied on the basis of FOIA exemption (b)(1)." Exemption (b)(1) covers material that is "currently and properly classified." The CIA was saying, in other words, that it couldn't furnish a copy of the already declassified and sanitized material in the CREST database because the material was classified. That didn't make sense. Smathers didn't appeal the rejection, though; he stopped asking for documents from the CIA and moved on to other things.

At MuckRock, Michael Morisy talked over the possibility of a lawsuit against the CIA with a FOIA lawyer, Kel McClanahan. They filed it in June 2014. "The Central Intelligence Agency has a track record of holding itself apart from, and largely above, the Freedom of Information Act, consistently ignoring deadlines, refusing to work with requesters, and capriciously rejecting even routine requests for what should be clearly public information," Morisy wrote on MuckRock's website. "We hope to change that." MuckRock, in its suit, asked for a number of things having to do with the CIA's declassificational methodology—and then, in July 2014, in an amended complaint, Morisy and McClanahan demanded all of CREST in electronic form, just as Jason Smathers had: "As of this writing," wrote Michael Morisy in his FOIA letter, "the only way to access most of the information in the CREST database is to travel to the National Archives and conduct a search on a machine physically located there. Once the CIA releases these records and we post them on the Internet for free public access, anyone will be able to perform searches of these records at their leisure, significantly improving the public's understanding of government activities and operations." Morisy specified that the CIA did not need to reprocess any records—he wasn't asking for further review. "This request is for the records AS THEY APPEAR IN CREST."

Martha Lutz, the CIA's chief of litigation support at CIA, told the court in January 2015 that MuckRock's request for all of CREST was unreasonable and unduly burdensome. Lutz estimated that it would take someone twenty-eight years to review and groom every document in CREST, stripping metadata and double-checking that nothing sensitive survived in the digital files, where it might be found by "hostile adversaries." Her estimate assumed one employee working full time, taking five minutes to inspect each of seven hundred thousand documents—and she added that since the CIA could not assign an employee to work full time on this one project, it would actually "take significantly longer to complete the metadata deletion."

A month later, while Kel McClanahan was working on his legal rebuttal, Lutz filed a supplemental declaration to the judge, announcing that her team had located a full backup of CREST on twelve hundred compact discs, and in light of the "extremely unique" nature of the CREST collection—unique in that all the documents had already been sanitized and declassified and released to the public—the copying project wouldn't take twenty-eight years, it would only take six years. It would still, however, "impose an unreasonable burden on the Agency." And it would cost MuckRock $108,000, prepaid.

"CIA has intentionally decided that it is going to insist on taking the most convoluted, most burdensome, most unnecessarily slow path to filling this request, because it simply doesn't want to process the request at all," Kel McClanahan told Josh Gerstein, a writer at *Politico*. "We plan to demonstrate this to the judge, and we hope to show exactly how unrealistic these baseless assertions are."

As *MuckRock v. CIA* progressed—very slowly—Emma Best, another MuckRock user, announced that they would begin printing out CREST documents one by one at the National Archives. Best would scan the documents, run them through optical character recognition software, and upload them to the Internet Archive. "There are nearly 13 million pages of CIA documents that have never seen the light of day," said Best's Kickstarter page. "It's time to change that." They raised $15,000, bought a high-speed scanner, and drove to Washington several times a week, printing out and scanning thousands of pages. It went well for a while—they uploaded masses of important records—and then things began to go wrong with the CIA's printer. It would run out of toner and not be replenished, or it would need service and nobody would fix it. Best would arrive, ready to go to work, and none of the four CREST terminals would be available.

Meanwhile Jeffrey Scudder entered the picture. Scudder is a tall, bluff, impressive person—a good talker, a believer in covert action, a former head of the Architecture and Systems Engineering staff of the CIA's National Clandestine Service. He spent much of his working life at the CIA, where, beginning in 2010, he got involved in a complicated kerfuffle with the Agency. During a two-year tour at CIA's FOIA office, working with its declassification software—which is called CADRE, for "CIA Automated Declassification and Release Environment"—he got to know and admire the work of the CIA's Historical Collections Division. He discovered that there were a lot of old articles in *Studies in Intelligence* that deserved to be more widely available. (*Studies in Intelligence*, the CIA's in-house journal, was founded by Yale historian and OSS legend Sherman Kent.) The articles had already been digitally scanned, and many were already declassified, but they were inaccessible to the public. After Scudder moved to a different IT job at the CIA, at the Counterintelligence Center, he had an idea—a brilliant and self-destructive idea—which was to submit FOIA requests, as a CIA employee, for the inaccessible, historically interesting articles that he knew were languishing right down the hall.

"I didn't talk to anyone at Historic Collections Division," Scudder told me. "I wanted to make sure, if there was blowback, none of them knew about it. To kind of protect them." His wife said, "I just don't think you should do this." In December 2010, Scudder submitted three FOIA requests, asking for electronic copies of about two thousand articles from *Studies in Intelligence.*

Scudder's FOIA requests, coming from within, were not well received. They set off a chain of dire events: a meeting with counterintelligence officers, a visit and house search from the FBI, bagging and tagging of evidence, and the confiscation of Scudder's computers. (Also his daughter's computer, a Nintendo Game Boy, and his wife's journal.) Eventually, with the help of lawyer Mark Zaid, Scudder was able to clear his name and find a new job at the Department of Commerce. He began to get his life back. Sadly for him, though, he lost his security clearance. He got a crestfallen look when he told me that. (We were sitting in a restaurant in Virginia that Scudder said was a CIA hangout.) If you have a security clearance in Washington you breathe a different atmosphere.

In June 2016 Scudder joined the MuckRock lawsuit. "Staples sells a 1TB portable hard drive for $69.99," he wrote, in a withering court document. "The entire CREST library could be copied to one hard drive for $70." It would be maybe a day's work to reassemble the TIFF image files, he contended, using a simple script. "Any high school student who took an intro to programming course could write this script." The concern about the possibility that "hostile adversaries" might discover lingering metadata in TIFF page images was disingenuous: "It cannot be stressed enough that when documents go through the 'burn' process in CADRE, all metadata is stripped from the file and the final TIFF image is without metadata." The insistence on inspecting every file was a way of ensuring that the whole database-copying process was "slower and costlier," Scudder said. "CIA has introduced inefficient and cumbersome processes to make every FOIA request a laborious process and large requests virtually impossible."

Suddenly one day Emma Best, arriving at the CIA CREST station at the National Archives in College Park to do some more printing, saw a new notice on the computer terminals. "As of 26 January 2017, this CREST kiosk will be decommissioned. All CREST content will be available electronically on the CIA Electronic Reading Room." That was it—the CIA had folded. They didn't say, We're sorry, or, We radically misled the judge about how long it would take. They just splashed everything up on the internet for the world to read. Michael Morisy and MuckRock had won—MuckRock, this small outfit, with its offices in the Old Cambridge

Baptist Church in Cambridge, won over a multibillion-dollar monolith in Langley. Emma Best won, Jason Smathers won, Jeff Scudder won, and Kel McClanahan won. History won. It was massive.

Even so, the CIA congratulated itself in a January press release. "Moving these documents online highlights the CIA's commitment to increasing the accessibility of declassified records to the public," the release said.

I DISCOVERED THE ARRIVAL of CREST on the internet by chance. On February 26, 2017, I was using Google to search for "bacteriological" and "Korea" on the CIA's website, and suddenly there were hits that hadn't been there before—many hits. I also searched Google for:

> "BW" "1952" site:cia.gov

and I got hits. And when I clicked on the links, I saw that I was retrieving new classes of documents—minutes of CIA director's meetings, planning memos, and intercepted enemy field communications, which said SUEDE TOP SECRET, in big letters, on top.

The Suede reports were remarkable. They were transcripts of Chinese or North Korean military radio or field-telephone communications intercepted by the 501st Communications Reconnaissance Group in Korea, and by other listening posts on islands and on the mainland—all of them under the direction of the Army Security Agency, predecessor of the National Security Agency.

On February 26, 1952, the 501st Communications Reconnaissance Group intercepted this message:

> *Chinese unit in Korea reports UN bacteria drop*: An unidentified Chinese Communist unit on 26 February reported that "yesterday it was discovered that in our bivouac area there was a real flood of bacteria and germs from a plane by the enemy. Please supply us immediately with an issue of DDT that we may combat this menace, stop the spread of this plague, and eliminate all bacteria."

This Suede message was turned over to the CIA, whose analyst slanted it thus: "Reports such as this from enemy field units provide the Communists with the 'proof' which they apparently require to support a propaganda campaign. This is the second instance during the current BW scare that a Communist field unit has actually reported the discovery of UN bacteriological agents."

I stared at my screen for a while the first time I read this document. In February 1952, Communist Chinese forces in the field were overheard asking for DDT—meaning they were contending with insects. They wanted help combating a plague. Are we really supposed to think they were engaging in an elaborate ruse? A ruse carried out not at the command level, or at the Chou En-lai level, but at the army field-unit level? Why did the CIA's commenter put "proof" in quotations marks?

HERE'S ANOTHER RAW INTERCEPT, dated February 16, 1952, followed by the CIA's comment:

> *North Korean coastal unit reports UN bacteriological warfare*: "The spies are putting poison into the drinking water" and are distributing "paper" that causes death to anyone "using those papers for the nose," a battalion of the 7th Railroad Security Regiment reported on 16 February. This battalion, stationed somewhere in the Wonsan-Hamhung area, also noted that "Chinese units" captured a downed US pilot northeast of Hamhung. (SUEDE 501st Comm Recon Group Korea, 15 RSM/6456, 16 Feb 52)
>
> *Comment*: Communist messages such as this, accusing the UN of employing Japanese and Chinese Nationalist troops and of engaging in bacteriological and chemical warfare, have frequently forecast a new propaganda outburst of charges of UN atrocities in Korea.

Here are two separate SUEDE reports for February 27, 1952:

> A North Korean battalion commander was ordered on 27 February to take special precautions to avoid contamination of his unit's food and water because "the enemy dropped bacteria" in central Korea.

Covering wells and disinfecting United Nations leaflets were additional recommendations.

Another message from a Chinese Communist artillery regiment reported on 27 February that "we have now fully obtained the vaccine required for smallpox in the spring time, malaria, and bubonic plague." The sender notes that the smallpox and malaria shots have already been given, but queries, "How shall we administer the bubonic plague shots?"

Two more, covering February 28 and February 29, 1952:

The seriousness with which the enemy is treating the charges of BW is evident from a series of 28 and 29 February North Korean messages which contained such instruction as "the contaminated area must be covered with snow and spray . . . do not go near the actual place" and which ordered that "injections with number nine (unidentified) vaccine will be made." Another message stated that "the surgical institute members left here to investigate the bacteria bombs dropped on the 29th.

A Chinese Communist artillery unit was informed on 29 February that "all personnel will be reinoculated at once" with bubonic plague vaccine. Healthy individuals, however, are to take only a half-strength shot or may "temporarily not be inoculated."

Here's an intercept from March 1, 1952:

KOREA. Bacteriological warfare in Korea now major Communist propaganda theme: A North Korean east coast defense unit was alerted on 1 March to hold protest meetings among the troops to intensify "hostile feelings" against alleged bacteriological warfare by the UN forces. The addressee was admonished to "make sure they (the troops) are awake at the lecture."

Almost a full month later, the reports of bacterial drops are still coming in from the field:

Enemy units still reporting BW agents in Korea: An unidentified North Korean regiment notified its battalions on 30 March that "the enemy

is actively dropping bacterial weapons in general now." All units were
to report promptly UN biological warfare attacks.

A Chinese Communist artillery division reported the formation of
a five man "health program" committee "in an attempt to check the
spread of bacteria."

Preventive measures are still being pushed actively in North Korea
as indicated by continuing reports of unit inoculations. One Chinese
Communist unit on 24 March reported, however, that inoculations
had not been made and that a "grave situation" has developed because
"the friendly troops (probably North Koreans) have developed (some
sort of disease?)." (SUEDE 501st Comm Recon Grp Korea, SK-H-
1226, 30 Mar; K-1813, 26 Mar; K-1729, 29 Mar 52)

It may be that later on, lab diagnoses and biological bombings were faked,
but it's hard not to conclude that in these first months of 1952 something
real was going on within Communist army units—that soldiers were
panicked and that they were sometimes getting sick.

April 18, 2019, Thursday

Cold today, all clouded up. Occluded. No blue. I woke up before dawn thinking about major agricultural disasters. Two of them, both possibly man-made. One was the failure of the rice crop in Japan in 1945, and the other was the failure of the durum wheat crop in the United States in 1950. Neither is secret. Both were in the newspapers.

IN APRIL 1945, the crop killers at Camp Detrick had figured out how to use a new sort of bomb, the "SS bomb," filled with plant disease, in order to spread Agent E, which was a malady called brown spot of rice. The SS bomb, or shotgun-shell bomb, was a 10-gauge shotgun shell into which fit an aluminum vial holding about eight ounces of either liquid or powder. One hundred and ten SS bombs fit into one cluster adapter. "Small bombs were desired which would produce a rapidly settling, highly concentrated cloud of 'E' spores," wrote Herbert Tanner in his report on munitions. "Preparations were being made for field tests with actual agents in experimental rice fields, but cessation of hostilities cancelled the experiments." Tanner had himself designed and built a machine that could fill thirty SS-bomb vials of Agent E at a time. "The filling cycle required about 15 seconds, hence the estimated machine production capacity was 7200 vials/hr." The shells, 110 of them, would go into an M16 cluster adapter, usually used for butterfly bombs, which were horrific delayed-action bombs that had two spinning wings. (Americans had copied the butterfly-bomb design from the Nazis, making slight improvements.) Tanner's efforts were going on in parallel with the efforts by others to spray a solution of VKA, vegetable killer acid, from the M10 airplane spray tank.

The idea of destroying Japan's rice crop reached the newspapers by May 1945. "Advocates of bombing the rice paddies point out that the havoc wrought among the peasants would be felt throughout Japan and the morale of the army as well as the people would be severely shakened," said an editorial in the *Rocky Mount Telegram*. In June, syndicated *Washington Post* columnist Ernest Lindley wrote: "Special measures might be taken to reduce the Japanese food supply—such as by bombing the rice paddies and so causing them to drain and by concentrated attacks on the Japanese fishing fleets." A Montana newspaper said, "While the naval blockade is being enforced the bombers will be over Japan in sufficient force to throttle war industry and quite possibly destroy even the Jap rice crop, the principal food of the Japanese people." An editorial in the San Bernardino *Sun* asked: "Is it possible to drop chemicals on Jap rice fields that would destroy the rice crop?"

Around that time Victor Bertrandias made his detailed proposal to Hap Arnold to poison the rice with ammonium thiocyanate in order to "reduce the Japs in the home islands to near-starvation." Then came another suggestion for "giving pain to the Jap," from Claire "Leatherface" Chennault, in a letter sent to bomber commander Curtis LeMay on July 9, 1945. "I have heard the War Department experts are working on the broad principle of my scheme, but I have been mulling it over for a long time, and should like to call it to your personal attention," Chennault wrote. His idea was simple: just spray Japan's rice paddies with diesel oil. "The only agent which I know will kill the rice is ordinary fuel oil," he said. "Only a very small amount is needed per acre." The plants were more delicate, he added, when they were "young and tender." "If the rice crop this year is reduced even by as much as 20 per cent, millions of Japanese will face starvation next winter." Chennault closed by complimenting LeMay on the magnificent job he'd been doing in Japan, using "incendiaries en masse" and flying in at low altitude. "With warm personal regards, I am sincerely, C. L. Chennault."

At the Office of Strategic Services there was a further line of antirice inquiry. Captain Donald Summers, one of the OSS's unconventional warriors, visited plant pathologists in April 1945 at the Department of Agriculture's research center in Beltsville, Maryland, to find out what they knew about "the feasibility of sabotaging Japanese grain supplies by means of bacteria, mold, or fungus." They knew a good deal, as it turned out, and they offered to help in any way they could; W. W. Diehl, who'd consulted at Camp Detrick, claimed that he was the person who had originally had the idea of using fungal diseases on rice crops back in 1942. Summers took notes on brown spot of rice, which attacks seedlings, and rice blast, which causes death, he wrote, "by rotting areas near the neck of the plant causing a breaking over of the plant stalk."

While all of this proposing and testing and evaluating was going on, actual rice fields had been under attack since March 1945 in doomed outlying islands in the Pacific Ocean—the so-called "bypassed islands"— where Japanese troops were stranded and starved while American forces, now in control of all sea traffic, closed in on Japan proper. The *St. Louis Post-Dispatch* described the "crop-dusting" of rice paddies and other food plots. A certain Lieutenant Mabrey Donovan was "flying low to spray diesel fuel over Japanese crops" on the island of Bougainville. The work was "a lot of fun," said Donovan, because there was no antiaircraft fire. "That oil really killed the stuff, or if it didn't, their carrots must have tasted funny." Another newspaper described "sprinkling" rice paddies with oil. "Then they shot tracer bullets into the oil and set it afire."

Trapped on remote islands, the Japanese garrisons were effectively prisoners of war. Toward the end of the war, Christian F. Schilt, commander of Marine flyers on Peleliu island, surmised that (as reported in *The New York Times*) "many Japanese in the northern Palaus must be dying daily of starvation as a result of persistent firebombing attacks of all likely garden plots around their uneasy homes." All food sources, crops, and fishing boats were held to be "legitimate military targets," the *Times* said.

By August 1945, thousands of Japanese soldiers had died of hunger on the bypassed islands. Their death was intentional. "Let them starve to death slowly and painfully," Admiral Bull Halsey had announced to startled newsmen in February 1945.

The destruction of Hiroshima on August 6 and Nagasaki on August 9 should have brought an end to the ravagement of the Japanese nation. But it didn't—ruin had its own momentum. On August 11, the Associated Press reported that its war correspondent, Vern Haugland, had heard that the Twentieth Air Force had further B-29 devastation in mind. "Haugland mentioned another possible weapon not yet used by the Superforts—fuel oil sprayed on rice paddies, to starve out the blockade-strangled enemy." From August 14, 1945, to the morning of August 15, close to a thousand Superfortresses and fighter planes bombed and strafed Japanese targets, "while the world awaited the Emperor's answer to Allied surrender demands." It was a "maximum effort" raid, said the Associated Press. The war ended that day, finally, with unconditional surrender.

AND THEN THE Japanese rice crop failed.

It didn't just fail, it failed disastrously. It was the worst rice harvest since 1909. "As a climax," wrote Jerome Bernard Cohen in 1949, "the 1945 rice crop proved to be a disastrous failure totaling only 6.4 million metric tons. Had the war continued, there would have been starvation in the urban centers of Japan during the winter of 1945–46." In October 1945, said the *Los Angeles Times*, "a leading Jap financier said famine and rice riots are in prospect for this winter because of the poorest rice crop in history."

Why had the rice failed? It wasn't because there was a shortage of laborers to tend the rice—many people had fled the napalmed cities, so there was more labor, not less, in rural areas. Some said it was unseasonable weather, and there was a typhoon in September—but the crops were already failing before September, and there had been many typhoons over the years. Natural misfortunes can't account for so drastic a shortfall.

Hanson Baldwin, *The New York Times*'s military analyst, learned that a shipment of rice-killing agent had been in transit when the Japanese capitulated. "We had dispatched to the Marianas a cargo of biological agents which we intended to use against the rice crop of Japan had the war continued, to cause that crop to rot and thus to add to the starvation blockade of the Japanese," Baldwin wrote in 1950. And Pentagon luminary Robert Lovett, in an oral history, described a program that he recommended called "B and B," or bombing and blockade:

> We had not only the A-bomb to use if we needed it, but we had a new hydrostatic fused mine, and we had a crop destroyer, which we could use in September and October, the rice-growing period in there, and pretty well keep food from coming in from the outside and destroy the food sources inside—keep the fishing fleet inshore, nail them down until they sued for peace. A very logical enterprise, in my opinion, and, as I said, we recommended it.

Captain Summers of the OSS learned early in August that the Joint Chiefs of Staff had at some earlier point approved the use of "plant BW" at the discretion of the theater commander. So they had military approval.

Here's what I believe happened. One or more of the several methods of rice destruction—the diesel fuel method proven to be effective on the bypassed islands, or the vegetable killer acid method, or the shotgun-shell method, or the ammonium thiocyanate method, or rice blast disease (code-named "IR" and studied intensively at a USDA station in Beaumont, Texas, under contract with Camp Detrick)—was surreptitiously employed in Japan, perhaps beginning in April, in the lull between firebombings, while hundreds of American planes roamed Japanese airspace unopposed, looking for things to damage, or after the atomic bombings. The collapse of the rice harvest was overdetermined. The American people wanted it to happen. The only reason Japan didn't starve was that General MacArthur, supreme commander for the Allied powers, was prevailed upon to import a great deal of food in the ensuing months.

After the war, when the rage went away, America's starvation plans for Japan came to seem barbaric and were deemphasized by the Department of Defense. This was "a matter that I asked you to say nothing about," Alden Waitt wrote to a journalist from *Life* who had sent him a draft of a bioweapons article that mentioned one of the 1945 rice-killing plans. Vannevar Bush, MIT's germ warrior, put in a call to the magazine to ask them to tone it down. "Virus rice disease and self-propagating potato blight might prove equally hard to eradicate," *Life* said, vaguely, in the final version, "leaving the victor with the problem of feeding not only himself but the vanquished as well."

RICE IS SO IMPORTANT. One of the Korean War SUEDE intelligence intercepts, from February 22, 1952, says:

> A North Korean message of 22 February—possibly between two rear-area units on the east coast—listed the foodstuffs on hand for three battalions and the number of days the provisions are to last. Each battalion had approximately 11 days supply of rice on hand and a ten-day supply on requisition.

A week and a half later there was talk of "starvation conditions" as a result of germ contamination:

> *North Korean east coast unit claims BW caused hardships*: A North Korean coastal security unit in eastern Korea reported on 3 March that UN bacteriological warfare agents in the surrounding area had prevented the movement of transportation since 21 February. Later in the day the unit reported to Pyongyang that "Pupyong (just southwest of Hamhung) . . . is the contaminated area. According to the correct news, no one can pass through it. If you do not act quickly, the 12th and 13th guard stations will have fallen into starvation conditions."

THE MUELLER REPORT is out today, blackened with redactions. Here it is—the most eagerly awaited legal document to be released in years—and the people are not allowed to read it. "HOM" is on many redactions. "Harm to ongoing matter." The harm to ongoing matter is that people can't be allowed to sully their eyeballs with what the government publishes. Harm to ongoing knowledge!

I'm so damn sick of redaction at this point. The black cape of ignorance drawn over page after page of this pointless inquiry, as it is over decades of activity—whole tranches of text held in abeyance. In order to protect what? An ongoing matter? Here we are in the land of the free—free not to know what people actually said or wrote while in government employ. Free to stare at a devil's checkerboard of blackouts. The garbage bag of ignorance stretched tight over paragraphs and pages of national torment.

I despise the loathsome chickenshittedness of a euphemistic cop-out. HOM! HOM! You are throttling public knowledge! And you call yourself lawyers!

It's time to rage against redaction! Rage against the malign succotash of self-blinkered ignorance!

April 19, 2019, Friday

I've been eating noodles for an hour. *Unredacted*, the blog of the National Security Archive at George Washington University, wrote a post about "dubious secrets" and the Mueller report. "The release of the redacted Mueller report today focuses new public attention on the systemic problem of over-classification and the routine overuse of exemptions to the Freedom of Information Act that are supposed to be reserved for protecting true secrets." They reproduce some examples of redactional inconsistency from their archives. I've been reading them shaking my head.

An upbeat 1975 biographical page on Chilean general Augusto Pinochet, for example, published by the Defense Intelligence Agency, said that Pinochet was intelligent and competent and "widely admired and respected by fellow officers." In 1999, this document was declassified in full. In 2003, however, another declassifier blacked out the laudatory prose on the page—possibly because by then the role of President Nixon and the CIA in ousting Allende and installing Pinochet, a murderous dictator, was embarrassing.

The *Unredacted* blog also reproduces two versions of a 2004 CIA Inspector General's report that includes a page from the Agency's primer on "Enhanced Interrogation Techniques." In 2008, a redacteur blacked out every word on page 15 except the phrase "the waterboard technique." The 2009 version of page 15 lifts the inky curtain, so that we can read that there were several enhanced techniques listed on that page, including the "insult slap," confinement in a small dark box, confinement in a small box with insects, and sleep deprivation, which will, however, "not exceed 11 days at a time."

It's time to understand what this use of redaction does to rationality. It's not always that what is blacked out or whited out is earthshaking, individually considered. There is sometimes another function. If you blank many proper names and sections of many paragraphs, the import of an entire document becomes blurred. What it is actually trying to say, even in summary, is lost. Redaction is a way of muffling the impact of something powerful. Sometimes it works like loud, crackly static.

MUCKROCK'S BLOG, TOO, has something relating to the Mueller report. It's about Attorney General William Barr, who, while he was working as in-house legal counsel for the CIA in May 1976, drafted a letter for director George H. W. Bush to sign. The letter informed Senator Mike Mansfield that the CIA was lifting its moratorium on records destruction, imposed by the Senate Select Committee on Intelligence. The CIA now planned to "destroy records which were collected and maintained by the Agency and which were subject to investigation by the Rockefeller Commission and the Select Committee." The destruction would, he said, be consistent with all applicable laws. "I trust you agree that this action is now necessary and appropriate."

WE NEED SOME SORT OF CIVIL PENALTY for over-redaction. You can get in bad trouble for revealing government secrets—you can go to jail, as Chelsea Manning discovered, and no whistleblower law will help you. But if you keep something secret that ought to be known by blanking it out, there is no penalty. Anyone who hides a paragraph that could have helped us avoid serious mistakes of historical interpretation, or disasters of foreign policy, should be charged with a crime and made, at the very least, to perform some kind of beneficial penitent public work, like ladling soup for refugees from one of the countries that the United States has destabilized in recent decades.

And what about when a person blanks out records permanently and irrevocably, by destroying them? Take Jose Rodriguez, for instance. Rodriguez, former director of the National Clandestine Service—which is what Frank Wisner's creation came to be called—destroyed ninety-two "enhanced interrogation" tapes because, he said, if the tapes got out it would be devastating to the CIA. It would make the Agency "look terrible," he said. Well, the Agency did terrible things, and therefore it must be allowed to look terrible. Rodriguez ought to have been charged with a crime—say, "extreme prejudicial disloyalty to the principles and practices of a working democracy." Or maybe just accessory after the fact?

During Rodriguez's time at the CIA, in 2003, a 9/11 detainee, Gul Rahman, froze to death after one torture session, while chained to the floor semi-naked. In 2007, another detainee, Muhammad Rahim, was subjected to a series of sleep-deprivation sessions. They were unproductive of intelligence. Rodriguez wrote that he didn't think Rahim should be held for another sixty days. "I do not believe the tools in our tool box will allow us to overcome Rahim's resistance techniques," Rodriguez said. Regardless, Rahim's torture continued. "CIA interrogators conducted an eighth sleep deprivation session, lasting 138.5 hours, in November 2007," said a Senate report. Rodriguez was praised for his CIA service, he took a job in the private sector, and in 2012 he wrote a book, *Hard Measures: How Aggressive CIA Actions after 9/11 Saved American Lives*. "I did what needed to be done," Rodriguez wrote about destroying the tapes.

Rodriguez knew all the tools in the toolbox, he allowed the torture to happen, he destroyed the evidence, he kept the secrets. There is a direct line between what Frank Wisner's heedless cocktail-sipping gigglers were doing in the 1950s and what Rodriguez's people were doing in the double-0s.

ONE AGENCY, one hypersecretive root nodule of an aberration of the hopeful human project, has been able to get away with murder for more than sixty years, using denials and redactions and national-security mumblings to control the slow doling out of its own past misdeeds.

"We have been unable to conclude that, on balance, all of the covert action programs undertaken by CIA up to this time have been worth the risk or the great expenditure of manpower, money and other resources involved," wrote Eisenhower's Board of Consultants on Foreign Intelligence Activities in 1961.

Nicholas von Hoffman, who died last year, reviewed Tim Weiner's sharp-cornered, fast-moving, indispensable history of the CIA for *The Observer*. "The organization has a history of having always been more or less out of control, going to excesses and plunging into ill-judged, often imbecilic ventures on its own," von Hoffman wrote. "Running around the world, spinning intrigues, overthrowing governments (or trying to), involving itself in frequently ludicrous adventures has worked out to mean that the Central Intelligence Agency was neither central nor intelligent but has often been an agency of mindless international chaos."

Weiner, quoting Eisenhower, called his book *Legacy of Ashes*. In many countries, though—in Korea, Iran, Guatemala, Syria, and Iraq, for instance—the fires are still burning.

In 2004, former CIA consultant Chalmers Johnson wrote: "I believe the CIA has outlived any Cold War justification it once might have had and should simply be abolished."

April 22, 2019, Monday

Today before I got up I looked down the list of books reissued by Mark Crispin Miller called Forbidden Bookshelf. One of the books is I. F. Stone's classic account of the Korean War, rejected by twenty-eight publishers. And one is by Kati Marton, about the murder of George Polk, a CBS journalist, in 1948. "For over half a century," Miller writes in a foreword to the series, "America's vast literary culture has been disparately policed, and imperceptibly contained, by state and corporate entities well placed and perfectly equipped to wipe out wayward writings." Some books, Miller says, were "vaporized" by threats of litigation. "But it has mainly been the press that stamps out inconvenient books, either by ignoring them, or—most often—laughing them off as 'conspiracy theory,' despite their soundness (or because of it)."

George Polk was shot in the back of the head, bound hand and foot, and dumped in Salonika Bay. His death was blamed on Communists, but Kati Marton argued that the murder was committed by right-wing vigilantes connected to the Greek government—a government that was supported by American military aid and CIA advice. An investigation by William Donovan, founder of the Office of Strategic Services, was a whitewash.

I looked up George Polk in the CREST database and found a letter from 2007 to the National Archives from the CIA's Office of Information Management Services. Someone at the National Archives had written the CIA to ask whatever had happened to nine documents involved in a FOIA request relating to George Polk's murder. Edmund Cohen, chief of information management, replied: "The Agency generally disposes of documents released to FOIA requesters and the associated source documents five years after the Agency's response to the requester." In other words, the FOIA-related copies of the original documents that were denied in connection with the FOIA request were thrown out. No records kept.

Not only that, Cohen said, but the original documents were now lost as well. "Notwithstanding our exhaustive search, we did not locate the nine documents or anything that would otherwise reveal their disposition." Cohen said that the CIA took seriously its record-keeping responsibilities. "It is unfortunate, given our otherwise excellent history of meeting our FOIA obligations and our engagement with the National Archives to make available millions of pages of significant materials on or involving the Central Intelligence Agency, that we are unable to find these nine documents."

There was one other hit for Polk I came across in CREST. The CIA's Office of Legislative Counsel, on March 28, 1978, made a phone call to Representative Sam Hall, a Democrat from Texas, to discuss matters relating to George Polk's murder. A constituent had written Hall that he had seen someone—a "CIA representative"—"kill CBS correspondent George Polk." The CIA lawyer who made the phone call is nameless—his name is redacted—but what he said to Hall's secretary was that "the agency had two FOIA requests in for information on the CBS correspondent and in our efforts to be responsive to these requests, we wished to alert the Congressman so that he could either agree to or deny release of the correspondence"—meaning the letter from the constituent saying that a CIA representative had killed George Polk. The CIA person also said that *60 Minutes* was working on a segment on "the confusion still surrounding George Polk's murder."

What I got from this was that the CIA had some level of discomfort in connection with Polk's murder, and that documents about the incident had been successfully mislaid.

Think about it. *The Agency does not keep a record of what turns up in connection with denied FOIA requests.*

THE CENTRAL INTELLIGENCE AGENCY, understandably, is bent on self-preservation, and self-preservation requires forgetfulness.

"The destruction process is not mindless," Edmund Cohen told Tim Weiner in 1997, in Weiner's *New York Times* piece on the CIA's lost records of the coup in Iran. No, it isn't mindless. It's deliberate. Nick Cullather, who wrote a redaction-spattered in-house history of the Guatemala coup, told Weiner that there was a "culture of destruction" at the CIA. Brian Latell, then head of the CIA's Center for the Study of Intelligence, said that officials in the early 1960s told the keepers of the Iran records that "their safes were too full and they needed to clean them out."

One famous records-destruction moment in the CIA's history came just as Director Richard Helms was leaving the agency in 1963. Helms didn't want the public to know about the mind-melting work of MKULTRA, ever. Someone whose name is whited out wrote, in a CREST database document from January 17, 1975, "Over my stated objections the MKULTRA files were destroyed by order of the DCI (Mr. Helms) shortly before his departure from office." Helms himself told David Frost why he had seven boxes of MKULTRA progress reports destroyed: "It was a conscious decision," Helms said. The CIA had a "fiduciary relationship" with the Americans who had helped the Agency perform the experiments, he believed. "We kept faith with the people who had helped us and I see nothing wrong with that."

Helms also destroyed tapes of his phone calls and tapes of conversations held in his office. "These tapes contained material having to do with foreign policy and US intelligence; they would have been damaging to our foreign policy, if they had gotten into the public domain," Helms said. "I thought that then, I think so now. I would do the same thing today."

The CREST files memorialize other moments when important records were burned or otherwise lost. "On Saturday the 10th of December the undersigned came in to work to assist the Chemical Branch in the destruction of some of their files," wrote ▭ in December 1960, in a document declassified in 2012. "A safe located downstairs was cleaned out and the contents destroyed." The destruction, ordered by Ray Treichler, then chief of the Chemical Branch, was thorough:

> Burning was initiated at 10:45; by 11:45 all 120 pounds were deposited in the burning chamber. At 12:15 the fire was completely out and complete destruction (100%) had been attained. There wasn't even one little uncharred piece remaining for the undersigned to peek at.

After the fires had cooled from the weekend, ▭ came in on Monday to vacuum out the incinerator. "Several coins were found which indicate that some money must have been included in this super secret material."

TODAY AN ENVELOPE came from the CIA, postmarked April 18. It was sealed, as always, with a brown width of string-reinforced tape over the flap. I slit open the top to read two letters from Riggs Monfort, a new information and privacy coordinator. Both letters were dated April 2. It took from April 2 to April 18 for the CIA to mail the letters—Daniel Alcorn, a FOIA lawyer I interviewed in 2017, said this is called "slow walking."

No matter—I'm delighted. I have two actual reference numbers now: EOM-2019-00512 and EOM-2019-00513, one for the intelligence memo on "Foreign Activities in the Field of Biological Warfare"—the one with a number of blanked pages and paragraphs—and one for project 146 of MKULTRA, the one seeking the identity of an internationally respected expert in sugarcane disease. I wonder if it's significant that these were both submitted as Mandatory Declassification Review requests, and not as FOIA requests. Probably not.

NOT ALL OF THE RECORDS destruction is intentional. Some of it is the result of the CIA's enduring fascination with microfilm and novel forms of indexing and retrieval. In the 1950s, the Agency entrusted some of its records to an innovative but, as it turned out, perishable, sometimes eventually illegible, film-based method of information storage. The Intellofax System, which lasted from 1948 to 1967, was accompanied by an elaborate "Intelligence Subject Code," created and refined in close consultation with the CIA's analysts. "The subject code for Plant Pathology (632.4) was subdivided into 68 different codes for wheat, rye, barley, oats, and miscellaneous crop diseases," according to an in-house history—a history, by the way, that has nine full pages blacked out.

In 1972, a CIA staffer opened some cans of stored microfilm. "On opening the metal cans in which the microfilm was contained, we have found the cans to be severely rusted (a sample is enclosed), with rust extending to the metal reels and in some cases flaking onto the microfilm itself," ⬜ wrote. "It indicates to us that the temperature and humidity conditions in Records Center are insufficiently controlled to meet standards for the storage of microfilm." A blanked-out page follows.

In 2001, Paul Wolf, a human rights lawyer, sued the CIA for access to records having to do with the assassination of Colombian politician Jorge Gaitán in 1948. After years of litigation, the Washington, D.C., Court of Appeals said that Wolf was permitted to see thirteen responsive documents from 1948. "It was at this point that the CIA admitted that its 'Post WWII Era Records' are on microfilm, and that their microfilms are indexed by an old IBM-type punch card computer which is no longer operational," Wolf wrote in *Counterpunch* in 2008. "The CIA is demanding $147,000 to find the missing reports." Other relevant CIA records, Wolf said, appeared to be "outside the reach of the Freedom of Information Act."

The assassination itself is a mystery, Wolf contends. "Many Colombians believe that the United States, through its Central Intelligence Agency, orchestrated the murder of Jorge Eliecer Gaitan." Wolf, however, says that there is "really no evidence of US involvement."

Actually there is some evidence. The story is this: In April 1948, Gaitán, a liberal hero, was the leading candidate in the Colombian race for president. He looked as if he might win. Then somebody shot him.

It happened in the middle of an important American-run international banking conference, the Inter-American Conference, attended by Secretary of State George C. Marshall and his CIA-connected aides, Vernon Walters and Marshall Carter. The CIA office in Bogota had heard beforehand that terrorists planned to bomb Secretary Marshall's car as he was driven from the airport, so they were on the alert. Meanwhile Fidel Castro, who was in town, met Jorge Gaitán in his law office and outlined a counterconference of protest he had in mind, to happen while the Inter-American Conference was meeting. Gaitán and Castro arranged to get together again soon.

Before that could happen, a gunman, Juan Roa Sierra, a man who'd previously spent time in a clinic for the insane, shot Gaitán as he was leaving his law office. Police chased the shooter, but as he was being taken away, an enraged mob grabbed him, beat him with shoeshine boxes, and kicked him to death. They dragged his broken corpse to the street in front of the presidential palace.

Grieving citizens dipped their fingers and their handkerchiefs in Gaitán's blood. Looting began. "Armed individuals and bands began looting shops, with determined attacks on hardware shops to obtain weapons, including machetes, iron pipes, guns, etc.," Ambassador Willard Beaulac reported. Leftist voices on the radio, including Castro's, urged the country to march on Bogota in an "organized revolution."

The mob broke into the Capitolio, where the Inter-American Conference had been meeting, breaking furniture and smashing typewriters. "They killed our leader, Gaitán!" they shouted, overturning streetcars and setting them on fire. A bomb was found at the Edificio Americano, where the delegation was staying. It was "an orgy of burning, sacking, and killing," reported Mac R. Johnson of the *New York Herald Tribune*. Johnson watched a government tank crush a protester. "We can still see the body of Gaitan's murderer in the gutter in front of the palace," he wrote. "Police have thrown a tarpaulin over the body, but the feet and hands stick out."

"It was explained," said *The New York Times*, "that Dr. Gaitán was regarded virtually as an idol and that when word of his death circulated the people 'went mad.'"

Edna Pawley and her husband, William Pawley, cofounder of Chennault's Flying Tigers and former ambassador to Brazil, were planning a shopping trip to the Plaza Bolívar when the shooting happened. "Fortunately Secretary Marshall drove by the house for a visit," she said. "Otherwise we would have been in the midst of the rioting." Colombia's president issued a statement on the radio at 8:20 p.m. The conservatives were once again in control of the city, he said. Gaitán had been killed by "a person apparently of Communist affiliation." Then the radio went off again. Rioting continued all night. Ambassador Beaulac said that the "mob remains in control in Bogota." Edna Pawley's cook left and didn't come back. For three days the Pawleys couldn't leave the house. They were reduced, she said, to eating pâté de foie gras and drinking champagne. William Pawley was CIA.

Many years later, an American covert agent and soldier of fortune, Captain John M. Spirito, who'd served in Castro's army in 1959, gave a taped interview in Cuba. Jorge Eliécer Gaitán, Spirito said, had been killed under orders of the American embassy.

Perhaps it was a false confession, forced on Spirito by the Castro government. Or perhaps he was telling the truth. Gaitán's daughter, Gloria, believed he was telling the truth—that the taped interview was evidence of CIA involvement.

The rioting, called El Bogotazo, began an era of instability and violence in Colombia that lasted for decades.

April 23, 2019, Tuesday

I t's wet and cold here. I'm looking at a bowl of tangerines on the kitchen table.

Cedric has injured himself somehow. He limps around, favoring his front right paw, sniffing the wet grass.

THE OTHER DAY I was going to tell you about the mysterious American epidemic of wheat stem rust in 1950, and then I didn't. I think it's worth getting on paper. During World War II, plant scientists H. A. Rodenhiser and J. J. Christensen studied wheat stem rust at Camp Detrick, as a means of reducing enemy food supplies. Rodenhiser was a student of a famous plant pathologist, Elvin "Stak" Stakman, of the University of Minnesota, avid softball player, world traveler, and grandfather of the green revolution.

Professor Stakman had devoted his life to the hybridizing and testing of disease-resistant varieties of wheat, and he had managed an epic barberry-bush eradication program in the 1920s for the Department of Agriculture—barberries being an alternate host and a reservoir for stem-rust fungus. "If you saw a mob of wild-eyed anarchists running amuck with firebrands and destructive intent, what would you do?" Stakman wrote in a 1919 USDA pamphlet. "The common barberry is a red-handed anarchist bush." It must be dug up immediately and burned wherever it is found, Stakman told farmers. "KILL THE BARBERRY NOW." More than 400 million barberry bushes were rooted out by Stakman's diggers in a swath covering eighteen states. (The barberry hedges served as windbreaks—I idly and perhaps unfairly wonder if the dust storms of the 1930s were made worse by the sudden loss of so many miles of dense foliage.)

Stakman also consulted steadily for Camp Detrick throughout his career, and he was an influential behind-the-scenes advocate for its crop-destruction research. "Biological warfare can be horrible," he said in his oral history:

> And yet we've got to think in terms of what our enemies might do. If they do horrible things, I don't think we can be gentle with them either, if we want to survive. I'm not sure that people starving to death or dying of hunger is much worse than having them spattered over about ten square rods of territory in bits so small that you can't pick them up and piece them together again.

In the late 1940s, Stakman, Rodenhiser, Christensen, and Ian Tervet, a Scottish-born plant pathologist who'd been another of Stakman's star students, labored to come up with a standardized, weaponized version of wheat stem rust, scientific name *Puccinia graminis tritici*, code-named TX. Their task was complicated by the fact that wheat stem rust comes in dozens of subvarieties, then called "races." Some races attacked one kind of wheat, some attacked another; some were more virulent, some less. Sometimes the races mingled and mutated, and sometimes they were exceedingly hard to tell apart. In 1935, one stem-rust variant, race 56, had caused what was called the worst wheat-rust epidemic in American history (despite the extirpation by then of millions of barberry bushes): 160 million bushels were lost, about half the national crop. Minnesota and the Dakotas were especially hard hit. Stakman and his fellow scientists outsmarted race 56, however (so they believed): they promoted one of their own wheat crossbreeds, a cultivar called Thatcher, which was race 56 resistant. Then, having witnessed firsthand the extensive harm it could do, they chose race 56 to sprinkle on Russian wheat.

Wheat stem rust, or red rust—so named by the Romans, who celebrated Robigalia in April, a feast and dog sacrifice meant to placate Robigus, the wheat-rust god—forms parasitic pustules on the stalks of growing plants; in the summer the pustules are red, and in the autumn they are black. The disease is carried by infinitesimally tiny wind-borne spores, called uredospores. "A single rust pustule may produce 350,000 spores," according to a USDA report from 1954, "hence the disease can spread very rapidly under favorable conditions." Because the spores are so small and so light, the wind can take them great distances. "They may be carried in short hops, about a state at a time, following the development of the wheat crop," the USDA explained. "Or, they may rise on a high-level wind to 10,000 feet altitude or more, and ride in one nonstop flight from Mexico to Canada. Or they may blanket the wheatfields by both local and nonstop flights."

Stakman and his colleagues had collected spores on airplane flights, miles in the air; all the wheat pathologists knew firsthand how migratory and mobile—how opportunistic—the spores they were working with were. Nonetheless, they inoculated wheat fields in Maryland with disease, and, when the pustules had spread and matured, they harvested the spores, initially by hand, and stored them in glass jars, where the disease had a shelf life of about six months.

After 1948, the National Security Council's plan to destroy the Soviet wheat crop moved up on the priority list, and Detrick needed more spores, pounds of them, not ounces. Ian Tervet and a colleague, Robert C. Cassell, developed a spore-disseminating and harvesting device they called the cyclone, which they used on wheat at Camp Detrick:

> Rust spores can be produced on field-grown plants; several models of field harvesters have been designed, constructed and field tested. The most effective, which is mounted on a trailer, will harvest a six foot swath. A total of over 50 lbs. of rust spores was collected in the field this season, with an average yield for combined harvests of about 25 lbs. per acre.

One Air Force lecturer described the cyclone harvester as "a complicated vacuum cleaner on wheels."

The cyclone was risky, though. The mass production of wheat disease had never been tried before. "Precautions against contamination must be observed," advises a 1984 textbook on the artificial cultivation of *Puccinia graminis*—and yet, in Detrick's farms, or antifarms, scientists incautiously cycloned clouds of stem rust in open-air wheat plots. Contamination was inevitable. Greenhouse space was "critically inadequate," said a 1949 progress report; the antiplant scientists needed more acreage of wheat to infect than Detrick's sealed greenhouses could accommodate. "In 1949, Detrick worked on developing the best methods for harvesting plant agents and intentionally infected cereal plants with rusts on several moderate size fields," according to a later Army report. The tests included explosive prototype munitions; there were "experiments using shotgun shells and 20 mm projectiles in 1948 and 1950 to disperse a cereal grain rust (wheat stem rust)."

The phytopathologists took some precautions to avoid causing local outbreaks, says this Army report, "planting infected crops later in the season, after plants in the community passed the point of infection (i.e., growing a spring-type cereal crop in areas where winter-type versions of those crops are grown)."

But in 1949 and 1950, something went wrong. Or so I think. Perhaps Ian Tervet's cyclone spore harvester harvested and then disseminated the wrong spores, or the shotgun shelling of wheat fields included contaminants, or the feather bombing of oat fields in Upstate New York included wheat rust spores as well—or maybe Tervet loaned one of his new cyclone machines to Stakman and his students at the University of Minnesota for field-testing. Somehow or other a formerly untroublesome race of stem rust, race 15B, began growing pustules on wheat plants on hundreds of midwestern farms. Nobody could explain its sudden appearance. "Two races of stem rust, never before important in the Midwest, today threaten Minnesota's entire wheat and oats acreage," said the *St. Cloud Times* on September 5, 1950. "The races—race 15B of wheat and race 7 of oats—were found in abundance in the area for the first time this year by E. C.

Stakman, chief of the division of plant pathology of the University of Minnesota." Eventually the epidemic—or "epiphytotic," as plant-based epidemics are called—reached twelve states. "Race 15B, which had lurked among the barberries for eleven years, was on a rampage," said a USDA pamphlet. Race 15B "astounded everyone," wrote Stakman and Rodenhiser some years later, in a volume edited by former Detrick crop spoiler Geoffrey Norman. "All of a sudden it was everywhere," wrote green revolutionist Norman Borlaug. "How it spread so rapidly no one knows." (Borlaug was another student of Stakman's.) "Durum wheat, used for making spaghetti, was hardest hit," said *Time* magazine, "with 10 million bushels lost."

Stakman got in touch with spore cyclonist Ian Tervet at Camp Detrick to try to find out what was going on. "It was too dangerous in 1951 to use race 15B for artificial field inoculations in the continental U.S.," explained a University of Minnesota newsletter called *Aurora Sporealis* years later. "Stakman went to I. Tervet (a former faculty member) who was with the Biological Warfare (BW) unit of the US Army and encouraged him to do the needed testing. The first nursery was grown at an army base in Puerto Rico and inoculated with the U.S. race 15B. This nursery was confidential so little is known about it, however, since Stakman had security clearance as an advisor to the BW unit, it seems likely he had a big hand in it. Out of this effort the Puerto Rican Rust Nursery program grew."

The epiphytotic carried on in 1952 and 1953. "It caused disastrous epidemics for four successive years between 1951 and 1954," wrote Norman Borlaug. In 1954 a quarter of the bread wheat and three quarters of the pasta wheat were destroyed in the United States.

Perhaps this was a natural phenomenon. I don't think so, though. One 1952 Air Force report reveals that U.S. government spore ranchers were busy blighting fields of wheat in South Dakota, Idaho, Montana, Puerto Rico, and "three locations in Wisconsin." "The spores migrate like wild birds," a USDA spokesman told *Time*. "Like balloons," said the Minnesota Agricultural Experiment Station, "they are so light that they are at the mercy of every current." This was blowback, literally. Project Steelyard was aimed, Air Force documents said, at the Russian "bread basket." But it looks as if the first actual victims of the anti-Communist anticrop program were the farmers of the United States.

I HEARD FROM Steve Endicott's daughter. Steve's been in terrible pain for several years, and recently he fell and crushed something in his already injured back.

MAYBE IT DOESN'T MATTER whether the race 15B disaster was natural or man-made—its effect on Camp Detrick was to spur the crop killers on to further research. The intensity and wide extent of the infection in the United States was proof of concept. In June 1953, H. A. Rodenhiser told someone from the Air Force's Biological and Chemical Warfare Division that the Research and Development Board wanted more wheat disease: "On the recommendation of the Crops Panel of the RDB, TX races 56, 17, and 38 are now being 'stockpiled.'" But not race 189, found in China and South America; race 189 was so virulent that "it would be undesirable offensively because of the possibility of contaminating crops of allied nations."

From 1952 to 1957 an Army worker named Tom West cultivated quantities of wheat disease on plots the size of football fields at an unused military airfield in Boca Raton, Florida—now the site of the Boca Raton Airport. West and other farmers sucked the spores off the plants with vacuum cleaners, packed them in vessels that looked like pressure-cooker pots, and sent them off to be mixed with feathers. In 2002, West told Eliot Kleinberg of *The Palm Beach Post* that he had no idea what part of the Soviet Union would be feather-bombed, but he thought the strategy of undermining Soviet leadership by starving the citizenry was a "feasible, good plan." "When you're starving, you can't fight too well," West said.

The antiwheat research, paid for and planned and pushed by the CIA, and approved of, or at least tolerated by, four presidents, continued into the 1960s. In 1963, the Air Force flight-tested the A/B 45Y-4 anticrop "dry disseminator" for high-speed planes. Also in 1963, according to a special-weapons list in the National Security Archive, "a massive cloud of wheat rust spores 'disappeared' because of climatic conditions and/or a mistake in dissemination." For six years, from 1960 to 1965, a team of Detrick employees intentionally infected several acres of wheat in Hays, Kansas (home of a wheat research and improvement station), with race 56 of stem rust. They charted the number of pustules per culm, studied the best times to introduce spores, and compared the yield of diseased wheat with a nearby control field that they'd sprayed with fungicide. Damage was severe almost every year, but especially in 1965: "Yield was reduced from 62 bushels per acre in the control area to 18 bushels per acre in the rusted area." The scientists don't seem disconcerted by the implications of their next sentence: "In this same year, 1965, a natural epidemic of stem rust severely damaged wheat in much of Kansas and Nebraska." They stopped the experiment after that. Was the epidemic natural? What is natural? If all of Kansas and surrounding states are turned into a plein air crop disease laboratory, what can "natural" possibly mean?

In October 1967, Ray Treichler, chief of the Biological Branch of the CIA's Technical Services Division, listed some of the accomplishments of MKNAOMI, the Agency's germ-war research initiative, carried on in collaboration with Detrick's Special Operations Division. There was, Treichler wrote, the development of the silent microbioinoculator. Also the experimental attack on a subway system. And the building up of a germ stockpile for CIA use composed of fifteen different biological agents and poisons, some of which were being further upgraded to achieve "improved stability and resistance to antibiotics." And then, finally, there was the design of "anticrop dissemination kits," Treichler said. "Three methods and systems for carrying out a covert attack against crops and causing severe crop loss have been developed and evaluated under field conditions."

Dr. Treichler doesn't specify what those three covert methods were, but in 1999 one of Fort Detrick's retired anticrop scientists set secrecy aside while talking to *Philadelphia Inquirer* reporter Steve Goldstein. The scientist was Charles "King" Kingsolver, former saxophonist and leader of a regional swing band; he had arrived at Camp Detrick in 1951 wearing a tie with a feather pattern that disconcerted his interviewer, and he had worked on the six-year wheat-stem-rust study in Kansas in the 1960s. The three methods of destroying the Russian wheat crop, according to Kingsolver, were (1) the feather bomb, (2) the balloon bomb, and (3) the spray tank mounted on a fighter plane. "When I came to Detrick, the feather bomb was already considered *the* weapon," he said.

April 24, 2019, Wednesday

I'm up. I've been reading my notes for an hour, looking for answers. The world: asleep. History: asleep. Knowledge: partial, fallible.

I'm pushing myself past what I can do. My mind can't hold, all at the same time, so many countries, so many diseases, so many bombs and cluster adapters. Lieutenants, majors, captains, generals, brigadier generals, temporary colonels. Whiskey colonels. The pathology of military rank. And medals. So many medals. Kay Summersby, I think it was, Eisenhower's chauffeur and mistress, remembered when General Eisenhower was given a medal by a foreign government—the grand cross of the order of the etcetera. Eisenhower said something like, "Kay, I need this like a hole in the head." What Eisenhower liked to do was to smoke and golf and read cowboy novels. And play poker. It's funny that one of the few things that Harry Truman and Eisenhower had in common was that they took joy in poker.

They both understood the idea of bluffing. Faking it. Lying. Eisenhower built on the covert machinery that Truman had okayed. Yes, do it, Truman told Bedell Smith. Do the crazy underhanded things. Sneak into Tibet and set up a little spy station. Infiltrate, arm, bombard with radio propaganda. Truman once wrote out a blanket pardon letter, when Smith was worried. Truman and Eisenhower were both ambulatory expressions of a national paranoia. Allen Dulles would cajole and wheedle and pipe-puff until Eisenhower said yes to some further CIA inanity—more guns and money to Tibetan "resistance fighters," for instance, or another risky U2 flight over Russia. When, in May 1960, the Soviets shot down one of the presidentially preapproved CIA spy flights, Eisenhower instructed NASA and the State Department to issue disinformational statements, prepared with CIA help, alleging that the U2 spy plane was engaged in nonmilitary research into "gust-meteorological conditions at high altitude," and that it had accidentally drifted off course after the plane's oxygen equipment malfunctioned, causing the pilot to lose consciousness. "Our assumption is that the man blacked out," said a State Department spokesman. "There was absolutely no—N-O—deliberate attempt to violate Soviet air space." NASA, covering for the CIA, distributed a fake flight plan, published as a map in *The New York Times*, showing the mission's blameless crisscrossings of Turkish air space in quest of weather data.

In the Kremlin, Premier Khrushchev then announced to the world that the downed pilot, Frances Gary Powers, was alive and healthy, and he read extracts from Powers's confession. Powers said, according to Khrushchev, that he worked for the Central Intelligence Agency, and that, after taking off from Peshawar, Pakistan, he had intentionally flown thousands of miles over Russia to take photographs of industrial and military installations. All of which was true. Khrushchev, growing animated, flourished prints of reconnaissance photographs taken during the flight; a week later, denouncing America's "provocative actions," he abruptly ended a planned rapprochement and four-power summit in Paris. "IKE, NIKITA CLASH; SUMMIT COLLAPSES," was the headline in the *Nashville Banner*. "PESSIMISM GROWS," said *The New York Times*. As a result of the CIA's adventurism, the Cold War darkened and lengthened, and President Eisenhower was left "hopelessly impaled on a lie," as David Wise wrote in *The Politics of Lying*. "I didn't realize how high a price we were going to have to pay for that lie," Eisenhower told a reporter in 1962. "If I had to do it all over again, we would have kept our mouths shut."

———————

IT'S NOW ONE MINUTE before five o'clock in the morning. I'm worried that the dogs will wake up and want to jump down off the bed onto the floor. I don't want Cedric to jump because jumping will further injure his paw or shoulder. Last night I built a step at the foot of the bed, using a box over which I draped an old rug.

M. came into the kitchen wearing a flowery shirt. Her hair was wet from her shower. She looked down at both dogs, smiling. "This one's blinking his shiny eyes at me," she said.

IN JULY 1949, Alden Waitt, head of the Chemical Corps, was testifying at a hearing before the House Armed Services Committee. Camp Detrick needed money for a new aerobiology building, and money for better ways of handling infected large animals. Sewage was also a problem. "Existing decontamination facilities are inadequate and construction of new additional facilities are essential," according to Waitt's budget document. (General Waitt, who had recently installed a fancy bathroom and kitchenette in his office, was soon to be fired for influence peddling.) Detrick's sewage was unique, Waitt's document explained, because it was "extremely virulent." "Operation of the existing facilities at over capacity is a definite safety hazard."

Also urgently needed, Waitt believed, was a pilot plant for "crop studies." The context was too secret to discuss in open hearings, but "the crops under study must be isolated from one another and must be carefully controlled to prevent all possibility of the escape of infectious diseases of crops."

Representative Sterling Cole of New York said, "May I inquire, What is a pilot plant for crop studies?"

General Waitt answered, "One of the agents that we are interested in is an agent"—and then he stopped. "We are getting into very classified material," he said. "May I talk to you off the record?"

The words "wheat" or "stem rust" or "Russia" were not said in this open hearing. Waitt did not tell the congressmen that virulent, far-floating crop-disease spores were being harvested from open-air fields using experimental high-volume harvesting machines. Nobody mentioned that there were indications that very year of a growing American stem-rust epidemic involving the durum wheat crop. There was only Waitt's request for a pilot plant, and that phrase about the possible "escape of infectious diseases of crops."

THE FIRST PEOPLE WHO SUFFER from a weapon are the people who develop it and test it.

The history of Detrick is a history of self-infection, suicide, and animal sadism.

In 1948, five staffers at Detrick got sick with rabbit fever, and fifteen came down with brucellosis. In 1949, five more got rabbit fever. Ten got brucellosis. A sewage-plant decontaminationist got cutaneous anthrax. Nobody died, but some were very sick. "This amount of tularemia and brucellosis shows that this installation is far from ready to handle more infectious agents or agents which produce more severe infections in man," wrote Detrick's head of safety, Arnold Wedum. "During the past year several persons have contracted chronic illnesses which may persist for many years."

There were two laboratory machines that caused problems. One was the centrifuge—"it was found that each step in the preparation of concentrated cultures by means of centrifugation produced aerosols"—and one was the Waring blender. "Investigation into the hazards associated with the Waring blender revealed that the blender leaks around the bottom bearing," Wedum wrote. "When the blender is used to cut up highly infectious tissue, the aerosol, and leakage from around the rapidly rotating drive shaft, become very dangerous to the operator." Both these machines rely on spinning motions to achieve their laboratorial end—which is one reason why I'm also suspicious of the cyclone spore harvester.

In October 1950, Harold Isbell, commander of Camp Detrick, gave an upbeat talk at the Francis Scott Key Hotel in Frederick, Maryland, for the local Kiwanis Club. Five hundred local people were employed at the installation, and new construction was in the works, Isbell said; Detrick's research product was a "big stick" on the international stage. "We're doing a job not only for the United States but for the entire world." A month later Isbell was found dead in his car in a remote part of the base. His hand held a gun, and he'd been shot through the head.

The year 1951 was a bad year for safety. Forty-four people got sick, and thirty-six ended up in the hospital. One microbiologist, William Boyles, died "during study of the foaming process involving B anthracis," wrote Wedum in one of his safety reports. The Army didn't tell Boyles's wife that he was an anthrax victim. "Death was due to acute bronchial pneumonia after a very short illness," reported the Frederick *News*, incorrectly.

The foaming method of spore concentration led to a general, buildingwide contamination: anthrax was found in the main hallway, on raincoats worn in the building, on tool cabinets, on the instrument control panel, on shoes, and on the foot pedal of the drinking fountain.

Also in 1951, Arvo Thompson, one of the interrogators who'd coaxed germ-warfare secrets from Japanese scientists, shot himself in the forehead in a hotel room in Tokyo.

"Several Virus Pilot Plant operations are fundamentally unsafe," Wedum believed. "Infections occur with monotonous regularity."

In 1964, Albert Nickel, a veterinary worker, was bitten by an animal and got sick. His doctor told him to take aspirin, but he didn't get better. "I watched him die through a little window to his quarantine room at the Detrick infirmary," said Gladys Nickel, his widow. "When I asked officials why he died, they told me they didn't know, but would tell me when they found out." The officials never told her. Nickel died of machupo virus, also known as Bolivian hemorrhagic fever.

"The aquifer underneath the Fort Detrick Area B Ground Water site is among the most contaminated aquifers in the nation," wrote the EPA in April 2009.

April 25, 2019, Thursday

One of the first things that struck me, reading Ned and Steve's book, was that they found a document, produced by the Joint Chiefs of Staff, called a "BW Cover and Deception Plan." Turns out that "cover and deception plan" is a stock phrase in intelligence. Sometimes they shorten it to "C&D." The Trojan Horse is probably the best-known cover and deception plan in history. Operation Overlord, the Allied attack on France in World War II, was attended by several cover and deception plans, including the diversionary bombing of places that didn't need to be bombed, and the dropping of three-foot-high, self-immolating, straw-stuffed parachutist dummies over parts of Normandy where real paratroopers weren't going to land.

There were cover and deception plans for Iran and Guatemala—many, in fact. "The importance of cloaking the U.S. hand in PBSUCCESS needs no particular emphasis for it is self-evident," said a memo from "Jerome C. Dunbar" (a cover name) in May 1954. One Guatemalan deception plan, Operation Washtub, was the hiding of a fake Communist cache of arms and ammunition that was then "discovered" by Nicaraguan president

Somoza, who was photographed peering through a magnifying glass at a gun decorated with a hammer-and-sickle seal. (It was a "very serious business," Somoza told reporters.) Another ongoing deception involved the location of the revolutionary radio station Radio Liberación. Supposedly it was operated on a shoestring by hardy freedom fighters in the Guatemalan jungle, when actually it was an American-run outfit transmitting from outside the country, using scripts written in the United States. (Radio Liberacion announcers excoriated the "red octopus" and read lists over the air of Communist leaders—"traitors whom we should kill"—and there was energetic song singing, sometimes about the assassination of President Arbenz: "Like a coward, you killed by iron, and by iron you will die. They're going to kill you like a dog, and the very day will arrive.") "From the first day of broadcasting, the claim was incessantly reiterated that the station was within Guatemala," David Atlee Phillips, chief propagandist, wrote in a CIA debriefing. "It was the Big Lie."

So the cover and deception plan for biological warfare was some sort of organized, agreed-upon set of lies and tricks and half-truths meant to lead a target group to believe one thing had happened in the realm of biological warfare, when, in fact, something else had happened. But what, specifically, was the plan?

THE BASIC PROBLEM IN WRITING about the "BW Cover and Deception Plan," code-named Plan CLASSROOM—approved by the gathered admirals and generals of the Joint Chiefs of Staff on September 8, 1948, during the Berlin blockade, and then amended by the Joint Chiefs of Staff on September 28, 1949, shortly after the Soviet Union first exploded an atomic bomb—is that the copy of it that Ned Hagerman and Steve Endicott finally managed to extract from the U.S. government was so heavily blacked out that it isn't easy to figure out what's going on.

The only way to know that JCS 1927/3—which is the number of this Joint Chiefs of Staff document—had to do with three very different cover and deception plans proposed by the Joint Strategic Plans Committee of the JCS, one of which involved biological warfare, is by cross-referencing it with other, differently redacted documents. By doing that, we learn that:

THE EMPLOYMENT OF ⬚IN SUPPORT
OF U.S. MILITARY POSITION AND POLICY

actually reads

THE EMPLOYMENT OF COVER AND DECEPTION IN SUPPORT
OF U.S. MILITARY POSITION AND POLICY

The three plans, Plan A, Plan B, and Plan C, were presented orally (not on paper, so secret were they), to James Forrestal, the secretary of defense, who approved them. They were also presented to Secretary of State George C. Marshall. Marshall wasn't sure what to do and deferred action. Everyone then decided to hold the plans in abeyance, except for Plan B: "Authority was granted to continue initial preparations with respect to the plan in Annex 'B' to Appendix 'B' to J.C.S. 1927, in order to permit ready implementation when directed."

Plan A, code-named THUMBTACK, was a scheme of some kind, possibly first pushed by Frank Wisner (who was reportedly in favor of a commando raid on Berlin), to "indicate firmness" in the face of the Berlin blockade of 1948. Plan C, called BOYHOOD, I know nothing about.

Plan B, CLASSROOM, is the one that has to do with germs, or the exaggerated threat of germs, and a plan to render Russian scientific research "unproductive and wasteful in nature." "This plan is still applicable," wrote the Joint Strategic Plans Committee. "It requires only minor changes in wording and form." Plan Classroom was approved by Forrestal, but then Forrestal killed himself. Eventually it was resubmitted to the new secretary of defense, Louis Johnson, a temperamental lawyer who had raised a lot of money for Harry Truman's campaign. The memo describing Plan Classroom was unusually important, marked: "To be hand-carried by the Chairman of the Joint Chiefs of Staff."

Let's flip to the plan itself, in the appendix. Here are the first two pages.

A P P E N D I X

)SP(b)(1)(a)(1) JOINT ███████████ PLAN
███████ THE USSR IN THE ███████
Short title: CLASSROOM*

I. GENERAL SITUATION

1. In the present critical world situation the United States is attempting to maintain a favorable capability for employing ████████████████████████ This favorable capability can be maintained by:

D (1)(a)(1)   a. Building up the ████████████ of the United States.

   b. ████████████████████ of the USSR to improve ████████

   c. A combination of a and b above.

2. The Department of Defense is currently undertaking measures which are designed to build up ████████████ of the United States. The extent of such a build-up is dependent upon and limited by amounts allotted for this purpose in the U.S. military budget.

3. No significant effort is now being made by the Department of Defense or other U.S. agency to exploit the possibilities of maintaining a favorable ████████████ by the economical method of systematically ████████████████████████ ████████ of the USSR. Particularly profitable opportunities are being passed up in the field of scientific research and development.

4. One feasible way to maintain U.S. ████████████ is to ████████ the USSR, ████████████████████ ████ which will tend to ████████████ the Soviet scientific ████████

Sd(b)(1)(a)(1) 5. The Chairman of Committee ████ of the Research and

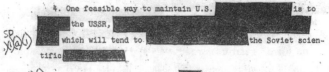

* Code name will be eliminated when plan is submitted to the Secretaries of Defense and State.

Development Board has examined the possibility of preparing ████████ ████ which, ██████████████ would ████████████ and result ██████

6. As a result of this examination, the Chairman of Committee ██ has prepared an informal report on the use of _____ * ████████████████████ This report indicates U.S. development of methods of producing ████████████████████████████████████ ██

7. The Chairman of Committee ████ believes that the material presented in this report will stand scientific scrutiny even though, ██████████████████████████████████████ ██

8. The Chairman of Committee ████ further believes, from a scientific standpoint, that the material in his report ████████ ████████████████ scientific potential ████████████

9. The existing security in the ████████ is considered adequate to forestall ████████████████████████████████ ██████

II. MISSION

10. To cause the USSR ██████████████████████████ the USSR ████████████████████████████ and ████████████████████ in order to maintain a favorable balance of ████ with respect to the USSR.

* Omitted for security reasons

Joint Chiefs of Staff, Appendix to JCS 1927/3, JCS Subject Series Papers, RG 319, entry 33, box 311.

There is no way, looking at these pages, so thoroughly are they redacted, that anyone would know that they're about deception, nuclear weapons, or biological warfare. But they are. The official title of Plan Classroom, as revealed in a different record series in the National Archives—in folder 93 of box 6 of the "cover and deception" folders of the Army's assistant chief of staff of operations, stamped in red "HANDLE AS EYES ONLY"—is given as "Cover and Deception Plan to Misguide and Waste Scientific Effort of USSR in Biological Warfare Field." Plugging those words into the blacked-out areas of the title shows that, with the addition of the word "the," they do indeed fit:

JOINT COVER AND DECEPTION PLAN TO MISGUIDE
AND WASTE SCIENTIFIC
EFFORT OF THE USSR IN THE BIOLOGICAL WARFARE FIELD.
Short Title: CLASSROOM

I'll try to loosely paraphrase what the document might actually say, despite the redactions, because what it says is important to the history of the biological arms race. (My Mandatory Declassification Review request for this document, submitted two years ago, has produced nothing except a reference number from David Fort at the National Archives; paraphrasing and guessing is all I can do at this point.) Guesses are in bold. They're approximate—I haven't tried to fit words exactly into the typewritten spaces.

The document says that the United States, in the current critical world situation, is attempting to maintain a favorable capability for employing **atomic weapons**. This capability can be maintained one of two ways, either by building up the **atomic stocks** of the United States, or by **reducing the nuclear weapons stocks** of the USSR, in order to improve **our relative strength**.

Currently the Department of Defense is building up its **atomic stockpile**. This is expensive.

What the United States is not doing, however, is exploiting the possibility of maintaining a favorable **nuclear balance** by the cheaper method of systematically **causing the Kremlin to squander the resources**

and industrial potential of the USSR. Opportunities in scientific research and development are being passed up.

One way to maintain U.S. **nuclear leadership** is to **convince** the USSR, **using exaggerated claims of BW advances, that they must keep up,** which will tend to **misguide and waste** the Soviet scientific **nuclear effort.**

That's the best I can do.

Page 2 is so heavily redacted that it's not possible to paraphrase redactions with any hope of accuracy. But the general idea seems to be that the Biological Warfare Committee of the Research and Development Board has studied the possibility of coming up with some plausible-sounding but exaggerated research results in the field of biological warfare. These (untrue, or only half-true, but credible) reports of novel weapons systems will create a state of deep concern in Soviet circles and cause directors of scientific research to redirect their funding away from nuclear weapons and toward biological weapons. Page 3 continues with more specifics of the plan, but with almost everything blacked out. A footnote says, "Details as to ⌐⎯⎯⎯⎯⎯⌐ are omitted for security reasons."

My guesswork is helped (slightly) by two other documents, both also heavily blacked out. I found them in Washington just a few weeks ago, in the HREX files. One is a letter from Frank Wisner to Colonel Ivan Yeaton, a former military attaché who advised the Joint Chiefs of Staff. Wisner is announcing to Yeaton that he's setting up a scientific steering committee to advise on means of ⌐⎯⎯⎯⎯⎯⎯⎯⎯⎯⎯⎯⌐.

This objective will be accomplished in two ways, namely: (a) ⌐⎯⎯⌐. And (b) ⌐⎯⎯⎯⌐.

That's not terribly helpful, but the document that follows—a set of minutes for the first-ever meeting of the Scientific Steering Committee of the Office of Policy Coordination—sheds some light. Eight people were there, one "Col.," three "Dr.'s, and four "Mr.'s. All names are blacked out except for Frank Wisner's. And yet today I noticed (zooming in on my phone's screen) that the redacteur didn't do a perfect job in felt-tipping out three names on the third page. The names hidden behind some of the blackouts were Dr. Bush, Dr. Compton, and Col. Black.

So it was a high-powered meeting: Vannevar Bush, the Department of Defense's chief scientist, head of the Joint Research and Development Board, napalmist, atomic concocter, envisioner of the all-knowing Memex microfilm retrieval system, avid fly fisherman, anti-Kremlinist, carver of pipes. And Karl Compton, former president of MIT, atomic administrator, ardent campaigner for universal military training, who'd debriefed the Japanese germ scientists just after the war. And (possibly) Col. Edwin F. Black, of the Joint Research and Development Board. The three of them were there with the others in order to discuss the kinds of underhanded psychologically tricky things that Frank Wisner's new organization was charged with doing.

The meeting convened at one in the afternoon on September 30, 1949, over lunch at the Statler Hotel in Washington. Wisner began by describing the history and the activities of the Office of Policy Coordination. Then they took up the troubling news: the Russians now had the atomic bomb. The Americans had been off in their timetable. They'd thought they had more months or even years. "At this point, after a brief discussion of the means and degree of certainty of the results, the subject changed to a method of ⸏⸏⸏⸏⸏⸏⸏⸏⸏⸏⸏⸏⸏⸏⸏⸏."

What the committee discussed seems to be related to the deception plan that had just been approved by the Joint Chiefs of Staff: "Although it was the opinion of Drs. Bush, ⸏⸏⸏⸏, and ⸏⸏⸏⸏⸏⸏ that ⸏⸏⸏⸏⸏⸏⸏⸏ were unreliable, it was felt that we might highlight our work in ⸏⸏⸏⸏⸏⸏ field as a means of confusing the Russians." Which, partly unredacted, could possibly read something like "Although it was the opinion of Drs. Bush, ⸏⸏⸏⸏, and ⸏⸏⸏⸏ that **toxic weapons** [or maybe **BW/CW weapons** or **CEBAR weapons** or **CBR munitions**?] were unreliable, it was felt that we might highlight our work in **this novel** field as a means of confusing the Russians." At the meeting, one of the scientists called what they were proposing a "false trail approach." Another scientist thought that magazine articles might be arranged that could help spread misinformation. Everyone seemed to think that the false-trail approach was a good idea.

I wonder now if Dr. Haskins was one of the blacked-out names.

After the false-trail discussion, the steering-committee members went on to weigh the possibility of arranging for some "⸏⸏⸏⸏⸏⸏⸏⸏⸏"—some spurious, forged documents or fragments of weaponry, perhaps—to "fall into the hands of curious people in areas adjacent to Russia, such as Azerbaijan and Iran. These could be made to look old and could be purposely damaged." Five blacked-out lines follow this bit of potential deception.

Meeting over. So much work for the redacteur to have scribbled over all those names and all of the actual substance of the meeting—and then he or she did not do quite enough scribbling on page 3.

If I'm right about what's going on behind the redactions, the deception plan involved trying to convince the Russian government that the United States was in the middle of developing a new kind of biological weapon, or combination of weapons—a worrisome hybrid superweapon. This would cause them to send scientists down a false trail of research, allowing the United States' scientists to stay ahead.

My guesses could be wrong—and it's easy to find out if I'm wrong. Just fully declassify JCS 1927/3, Plan Classroom, and related documents. No more guesswork about something this important.

THERE'S EVIDENCE IN THE PRESS that the deception plan was carried out, and that Dr. Compton, chairman of MIT, lent his name to it. On October 6, 1949, a number of newspapers carried an unsigned editorial: "The United States has not been backward in attempting to develop a long-range rocket," it said. "Five thousand miles is within the range of possibility, according to Dr. Karl T. Compton, of the Defense Department's Research and Development Board." In November 1949, *Liberty Magazine* published a report on atomic-powered guided missiles with biological warheads, again quoting Karl Compton. "Screaming and thundering at 6,000 miles per hour 250 miles high, out of sight and out of hearing, atom-powered missiles will search out with robot precision a target smaller than the Pentagon, smaller than the Kremlin, from any point on earth," the article said. "And there's the weird, but entirely feasible, conception of biological warfare, with guided missiles carrying the most frightful of epidemic disease in their warheads." The article was breathlessly written up in newspapers, which talked of tests at Cape Canaveral of an atomic-powered missile "so lethal, so total, that fear of a retaliation alone will forever ban its use." One surmises that these articles were planted as part of Frank Wisner's false-trail campaign. On January 30, 1950, Defense Secretary Louis Johnson made broad hints in his annual report about the "armed forces special weapons project" and attendant biological, chemical, and radiological research: "The United States must be adequately equipped for this type of warfare," Johnson said.

In response, the Soviet Union said that biological weapons were barbarous, and that the United States had begun a "new wave of war hysteria." The attempt to frighten, said *Pravda*, would fail. "People who have made three revolutions and who have crushed hordes of interventionists in two wars do not yield to fright. People educated by the party of Lenin and Stalin will not be frightened." But the Russians were frightened, actually; they subsequently vastly ramped up their own biological-weapons research program.

The false-trail campaign was taken up again in the 1970s, when a double agent named Dmitri Polyakov—his FBI cryptonym was Top Hat, and his CIA cryptonym was Bourbon—leaked fake intelligence to the Russians that was meant to imply, misleadingly and alarmingly, that the Americans were still secretly at work on offensive biological weapons, even after Nixon announced that he'd shut down the program and had signed the Biological Weapons Convention in 1972. In reaction to this "successful" American deception operation, the Russians created a gurgling marsh monster of biowar research, the Biopreparat, engineering the very anthrax-laden missile warheads that the Americans had hinted at in their deception campaign in 1949. "Not only did the U.S. disinformation program lead to unexpected and undesired Soviet achievements in developing chemical and biological weapons," wrote Raymond Garthoff, a former CIA analyst, in 2000, "it also contributed to mutual fear, suspicion, and tension."

THE GRASS TURNED GREEN TODAY. A detonation of bright green grass. It shocks the eye, and it happens every year—this sudden prestidigitational tablecloth-pull from dun to green. Each year I like it more, and need it more.

April 26, 2019, Friday

I've been thinking how important people's names are. When Eileen Welsome was a reporter for *The Albuquerque Tribune*, she read an Air Force report about toxic-waste sites, and she noticed that radioactive animal carcasses were listed as having been buried in one of the waste sites at Kirtland Air Force Base, near the Albuquerque airport. "Although this didn't seem like much of a story, I have always loved animals and the disclosure caught my eye," she wrote in *The Plutonium Files*. At the Special Weapons Laboratory in Kirtland, she read through records of experiments in which dogs were injected with plutonium. A footnote mentioned a human plutonium experiment. "I wondered if the people had suffered the same agonizing deaths as the animals."

She filed FOIA requests with the Department of Energy for records of human radiation experiments and got almost nothing. The DOE sent her "a few scraps of paper"—sanitized. The names were deleted. "I knew from my reading that there was much more information available and that the DOE was not complying with either the letter or the spirit of the Freedom of Information Act," she said. One day she noticed the name of a very small town in Texas where a code-named plutonium patient lived.

"CAL-3," who had lost a leg to a plutonium injection, lived in Italy, Texas. Italy, Texas. "Two words that the censor failed to obliterate unlocked the entire story," she said to me when I called her in February 2017. She went to Italy, asked around, and heard a name, Elmer Allen. She talked to Elmer Allen's wife and his friend. "They guinea-pigged him," said Allen's friend. "They didn't care about him getting well."

An attorney for the Albuquerque paper, Loretta Garrison, filed a new Freedom of Information request and began petitioning the DOE for documents. Everything followed from Welsome's initial trip to Italy, Texas, but it required a lawyer to bring about actual disclosure. "I got nothing from the Department of Energy, filing as a newspaper reporter," Welsome told me. "It was only after the newspaper hired a lawyer that the documents began to flow." In the documents were more names, more human stories to discover.

History is about individual people doing things—and having things done to them. These people have names. That's what's so terrible about name redaction. You have the minutes of a meeting, and a paraphrase of what was said, but the heads are all lopped off. Name redaction is the decapitation of history.

IN A 1982 SPEECH to retired intelligence officers, William Casey, director of central intelligence, offered a mini-history of the Agency. "Bedell Smith and Allen Dulles put flesh and bone on the CIA," Casey said. "Dick Helms and Frank Wisner devoted their professional careers to the creation and development of our human intelligence capability. Bill Colby took the heat and fought hard to maintain an effective intelligence service in the midseventies. George Bush then stepped in and began the long process of restoring confidence and regaining public respect."

Casey himself was appointed by Reagan. He funded the contras in Nicaragua, sold weapons to Iran, gave money and Stinger missiles to the mujahideen in Afghanistan (in Operation Cyclone, begun by President Carter), and—*and*—in 1984 he shut down FOIA inquiries into the CIA's "operational" files so that nobody could know what the clandestine division had been up to. The CIA used a clever argument to win that debate. If you allow us to keep secret our "operational" files, the Agency said—our covert-action, chaos-creating files, the ones that chronicle how we disrupted and disimproved entire countries and indeed whole regions of the planet—we will be freed up to respond with more speed and efficiency to our current multiyear backlog of FOIA requests. We hardly ever respond to requests for operational files anyway, so this is just a technical adjustment. By allowing us to hide black operations, more information will have more freedom faster. The American Historical Association, the Newspaper Guild, and the Society for Professional Journalists weren't convinced. But somehow the CIA got the American Civil Liberties Union, of all groups, to endorse the bill ("Protection of Operational Files of the Central Intelligence Agency," amending the National Security Act of 1947) and it marched onward toward a vote.

Speaking in opposition were two congressmen: Ted Weiss from New York, and John Conyers from Michigan. (I found their remarks in a copy of pages from the published *Congressional Record* in the CREST database.) "The CIA's record of responding to requests under the Freedom of Information Act has been appalling," said Congressman Weiss in a speech on September 17, 1984. "Individuals filing FOIA requests commonly face a host of tactics that delay and impede legitimate access to information." Had the operational files exemption been part of the original Freedom of Information Act, Weiss observed, the country might never have discovered the CIA's spying on Martin Luther King, or the thousands of pages of Guatemala records that the CIA illegally withheld from Stephen Schlesinger. "This legislation would dangerously intrude on the powers of the courts to review the actions of the Central Intelligence Agency and would likely limit legitimate public access to CIA documents."

Congressman Conyers said that the Agency was making a major, "unprecedented" change under the guise of a minor procedural reform. "Essentially, the CIA is asking us to respond to its current intransigence to and phobia of releasing information by enshrining it into law," Conyers said. "Under current law, the CIA must answer each FOIA request, if not by actually releasing documents, then by listing all existing documents and providing a justification for the withholding of these documents." The new law would remove that requirement. Nobody would know what the CIA had. "I urge my colleagues to judge this bill on its actual merits, not on the desire for clean desks claimed by its proponents. H.R. 5164 represents an attempt to roll back the rights of information which have been obtained so recently, and the bill should be judged as such."

The bill passed, but Conyers and Weiss were right. A midden full of black operations, former and current, stayed buried. Meanwhile, the FOIA delays lengthened. The bill was just a tricky way of hiding crimes.

I KEEP THINKING about finding "Bush" behind one of the scribbled blackouts yesterday—this man who used all of his brilliance to invent new ways to do harm. There, lurking behind the redaction, was his name once again, surfacing like the fortune in an old Magic 8-Ball fortune-telling toy. *Dr. Bush.*

In November 1949, Vannevar Bush sent an inscribed copy of his new book, *Modern Arms and Free Men,* soon to be excerpted in *Reader's Digest,* to Earl Stevenson, president of Arthur D. Little, a consulting firm just down the road from MIT. Arthur D. Little had a contract, or was soon to have a contract, with the Chemical Corps to produce an infectious aerosol generator. Earl Stevenson, an enthusiast of the wartime bat-vector bomb (a cluster of 1,030 live Mexican free-tailed bats fitted with napalm vests that were meant to burst into flame under the eaves of Tokyo houses), wrote Bush a thank-you:

"Dear Van, I am most appreciative of having received an advance copy of your book, *Modern Arms and Free Men* with your autograph, and I have greatly enjoyed your informative account of the present status of new weapons." Stevenson then invited Bush to help him with a new ad hoc committee on biological, chemical, and radiological weapons. "Tell him I'll fit him in," Bush wrote in the margin to his assistant. Bush helped kick off the committee. There was a dinner at the Cosmos Club on Thursday, January 5, 1950, and then the bacteriophiles convened at the Pentagon at nine in the morning the next day.

The meetings continued for months—William Creasy, Caryl Haskins, Karl Compton, James Conant, and insiders from the Pentagon, the CIA, and Camp Detrick made presentations—and eventually there emerged the Stevenson Report, which is the most influential governmental paper ever published about unconventional weapons. It was submitted on June 30, 1950, five days after the beginning of the Korean War. It was full of urgency and conviction. "The United States must not arbitrarily deny itself the use of weapons, such as chemical, biological, and radiological agents, which take advantage of this nation's great technical and industrial potential," said the Stevenson Committee—composed of Willis Gibbons, of U.S. Rubber, soon to be head of the CIA's Technical Services Section; Gordon Arneson of the State Department, who'd ghostwritten the Merck Report about World War II biological warfare research; Eric G. Ball of Harvard Medical School, Arthur Page, a PR maestro who wrote President Truman's "rain of ruin" announcement of the dropping of the bomb on Hiroshima; and several others. They recommended the immediate construction of factories that could produce "virulent biological organisms in quantity" and "militarily significant quantities of G-agents ('nerve gases')." "THE UNITED STATES SHOULD BE PREPARED TO WAGE BIOLOGICAL WARFARE OFFENSIVELY," said the report, in capital letters, at the top of page 15. Germ agents were as yet incompletely explored, the authors conceded—"however the potential worth and the dangers of BW appear to be great." Field tests had already demonstrated that biological aerosols would "drift with the wind over bodies of water and enter ships through their ventilating systems." Data on natural epidemics, along with "the results of laboratory accidents," could be useful in predicting the effects of biological agents. As for war gases, we needed them to counter Soviet troops, which threatened to overrun Europe. "The saturation of transport centers and bottlenecks with mustard gas, and the strafing of troop concentrations with the more lethal gases would, in the opinion expressed by those who will have to combat such enemy action, be an effective support to render to our allies in the opening phases of another war."

The committee's primary goal was to change attitudes at the highest levels of the Truman administration about whether the United States could permissibly use gases, germs, and radioactive dusts whenever the president wanted to, or whether the president had to wait until the country was attacked by a certain type of weapon in order to retaliate in kind. "We do not believe that any useful distinction can be made between weapons on a moral basis," the committee said. "The security of the United States demands that the policy of 'use in retaliation only' be abandoned."

The Stevenson Report, declassified with redactions in 1987, and declassified in full in 1996, was one of two major developments that accelerated the biological-warfare program. The other was the Korean War. "The outbreak of war in Korea and the Stevenson Committee's report (Secretary of Defense Ad Hoc Committee on Chemical, Biological, and Radiological Warfare) caused the R and D budget to be increased from $10,000,000 to $30,000,000," according to a summary history of the Chemical Corps from October 1951, declassified more than forty years later. About 2,000 people worked in research and development at the Chemical Corps in June 1950; by September 1951 that number had risen to 3,700. "The Korean conflict, as well as the world crisis in general, revived interest in toxicological warfare," the report said.

April 27, 2019, Saturday

I lay awake thinking about people at the ends of their lives. Steve Endicott is in pain in Toronto. He's in a bad way. I thought of his back and how fragile it is. That was the word his daughter Marion used: "fragile." He's in a constant state of agony.

I started to write him an email, saying that I'd been thinking a lot about him while I was holed up trying to finish a book that was originally inspired by his book. "You've been my wise tolerant travel companion and guide as I hike through strange lands of redaction and partial disclosure," I wrote. How do you write someone who is in pain and has given up—and is contemplating death?

I THINK OF STEVE'S LIFE. He spent his life teaching history and writing history. And now Steve is coming to the end. He has not killed a single person. Contrast that with the germ-warfare people—Vannevar Bush, Dale Jenkins, William Creasy, Earle Partridge—they were all killers. Killers of people, killers of villages, killers of monkeys and dogs. They devoted themselves to finding improved ways and means of killing. It's worth pointing out this basic difference.

There are two ways to live. You can live in a way in which you do your best not to kill people, or you can live in a way in which you attend meetings and perform experiments that are aimed at refining ways to cut lives short.

IT'S NOW 4:00 A.M. Minerva the cat has padded into this dark kitchen, lit only by the streetlight outside, and she's crunching her way through the kibble. I picked her up yesterday and marveled at the softness of her fur.

After this book I am going to teach myself how to paint. I have maybe twenty years of life left—time to fit in a little painting.

HERE'S ANOTHER PIECE of SUEDE communications intelligence, dated March 11, 1952:

> Two coastal security stations in northeastern Korea reported on 11 March that "the bacteria bomb classified as mosquito, fly and flea were dispersed" and "an enemy plane dropped ants, fleas, mosquitoes, flies and crickets."
>
> A Chinese Communist unit commander in western Korea demonstrates his conviction that BW is being employed against him in his order to a subordinate unit who captured some UN soldiers. The subordinate unit is instructed to ask the prisoners what "type of immunization shots were administered recently . . . in preparation for defense against what disease," and "what type of common literature (was) made available regarding disease immunization and prevention."

Teams of Chinese doctors were sent to the front, said Henry Lieberman in *The New York Times.* "Communist dispatches reported today medical teams were now being organized throughout Red China to go to Korea to help combat disease among Chinese and North Korean troops," Lieberman wrote. "Maintaining its 'germ warfare' propaganda at a shrill pitch, the Peiping radio charged tonight in an overseas broadcast that 'sixteen kinds of bacteriological weapons' had been used against Chinese Communist troops."

IN APRIL 1952, a new and personal note entered the propaganda war—the Chinese began broadcasting and publishing (sometimes in handwritten facsimile) statements by Air Force and Marine Corps prisoners of war who said that they had participated in germ-warfare combat missions. The statements seem to be a mixture of truths and plausible fictions, obtained under duress and, in some cases, torture. The later confessions, especially— there are about thirty of them—sound similar, as if some of the downed American fliers had learned from other POWs that producing a good germ-warfare confession was a way to get through the interrogation phase of captivity faster.

Floyd O'Neal's statement, filmed and included in one of the Chinese propaganda films, and republished in part in *Time* magazine, is surprising and moving, though, whether or not it's true. Lieutenant O'Neal, a reservist with a master's degree in chemistry from Tulane, describes attending two training lectures on biological weapons, one in the States and one in Korea. Then O'Neal is asked what he felt like when he went out on his first and only germ-warfare mission. "Frankly," says O'Neal, "I was, I think, the most nervous I have ever been in my life. I also felt like it was a funeral rather than a usual mission."

He's asked how his fellow officers took the news that the United States was engaged in germ warfare. "Well sir, I can only describe the feelings which I observed in the fellow pilots who attended the second lecture— the other three pilots—because those are the ones whom I observed reacting immediately after we found out that the U.S. forces were using germ warfare in Korea. Among those men and myself, I think the main thing was a sense of horror, of abhorrence." After the lecture the four of them walked in stunned silence. "I know I was wondering myself why on earth we were using this terrible weapon in Korea, even while the peace talks were going on at Kaesong, when the war was practically stopped."

O'Neal has this closing thought: "When I think of my future, when I think of someday—though I'm not married, I intend to be—when my son asks me what I did in Korea, how can I tell him that I came over here and dropped germ bombs on people, destroying them, bringing death and destruction? How can I go back and face my family in a civilized world? How can I tell them these things, that I—I am a criminal in the eyes of humanity? They're my flesh and blood. It's the most difficult thing, to really give a man's feelings a vocal expression. I can't try, I can only tell you somewhat of how I feel."

When O'Neal was released, he recanted completely. "I did sign a confession relating to germ warfare," he said, "but the statements contained in this confession were false. They were obtained under duress." The duress, he said, consisted "mainly of standing at attention, having my face slapped once in a while when I failed to respond to what they wanted me to." O'Neal was also denied sanitation privileges, fed bad food, fed dirty water, and "denied medical facilities when I was ill." His interrogators spent many hours "wrangling and haranguing," he said, "attempting to break down my willpower."

Ten years ago, I wrote O'Neal a letter asking him about his experiences. I said, "Your filmed response to questioning from the scientific commission is one of the most moving things I've seen."

In reply he sent a long, interesting, confusing letter. He said his statement was scripted by a Chinese handler, with the possible help of Wilfrid Burchett, an Australian journalist who wrote for a Paris newspaper and was sympathetic to Communist causes. (I'd asked him in my letter about Burchett.) He said:

> The germ warfare charge was totally false and a propaganda device. There was not a word of truth by my knowledge in any of the allegations about germ warfare that I wound up placing in my confession and in the stage show for the commission.

O'Neal specifically denied that he had any training sessions of the sort he'd described: "I had never had ANY information given to me by AF or other armed forces personnel about germ warfare. I thought most of the material was science fiction or very poor science." His combat missions were varied, he said—they included "bombs, strafing and napalm," as well as reconnaissance and rescue. "I viewed my journey to Korea as my opportunity to help in preserving non-Communist values." His goal was to fly his fifty missions, "do a barrel roll over the runway," and go home.

The confession, he said, came about after he lost his temper during an interrogation. "I slapped the handler hard enough to knock him off his stool and onto the floor. What they did for the next days I don't care to discuss but I finally agreed to sign their confession."

THE BEST-WRITTEN CONFESSION was by Colonel Frank Schwable, commander of the First Marine Aircraft Wing, recipient, before he broke, of four Distinguished Flying Crosses and two Legions of Merit. He was shot down in Korea on July 8, 1952, interrogated, badgered, held in solitary confinement, not allowed to bathe or shave, and given bad food. "It wasn't a method of physical torture so much as mental torture over a long-drawn-out period of time," he said afterward. "We were always in solitary confinement." His captors made him write and rewrite his statement, which is long and filled with the names of superior officers. Here's a passage near the beginning:

> Toward the end of January 1952, Marine night fighters of Squadron 513, operating as single planes on night armed reconnaissance, and carrying bacteriological bombs, shared targets with the B-26s covering the lower half of North Korea with the greatest emphasis on the western portion. Squadron 513 coordinated with the Third Bomb Wing on all these missions, using F7F aircraft (Tiger Cats) because of their twin engine safety.

In June 1952, Schwable said, they began creating a "contamination belt":

> During the first week of June, Squadron 513 started operations on the concentrated contamination belt, using cholera bombs. (The plan given to General Jerome indicated that at a later, unspecified date—depending

on the results obtained, or lack of results—yellow fever and then typhus
in that order would probably be tried out in the contamination belt.)

Schwable was told to refer to the intermittent biological missions as "Super-
propaganda," or "Suprop" missions. He closes with this:

> I do not say the following in defense of anyone, myself included, I
> merely report as an absolutely direct observation that every officer
> when first informed that the United States is using bacteriological
> warfare in Korea is both shocked and ashamed.
>
> I believe, without exception, we come to Korea as officers loyal to
> our people and government and believing what we have always been
> told about bacteriological warfare—that it is being developed only for
> use in retaliation in a third world war.
>
> For these officers to come to Korea and find that their own
> government has so completely deceived them by still proclaiming to
> the world that it is not using bacteriological warfare, makes them
> question mentally all the other things that the government proclaims
> about warfare in general and in Korea specifically.
>
> None of us believes that bacteriological warfare has any place in
> war since of all the weapons devised bacteriological bombs alone
> have as their primary objective casualties among masses of civilians—
> and that is utterly wrong in anybody's conscience. The spreading of
> disease is unpredictable and there may be no limits to a fully developed
> epidemic. Additionally, there is the awfully sneaky, unfair sort of
> feeling of dealing with a weapon used surreptitiously against an
> unarmed and unwarned people.

Everyone who hears of it is horrified and stupefied, Schwable wrote:

> Tactically, this type of weapon is totally unwarranted—it is not even a
> Marine Corps weapon—morally it is damnation itself; administratively
> and logistically as planned for use, it is hopeless; and from the point of
> view of self-respect and loyalty, it is shameful.

And then, when he was released, he denied all of it. It was all false, he
said—a "bogus confession."

April 28, 2019, Sunday

Right now the sun is warm on my face. My fingers are numb from the cold, but the river is as shiny as a piece of Juicy Fruit tinfoil that's been carefully flattened, moving, moving.

And in the dead leaves along the edges of the street, thousands of little maple seedlings, with floppy dog's ears of dicotyledons, are coming up. All of them about an inch high.

April 29, 2019, Monday

It seems wrong to be itemizing long-ago dark deeds when daily life is full of thoughts of mortality.

Sometimes history recedes, because the now drowns it. But it's always there later, like seaweed with bits of things caught in it, waiting to be thought through again.

YEARS AGO I INTERVIEWED Robert Stinnett, whose book *Day of Deceit*, about Pearl Harbor, is dedicated to John Moss, creator of the Freedom of Information Act. I remember sitting in his beautiful Oakland bungalow, at an oak table in his dining room, eating a crunchy baked good, talking to him about his years of research. His wife was very elegant. Stinnett seemed old to me then. But not tired. He took me down to the basement and showed me his row of file cabinets filled with code-breaking documents. He had a crispness of speech, an air of wanting to find truth. He'd been a reporter for the *Oakland Tribune* for years, and before that he'd been on an aircraft carrier in World War II. His voice was deliberate and gravelly.

Somewhere I have a tape of that interview. I remember asking him if there were any documents now that he really wished he could see, ones that were still classified. He thought for a moment. Then I think he told me some, but the names didn't mean anything to me because I didn't know anything about the documentary history of Pearl Harbor. The interview tape is in a box in a storage place two hours' drive from here.

I like that Stinnett dedicated the book to John Moss. And I'm glad he was able to get so many documents from the Navy. "Without the FOIA the information revealed in this book would never have surfaced." Of Stinnett's book, John Toland wrote: "It is disturbing that eleven presidents, including those I admired, kept the truth from the public until Stinnett's Freedom of Information Act requests finally persuaded the Navy to release the evidence."

I'm now going to look Stinnett up, braced to find out that he's died—hoping he hasn't.

Yes, he died in November of last year. This is what happens, I have learned. People come to their end. I have wasted so many opportunities, though. I could have gotten to know Stinnett better and asked him better questions. I could have written about him.

Here's how Stephen Budiansky, who disagrees with Stinnett, begins his refutation of *Day of Deceit*: "Robert Stinnett is hardly the first author, and I am sure he will not be the last, to advance a sensationalistic conspiracy theory concerning the Pearl Harbor attack." There it is—the haughty tone, the empty high-flown phrasing, the received put-down. Stinnett's book must be junk because his theory is not a theory, it's a "conspiracy theory." Just call it a theory. Inserting "conspiracy" in the middle is a way of trying to shut it down without thought. "Conspiracy theory" has ridicule built into it.

Budiansky is himself an intelligent man, but he fails to acknowledge that Stinnett thought hard and teased truths out of hiding places and, above all, that he put fresh documents out for public view. Budiansky then goes on to attack Stinnett for errors: "elementary mistakes." "He gets basic cryptologic facts wrong." He bases this not on his own knowledge but on a "devastating" review by David Kahn, author of *The Codebreakers*. This is the "riddled-with-errors" gambit, used to undermine people who say things you don't like. All historians make elementary errors sometimes. There's a lot to know.

AFTER JOSEPH MCCARTHY, the biggest conspiracy theorist of the Cold War was Harry Truman. He enjoyed talking about the Communist conspiracy—and how he'd destroyed it with the help of the FBI. "The Communist conspiracy is a definite and disciplined group of people who are fanatically dedicated to carrying out the purposes of the Soviet Union," he said in 1951, on Citizenship Day. "These people can be identified, isolated, and prosecuted in many cases, and rendered harmless." Not everyone one disagrees with is a Communist conspirator, though, the president added. "We are not engaged in an effort to stamp out differences of opinion, but to root out a conspiracy."

On September 29, 1952, on a whistle-stop tour in Minnesota, Truman said, "We've crushed the Communist conspiracy in this country. And we've stopped the advance of communism all over the globe." The next day, in Montana, he said, "We moved in and stopped the Communists in Korea. This cost us money and effort, and worst of all, the lives of many of our finest young men. But it checked the plans of the Communists and the Kremlin for world conquest, and blocked their conspiracy against this country." At Symphony Hall in Boston in October 1952, he said, "Skillfully and systematically, the FBI and the Department of Justice have been breaking up the Communist conspiracy in the United States. They have caught Soviet espionage agents. They have sent the principal leaders of the Communist Party to jail for conspiring to advocate the overthrow of our Government by force and violence."

In the book I was in the middle of writing before I put it aside to write this one, Harry Truman is a major figure. I found I really came to despise him sometimes. Other times I thought he was charming and even occasionally brave. But he was such a horrendous racist and bigot. Honestly. The truths about Harry Truman's bigotry aren't classified, but they're not discussed—they're well-kept secrets (recently scrubbed, in fact, from the Truman Library website)—because they're simply too awful. When he was a young man, he wrote, "I think one man is just as good as another so long as he's honest and decent and not a nigger or a Chinaman." New York City he referred to (while self-censoring an expletive) as "this —— kike town." After a phone call from Henry Morgenthau, Truman wrote: "The Jews, I find are very, very selfish. They care not how many Estonians, Latvians, Finns, Poles, Yugoslavs or Greeks get murdered or mistreated as DPs"—displaced persons—"as long as the Jews get special treatment. Yet when they have power, physical, financial or political neither Hitler nor Stalin has anything on them for cruelty or mistreatment to the under dog." In March 1948, Drew Pearson, the columnist, wrote:

> Ordinarily, Negro voters would be out shouting and drumming up votes for Truman as a result of his civil-rights message. But too many times the president has talked to his intimates about "the —— niggers" in exactly the same way he talked about "the —— Jews." These conversations leak out.

Once, sitting at his desk in Washington in 1940, Truman killed a cockroach. "He walked right out on the arm rest where I'm writing this," he wrote his wife, on U.S. Senate stationery, "as impudently as a sassy nigger."

Truman has a reputation now for telling it like it is, but he frequently told it like it wasn't. He authorized all sorts of CIA underhandedness, and then, late in life, he said, "I never had any thought when I set up the CIA that it would be injected into peacetime cloak and dagger operations."

No, Harry, you're not going to get away with that. One of Truman's early cloak-and-dagger initiatives involved spending some of the $75 million from his anti–Communist China fund. In October 1949, the president showed James Webb, acting secretary of state, a map of Russia, color-coded to indicate where Muslims and Buddhists were to be found: they formed a wide belt across southern Russia. Both groups were antagonistic to the Soviet regime, Truman pointed out to Webb; perhaps they could be induced to make trouble at the border? "He wanted us to try to develop some plan by which part of $75,000,000 might be used to penetrate these peoples if such was feasible through covert activity," Webb wrote. Webb sent a copy of notes on his meeting with the president to the CIA and to counterinsurgency specialist Dean Rusk. And that was the beginning of the end for Tibet.

In the fall of 1950, President Truman authorized Wisner's reckless use of General Li Mi and his army of Nationalist "irregulars" in Burma to attack the Chinese Communists, as a way of forcing the Chinese to draw off some troops from North Korea. The head of the CIA, Bedell Smith, said it was a bad idea—Truman countermanded him. This I learned this morning reading a paper by Victor S. Kaufman in *The China Quarterly*. "Interestingly," Kaufman writes, "the CIA's director, Walter Bedell Smith, opposed the plan, considering it too risky. But President Harry Truman saw merit in the OPC's proposal and approved it. The program became known as Operation Paper."

And then there he is, late in life, saying he had no idea that his intelligence organization was going to be doing sneaky things. What a total, spread-eagled lie.

The Nazi War Crimes Disclosure Act forced out some of the documentary record on General Li Mi: there was evidence that his counterinsurgency operations were paid for with Nazi gold, channeled by Wisner's operatives. On July 31, 1951, Wisner was on the hot seat at the Department of State, in the office of H. Freeman Matthews, offering background on OPC projects all over the world, including General Li Mi's attack on China from Burma, which had been in all the papers. ("A Chinese Nationalist Army has struck 65 miles into Red China from its refugee base in Burma and seized a 100-mile-long frontier strip in Yunnan Province," the Associated Press reported on July 28, 1951, without disclosing that the CIA had ordered and financed the attack.) Livingston Merchant, a Far East specialist, ventured to suggest that General Li Mi's attack on China might "create difficulties," and suggested that the Office of Policy Coordination disengage from the operation.

Wisner didn't think that was necessary, the meeting minutes record. "Mr. Wisner stated that OPC was in a position to deny official American responsibility in connection with the operation."

And there it is. You mount a complicated paramilitary campaign, you write memos, send cables, leak tidbits to the press, spend money (perhaps

Nazi money), train and arm a small army on the other side of the world—
and then you are "in a position" to deny the whole thing. How can this be?
What Wisner was implying by saying that the Office of Policy Coordination
was in a position to deny was simply that Truman himself had okayed the
operation. It had gotten the presidential green light, so it really didn't
matter what H. Freeman Matthews or Livingston Merchant thought.

On October 23, 1951, Truman authorized NSC 10/5, "Scope and Pace
of Covert Operations" (declassified with one redaction in 1994), which,
while reaffirming the "responsibility and authority of the Director of Central
Intelligence for the conduct of covert operations," stepped up their pace and
widened their scope. The document called for an immediate expansion and
intensification of covert activities, in order to place "maximum strain on the
Soviet structure of power." China was specifically mentioned as a locus
for "expanded guerrilla activities," although that line was blacked out for
another decade, until a State Department *Foreign Relations* volume came out
in 2007. The covert activities would include, where possible, the establishment
of bases for "underground resistance" to be held in readiness for military
action in wartime.

This was a big step—it set up the covert machinery for everything that
happened later under Eisenhower, Kennedy, Johnson, Nixon, and onward
to Reagan and beyond. Approved by President Truman, and then kept
secret from the public for four decades: "It is requested that special security
precautions be taken in the handling of this report and that access be
limited strictly to individuals requiring the information contained therein
to carry out their official duties."

WISNER, TRUMAN'S SHADOW WARRIOR, exerted himself, throughout
Truman's presidency, to bring needy Nazis to the United States under special
visas, as part of a program called Operation Paperclip. Wisner was strangely
drawn to neofascism. On June 3, 1950, he got a cable from one of his people
in Frankfurt: "Most interesting possibility presents itself of getting on
ground floor of well-led youth organization," it said. The organization
was the League of German Youth, or Bund Deutsche Jugend, code-named

KMPRUDE. The membership was Western oriented, said the cable—mostly junior officers from the German army, along with some Hitler Youth. "We wish to subsidize organization with working capital to get it going on a larger scale."

As a first trial of KMPRUDE's effectiveness, the cable said, the organization would be asked to interfere with the TPSTALL (East German) elections. Under consideration was the idea of "kidnapping" ballot boxes in order to check on actual results. Outright election fraud was another possible course of action: "production of ballot boxes notionally kidnapped, actually stuffed by us."

"Proposal regarded favorably," Wisner cabled back. The "counter-election work" proceeded, paid for with ZRCANDY—Marshall Plan money.

KMPRUDE grew and was absorbed into something bigger called LCPROWL, which engaged in psychological warfare and spun off a network, or "Technical Service," of paramilitary and sabotage teams whose job was to hoard weapons, train with CIA trainers, make liquidation lists of prominent Communists and Socialists, and wait for World War III. "In the light of recent developments in Korea," one memo from August 1950 said, "the necessity of laying—at the earliest possible time—the ground work for the training of personnel for guerrilla and sabotage operations in Germany has become apparent." Everything would be most secret, of course. "All necessary security precautions, such as cover and/or deception, will be employed in order to avoid any connection with the U.S. Government even by implication with this undertaking."

KMMANLY, a project to neutralize the German peace movement, was another of OPC's psychological projects—it aimed to encourage West German rearmament by funding rightist veterans' groups and magazines. (Magazines staffed, as it happened, by former Nazis and SS men.) Then there was so-called nerve-war activity, which involved harassment, intimidation, and fear. A memo sent in March 1952 from the chief of the Eastern European Division to Frank Wisner described some of the CIA-instigated nerve-war actions taken against East German Communists, including anonymous letters and phone calls. "A hangman's noose and death sentence were mailed to a Communist judge," said the memo, "with the admonition that the actual judgment was to be carried out in the future in retribution for needless sentencing of East Germans to Siberian exile."

A related project, DTLINEN—which began in May 1949 as Operation Earthenware—mounted "several poison-pen campaigns directed specifically against Communist functionaries in the Soviet Zone." The effect of these letters was "remarkable," the memo said: they created such fear of retribution that they forced some Communists to become CIA informants.

These documents and thousands of others, including many boxes of OSS files, were kept secret until the passing of the Nazi War Crimes Disclosure Act of 1998.

WHAT THE CIA ACCOMPLISHED under Wisner and Dulles, with Truman's blessing, was the postwar renewal of Europe's fascist underground. Groups of right-wingers at loose ends were paid, housed, trained, indoctrinated, armed, and grouped into small "stay-behind" squads, ready for action when war with the Kremlin came. LCPROWL's cover was blown in October 1952, when the guerrilla-training network became front-page news all over Germany. The *Frankfurter Allgemeine* ran a long article with the headline "A Secret Organization Unearthed." "Partisan training courses were held in secrecy under American supervision," the newspaper said:

> Membership was believed to amount to 1,000 to 2,000, most of them former Luftwaffe, Wehrmacht and Waffen SS officers ranging in age between 35–50 years. Neo-fascist tendencies were officially denied. The police found arms of German, Russian and American origin, machine guns, explosives and sabotage equipment. Also among the confiscated material were accounts which attested to ample financial means. Allegedly the organization received 50,000 DM monthly from American agencies via a camouflage business firm.

What especially alarmed German moderates was that prominent Social Democrats were included on liquidation lists as well as Communists. "All measures taken must be stern and resolute," said one of the Bund Deutsche Jugend documents. "Early bloodshed may prevent much bloodshed later."

DANIELE GANSER, a Swiss PhD student working on a book about the CIA's stay-behind operations in Europe and their links to later acts of terror, sent a FOIA request to the CIA in December 2000. The reply was prompt: "The CIA can neither confirm nor deny the existence or nonexistence of records responsive to your request," the letter said—but if the records existed, their release would be withheld under FOIA exemptions (b)(1) and (b)(3). "We regret that we cannot assist you with your request." (This is called the Glomar response, referring to the CIA's refusal to confirm or deny records relating to the *Glomar Explorer*, a ship that the Agency built in order to try to salvage a Russian nuclear submarine in the Pacific Ocean. The *Glomar Explorer's* cover story was that Howard Hughes planned to use the ship to mine undersea manganese nodules.)

Ganser appealed the CIA's rejection, citing many books and articles, along with a BBC documentary TV series, that described stay-behind networks and arms caches financed by the CIA, all part of something called Operation Gladio. The Agency accepted his appeal: "Arrangements will be made for its consideration by the appropriate members of the Agency Release Panel." The letter warned, however, that there were 315 appeals in line ahead of Ganser's. "In view of this, some delay in our reply must be expected, but I can assure you that every reasonable effort will be made to complete a response as soon as possible."

Years went by. Ganser heard nothing. His book *NATO's Secret Armies: Operation GLADIO and Terrorism in Western Europe* came out in 2005, whereupon the CIA published a brief review of it in *Studies in Intelligence*: "Although Ganser's sourcing is largely secondary—newspapers and the like," wrote Hayden Peake, a former CIA operations officer and curator of its Historical Intelligence Collection, the book was convincing, he said, in establishing that some GLADIO members became right-wing terrorists, "responsible for hundreds of terrorist attacks whose real purpose was to discredit the Communists." What the book lacked was documentary evidence, Peake felt. "Ganser fails to document his thesis that the CIA, MI6, and NATO and its friends turned GLADIO into a terrorist organization."

It's now more than eighteen years since Ganser filed his FOIA request. The CIA is still shielding its Gladio documents.

April 30, 2019, Tuesday

An envelope came from the CIA. They've assigned me another reference number. Now I have four, I think, actual reference numbers.

I want to tell you about nerve war, the CIA's strategy of driving the enemy crazy. Nerve war, or "psychiatric warfare," was a particular interest of CIA consultant Paul Linebarger, of Johns Hopkins, famous now because as Cordwainer Smith he wrote about scanners, about the deep pain of space, and about the brain-searing powers of hostile telepathy. Linebarger gave a talk on psychiatric warfare one afternoon in January 1952. Psychiatric warfare, he said (to the War College Wives in Newport, Rhode Island), was a fiercer, more destructive subform of psychological warfare. It destroyed people's brains and personalities and rebuilt them in new patterns. The Chinese practiced it when they performed a "brainwashing," Linebarger said. Linebarger's follower Lieutenant Gerald L. Geiger, chief of psychological warfare and training at the Air Resupply and Communications Service headquarters in Washington (nominally Air Force, but underwritten by the CIA), published a pilot paper in April 1952 on the use of psychiatric warfare against Communist leaders. The idea was to employ black or gray "poker-faced propaganda" to create a situation of prolonged mental stress, and then to intensify that stress through "subtle, nerve-corroding verbal needling." The end result might be paranoia, or anxiety hysteria, or some other form of mental disease—or violence. "Psychiatric warfare is psychiatry used in reverse to create sickness," Geiger wrote. "It is intended to produce the nervous breakdown of enemy personality, individual as well as collective."

In 1954, the CIA distributed a nerve-war manual to its Guatemalan coup plotters, in English and in Spanish translation. It was called "Guerra de Nervios Contra Individuos"—"Nerve War Against Individuals." (Was it written by Paul Linebarger? Possible.) An enemy's strength consists of its key individuals, the manual said—its military leaders, its writers, its cabinet members, and so on. Therefore any effort to defeat an enemy must concentrate on those individuals:

> If such an effort is made by means short of physical violence, we call it "psychological warfare." If it is focused less upon convincing those individuals by logical reasoning, but primarily upon moving them in the desired direction by means of harassment, by frightening, confusing, or misleading them, we speak of "nerve war." Such a nerve war can be waged against an entire nation or against major groups of the population.

To destroy a man mentally, the manual said, it's a good idea to choose a time when he is psychologically vulnerable—his birthday, for instance, or when he is depressed. Some options were: calling him in the middle of the night, when his resistance is low, painting "threatening texts" on the wall of his house—e.g., "You have only 5 more days," or "Your secret life has been discovered"—or "sending a phony bomb through the mails." Forged letters may assist the campaign, and "el beso de la muerte" (the kiss of death) can be useful—that is, public praise coming from a despised source. "Whichever method you choose, you'll have to pursue your campaign relentlessly and methodically, until your target either gives in—or, on the contrary, until you recognize that this is, for the time being, a hopeless case and that you are wasting your effort." Never give your target time to recover: "Repetition is one of the strongest devices in all propaganda."

PBSUCCESS, the CIA's Guatemalan coup, the most thoroughly documented of all CIA's interventions (Frank Wisner wanted the record to serve as a guide), relied heavily on the recommendations in the nerve-war manual. One document I found from May 1954 (in CREST, declassified in 2003) said that nerve war might include:

> (a) sending death notices
> (b) Telephone calls—preferably between 2 and 5 A.M.—whispering a threat or a warning (either against impending purge by PGT or government—or against being blacklisted by Liberation Movement)
> (c) Marking subject's house "here lives a Moscow agent" or the like (luminous paint?)
> (d) Sending cardboard coffin or hangman's noose through mail or depositing before subject's house or office.
> (e) Sending subject a fake summons, asking him to appear in Guatemala City to answer charges of deviation from the party line (if a PGT member), or embezzlement or betrayal of government secrets (if a government official).
> (f) Informing subject's wife that he is in danger and that she must see to it that he seeks safety.

Another memo, sent on April 28, 1954, from "Jerome C. Dunbar" (cryptonym for Albert Haney, chief of PBSUCCESS headquarters in Florida, formerly chief of station in Korea), requests another death-notice operation, "right now":

> Only, we would like to have the death notices announce the deaths of ARBENZ, Mrs. ARBENZ, FORTUNY, GUTIERREZ, PELLEGER, Jaime ROSENBERG, Alfredo GUERRA Borges, Jaime DIAZ Rozzotto, Humberto GONZALEZ Juarez, Francisco MORAZON and others of their ilk, rather than the deaths of foreign Communists. The date of death should, in each case, be listed as October 1954, with convenient variations as to the specific day of the month.

Dunbar wanted the death cards, five hundred of them, to go to all the named victims, to newspapers and radio stations, and to "crypto-Communists," prominent citizens, and Arbenz supporters.

A few weeks later, a cable from Guatemala City said: "Request forward soonest dozen fragmentary and dozen concussion grenades preferably of Czech, German or other manufacture." The idea was to back up certain letters with "persuasive measures," the cable said, so that their threat wouldn't seem idle. "Plan scare not kill."

May 1, 2019, Wednesday

Well, it's the first of May. This morning I sat in the sun and wrote about very sad things that have nothing to do with this book. Carroll, my mother-in-law, is not doing at all well.

We are on a river, my son said the other day.

TOWARD EVENING I LOOKED at the light in the trees and tried to push myself to write about the balloon bomb, but I couldn't.

May 2, 2019, Thursday

The sheltering dark. I woke up after a dream of paging through a new issue of a magazine that was thick with articles and ads, laid out like *Vogue* or the old *Harper's Bazaar*.

This morning is the first morning I can hear the early birds. I can also hear one of the dogs snoring.

CHEERIOS BEGAN AS A PRODUCT called Cheerioats in 1941. General Mills got into unconventional warfare during World War II, when the company made room for B. F. Skinner's pigeon-bomb project. Skinner, inventor of the Skinner "Air Crib," a sealed, soundproofed, glass-fronted, climate-controlled confinement unit for babies, had the idea of conditioning pigeons, through rewards and punishments, so that they would peck at the directional controls of a glide bomb and aim it at a target.

After the war General Mills's president, Harry Bullis, a friend of Allen Dulles, began a balloon program, General Mills Aeronautical Research Laboratory. Abbott Washburn, General Mills's head of public relations, became director of an ostensibly private undertaking, the Crusade for

Freedom, which used CIA funds channeled through the National Committee for a Free Europe to launch thousands of leaflet-bearing balloons into Czechoslovakia and other countries of Eastern Europe. There were big balloons and pillow-sized balloons. These "friendship balloons" were widely covered in the United States. Drew Pearson, muckraking columnist, was won over by them: "The current experiment in penetrating the Iron Curtain by balloons may be a great success or it may fail. It is too early yet to say. But the important thing is that it's an attempt by private individuals under the free-enterprise system to try out certain methods of psychological propaganda—or call it psychological warfare if you will—which governments will not and perhaps cannot tackle."

The CIA's leaflet balloons were not always friendly. Some carried parody banknotes and anti-Soviet messages. "The regime is weakening and is afraid of you," one Czech leaflet said. "The power is in the people and the people are against the regime. Unite and mobilize your forces!" The leaflets themselves also functioned as a simulant for other payloads: they gave the CIA and Air Force targeters information on the flows of air high over Europe.

And that in turn fed into the covert plan to destroy Communist food sources, using high-altitude "balloon disseminators" filled with heated containers of wheat stem rust and hog cholera. Engineers at General Mills studied Japanese incendiary balloons and began a feasibility study for a biological balloon bomb in 1950. A memo from 1951, which I found in Air Force files, describes the balloon-bomb development program: "For some time there has existed an apparent need for an inexpensive method of air delivery of certain BW munitions to potential enemy area targets," the memo begins. "This investigation consisted of a feasibility study by General Mills Inc., which is now complete. This study indicates that an unmanned free balloon can deliver BW agents (anti-crop, anti-animal) to an area target at distances up to 1500 miles from the launching point with acceptable accuracy at extremely low cost." By September 1952, Marvin Sandgren, a balloon engineer at General Mills, had developed a prototype. It had some problems, though—the heater malfunctioned, baking the agent or allowing it to freeze. Camp Detrick handed the problem over to

Ralph E. Stine, an engineer in the M division (M for munitions), for improvements. After tests at Dugway Proving Ground in February 1953, the bomb was pronounced "very satisfactory." It was called the E-77 biological bomb.

The balloon itself was big—twenty-five feet in diameter—and made of polyethylene; when inflated with hydrogen it could carry an eighty-pound gondola full of crop disease for fifty hours at a constant altitude. "This munition is expressly designed for dissemination of pathogenic anticrop agents (TX-1) over large target areas of cereal crops," wrote Ralph Stine in a status report, "Biological Bomb for Balloon Delivery," dated May 15, 1953. (The report was signed by John L. Schwab, former head of the Special Operations Division, now director of Detrick's Biological Laboratories.) "It consists of an insulated fiberboard 'hatbox,' 32 inches in diameter and 24 inches high, opening in clamshell fashion about the vertical centerline to distribute the agent packages," wrote Stine. The hatbox, made of nonmetallic materials to avoid radar detection, was lined with Styrofoam, and the packages, five of them, were grouped around a heating element, so that the six-mile-high cold wouldn't kill them. If the balloon malfunctioned, suddenly losing altitude, a gas canister would kill the spores. "There are many agent candidates that may be carried in this balloon," Stine wrote. "By adding of suitable antianimal fill such as a pellet, the bomb could be transformed into an antianimal munition."

A timer, a custom-adapted Lux Clock Model 1060, triggered the release of the bomb gondola. Parachutes popped out to slow its descent. When the gondola reached a low altitude—somewhere between one thousand and five thousand feet—it opened like a clamshell, ejecting five fiberboard containers. In each container, a small bottle of pressurized carbon dioxide blew a sliding disk that pushed the spore cloud and its feathers or other carriers into the air. The spores would gently land on the stems of wheat plants, forming pustules.

On November 1, 1952, the Air Resupply and Communications Service activated the 1300th ARC Squadron (Special)—a joint Air Force–CIA balloon-launching group. The ARC squadron reportedly launched more than 2,400 E-77 anticrop test balloons, according to one Air Force

document from April 1953—although that number seems high; the
launching sites included Edwards Air Force Base in California, a naval air
station in Vernalis, California, and another naval air station in Tillamook,
Oregon. Not surprisingly, there were many UFO sightings in 1953.

MEANWHILE OTHER BALLOONS, also made by General Mills, began taking
aerial photographs over the Soviet Union—photographs that were sent to
the Library of Congress's Air Research Division for target analysis. And in
Germany, DTLINEN's covert warriors—aiming to "harass and weaken
the Soviet administration in East Germany"—continued to launch General
Mills's propaganda-bearing balloons into East German airspace as late as
1957. The poison-pen letter campaigns and "confusion operations" continued,
as well—needling the government with operations designed to "ridicule,
confuse, and undermine" its leadership. "These operations appear to be the
most infuriating to the East German regime," reported the head of the CIA
station in Berlin, and "regularly result in significant press and other reactions
in East Germany and often cause negative reactions from weak-kneed or
fellow-traveling West German politicians and/or functionaries." Psychiatric
warfare.

IN VANNEVAR BUSH'S PAPERS at the Library of Congress is the draft of an
unfinished essay for *Reader's Digest* on unconventional weapons. He wrote
it early in January 1951, when he was no longer in charge of the Defense
Department's Research and Development Board, but when he still played
an avuncular role in the intelligence world, meeting with Allen Dulles and
other pipe smokers at meetings of the Princeton Consultants to talk over
the Soviet menace. The Russians were "inclined to be devious," Bush wrote
in his draft. "They are unscrupulous, and will employ any means whatever
to gain their ends." The fourteen men in the Kremlin wanted to dominate
the globe, he held. "They are at war with us, constantly and unremittingly.
They have been ever since 1945," he said. They had shut off their own
people from the truth,

and fed them a mass of lies. At the present moment the peoples of half of Europe and half of Asia are being deluged with the repeated story that America is bent on conquering and enslaving them, and must be resisted at all costs. Emotions are being stirred and vast hordes prepared for great sacrifice.

We surprised the men in the Kremlin, Bush said, when we resisted them in Korea. In doing so, we suffered a terrible defeat. "It took Korea to really wake us up," Bush believed. "It was the defeat in Korea, the retreat from overconfidently advanced positions, the casualty list of American boys, that brought us to our feet." Now we were arming. "Conscription, to bring in young men by the millions, billions of dollars for purchase of war equipment, controls, rationing. We know the pattern well enough, and are plunging into it." All that was absolutely necessary, Bush believed. But we needed to do more. We needed to arm our allies. And we needed unconventional warfare. One unconventional avenue was propaganda. Another was sabotage—"the subversive wrecking of machinery, plants and vehicles, and this is full of possibilities." In the passage that followed, he paused, and made a correction. "But there are other more sinister forms," he said:

> The spreading of disease among food plants and animals could readily be done, and would be very difficult to counter. It ought even

After Bush crossed out "It ought even," he continued:

> It might even extend to the poisoning or infecting of milk or water supplies, or other forms of murder. There are plenty of forms of deviltry.

Then he took a break, removing the paper from the machine. He was getting into uncomfortable territory. The spreading of disease among food plants and animals? Who was he talking about? Who "ought" to be planning to infect milk or water supplies? Was he writing about the Kremlin? Or about the Truman White House?

Bush resumed work on the essay later, again describing the evils of the Soviet system and the importance of unconventional retaliatory strength.

Russia, he said, "refrains from spreading rinderpest among our cattle, for her own herds and wheat fields are vulnerable." He stopped again. Perhaps it occurred to him that he was on the verge of publishing military secrets, threats to Russian livestock and Russian wheat, in the pages of *Reader's Digest*, a magazine with millions of readers. That wouldn't be a good idea. He set the essay aside.

May 3, 2019, Friday

I'm parked in the graveyard.

What amazes me about the history of weapons is that there seems to be no stopping them—and then they stop. Huge, seemingly irresistible forces of momentum keep a research-and-development program in process, and eventually even huger forces shut it down.

All through the 1950s, Dale Jenkins and other Fort Detrick scientists worked on ways to use mosquitoes and other insects to make people sick. And Elvin Stakman, Charles Minarik, Ralph Stine, and others worked on ways to destroy plants. The balloon bomb was tested and built, and squadrons of balloon launchers mastered the complexities of launching balloons from trucks and submarines. (Hydrogen was dangerous in submarines, so they used helium, even though it was more expensive.) In May 1955, Minarik, head of Detrick's anticrop program, invited Professor Stakman to join him for a conference to discuss "certain problems in the field of plant pathology." In June 1956, Minarik wrote Stakman to say how pleased he was that Stakman's consulting contract at Detrick had gone through. "We are planning some field studies at Avon Park next November and would like to have you visit at that time," Minarik wrote. "If you could plan to spend two days at Detrick prior to two or three at Avon Park, this would bring you up-to-date on our activities in the cereal rust field." In January 1958, however, the entire anticrop program came under attack: a report by the Operations Research Office said that plant killing was inefficient and costly. The anticrop program was put on hold. Production of Agent SX, rice blast, continued, but it was paid for a different way, via an industrial-preparedness measure.

Minarik turned to Stakman for help. "I was wondering if you would be able to come to Fort Detrick for about 3 days to read the ORO report and prepare some comments," he wrote. "Dr. Schwab feels confident that our program will be reinstituted if we can refute the ORO report and have it withdrawn." Stakman obliged: "I will be happy to come to Fort Detrick within the next couple of weeks, as you suggest." And then he wrote a critique of the ORO study. Other anticrop scientists came to the defense of Detrick's team. "An ability to induce famine by antifood warfare can provide a strong deterrent to aggression," wrote Edgar Tullis, who'd been engaged in finding ways to spread rice blast disease since 1942. "Mainland China appears to be particularly vulnerable to antirice warfare."

"Dear Stak," Minarik wrote in October 1958. "Just a hasty note to let you know that our program has been reestablished." The money was flowing again. "A great deal of credit for getting the program going again is due to you for your excellent comments on the ORO Report." Minarik said they were hoping to hire twenty anticrop researchers next year. "If you can send any people our way, we would appreciate it very much. Kindest regards, Charlie."

So the antiplant program was saved—and it thrived. Stakman's former student Clyde Christensen studied "molds that deteriorate grain in storage." In 1961, General Maxwell Taylor, President Kennedy's military adviser, endorsed "the use of chemicals to attack the rice and manioc crop in carefully selected mountain areas where the Viet-Cong buildup depends on their own plantings to supplement a thin local food supply." On November 30, 1961, Kennedy approved a "food denial" plan for Vietnam, using Agent Orange and other defoliants developed by Charles Minarik.

One of the classified Pentagon Papers documents, a memo by McGeorge Bundy, leaked by Daniel Ellsberg, tells the story:

> The President has approved the recommendation of the Secretary of State and the Deputy Secretary of Defense to participate in a selective and carefully controlled joint program of defoliant operations in Viet Nam starting with the clearance of key routes and proceeding thereafter to food denial only if the most careful basis of resettlement and alternative food supply has been created.

Thus began the creeping catastrophe of Operation Ranch Hand. "The most effective way to hurt the Viet Cong is to deprive them of food," Secretary of State Dean Rusk explained to Kennedy in the summer of 1962. "Food is scarce in their mountain strongholds and food destruction there can be most effective."

One anticrop scientist, Thomas Barksdale, studied the history of twenty-four rice blast epidemics to find a curve describing "the percentage of days favorable for disease development." In 1960, Barksdale inoculated Florida rice paddies with rice blast fungus and then counted the number of lesions he'd produced; in Okinawa and Taiwan, he used a "midget duster" to infect more experimental rice fields. Another anticropper, Marco Marchetti, developed a fungal rice-killing spray gun powered by compressed carbon dioxide. A third, M. M. Kulik, spread clouds of rice blast disease in Texas using a carbon dioxide pistol.

Paul Linebarger, aka science fiction writer Cordwainer Smith, was hired to study anticrop warfare in 1962. Linebarger and his colleagues wrote: "The advent of modern biological and chemical agents which can effectively attack and destroy a variety of crops now makes it possible to consider the delivery of such agents on a strategic scale to wipe out entire crops of a region or country, thus leaving the target nation in a state of famine and subsequent starvation." They listed some possible "target countries": Afghanistan, Algeria, Borneo, Bulgaria, Burma, Czechoslovakia, Egypt, Hungary, Indonesia, Iraq, Korea, Laos, Malaya, Poland, Romania, Sumatra, Syria, Thailand, the USSR, Vietnam, and Yugoslavia. China was an excellent anticrop target, they felt: "The people are ostensibly always on the verge of starvation," the report said, and "rice and wheat are the main crops and agents are available to destroy both."

In July 1963, Charles Minarik hosted a two-day defoliation conference at Fort Detrick. He invited contractors and scientists from all over the country to meet and give presentations and tour the test fields and greenhouses. Scientists from Monsanto, Dow Chemical, Pennsalt Chemical, the University of California at Davis, Purdue University, the Department of Agriculture, and the University of Illinois were there to investigate new and better ways to achieve leaf "abscission" (detachment) in support of counterinsurgency operations. "The need still exists to get herbicides or organic-type compounds that will do the job in a quicker period of time than we are able to do at present," said General Fred Delmore of Edgewood Arsenal, kicking off the proceedings. "Go as far as you can without committing your companies or giving away proprietary rights or your really deep secrets, but we must have some answers." Kenneth Demaree of Fort Detrick described the tree component of the defoliation-testing program. "We have a nursery at Fort Detrick consisting, at present, of about 1800 trees, and plans for another 18,000 to 20,000 trees to be planted this fall in blocks," Demaree said. "The species now in the nursery are dogwood, maple, pine, spruce, hemlock, bald cypress, and oak. We will reserve some blocks so that we can spray trees that are 10 to 12 years old. A logarithmic sprayer will be used on some plots to determine the minimum amount necessary for complete kill."

But things had begun, by then, gradually, to turn. In March 1963, Representative Robert Kastenmeier, a Wisconsin Democrat, asked President Kennedy to stop Ranch Hand and end "our present starvation tactics in Vietnam." William Bundy, assistant secretary of defense, replied that "denial of food and ambush is a wholly normal procedure in counterinsurgency warfare."

"It is a fair question to ask," said Kastenmeier, "if the continued existence of the Diem regime is worth the compromise of this nation's moral principles."

Joel Aber, one of the student protesters of Project Spice Rack, the

University of Pennsylvania's multiyear germ-warfare evaluation program, said in 1965 that the university was complicit in genocide by investigating "diseases of rice which, if used in Southeast Asia, would result in famine killing millions of people."

A former Fort Detrick employee, Helen Alexander, wrote a letter to the Frederick *News*, on May 18, 1968: "The more I learned about Vietnam and the type of terrible weaponry we have been using there, the more I realized too well how much I was part of the operation," Alexander said. Everyone at Detrick was a cog in the wheel of a conveyor belt, she believed, and the end of the belt was Vietnam:

> Many fine people who are opposed to our policy in Vietnam and the use of such terror weapons as napalm, white phosphorus, nerve gas, defoliants, soil poisoning agents, rice blast fungus, and anti-personnel bombs, will not speak because they are intimidated into the crime of silence. Meanwhile, they continue to earn their money at the expense and misery and destruction of the Vietnamese people.

Really, though, it was the pictures that did it. I remember opening *Life* magazine, or maybe it was *Look* magazine, when I was about eleven years old and seeing a photo of a completely defoliated mangrove swamp or rubber plantation somewhere. It was a nightmarish place, all the big formerly glossy green leaves curled and hanging. I was looking at death. This was what America was doing. Obviously it was wrong.

Arthur Westing, chairman of the Herbicide Assessment Commission of the American Association for the Advancement of Science, went to Indochina with a scientist from Montana, E. W. Pfeiffer, and the two of them surveyed defoliated moonscapes. One location of interest was in Cambodia—Senator Frank Church had heard that the CIA's airline, Air America, was responsible. Westing cabled a question to Ellsworth Bunker, ambassador to Vietnam: "Would you care to comment on the allegation by Senator Frank Church," he said, "that herbicide attack on Cambodia in the Spring of 1969 was carried out by the Central Intelligence Agency?"

"No repeat no defoliation operations were authorized in Cambodia,"

Bunker replied, in a document I found on CREST. "Nevertheless USG has recognized it is possible that one of its aircraft may have carried out this application despite fact no such application was authorized." (USG = U.S. government = CIA, I guess.)

Because the CIA is so careful about tracking its own press coverage, the CREST database is one of the best places to find obscure newspaper and magazine articles critical of the CIA. Sometimes the way they've been indexed or highlighted or subject-tagged is revealing. For instance, the University of Tennessee's newspaper, the *Daily Beacon*, ran a brief editorial in 1979 about the Pine Camp oat-stem-rust experiments, entitled "Rusty Cheerios and the CIA."

"According to research conducted by the American Citizens for Honesty in Government on recently declassified government documents, the U.S. Army and the CIA were experimenting in the 1950's with infected pigeons and turkey feathers to find out an effective means to wipe out cereal crops," the *Beacon*'s editorial said. "The fact that the government used tons of turkey feathers to contaminate the fields causes speculation that a bunch of naked army and CIA people were running around Washington at the time."

A handwritten note on the side reveals that the CIA indexed this document under three subject headings: "CIA2.050.1 FOIA," "ORG1 Scientologists" (because the Citizens for Honesty in Government was an offshoot of the Church of Scientology), and "CIA4.01 MKULTRA." Which is further confirmation that the CIA's plan to destroy Russia's wheat crop was part of MKULTRA or its predecessor MKNAOMI.

Another anti-CIA document in the CREST database is an issue of *Counterspy* that talks about Operation Paper and the opium trade in the Golden Triangle. "From 1948 on, American intelligence activities in the Golden Triangle were intertwined with the opium trade," David Truong says in *Counterspy*. "Infiltration routes for CIA commando teams into southern China were also used as drug smuggling routes for traffickers in Burma and Thailand." Truong cites Alfred McCoy's book *The Politics of Heroin*, a huge work that the CIA tried very hard to squelch. The CIA's general counsel wrote a letter to Harper & Row saying that McCoy's book was "baseless criticism designed to undermine confidence" in the government's antidrug efforts.

How weird to think that the easiest way now to get vintage copies of *Counterspy*, a publication hated, and secretly confiscated, by the CIA, is by searching for it on the CIA's own website.

May 4, 2019, Saturday

I fell asleep last night reading a scientific paper on my phone: "Population Structure of the Rice Blast Pathogen in Vietnam." When I woke up this morning it was there on my screen. What it says is that the pathotypes (races) of rice in North Vietnam are very different from the pathotypes found in South Vietnam. "Although the number of isolates analyzed is relatively small, the present results suggest that the fungal population is quite different between the two major rice production deltas." Different in two ways: the "virulence spectrum" is different, and the "blast population in the northern delta was more diverse in the lineage structure than that in the southern delta."

The plant scientists don't have an entirely satisfactory explanation for this. They have possible explanations but nothing definite.

I think I know why, because I know how interested Fort Detrick and its contractors were in the ways and means of infecting rice crops during the Vietnam War. The fungal pathotypes are different in the north, I think, because that's where the CIA was field-testing rice disease.

———————

I GOT AN EMAIL BACK from Marion Endicott, Steve Endicott's daughter. I'd asked Steve, through Marion, if there was a phrase or a saying that his father, Reverend James Endicott, used that had helped him when he, Steve, was working on the biological warfare book.

Marion took down what Steve said, as she and gathered family sat in Steve's living room. He said he remembered the big speech that James Endicott gave in Toronto in 1952, when he took the side of China and North Korea and said the germ-warfare accusations were true. James Endicott's father, Steve's grandfather, also a minister, had introduced his son by talking about the Bible story of Daniel and the lion's den, and how his son James was taking the side of Daniel.

The people around Steve then sang the old hymn, as best they could remember it:

> Dare to be a Daniel
> Dare to stand alone
> Dare to have a purpose firm
> Dare to make it known.

"At the moment a number of us are sitting around the living room and occasionally bursting into song," Steve then said. "It's a lovely way to go."

Marion wrote, "Thank you from him and our family for your friendship and your quest for the historical truth."

IN OTTAWA, ON MAY 13, 1952, the Canadian government considered charging James Endicott with treason. "Justice Minister Stuart Garson said in parliament that his legal experts would let him know 'very shortly' whether the treason laws, which carry a maximum penalty of death, applied to the former United Church missionary who charged the allies with using germ warfare against the Chinese Communists," reported a newspaper in Victoria, British Columbia.

Endicott's pamphlet quoted *U.S. News and World Report* from September 21, 1951: "New non-atomic weapons of fantastic design are talked of in Congress as being available for use in Korea." On the back, he printed the Canadian Peace Pledge: "I believe that there are no international differences which cannot be settled by negotiation," it says. "I am for the total abolition of all instruments of mass destruction of people, such as atomic, bacteriological, napalm and similar weapons."

Some news stories had called Endicott's speech anti-American, he wrote. "It was not. Neither is this an anti-U.S. pamphlet. Almost everybody in the U.S. is opposed to germ warfare. That is why its preparation is under such secrecy."

May 5, 2019, Sunday

There are individual deaths, and then there are unthinkably vast plans for killing. The most sweeping plan was for the eradication of the Jews of Europe, much of which was carried out. The worst year was 1942. The killing was sheltered and enabled by secrecy and long years of attritional war.

The second-biggest plan—that I can think of right now at least—was Operation Sphinx, a plan to kill or injure more than ten million people by air-dropping a hundred thousand tons of poison gas on Japanese cities. I learned about it a year ago, reading Jeanne Guillemin's book about Unit 731, *Hidden Atrocities*. Sphinx was not carried out. The plan was hidden until 1996, when military historians Norman Polmar and Thomas B. Allen got wind of it and filed a FOIA request. It was, wrote Polmar and Allen in January 1998, "a document kept under wraps for five decades."

General William Porter, head of the Chemical Warfare Service, submitted "A Study of the Possible Use of Toxic Gas in Operation Olympic" on June 9, 1945. (Somebody later inserted the handwritten word "Retaliatory" in front of the word "Use.") The plan envisioned an initial "gas blitz," according to the Sphinx document. Tokyo was to be drenched with phosgene at eight o'clock in the morning, when most people were at home—those whose homes had survived the March 10 firebombing, that is. The primary target was an area north of the Imperial Palace. "Almost a million people would be in that area at the time of the first strike," write Polmar and Allen. "Within two miles of the target area were 776,000 more Japanese; they probably would be in the path of wind-carried gas." The attack would use more than 21,000 five-hundred-pound gas bombs, or 5,420 thousand-pound gas bombs—depending on which was judged to be best.

After Tokyo, twenty-five cities were specified as "especially suitable for gas attacks." Later urban gassings would use mustard gas, hydrogen cyanide, and cyanogen chloride. Every six days would bring "refresher" gas attacks. One attack zone in Yokohama was described as filled with dense clusters of low houses, narrow streets, small stores, and theaters. "There are no large factories in this zone and comparatively few household shops." In all, said the planners, the gas attacks "might easily kill 5,000,000 people and injure that many more."

SO THERE EXISTED these gas warriors, Porter and Waitt and others— damaged sacks of misdirected rage—who had spent the war stockpiling fearsome substances without being able to use them. They'd watched tens of thousands of American soldiers die fighting over little islands in the Pacific Ocean. Why? they asked. When there is gas? The United States was producing sixty tons of war gas per day. "YOU CAN COOK THEM BETTER WITH GAS," said an editorial in the *Chicago Tribune* in March 1945, citing Alden Waitt's book *Gas Warfare*. When I first read about Operation Sphinx, in July of last year—first in Jeanne Guillemin's book and then in Polmar and Allen's paper—I felt trembly and disgusted at the same time. M. came in from outside, where she'd been using the tiny electric mower, really a Weedwacker attached to a wheeled base, on a patch of grass. She said, "How's it going?" I didn't want to tell her because it's too much to load on someone who's just been smelling the smell of cut grass out in the garden. But I did anyway. I apologized.

It's a horrible and disillusioning thing to know that your own country was passing around a paper like Sphinx in the Pentagon. I thought, At this moment I want to go away from here. Away from this country. It was 2018 and we had a president who was nakedly horrible. Who was at the end of a long line of completely hypocritical presidents. The earlier presidents weren't crassly stupid the way this one is—they got their speechwriters to write nice humanitarian things about the desire for peace, and freedom of expression, and liberty and justice, but they were all sitting on top of a mountain of weapons, and they used them all over the place, one president after another. Even Carter and even Clinton. When they got in the driver's seat, they couldn't resist. Eisenhower made that much-quoted speech at the end of his term, the one about the military-industrial complex, but he spent much of his presidency funding guerrilla actions that led to the deaths of thousands of people. He didn't want to send platoons of American soldiers to their deaths—he'd already done that in the big war. He wanted to use indigenous forces, non-American troops: hired mercenaries or corruptible factions.

And then comes Kennedy, who approves defoliation and food denial and Operation Mongoose. Kennedy appoints Henry Cabot Lodge to be ambassador to Vietnam. Ambassador Lodge becomes filled with a murderous sort of petulance in Saigon and writes to Dean Rusk and Robert McNamara in June 1964. "It would help here, and possibly in Laos and Thailand, if there were some screams from North Viet-nam that they had been hit," Lodge says. "There must be a number of different ways to make them scream." He mentions rockets, employed on the pretext that they were returning fire. One method he offers is redacted. Lodge uses the word "scream" four times in one telegram. Then comes the Gulf of Tonkin incident, and then in 1965 Lodge and the others convince Johnson to begin Rolling Thunder. "The war is in a new phase, thanks to the President's great decisions," Lodge wrote to Clark Clifford, delighted about the bombing.

More thunder, endless thunder. "Anything that flies on anything that moves," said Kissinger, relaying Nixon's order.

SOMETIMES I DON'T BELIEVE in the history of the United States. I don't believe that this place deserves to have any sort of moral standing in the world. As a country. It has been the source of incalculable disruption.

I understand that Americans individually have done good things—paintings, sitcoms, songs, cars, toasters, locomotives, buildings, bridges, billboards, sunglasses, topiary, dance steps, casseroles, no-hitters, corn mazes, speeches, ad campaigns, YouTube videos. *The New Yorker* of the Katharine White and E. B. White era is a great American achievement, no question. I always go back to the midcentury *New Yorker.* And there's John Singer Sargent. But Operation Sphinx—this homegrown American plan to kill 5 million human beings in the space of weeks, almost all of them civilians—is just too awful to think about.

I'M FORTUNATE TO BE MARRIED TO M. If you have a life companion, then when you come to some hideous surprise like Operation Sphinx that climbs out of the dead past and stands there in front of you, bleeding from the mouth, waiting for you to adjust to its presence, you can talk to your loved spouse and she will hug you and say, "That's bad, that's inhuman, that's awful."

As M. said, it didn't happen. It was just a plan.

AMNESIA IS THE CIA'S IDEAL—and the Air Force's ideal. That's what I'm understanding. By controlling their own records, and purging them, and cutting all the interesting parts out of them, they are forcing a state of amnesia on a whole country—on us—so that we don't know what we as a purportedly self-governing nation did. We can't remember what we did.

Historians are professional rememberers. They find ways through the thickets of specificity. They connect one name with another. They load a lot in their heads, more and more of it, until they feel themselves brimming over with too much, and then they put it all down in a book, which is an album of smoothed and aligned and combed-through memories.

Really secrecy is about mind control. It's about deliberately imposed historical amnesia. If you can suppress all knowledge of something like Operation Sphinx for decades, you allow the myth of American decency and goodness to endure. By the time the truth comes out, the shock is muffled. The outrage response is inhibited.

WHAT FRANK WISNER and Sidney Gottlieb and Cornelius Roosevelt were doing with MKULTRA was trying to figure how to get someone to do something—and then forget all about it after they'd created the behavior. MKULTRA had as one of its major goals the refinement of drugs and techniques that create a state of amnesia. Donald Hastings, an early MKULTRA scientist, studied the "guaranteed amnesia" of electroshock treatments. Dr. Carl C. Feiffer, a pharmacologist, was paid by the CIA in the 1960s to test LSD and other drugs on volunteers at the federal prison in Atlanta and at the reformatory in Bordentown, New Jersey; one of his tasks was to evaluate substances that would create amnesia and help people resist interrogation. Dr. Charles Geschickter, a cancer researcher at Georgetown Hospital, formerly a Navy pathologist and an authority on "benign and malignant diseases of the breast," was funded by the CIA in order to look into drugs that would create prolonged states of sleep and/or amnesia. (At congressional hearings in 1977, Dr. Geschickter testified that CIA documents were "absolutely false and inaccurate" when they implied that he had experimented with knockout drugs on advanced cancer patients.) The CIA and the Office of Naval Research paid for investigation into what someone called a "perfect concussion." This work seems to be related to MKULTRA work on "carefully controlled impacts deliberately delivered to the heads of experimental animals" in order to find out what type of nonpenetrating impact was instantly fatal, what caused a cranial hemorrhage, and what led to a concussion with attendant memory loss: the idea was to produce a "calibrated blackjack." There was, running throughout MKULTRA's research, a fascination with amnesia hypnosis—finger-snap forgetfulness.

People forget, or pretend to forget, but the documents remember, and some of them survive in out-of-the-way places. John Marks taught us that.

LAST YEAR, the CIA was still trying to administer a calibrated blackjack to the historical record of MKULTRA. John Greenewald, who began as a UFO inquirer and who is now a prodigious FOIA requester, runs a website called the Black Vault, where, in 2004, after years of waiting, he posted many hundreds of scanned MKULTRA records that he got by filing a FOIA request. He thought he'd gotten all the records on the CIA's MKULTRA index, but it turned out he hadn't; the Agency had held back more than two thousand pages without telling him. "I then began a 'FOIA Battle' with the CIA about this entire issue," he wrote. The CIA asked for $425.80 to supply the missing "behavioral control" MKULTRA records. He sent in a check. They replied that the amount they were asking for was incorrect. They really only needed $221.60. Could Mr. Greenewald please send in a new check? He did. And finally he got the documents and posted them online. They're free and they are not in the CIA's CREST database.

Today I spent some hours looking through Greenewald's 2018 release. That's where I found the document about the calibrated blackjack. Some rhesus monkeys, many cats, and some dogs were drugged with mind-altering chemicals, tortured, and killed in these CIA experiments—more cats than dogs simply because cats were less expensive. The CIA wanted to implant cats with microphones and tone-based guidance systems, on the B. F. Skinnerian model of reward and punishment, so that they could eavesdrop on Russian conversations. Or, perhaps, to deliver bombs. There's so much whiting out that it's not clear what all is going on with the cats and the dogs and the monkeys:

> It is felt that the ⬛ proposal for ⬛ should be undertaken at this time in order to begin studying mechanisms, both animal and hardware, to be used ⬛ and to do this covertly and in a nonattributable fashion.

> This project which has also been underway for approximately twelve months has two basic purposes. The first is to develop a prototype ⬛ system, totally ⬛ a cat, ⬛. We felt that a total system approach would assist us in determining what the real problems are in ⬛ cats or dogs for a variety of ⬛.

ONE DOCUMENT SAYS, "We are negotiating with a contractor to do a paper study on possible ways of guiding ⬛ animals over short and medium range distances." Domestic animals? Barnyard animals? Unarmed animals? Trained animals? Why is this secret? *What kind of animals?*

In one set of behavioral experiments, a whited-out doctor and colleagues tested whited-out drugs to see whether they would or would not inhibit a rage response in cats. The experimental means used to induce the rage response is whited out. The researchers also did something whited out to "mongrel dogs," and they studied the "shock-induced fighting response" in pairs of mice. Of the drugs they tested, they found that "⬛ was much more potent in inhibition of mouse fighting behavior ⬛ than was ⬛." The last page is altogether whited out except for five words: "To further screen candidate compounds." Perhaps it's about human testing.

All of this was paid for by us.

THE WHOLE POINT OF PLAUSIBLE DENIAL is that you must lie. You can't not lie. Your duty is to lie. To tell the truth is to imperil the covert nature of the operation.

May 6, 2019, Monday

So yesterday M. and I walked through a nature preserve with an overflowing brimming mirror of a river and green moss and beautiful reflections of trees, and it was a Sunday. I looked at my phone while we were walking and saw an email from one of Stephen Endicott's daughters, not Marion but Valerie. It said that Steve "was allowed the peaceful, happy death and 'long rest' that he so desired." It had happened at 1:00 P.M. on May 4. So by the time I wrote my reply to Marion's email about Daniel and the lion's den, Steve was already gone.

And there it is. All the memories of working on that book—all of the endnotes, all the knowledge of those Joint Chiefs of Staff documents, those trips to China, the days and weeks going through file boxes at the National Archives—poof, gone. Steve is gone, and Ned is gone, and all that is left is the book. It's a dense book. And they were attacked for it. Unfairly. But they wrote it and stood by it and that's what's left. "The continuing evasiveness and secrecy about what happened in those distant days make the Korean War a living part of the continuing debate on public morality and the waging of war," they wrote.

Right when I saw the email from Valerie Endicott, and knew that

Steve was dead, I was standing in front of a large stone covered with almost incandescently green moss, in a clearing. I took a picture.

IT'S A STRANGE STATE OF AFFAIRS: the CIA's history is parceled out in half a dozen places. Brill's Primary Sources is one important source—they have an interesting collection of documents curated by the late Matthew Aid, author of *The Secret Sentry*, about the National Security Agency. (Aid raised the alarm in 2006 when the CIA and the Air Force secretly reclassified more than 55,000 pages of declassified documents, some going back to World War II, which had previously been open to researchers at the National Archives.) Brill's is good but expensive: more than thirty dollars to use their database for a day or two, and then they don't let you download anything or even print it out. The Black Vault is another source—totally free. The National Security Archive at GWU has a huge collection of documents. And then there's governmentattic.org and ibiblio.com and maryferrell.com and rockymountainarsenal and memoryhole2 and MuckRock, which has joined forces with documentcloud. Plus the thousands of pages that FOIA voyager Emma Best has put on the Internet Archive.

And then of course there's the CIA's own Freedom of Information Act Reading Room, as they call it, where CREST resides. "Do UFOs fascinate you?" says the CIA's webpage. "Are you a history buff who wants to learn more about the Bay of Pigs, Vietnam or the A-12 Oxcart? Have stories about spies always fascinated you? You can find information about all of these topics and more in the Central Intelligence Agency (CIA) Freedom of Information Act (FOIA) Electronic Reading Room."

Nobody knows how much is held back. In 1994, Melvin Leffler, a historian, wrote a letter to the CIA's director of information management, on the letterhead of SHAFR, the Society for Historians of American Foreign Relations, of which Leffler was president. "As a group we applaud the publicly stated position of the CIA that it will extend greater access to its records and files," Leffler said. "On the whole, however, CIA actions have not comported with its rhetoric, and the agency has hardly complied with the spirit of the 1984 law calling for openness." The basic problem,

Leffler said, was that the CIA had not presented any overall description of its records or its filing system. "It has not done this even for the early years of the agency's existence. The public has absolutely no way to judge the significance of CIA releases of selected materials until it has a full and accurate listing of its records."

This letter was one of many released by the CIA in response to a FOIA request from Government Attic. Every ten years, under the provisions of the 1984 act—the one under Reagan that shut off access to operational files—the CIA is required to solicit letters from the public regarding its declassificational efforts.

David Corn, then Washington editor of *The Nation*, wrote: "While the CIA has made strides in its historical unit toward greater openness, the atmosphere in the FOIA office has struck me as being overly protective in almost a vindictive manner—to the extent that it is hard to trust the office when it reports it cannot find documents."

Patricia Mooney-Melvin, president of the National Council on Public History, wrote the CIA that "preselected groups of documents pulled from the files" won't do. "The principle that the sensitivity of a record declines with age should be a part of all access policies. A most troubling aspect of the current designation of files to be exempt from the Freedom of Information Act is that there is no consideration of the age of documents. Thus, a 1950 document is as inaccessible as one from 1990, if it falls within one of the exempted categories." Someone, name blanked, from the American Historical Association wrote: "We are troubled by the continued resistance of the CIA to making older records subject to FOIA requests." Arnita Jones, executive secretary of the Organization of American Historians, wrote that historians needed access to the CIA's old operational files. "We therefore urge that there be a full-scale revision of the operational categories defined in the CIA Information Act of 1984 in order that older records except for a few personnel files within all these categories will be subject to FOIA requests."

None of that has happened.

May 7, 2019, Tuesday

It's my daughter Alice's birthday and leaves are actually coming out on the trees. Yesterday M. washed the curtains. I took a lot of pictures of them slow dancing and salaaming on the clothesline. The dogs were tethered outside. They barked furiously at an innocent pedestrian and had to go inside in disgrace.

JUST NOW I WAS WONDERING how to end this book. You stop writing, I thought, not when you've found the answer, but when you're tired of wanting to know the answer. You end when curiosity dies. I'm still curious.

I'm curious, for instance, about the potato bugs in 1950.

SOME THINGS ARE WORTH SAYING. I thought of them yesterday while driving around.

First. The early "political warfare" phase of the CIA was something that came out of conversations between Allen Dulles and George Kennan.

Kennan wrote it up and pushed it at the State Department, but it was really Dulles's achievement. The creation of shell corporations, the fake private nonprofits—all that is Dulles, not Kennan, who had retreated to Princeton's Institute for Advanced Study to have deep thoughts about the history of diplomacy. Dulles pushed for Frank Wisner to be in charge, because he knew he had sway over Wisner, and when Eisenhower became president in 1953, Dulles assumed control of the whole of the CIA, as Wisner's sanity gradually crumbled.

SECOND. Wisner was the mad tortured soul. Richard Helms was the neo-Nazi. "Make economy scream," Helms wrote, in planning with Richard Nixon how to deal with the Allende regime in Chile.

THIRD. In 2009 I spent some days at the Eisenhower Library in Abilene, Kansas. I felt then that I understood more or less what had gone on. The CIA had tried out several germ-warfare experiments in a war zone, first late in 1950, and then in January and February 1952, and the Communists had discovered them almost immediately, launching in response a huge, coordinated propaganda campaign—a campaign that included some faked evidence. When Stalin died in March 1953, and Eisenhower took over the presidency, Eisenhower's top Cold Warriors—C. D. Jackson and Henry Cabot Lodge and the Dulles brothers—created a new, vitriolic campaign against the Soviet regime, in order to, as Lodge wrote in March 1953, "throw them right back on their haunches." The campaign would involve "press releases, movies, statements of denunciation by world political leaders, resolutions by organizations, magazine articles, public parades and demonstrations, and protests to Moscow," said Lodge, who had begun his tenure as ambassador to the United Nations by refusing to shake Ambassador Vishinsky's hand.

A central component of the new strategy was to neutralize the germ charges. "It is of the utmost importance for us to counter these charges and to dissipate to the fullest possible extent their harmful effects upon the attitude of those peoples whose confidence it is our purpose to win and maintain," wrote Ambassador Lodge to C. D. Jackson. "I know that attention is being paid to the matter in the State and Defense Departments as well as in CIA."

The Army began working out "deindoctrination procedures" for repatriated prisoners of war, and at the CIA Allen Dulles convened a committee of scientists and psychological strategists, headed by Detlev Bronk, president of Johns Hopkins, to "review evidence on Commie 'brain-washing' activities." They didn't get much accomplished; Bronk himself was induced to draft a statement about brainwashing for release to the scientific community, but it was "pitched in an extremely low key," according to an observer at the State Department—"so much so as to be of dubious effect." But Dulles himself gave a strong speech in Hot Springs, Virginia, to Princeton alumni entitled "Brain Warfare," copies of which he handed around to favored journalists, including *The New York Times*'s Arthur Krock, who wrote it up. The Soviet aim, Dulles said, was "the perversion of the minds of selected individuals":

> Parrotlike, the individuals so conditioned can merely repeat thoughts that have been implanted in their minds by suggestion from outside. In effect the brain under these circumstances becomes a phonograph playing a disc put on its spindle by an outside genius over which it has no control.

American prisoners of war had read over the radio "fictitious information regarding preparations for bacterial warfare in Korea," Dulles said to his fellow Princetonians in Hot Springs. And the brainwashing continued: "It is not beyond the range of possibility that considerable numbers of our own boys there might be so indoctrinated as to be induced, temporarily at least, to renounce country and family."

Meanwhile the Communists continued to insist that American planes were dropping insects on them. "The North Korean radio resumed its germ-warfare campaign yesterday after dropping the hate-propaganda theme during a mourning period for Stalin," reported the Associated Press on March 21, 1953. "A Pyongyang broadcast heard here said allied planes from January to mid-March 'made over sixty air drops of germ-infested insects' in North Korea."

C. D. Jackson, former publisher of *Fortune* magazine and psychological-warfare specialist, wrote President Eisenhower in April 1953 that he'd been puzzling over the question of why the Soviets had organized such a big and expensive germ-warfare propaganda effort. "It couldn't be just 'hate America,'" Jackson thought. "It couldn't be just preparing the way for their own use of bacteriological warfare. It couldn't be just a counter measure to our sending candy, soap, and food by balloon. It couldn't be just a device to discredit us in the U.N." Jackson believed that the Soviets' sinister purpose was to "plant the idea that maybe the Americans are morally capable of initiating germ warfare." If we were capable of germ warfare, Jackson wrote, we could be capable of anything at all. "I feel that it is terribly important that we should erase the mass impression that the Americans are capable of germ warfare."

Jackson wanted to create a "Committee of 100 Against Soviet Germ Warfare Lies," composed of eminent scientists, lawyers, and religious leaders, using funds from the U.S. government. "These could come from CIA, through a foundation such as the Rockefeller Foundation, which has a worldwide reputation for scientific research," he suggested to Eisenhower. Funding could begin at $100,000 and rise to $300,000. It was a matter of the highest urgency, Jackson wrote.

In 1953, American prisoners of war began arriving in the United States from Tokyo, as part of an exchange program with the Communists called Little Switch. The returning POWs were carefully vetted and assigned one of three categories—black, white, or gray. Black prisoners had signed several peace petitions or issued statements that indicated a level of cooperation with their captors. White prisoners had not collaborated. Gray prisoners had signed only one or two petitions. Some returnees were allowed to give interviews, but the hard-core collaborators, thought to be security risks, were isolated and flown to Valley Forge Hospital. While in transit at Travis Air Force Base, in an airplane with barred windows, they were surrounded by military police with machine guns.

"A planeload of repatriated American prisoners of war from Korea, designated by the Air Force as 'victims of Communist propaganda,' arrived here today under a cloak of military secrecy," reported the Associated Press on May 1, 1953. The pro-Red patients told a chaplain that they were unhappy over a headline in the Far East edition of *The Stars and Stripes*: "Communist Dupes Destined for High Level Psychiatric Treatment at Valley Forge."

The ad hoc committee issued a report on the isolated group of returning prisoners held at Valley Forge Hospital. Five were confirmed Communists, "considered irreclaimable and constituting security risks." Five were slightly indoctrinated and would need minimal "reorientation." Ten were "thoroughly indoctrinated" but would come around in time. There had been no outright torture of these POWs, the report said, and no brainwashing:

> Among this group there was no evidence of any of them having been subjected to "brainwashing" techniques, if this is interpreted to mean any special hypnotic, narcotic, medical injection, or any torture inflicted to impose the will of the Communists on these individuals. On the other hand, they were subjected to Communist indoctrination by the process of continual exposure to propaganda, the denial of truth or factual events, and by a system of rewards and punishments.

One prisoner, Carl Kirchausen, was diagnosed as having a "cyclothymic" (mildly bipolar) personality and frostbite in both feet. "This soldier, of Jewish extraction, was born in Germany, in an urban area. He fled Germany due to persecution by the Nazis at the age of 12." He'd written letters to Communist friends in Berlin and London, and he'd spent much time while at the POW camp reading Communist literature. He believed that the United States had engaged in biological warfare. "The Committee recommended that this man be closely surveilled by the FBI upon release from the Army."

DULLES, LODGE, and Jackson carried on their crusade against the germ-warfare charges. They called it "National Operations Plan to Exploit Communist Bacteriological Warfare Hoax, Mistreatment of Prisoners of War, and Other Atrocities Perpetrated by Communist Forces during the Korean War." Allen Dulles signed off on it in October 1953.

The plan aimed high, hoping to put out a documentary film or TV show, hosted by someone like Edward R. Murrow or Eric Sevareid, on the brainwashing—or "mind-murder," or "menticide"—of prisoners of war, with overall guidance coming from movie director John Ford. They also envisioned "a major 'quickie' paper-back book, possibly 'authored' by one of the returned officers." An MGM feature film, *Prisoner of War*, came out in 1954: Ronald Reagan, hearing the screams of the tortured, grimaces and says, "Every man has his breaking point." In the end, though, the government's biggest counterpropagandistic moment was a speech by Dr. Charles Mayo, son of the founder of the Mayo Clinic, delivered at the United Nations on October 26, 1953.

"It is not a pretty story that confronts us," said Dr. Mayo. "It is a story of terrible physical and moral degradation. It concerns men shaken loose from their foundations of moral value—men beaten down by the conditioning which the science of Pavlov reserves for dogs and rats—all in a vicious attempt to make them accomplices in a frightful lie." The germ-warfare campaign, Mayo said, was "part of a larger political program of Communist imperialism." Its aim was to "discredit the United States in the eyes of the free world and thus to help isolate it from its allies." The speech was ghostwritten by Wallace Irwin, Jr., a member of Henry Cabot Lodge's staff at the United Nations, and it relied on reports gathered by Philip Corso, a counterintelligence officer who had served under Charles Willoughby on General MacArthur's staff in Japan.

Ambassador Lodge wrote C. D. Jackson on the tremendous success of Mayo's address: "The statement was a good example of what can be accomplished by coordination between PSB, Defense and CIA and my advisers tell me that Colonel Philip J. Corso was primarily responsible for assembling this material. Colonel Corso should be commended for having performed this outstanding job which may prove to be the biggest setback the communists have suffered since the landing at Inchon." Corso believed that the Communists' treatment of prisoners of war was "an insidiously planned conspiracy with the far reaching goal—i.e, World Domination."

In later years, Corso became a UFO fantasist. He described a 1947 visitation at Roswell by "extra-terrestrial biological entities," and asserted that Kevlar, fiber-optic cable, integrated circuits, and the stealthy design of the B-2 bomber all came from materials found at the alien crash site. He claimed that he'd seen an alien body floating dead in a tank, minus sex organs. "I'll tell you about the time machine later," he said to John Hockenberry on *Dateline* in 1997.

I interviewed speechwriter Wallace Irwin, Jr., at a retirement home in Lexington, Virginia, a year before he died in 2010. He turned out to be a thoughtful, high-born Princetonian in a plum-colored cardigan—the son of newspaper humorist Wallace Irwin. The younger Irwin, writer of United Nations speeches for Adlai Stevenson and George W. Bush, and later editor of *Foreign Policy*, had unpleasant memories of Henry Cabot Lodge, who was brusque and dictatorial. Irwin told me that he came to understand later that Lodge's effort to invalidate the Communist allegations was based on untruths and "machinations." Charles Mayo, he said, was a nice man who'd been dumped into a situation he didn't know anything about. "This was, I think, about the only experience I ever had," Irwin said, "in which I was engaged in an operation which turned out to be based to a great extent on falsehoods."

Irwin said he'd had suspicions at the time that there might be some substance to the germ-war allegations. "Absolutely," he said. But he had a job to do, which was to make the government's case. "Probably some of these things were really done," Irwin said. "How many of them, which ones of them I will never know. And I don't really give a damn. The Cold War is over. We won. The heck with it." Both sides lied, he said, and the Chinese and the Russians lied to each other, too.

I said I couldn't help it—I wanted to know more. I wanted the documents to be declassified.

"I don't think it's going to happen," Irwin replied. "A lot of people want to protect their backside—and protect the institutional setting that they are still working for." He paused for a moment. "We don't admit that we lied," he said.

May 8, 2019, Wednesday

G arbage day. Dogs fed. Coffee is going.

So many hours and days I've spent gathering little facts about unknown people. There is a memo by Herbert D. Friedlander on the status of anthrax in the Air Force's Research and Development Program as of May 1952. When research began during World War II, Friedlander wrote, it took a million spores to infect a single monkey. "Improvement in anthrax strains led to an exposed dosage of 70,000 spores for monkeys. By adding a surface active agent the exposed dosage for monkeys became 8,000 spores."

My small question is: Was this Herbert D. Friedlander—this proponent of anthrax and plague weapons during the very apogee of international outrage over America's use of germs—the same person as the Herbert D. Friedlander who, as a sixteen-year-old boy, won first place in a glider contest in New York? "A new world's record for hand-launched model gliders was set yesterday by Herbert Friedlander, 16 years old, of 2,527 Cortelyou Road, Brooklyn, when his model craft made a timed flight of 2 minutes 58 seconds at a gliding contest held in Central Park under the auspices of the Metropolitan Model Airplane Council," *The New York Times* reported. The Central Park Herbert Friedlander also came in first in the rubber-band-powered competition. His rubber-band plane flew for more than four minutes. What a triumph. In 1944 he served as a bomber navigator in the war. I don't know if the glider-and-bomber Friedlander is the same as the anthrax-and-plague Friedlander, or not.

I READ UP ON THE WALK of the Quaker Action Group in 1970. The Quakers and Lawrence Scott went up against Detrick twice—once in 1959–1961, and once in 1970.

Nixon, hoping to be seen as a peaceable president despite Vietnam, had announced in November 1969 that he was putting a stop to offensive biological-weapons research (except for "research into those offensive aspects of bacteriological/biological agents necessary to determine what defensive measures are required"), but herbicides, riot-control gases, and various lethal toxins weren't banned. Existing stockpiles of disease weapons weren't destroyed yet, either.

On June 2, 1970, the Philadelphia office of the FBI sent a cable to FBI headquarters. The Quaker Action Group, they'd learned (from a Quaker mole, Mrs. Alenda Crymble), was planning a campaign against chemical and biological weapons, to begin with a demonstration in front of the White House, followed by a tree planting and a walk to Edgewood Arsenal and Fort Detrick, with minor acts of civil disobedience scheduled here and there. "All this will be tied directly to the demand for withdrawal from Cambodia and Vietnam as well as CBW weapons," the FBI noted. Military agencies and the Secret Service had been informed.

Mrs. Crymble had provided the FBI with a copy of the typed flyer for the campaign. "SPREAD THE STRIKE TO THE CENTERS OF DEATH," it said. "Herbicides, CN and CS gases, napalm and other products of Fort Detrick and Edgewood arsenal (both near Baltimore) have been used extensively in Vietnam. Now Cambodia and Laos are being devastated." A schedule of nonviolent mass demonstrations followed, with dates for street speaking, leafleting, and "guerrilla theater." The sponsors included A Quaker Action Group, the War Resisters League, the Catholic Peace Fellowship, the Jewish Peace Fellowship, and the Women's International League for Peace and Freedom. "We believe that nonviolent action has great possibilities for revolutionary change," read the flyer, which also demanded an end to the stockpiling of chemical and biological weapons, and called for the conversion of Fort Detrick to a "World Health Center."

The FBI followed the progress of the protest step by step; this surveillance is revealed in a bulky document held back, pointlessly, until the obligatory 2017 JFK records release by the National Archives. On June 12, 1970, about twenty Quaker Action protesters appeared at the Pentagon, where they engaged in guerrilla theater critical of the war and defoliation. Four protesters tried to hand out literature inside the Pentagon about the "weapon of starvation" and were arrested. On July 1, 1970, a group of forty, shadowed by two federal agents, gathered in Lafayette Park, across from the White House, and planted a tree at a Boy Scout monument. (They'd gotten permission from the Park Service.) They handed out leaflets:

> Herbicides and defoliants have killed a large percentage of crops resulting in starvation mostly among civilians. Gases—CS, CN, DM—are used to flush whole villages out of their shelters where they can be bombed. Studies have shown that poisoning and extreme birth defects result from some of these chemicals.

On July 5, 1970, three hundred people gathered at Fort McHenry in Baltimore. Pete Seeger and Stuart Meacham were there. "Speeches were anti-war, anti-chemical and biological weapons production oriented," the FBI's cable said. "Crowd sang several ecology type songs." On July 8, 1970, forty-five demonstrators gathered at Edgewood Arsenal, intending to stay for an all-night vigil. Some boarded a bus for Fort Detrick. They had two trees that they wanted to plant, but didn't. The next day "three white males and four white females" tried to plant a fourteen-inch-high tree at Edgewood but were arrested and driven off in a bus. A military police vehicle ran over the tree, according to the *Baltimore Sun*. More protesters entered to take away the broken tree and were themselves arrested. On July 13, 1970,

Lawrence Scott, the leader of the movement, and William Davidon, a physics professor at Haverford College, were arrested at Edgewood Arsenal—again for trying to plant a pine tree.

Later, officials at Edgewood Arsenal agreed to plant the tree. "Nonviolent action," said another leaflet handed out by the Quaker Action Group, "has the power to change men's hearts and minds and change outworn institutions which perpetuate the war in Vietnam." On October 1, 1970, Helen Alexander, the Detrick employee who'd written an antiwar letter in 1968, was arrested for trying to plant a tree on the grounds of the Pentagon, according to the FBI file.

STARTING IN MAY 1971, the Department of Defense began destroying its biological weapons stockpile: 220 pounds of anthrax, 804 pounds of tularemia, 334 pounds of Venezuelan equine encephalitis, 4,991 gallons of Venezuelan equine encephalitis in liquid suspension, 5,098 gallons of Q fever, and tens of thousands of bombs. At Rocky Mountain Arsenal, workers buried 158,684 pounds of wheat rust and 1,865 pounds of rice blast. Some of the wheat disease was homegrown at Rocky Mountain, and some was cultivated at Beale Air Force Base in California, north of Sacramento, "harvested by Air Force personnel dressed to look like farmers," according to a retired Chemical Corps employee.

Fort Detrick was repurposed. The headline across the top of the *Baltimore Sun* on October 18, 1971, was "Nixon Says Ft. Detrick to Be Top Cancer Research Center." The germ-warfare buildings were now at the disposal of the National Cancer Institute. Germ warriors would become cancer healers. "Where we have previously had scientists—some of the best people that we could possibly find in the United States—working on weapons of war, we now have scientists devoting their efforts toward saving life," President Nixon said. "For thousands of years, mankind has dreamed of turning swords into ploughshares and spears into pruning hooks. Today we mark another chapter in the realization of that dream."

May 9, 2019, Thursday

At about 11:00 A.M., my cell phone rang. A man from the CIA was calling with a question about one of the FOIA letters I'd sent. I'd asked for white-out removal in a March 6, 1952, document, but I'd mistakenly typed "May 6, 1952." Did I want March 6, or May 6? I said I wanted March 6. I thanked him for calling. "It's very kind of you," I said.

ON JANUARY 29, 1954, the Arbenz government in Guatemala exposed the American involvement in the coup plot by publishing a white paper that included actual intercepted documents between the plotters. Wisner and his team regrouped and plowed ahead nonetheless. Who cared if the operation was blown? Deception plans, assassination plans, terror, and harassment all would continue, and accelerate.

I REALLY THINK GUATEMALA is the key to Korea and germ warfare. The Guatemala records are complete enough that you understand how the men at the Office of Policy Coordination planned something and then shifted around when it was exposed, and how they then indignantly denied what they knew to be true: 1954 is the key to 1952.

Two things were preoccupying the CIA in 1954—one was countering Colonel Frank Schwable and the other Air Force fliers who'd signed germ-warfare confessions. The other was Guatemala. Indochina was perhaps a distant third.

Here are some things I found in my notes about events in January and February 1954:

January 9, 1954. The CIA's psychological-warfare team in Guatemala reported that they had made a "hit back" propaganda poster to counter attacks on United Fruit and foreign intervention. The poster showed an octopus with a skull face superimposed with a hammer and sickle. Each of the tentacles was labeled: one tentacle was *destruccion del trabajo y economia nacional*, and one tentacle was *intervencion extranjera*. They chose the octopus because United Fruit was known as "El Pulpo" (the Octopus) in Guatemala. The CIA's foreign interventionists were thus making a poster critiquing foreign intervention by appropriating a central image from the opposition—classic transformational psychological warfare.

January 10, 1954. *The New York Times* reported that the French were bombing Laos with napalm. Meanwhile, the CIA's Technical Services Section was rushing to meet the deadline for the necessary number of non-American rifles for Guatemala. "Supply has 8 new government sterile 22 cal rim fire single shot or box magazine foreign rifles."

January 13, 1954. A PBSUCCESS report came in about certain teams: "K teams," or "assassination specialists."

January 20, 1954. Someone whose name was whited out wrote J. C. King, the leader of the Guatemala operation. He was concerned about "the international consequences of visible signs of U.S. official support" for the coup—"especially in case the violent steps planned for the final stages must be carried out." He had a suggestion for a black propaganda operation: Make up an ad that looked as if it came from the Guatemalan Department of Agriculture. It would say "Only Guatemalan Coffee Is Free of the Injurious Tarbinaldehyde." Then send the ad to coffee buyers around the world. "This would help to discredit the target with other coffee-producing countries."

January 21, 1954. A cable from Guatemala: "Request maximum degree silenced guns." Also somebody with the code name of "Seekford" had mistakenly left incriminating papers about the planned coup in his hotel room.

January 22, 1954. In a deputy director's meeting, Allen Dulles said, "⬚⬚⬚⬚⬚⬚⬚⬚⬚." (The whole paragraph is whited out.) General Cabell recommended that all high-level names involved in PBSUCCESS use pseudonyms "in view of the sensitivity of this operation." Mr. Wisner said, "⬚⬚⬚⬚⬚⬚⬚⬚⬚." (The whole paragraph is again whited out.)

January 29, 1954. Guatemala's press office issued its five-thousand-word white paper, a pamphlet of ninety-eight pages, which claimed that President Somoza of Nicaragua and an unnamed "government of the north" were collaborating on a plot of subversion. Castillo Armas, the leader of the plot, had written incriminating letters. "Super saboteurs and assassins" were being trained on the island of Momotombito, under a United Fruit employee named Colonel Studer on loan from the U.S. Army. President Somoza's son Tachito was helping the plotters procure airplanes and napalm, paid for with "rivers of money."

"Guatemala Says Neighbors and U.S. Plot an Invasion," said the front page of *The New York Times*. Taken by surprise, the State Department first scoffed at the charges, reported the *Times*, saying that any further response would "give the story a dignity it doesn't deserve." Then Undersecretary of State Bedell Smith began a counterattack. The charges were "ridiculous and untrue," he said, in a press release. "This is additional proof of the length to which the international Communist conspiracy will go to break up hemisphere solidarity on the eve of the tenth Inter-American conference." Tachito Somoza, reached at a Kansas City hotel, said the charges were a lie. "Those people are just seeing monkeys in the air," he added.

The next day a cable went out from PBSUCCESS headquarters in Florida. "White paper has effectively exposed certain aspects of PBSUCCESS, probably more to come." Everything now must move forward urgently. "Our pressure, once applied, should not be released but intensified," the cable said. "The enemy has played a strong card which we must be prepared to counter and exploit or withdraw."

January 31, 1954. Newspapers carried more of Bedell Smith's testy denials from the State Department. Guatemala was engaging in an "increasingly mendacious propaganda campaign," said Smith, mendaciously. The propagandists of the Arbenz government "have a long record of circulating false charges, typically Communist in their technique."

February 1, 1954. Jerome C. Dunbar/Al Haney called for "character assassination materials": photos and signatures of people who were standing in the way of PBSUCCESS.

February 9, 1954. J. C. King, chief of the CIA's Western Hemisphere Division, wrote a cable. The white paper was, King said, "a Communist inspired provocation." He wanted articles and cartoons published in *Alerta* stressing that "Guat govt stooge USSR" and that "Guat Commie labor delegates recently returned from Moscow brought back order to take action possible to bring about hemisphere disunity through political action including elaborate trumped up charge of intervention by neighboring countries and disruption conference by physical disorders on 'Bogotazo' pattern." He had in mind a cartoon on a postcard of Malenkov holding a puppet labeled "Bogotazo," which he was lowering into the Caracas conference.

February 10, 1954. The CIA planned further discrediting attacks on the revelations of the white paper—even though the white paper was all basically true. One proposed counterclaim was that the documents were "fabrications and forgeries." A summing-up statement was proposed: "It is not surprising that the Guatemalan Government resorts to such desperate devices, because this type of fabrication so closely resembles the 'potato bug' and 'bacteriological warfare' lies of the Soviets, whose loyal servant the Guatemalan Government is."

February 13, 1954. The CIA's plotters held a big conference in Florida at ten o'clock in the morning, where they discussed the nine-week training course for paramilitary units to be handed over to RUFUS. (RUFUS was another cryptonym for General Castillo Armas.) Twenty-seven men were undergoing training, including four sabotage instructors and two "assassination specialists." Castillo Armas wanted to send some of his men to a CIA course for "low level saboteurs," to begin on March 5.

In June 1954, the CIA began bombing and buzzing targets in Guatemala. Tass, the Russian news agency, charged that the United States had made an "assault on the freedom and independence of the people of Guatemala." A P-47 plane crashed in Mexico after an alleged bombing run in Guatemala and two Americans emerged. In the United Nations, the Guatemalan delegate said that foreign mercenaries, with backing from the United States, United Fruit, and Secretary of State John Foster Dulles, were behind the revolt in Guatemala. Ambassador Lodge "hotly" denied the charges, according to the Associated Press. "The situation," Lodge said, "does not involve aggression, but is a revolt of Guatemalans against Guatemalans." Lodge had strong words for Russia: "I say to the Soviet delegate, Stay out of the Western hemisphere. Don't try to start your plans and your conspiracies here."

TODAY WAS A LONG, sad, worried day for our family. At noon I heard an airplane and was struck by how it sounded like a bowling ball moving across the sky.

May 13, 2019, Monday

Three times in the dark I stepped on a dog toy—a soft squid that made an unhappy squeak.

M. found a tick on Cedric's eyebrow and pulled it off. He gave a small yelp.

SPENT SOME TIME LOOKING AT LCPROWL documents and other things from CREST—pushing my brain to form words when it didn't want to. Finally I fell asleep on the naked bed, stripped of sheets. This journal is taking a toll on me.

But right now I'm sitting looking at the river—there's a young-leafed tree and some sliding clouds and a faraway color of blue.

ANNIE JACOBSEN HAS WRITTEN a very good book about Frank Wisner's early Nazi-emancipation project, Operation Paperclip. The Freedom of Information Act wasn't much help to her, she says: "To report this book, I filed dozens of Freedom of Information Act (FOIA) requests, some of which were honored, many of which were denied, and most of which are still pending." One of the Paperclip arrivals she writes about was Hubertus Strughold, who performed freezing experiments and high-altitude-simulation experiments (including experiments with epileptic children) on inmates at Dachau.

Strughold got a job in Texas, at the School of Aviation Medicine, and began launching captured German V-2 rockets into the sky with rhesus monkeys strapped into their nose cones. The first monkey was Albert, who weighed nine pounds. "The V-2 rocket carrying Albert traveled to an altitude of 39 miles," Jacobsen tells us. "Albert died of suffocation during the six-minute flight, but for Dr. Strughold, the monkey's voyage signified the momentous first step toward human space flight." I looked up what happened on later flights. A second monkey, anesthetized, went up in a V-2 on June 14, 1949. "That monkey survived the flight but was killed on impact," says a NASA historical pamphlet. "On September 16 a third monkey was killed when the rocket exploded at thirty-five thousand feet. In December 1949, a fourth monkey was flown, with data on ECG and respiration successfully telemetered, but the monkey died on impact." On a later flight, in 1951, a monkey lived for two hours after impact. Four of five monkeys, anesthetized with morphine, died in 1952 when their parachutes failed to deploy. Strughold lived to the age of eighty-eight, and was known as the father of space medicine.

Another Paperclip case was Kurt Blome, a bacteriologist with a dueling scar on his upper lip. In 1940, Blome established the Potato Beetle Research Station in Kruft, Germany, near Koblenz. Eighteen people worked there, ostensibly engaged in cancer research. One of Blome's colleagues, Martin Schwartz, bred potato beetles and dropped them from airplanes.

In 1942, Heinrich Himmler ordered the establishment of the Waffen SS Entomology Institute. Blome oversaw that laboratory as well. At Himmler's request, Blome built a medical institute in Poland, in order to perform plague experiments on humans. (Blome claimed at Nuremberg that he never actually carried out the experiments, he merely intended to carry them out.) Blome was interested in using mosquitoes to spread malaria, and in combining germ weapons with chemical weapons, which injured breathing passages. "When membranes are hurt," he told his Camp Detrick interviewers, "bacteria has a better chance to infect."

Blome was acquitted of war crimes charges at Nuremberg. In 1947, he began to pass on his biowar lore to scientists from the Special Operations Division of Camp Detrick. By 1950, he was working for the Americans. He performed work on an unspecified "special matter" at Camp King, a former agricultural college near Frankfurt that the CIA used as a spy outpost and interrogation facility. Camp King was run by Reinhard Gehlen; Gehlen was Frank Wisner's man in Germany. The Third Reich's former head of germ and insect warfare was, in effect, working for the CIA.

ON MARCH 26, 1950, Russian radio carried some news coming from Amsterdam. *De Waarheid*, "The Truth," a Dutch Communist newspaper, reported that the American government was paying scientists in Germany to carry out research on bacteriological warfare. "The Americans are supplying to German bacteriologists, engaged in this criminal activity, equipment, chemicals, and money," Tass radio said. Blome was a German bacteriologist.

On May 26, 1950, the East German news bureau issued a statement. American planes had flown over some fields near the town of Zwickau, the statement said, where they had dropped "large amounts of potato bugs."

This was a new twist, said *The Times* in London.

"Potato bugs were found in bunches of up to 100 after an American plane had passed," the broadcast said. "There is great indignation among the population about this criminal plot."

Airmen laughed when a reporter asked about the beetles. "We paint the four freedoms on the back of each bug," one allegedly said. Moscow took up the potato bug charge. German workers were outraged by this "new crime of the Americans," said Tass.

"Americans in Germany are incredulous at these charges of potato bug warfare and get the giggles when asked about them," reported the Associated Press. "In sober reflection they feel the potato crop in Eastern

Germany may have failed, causing the Communist leaders to look about for a scapegoat."

Walter Ulbricht, a top Communist official in East Germany, said the Anglo-American imperialists must go home. "Today they are dropping potato bugs," Ulbricht said. "Tomorrow it will be atom bomb!"

On June 30, 1950, the Soviet government delivered a formal note to the American embassy in Moscow. With it was a report by an East German commission on the dropping of Colorado beetles by "American occupation authorities in Germany." "Russian Note Insists U.S. Hurled Spud Bugs" was the headline in the Rochester, New York, *Democrat and Chronicle*. "In the present world situation, fraught with explosive tensions, the Soviet Government has chosen to poison the atmosphere even further with one of the most fantastic fabrications that ever has been invented by one government against another," said the State Department.

The Czech government complained, too—a Prague radio station said that the American use of the Colorado beetle had ruined the potato harvest. It was "an act of war and no longer cold war," said a Czech church official. Whereupon the American ambassador in Prague, Ellis Briggs, issued a statement denying the insect attack. "The embassy," the statement said, "ventures to suggest the inherent unsuitability of the potato bug (*doriphora decomlineata*) as an instrument of national policy."

Everyone thought this was very funny.

May 14, 2019, Tuesday

What I want to do is sue the CIA. I want to ask for something huge and simple. Bigger than CREST. I want all documents fifty years old or older. All of them. Unredacted, unreviewed. Any document created before 1969, the public can read. As a first step.

If I had $20 million, that's what I'd do. Sue the CIA—assuming they rejected my FOIA request—and sue the Navy and the Air Force and the Army and a few other branches of government, for all the fifty-plus years of paper in various records centers and in the big depot in Suitland, Maryland, and at the National Archives and in every other trove or storage facility that might hold evidence of what happened. And maybe I'd win. And then, maybe with the help of the National Security Archive and MuckRock, if they were interested, I'd hire a team to scan all the pages and we'd put them up on the Internet Archive. (Keeping the original pages, too, of course, at the National Archives: you always, always want to keep the paper.) And then this country would at least have a chance of knowing what happened. We would be able to move forward. Twenty million dollars is about the cost of buying, arming, and flying one Reaper drone for a year. It's less than 1 percent of the cost of one ridiculous Zumwalt "stealth" destroyer.

May 15, 2019, Wednesday

It's so darn cold today. It must be the coldest spring on record. It's 43 degrees right now, overcast and threatening more rain. I'm wearing a wool hat. Briney is sleeping with the blanket completely covering himself. At 12:30 I'm driving to Mike's Automotive to have my car inspected.

I've been going through this book from the beginning, wondering what I was thinking of. I felt a great misery and a physical shivering coldness and got in bed and M. carried Cedric in and put him on the bed with me. Seeing his little face peering over the lumps of the covers healed me. I'm astonished by how much love I have for this dog and his fringed ears and the tufts of fur between his toes.

May 16, 2019, Thursday

I lay in bed some of today reading more of this book, hating it, excited by it, embarrassed by it. M. came home from work and we drove to Mike's Automotive to pick up my car. Warmer today. Tiny leaves unscrolling themselves.

LET ME JUST BLURT OUT what I think happened with germs and insects during the Korean War. You may not be convinced, but that's okay. My aim is to open the files, not necessarily to convince.

First, though, this must be said: the war was not about germs, it was about fire. Napalm firebombs were the horror weapons of the Korean War, and never before or since—not in Japan and not in Vietnam—has there been such a steady, concerted, relentless effort to destroy an entire country as there was in Korea. As Bruce Cumings wrote years ago, by the end of the war, after years of napalm, the North Koreans were living in caves. There was very little left to burn.

Emmett "Rosie" O'Donnell, an Air Force bomber commander,

testified in congressional hearings on June 25, 1951, that there were "no more targets in Korea." He explained to the senators that he had proposed to General MacArthur very early in the war that the United States should "cash in on our psychological advantage" by destroying eighteen strategic targets and "burning five major cities in North Korea to the ground." MacArthur didn't allow him to do it, though—not at first. Senator Stennis spoke: "Now, as a matter of fact, Northern Korea has been virtually destroyed, hasn't it? Those cities have been virtually destroyed?"

"Oh yes, we did it all later anyhow," said General O'Donnell. "I would say the entire, almost the entire Korean Peninsula is just a terrible mess. Everything is destroyed. There is nothing standing worthy of the name."

There was no secret about the immensity of this destruction. General O'Donnell's testimony was quoted from and paraphrased in dozens of newspapers the next day.

Donald Kingsley, the American in charge of the United Nations Korean Reconstruction Agency, was stunned when he surveyed the damage. "I doubt that ever in the history of the world, since perhaps the sacking of Carthage, has there been such complete destruction as has occurred in Korea," he said on the radio, and in *The New York Times*, in May 1951. The destruction of thatched villages in the middle of the country was "almost total," Kingsley said; two million Korean civilians had died so far in the war, and there were another 3.5 million refugees. If the fighting stopped, relief could begin immediately, he said.

But it didn't stop. The war had never officially begun, as far as the United States was concerned—there was no congressional authorization for Truman's decision to send in planes and troops—and it has never officially ended. Any odd or disturbing or objectionable or irrational act that North Korean leaders may commit in our era must be understood in the context of unimaginable explosive and napalmic trauma inflicted by the United States Air Force between 1950 and 1953.

The Senate committee loved General Rosie O'Donnell, by the way. "I think you have demonstrated soldierly qualities that endeared you to the

American people," said the committee chairman, Georgia senator Richard
Russell.

SO FIREBOMBING WAS THE PERVASIVE CRIME. But even so, I believe that
something real and infectious happened in the last, subzero months of
1950, when things were going wrong on the American side. Commandos
spread around feathers, and people got sick in a localized belt along the
38th parallel—North Koreans and Chinese soldiers got sick, and so did
South Koreans and Americans. Some of them were stricken with a
gruesome new disease, Songo fever, one that had been studied and
weaponized by Kitano Masaji during World War II, now known as Korean
hemorrhagic fever. Kitano was, as the Soviets charged, consulting for the
Americans. Korean hemorrhagic fever, carried by the field vole, now
classified as one of the hantaviruses, is still a problem in Korea today.

The North Koreans and the Chinese lodged their formal charges of
bacterial warfare in May 1951, but the charges didn't take. "The State
Department used ridicule in combatting the campaign, and the number of
references dropped off after June," wrote a CIA analyst in 1952.

The Americans got away with what was a relatively small, covert
effort—which I suspect was overseen by someone like Hans Tofte or
Donald Nichols.

THEN, THROUGH THE SECOND HALF OF 1951, there was a crescendo of
increasingly urgent biowar preparation in the Pentagon. War planner
Donald Zimmerman suggested to General Stratemeyer that a request
from the Far East Air Force for "chemicals and biologicals" might help
things move along at Air Force headquarters, and there were meetings and
decisions and papers and prototypes and "short-range crash training"
programs, pushed along by Nathan Twining, William Burden, Jimmy
Doolittle, and Robert Lovett, all aiming at getting some sort of megascale
germ-delivery activity ready for the final battle with China and the Soviet
Union.

Then came the weird phenomena of February and March 1952—the wolf spiders and the springtails and the flies and the feathers and the voles and the clams and the modified leaflet bombs and the fragments of ceramic containers that were reminiscent of Ishii's plague munition. At the beginning of this period there were, in addition to the sinister-seeming menagerie, some actual germs involved. But once the operation was blown, I think, the CIA quickly mounted a bigger campaign that was biological only in the sense that living creatures were involved. The 1952 effort quickly became a psychological-warfare campaign, or a nerve-war campaign—a campaign to cause fear and confusion and revulsion. There were some outbreaks of disease early on, but mostly it was the implication of potential disease that the CIA was aiming for. They wanted people to discover the insects on the snow and panic, assuming that the insects carried germs.

It was a deception operation—and it was a lousy idea, a very CIA-style lousy idea. Perhaps this operation was what Bedell Smith was referring to on March 11, 1952, when he talked in a meeting about responding to the Communist propaganda charges by "using the bigger lie." The deception plan was meant to demoralize Chinese and North Korean troops, and trouble and overload public-health workers, by creating the impression that a massive germ attack was in progress, when, in fact, the attack was mostly composed of prototype bombs filled with untainted but scary masses of lab-reared insects and voles and spiders. The creatures did harbor some diseases that could be cultured in a petri dish—they came from Japanese or American pathology laboratories, after all—but only a small fraction were deliberately doped with germs. That's why there were no epidemics and why, by the Chinese scientists' own admission, relatively few people got sick. (Although there was a cluster of cases, some fatal to children, of a new, unidentifiable type of encephalitis of "extreme virulence" in Shenyang, possibly related to overflights by American planes on March 2, March 7, and March 13, 1952, which led members of the Scientific Commission to suspect "the artificial spreading of this disease by the American armed forces.") The North Koreans and the Chinese were telling the truth when they reported the bombs and the insects, it seems to me—the intercepted SUEDE reports were accurate—but the

Communists didn't understand that it was primarily a terror weapon they were dealing with, and they exerted themselves to find the taint of disease where it wasn't.

"Plan scare not kill," as one of the Guatemala nerve-war plotters said. Germ warfare was easily deniable in March 1952 because mostly it wasn't happening. What was happening was the aerial dumping of evil-seeming arthropods and rodents followed by intense, angry, gaslighting disavowals. That explains why the actual microscopic germy evidence of plague and other diseases was so hard to come by, and had to be faked. In his mea culpa, Wu Zhili, former director of the Chinese People's Volunteer Army Health Division, said in 1997 that it had been a "false alarm." "We had already dispatched men (including myself) to the reporting units many times to ascertain the situation, an investigation which concluded that there were insects and other objects dropped on the snow, but which did not discover people who had died suddenly or suspiciously fallen ill." The insects were real, but they were a trick, meant to make the Communists go crazy.

ONE MIGHT REASONABLY ASK whether there is any evidence for a CIA-managed unconventional-warfare deception plan of this type during this period of the Korean War. Well, there is. It's not about germs; it has to do with radioactive dust. I found it in the Truman Library in April 2017, in one of the covert-action appendices to something called Plan TAKEOFF.

Plan Takeoff, overseen by Gordon Gray and Tracy Barnes of the Psychological Strategy Board, was a big plan with many subcomponents, which went through a series of drafts in the summer and fall of 1951. It described what various elements of the United States government ought to do, concertedly, overtly and covertly, in the event of the breakdown in the peace talks that were in progress (though stalemated and full of mutual recrimination) between American and Communist negotiators. Ned Hagerman and Stephen Endicott wrote about Plan Takeoff in chapter 8 of their book, paying special attention to a last section, "Annex G," which, although it was heavily redacted, itemized some of the actions that the CIA might perform.

I've studied Plan Takeoff in some detail. It was "pushed through and approved in very short order," according to one participant, "at the urgent request of the White House." It aimed to create "interference, confusion, and disruption in all aspects of North Korean and Communist Chinese military operations." Proposed actions might include: increased guerrilla activity, disruption of rail lines and roads, "assassination by disaffected indigenous persons of Chinese and North Korean military and supporting civil officials," and "passive resistance stimulated through fear." The CIA was specifically charged with conducting "such additional bribery and sabotage activities as may achieve either action effects or psychological effects desired." Someone has crossed out the phrase "bribery and sabotage activities" and handwritten "guerrilla activities and special operations" in its place.

One of the specific operations that the CIA contemplated was a mass leaflet drop over Chinese cities. The State Department would be responsible for figuring out what the leaflet would say. "Such leaflets should carry the *implicit* message that they might have been bombs rather than leaflets," one draft of Takeoff said. (Some drafts have many pages blanked, some comparatively few.)

"There are signs that Operation Takeoff, which Gordon Gray signaled was to be handled on a 'need to know' basis, had some highly unusual aspects," wrote Ned and Steve. In 2009 I went through the Takeoff files, trying to figure out what else might be there behind the redactions. "It is necessary that both ⸤_____⸥ and psychological warfare be employed to the limit of our capabilities," said one draft. (Perhaps something like "sabotage activities" went here?) There were vague enabling phrases in the drafts: the CIA could perform "other covert activities," unspecified, and "additional 'other than usual' actions." Nothing about germs, though. I sent off copies of what I'd found in 2009 to Ned and Steve. Ned wrote back: "What is covered in those long stretches of totally sanitized material? And why so much activity across such a range of the upper military echelons over a leaflet drop? And why such stress and strain?"

When I went back to the Truman Library in 2017, more readable pages were in the "384.7 Korea" Takeoff file—though some still said "Page

Denied." Annex G, covering the CIA's responsibilities, now had three subsidiary sections. One section described the leaflet drop over China, one described "massive air drops of counterfeit Chinese currency" accompanied by the inciting of guerrilla activity, and one, declassified in 2015, was a "Special Task": "Exploitation of Psychological Possibilities of Covertly-Claimed Radiological Contamination." The goal of this deception plan (which existed in two typed versions in the file, one of which began with a redaction) was to "convince CHINESE troops in China and Korea by covert means that an area along the Yalu River has been contaminated by radiological warfare means." The action, it was hoped, would demoralize Chinese troops, by convincing them that (a) they couldn't return home, that (b) their food and supplies would be contaminated, and that (c) "to enter Korea from China is certain death."

> It is believed that the credulity [read "credibility"] of this covert propaganda theme should be established by an overt act which is otherwise inexplainable. In this case a flight of aircraft spraying an area extending for a considerable distance along or near the Korean bank of the Yalu River is indicated.

After the mysterious planes fly over, spraying fake radioactive dust, "covert rumor spreading should indicate that this area along the Yalu River has been contaminated by a slow reacting but concentrated form of radioactive dust," the special task document said. "Chinese troops should be similarly informed that while their officers will deny it, passing through this area will result in a slow but certain and lingering death. This should be woven into a general theme that Korea is a death trap from which none will return except by sea." The material sprayed from planes must be conspicuous but "inoffensive and difficult to analyze." The air crews must take extreme care not to be shot down, but if they were to be shot down, they then would become part of the deception: "Bombs and spray containers should be specially marked and handled and the crew given to believe that they were engaged in a special and unusual mission."

The rumored contamination would demoralize Chinese troops, slow down the movement of supplies, and "reduce by fear the available coolie manpower in the area," the CIA believed. And it was deniable. "The covert theme could be easily and truthfully denied by the U.S. if challenged. Early overt denial might even help to spread the rumors." *Early overt denial.* The Air Force would supply the planes and crews, coordinating its flights with CIA covert propaganda and rumor spreading.

My best guess is that late in 1951, some CIA planner, possibly Frank Wisner himself, improved on the deadly atomic-dust deception plan— which was based on an idea publicly proposed by Senator Albert Gore in April 1951 ("ATOMIC DEATH BELT URGED FOR KOREA" was the headline in *The New York Times*)—by substituting fleas, flies, springtails, spiders, voles, feathers, and mosquitoes for pretend radioactive dust. The insects and feathers were visible and frightening, whereas the dust would be hard to see. And everyone who'd been told the insects were (mostly) uninfected could deny the Communists' charge as fiercely and sneeringly as they wanted to.

Ned and Steve were right—Operation Takeoff did have "highly unusual aspects."

May 17, 2019, Friday

Overcast today.

May 18, 2019, Saturday

Frank Wisner had the first of several breakdowns in 1956, after the Soviets suppressed the Hungarian uprising. "That's when he first went nuts," according to his friend and CIA colleague Tom Braden. Wisner said that he ate some bad clams in Greece, which gave him a high fever and a case of "oriental fulminating hepatitis." At Georgetown Hospital he was cared for by two high-level doctors, Dr. Brick and Dr. Smadel. Dr. Irving Brick was a gastroenterologist; Dr. Joseph E. Smadel, weirdly enough, was the very same tropical-disease specialist who had written an early paper on Korean hemorrhagic fever—a paper written with information about human experiments supplied by germ warriors Kitano Masaji and Kasahara Shiro.

Wisner submitted a manic flood of words to Drs. Smadel and Brick about his symptoms, describing "the rather unusual character of my particular attack which appears to have been of exceptional virulence and to have come on very suddenly and which further appears to have run the course of the main phases of the disease rather more quickly than is normally the case in the lower grade infections which carry along for weeks and weeks before coming to a head, or becoming identifiable." Clams or no clams, Wisner was not in good shape mentally.

By January 1957, Wisner had recovered enough to answer some letters, keeping drafts and carbon copies that are now at the University of Virginia, unredacted. He wrote a friend, Ethel Fowler, that his malaise included depression and a sense of abandonment. He managed to get in some quail shooting, though, and he asked Ian Fleming to sign a copy of *Dr. No* for his friend Gordon Gray. At work, where colleagues covered for him, he began to fantasize about regime change in Czechoslovakia, and then, on orders from President Eisenhower, he helped plan political upheavals in Indonesia. (The CIA's Indonesian coup failed; decades of death and disorder followed.) In August 1958, Wisner again pivoted into mania and paranoia, hectoring his secretary and calling up people at all hours with strange ideas. CIA psychologists were consulted. He spent months in a private hospital in Baltimore undergoing, and then slowly healing from, mind-blistering electroshock sessions.

"Frank Wisner has had a very hard time of it," Allen Dulles wrote a colleague in December of 1958, "but during the past few weeks he has been showing very real progress and I hope it will not now be many weeks before he is out of the sanitarium." Dulles released an official memo: "In view of his protracted illness, Mr. Frank G. Wisner has been reassigned to the Office of Director pending eventual reassignment." Richard Bissell would take over as deputy director of plans, Dulles said, and Richard Helms would continue under him, as chief of operations.

There are in CREST several differently redacted versions of this brief announcement. In some the phrase "In view of his protracted illness" is whited out. In one the shorter phrase "his protracted illness" is whited out. Some show Richard Helms's name, some don't. Some white out Helms's new title—"Assistant Deputy Director (Plans) for Psychological and Paramilitary Operations"—and some don't. One blanks Bissell's name. A not insubstantial amount of work and time went into declassifying duplicate copies of an internal notice of a personnel change. This is the CIA's basic problem: fulminating redaction psychosis.

By 1962, recalled from London after further outbursts, Wisner was a forlorn figure. He did a little legal consulting, unsuccessfully recommending to the chiefs of Reynolds Tobacco that they diversify, in advance of the surgeon general's report on the health effects of smoking, by merging with Fannie Farmer Candies. He bought guns and went hunting. He reviewed Allen Dulles's bestselling book *The Craft of Intelligence* for the CIA's journal, *Studies in Intelligence*, where he argued for the existence of permasecrets: "Persons having the deepest and most legitimate insights into intelligence matters are most scrupulous in their trusteeship of such knowledge," he wrote in his review. "Mr. Dulles does not reveal secrets which are still sensitive (and many of which must always remain so)." Wisner dismissed sensational journalists—those "charlatans and pretenders who scavenge along the flanks of the intelligence enterprise"—by which he meant people like David Wise, coauthor of *The Invisible Government*, a bad book with a fraudulent premise, in Wisner's view. "There should be a greater public willingness to give those brethren who are 'serving the rice' some benefit of the doubt," he believed. In one teasingly, almost playfully paranoid paragraph, Wisner suggested that Americans be on guard against an insidious sort of pinpoint psychological attack mounted by Communists on "selected individuals in positions of power." An individual's suspicion that he is being "victimized or duped" by the enemy is almost impossible to prove, Wisner said, "once the infection has spread to the bloodstream."

On May 4, 1965, John Chancellor narrated an hour-long NBC News special on the CIA, "The Science of Spying," which peered into some of the spidery shadows of Wisner's operations—especially the Guatemalan overthrow, which Wisner had once thought of as his great triumph. "The American government, through the CIA, made an alliance with Arbenz's opposition, and as of that moment, he was doomed," Chancellor said. There's an interview with a CIA "air attaché" named Fred Sherwood who talks about arranging for help from anti-Communist vigilantes and "night riders":

> There was a group that tried to bring in some Puerto Rican and Cuban gangsters, who made an offer—a package deal so to speak—to kill or assassinate any twelve Communists within the country for fifty thousand dollars. We went around, trying to raise money, but we were only successful in raising a part of it, so it never came off. But this demonstrates the desperate situation the country was in.

Sherwood says that the United States "provided the know-how to organize a successful revolution," furnishing pilots, demolition teams, and psychologists who created rumor networks. It can't have helped Wisner's gloom to see what he'd done in Guatemala X-rayed so completely on TV, and then held up as an example of a CIA-devised political disaster. Or to hear his orotund, soulless replacement, Richard Bissell, drawlingly say, of covert operations, "I will not deny that there were occasions when the Americans that were involved in these, as it were, out on the front had—as people do in wartime—to undertake actions that were contrary to their moral precepts." There is a complete script of the NBC TV show in CREST, and you can watch it on YouTube.

"FRANK GARDINER WISNER, a former New York lawyer and for many years a top official of the Central Intelligence Agency, died at his farm in nearby Galena, Maryland, today," said *The New York Times*, in an article datelined October 29, 1965. "According to the police in Kent County, Md., Mr. Wisner shot himself in the right temple with a 20-gauge shotgun." He was only fifty-six. *The Washington Post* added a crucial detail: "Mrs. Wisner was downstairs when she heard the fatal shot." In an editorial, the *Post* praised Wisner's "extraordinary devotion." "Frank Wisner deserves to be remembered gratefully," the editorialist wrote.

The *Daily Worker*'s editor, James E. Jackson, wrote a letter to the *New Times*, an English-language paper published in Russia. The CIA employed bandits and cutthroats, "practiced hands in the underworld crimes of subversion, sabotage, and assassination," Jackson wrote. "The terror against the Guatemalan people and the total suppression of popular liberties still persist after eleven years. This is the legacy of Frank Wisner, CIA agent par excellence."

"There has passed the greatest cold war soldier in American history," said the *Blade-Tribune*, in Oceanside, California, in a clipping preserved (along with the one from the *New Times*) in the CREST database. "It was Wisner who set up clandestine radio stations; Wisner who arranged for the uprising in Guatemala; Wisner who kept in touch with the dissident Poles, the dissident East Germans; Wisner who planned the defection of Russian agents; Wisner who answered 'yes' or 'no' when the National Security Council asked whether the clandestine services could do the job." Wisner knew each agent and each mission, the obituary said—"knew who was dead, who was 'blown,' who had his hand in the till, who was good and who was tired. Eventually, he wore himself out."

THAT'S ENOUGH. I've worn myself out. I need to take a break from thinking about germs and spies and balloons and generals and coups and death by starvation. Life is green and grassy.

Walked the dogs with dear M. The dandelions are coming up everywhere. Little spiky explosions in the grass—a dollop of yellow pigment seen through tears.

It's finally really spring.

Epilogue

That's what I thought about in March, April, and May of 2019. I've done some rewriting and interpolating and cutting. But that's basically it.

Except for one huge omission: While I was writing this book, my mother-in-law, Carroll Brentano, died. Her last weeks of life were too fraught and too painful to be included in this record. Carroll was a peace-marching, football-loving art historian who founded and edited a journal of the history of the University of California. Her desire to live showed me how big and intimate and personal death was, and how miraculous life is. How many trillions of very small things have to go right, all the time, for life to continue.

SINCE MAY, I've filed more FOIA requests, and I've waited. All the Air Force documents that I asked for in 2012 are still held back, no explanation given. The CIA sent some meeting minutes from the early fifties with tiny snippets unredacted, but whole passages and pages are allegedly too sensitive to be disclosed. Concerning two documents that I asked for, the CIA claims that they can't be found: the blacked-out copies are all that's left, even though one document is stamped "DO NOT DESTROY." The ancient secrets fester and liquefy.

Sometimes the system works, however. On March 5, 2020, just as this book was going to press, an envelope came from the National Archives. In it, miraculously, was an unredacted version of Plan CLASSROOM, JCS 1927/3, the deception plan developed by the Joint Chiefs of Staff that I'd requested three years earlier. Some of my guesses about what was behind Plan Classroom's many blackouts were wrong, it turns out, but most were right. I'd thought that the Defense Department wanted to slow down Soviet progress on their atomic bomb by distracting Kremlin war planners with false documents about U.S. biological weapons. In fact, the plan, devised by MIT's Karl Compton and others, was more tightly focused than that: its mission, according to the now unredacted text, was to

> cause the USSR to waste considerable scientific potential in the BW field, by inducing the USSR to undertake research and development on BW projects which are dangerous, and unproductive in nature, in order to maintain a favorable balance of BW capability with respect to the USSR.

The idea was to maintain American preeminence in the field of biological warfare by passing false documents to Russian intelligence, with the help of U.S. and British spy agencies. These documents were aimed at getting the Russians to believe the following (untrue) story:

> The Research and Development Board of the Department of Defense has developed methods of producing mass cultures of the _____ bacillus of high virulence, methods of stabilizing the organism for distribution, and methods for procuring solid immunity in humans against the organism.

The specific name of the bacillus was omitted by the Joint Chiefs of Staff.

Plan Classroom, kept secret for seventy years, aimed to trick and frighten the Russians into entering into a hazardous, large-scale bioweapons arms race with the United States. The plan worked all too well: the

Russians were deceived, the biological arms race intensified; germy stews were cooked up in unsafe laboratories around the world.

Bit by bit, as with this one tiny release of a single Defense Department plan from 1949, we begin to understand how we got to where we are. But the process of disclosure has been too slow. *Every U.S. government document that's more than fifty years old should be released in full, right now. No redactions. As a first step.*

Notes

ACHRE: Advisory Committee on Human Radiation Experiments

AFOAT BW-CW: Air Force Office of Atomic Energy, Biological and Chemical Warfare Division

AP: Associated Press

CREST: CIA Records Search Tool; CREST is the CIA's incomplete online database of declassified documents.

DPG: Dugway Proving Ground

DTIC: Defense Technical Information Center

FRUS: *Foreign Relations of the United States*, historical volumes published by the Department of State

INS: International News Service

IWG: Records of the Nazi War Crimes and Imperial Japanese Government Interagency Working Group

JCS: Joint Chiefs of Staff

JWC: Select Documents on Japanese War Crimes, as compiled by William H. Cunliffe at the National Archives

LC: Library of Congress, Manuscript Reading Room

NA: National Archives, College Park, Maryland

NSC: National Security Council

NYT: *New York Times*

UP: United Press

March 9, 2019, Saturday

1 **"an Air Force-wide combat capability"**: Arthur E. Hoffman to Chief, Control Division, D/Operations, DCS/O, "Establishment of Priority for Project BASELESS," October 10, 1951, AFOAT BW-CW, RG 341, entry NM-15 199, 1951, box 1, file 373, NA. Hoffman, acting chief of the BW-CW Division, cites several pieces of earlier correspondence and then says: "Reference 1a directed the achievement of an Air Force-wide combat capability in biological and chemical warfare at the earliest possible date and with the same priority now accorded the atomic energy program. Reference 1b placed biological warfare operations in Group I category of importance. References 1c and 1d established the code word 'BASELESS' (Confidential) for use in referring to the USAF program for achievement of an Air Force-wide combat capability in biological and chemical warfare at the earliest possible date." See also Leonidas Baker, memorandum for record, "Related Meaning of Code Word," October 29, 1951, RG 341, entry NM-15 199, box 1, file 373, NA.

2 **"with all practicable speed"**: "Freedom of Information Act Statute," FOIA.gov, www.foia.gov/foia-statute.html.

3 **"Old enough to rent a car"**: Lauren Harper, "Government's Oldest FOIA Request Even Older than Reported," *Unredacted: The National Security Archive Blog*, National Security Archive, March 28, 2019.

March 10, 2019, Sunday

5 **The Pentagon instituted its secret crash program**: Nathan F. Twining, Memo to Deputy Chiefs of Staff, "Biological and Chemical Warfare," October 20, 1950, Air Force, Plans, RG 341, entry 335, box 581, NA.

5 **"a new monstrous crime"**: U.S. Department of State, "The Bacteriological Warfare Campaign," Appendix B to "The Soviet Hate America Campaign," Soviet Affairs Note No. 140, November 28, 1952, 9–10 (hereafter "Soviet Hate America Campaign"). Held at U.S. Army Heritage and Education Center, Carlisle Barracks, Pa., HM263 .S68 1952.

5 **"Foe Charges Use of Bacteria"**: NYT, May 9, 1951.

5 **"A charge that U.N. forces employed"**: Peter Kihss, "North Koreans Accuse U.N. of Germ Warfare," *New York Herald Tribune*, May 10, 1951, 5; "Reds Accuse U.N. of Using Germs in Korea War," *Washington Post*, May 10, 1951, 17.

6 **a long cablegram**: *Year-Book of the United Nations*, 229.

6 **"It has been established by medical experts"**: "Soviet Hate America Campaign," 9–10.

6 **"flatly denied" the charges**: AP, "Reds Lay Blame for Smallpox on MacArthur, Ridgway," *Daily American*, Somerset, Pa., May 9, 1951, www.newspapers.com/image/511416938.

6 **"According to precise information"**: "Soviet Hate America Campaign," 18. This is a State Department translation into English of a Russian translation of the Korean original.

7 **"North Korea's foreign minister has accused"**: AP, "U.N. Accused of 'Germ' War," *New York Herald Tribune*, February 23, 1952; "Red Charge on Buggy Side," *Newport Daily News*, February 22, 1952, www.newspapers.com/image/57430684.

7 **"deadly insects were dropped"**: UP, "Charge U.S. Planes Dropping Disease-Laden Insects on Reds," *News-Record*, Neenah, Wisc., February 22, 1952, www.newspapers.com/image/444612574/.

7 **"Reds Claim U.S. Planes Drop Bed Bugs"**: *Waterloo Daily Courier*, Waterloo, Iowa, February 22, 1952, www.newspapers.com/image/357695715/.

7 **"The claim recalled Communist charges"**: UP, "Charge U.S. Planes."

7 **The insects were wrapped in paper bags**: UP, *Boone News-Republican*, Boone, Iowa, February 22, 1952, newspaperarchive.com/boone-news-republican-feb-22-1952-p-7/.

7 **"torrent of propaganda"**: UP, "Truce Talks Totter; Germ Tests Claimed," *Greenville News*, Greenville, S.C., February 25, 1952, www.newspapers.com/image/188004915/.

7 **"Refusing to acknowledge their defeat"**: "Soviet Hate America Campaign," 19. This is a

State Department translation of a Russian translation (from *Pravda*, February 27, 1952) of a Chinese original.

8 **"unspecified deception matter"**: Director's Meeting, February 25, 1925, CREST, https://www.cia.gov/library/readingroom/docs/1952-02-25b.pdf.

8 **"be prepared to employ BW whenever"**: Howard Bunker, Memo for W. A. M. Burden, "BW-CW Program," March 6, 1952, AFOAT BW-CW, RG 341, entry NM-15 199, 1952, box 1, file Finis #4, NA.

8 **"The research and development program is being expedited"**: Joint Chiefs of Staff, JCS 1837/29, February 26, 1952, RG 218, NA.

8 **"In violation of all principles of human morals"**: "Soviet Hate America Campaign," 20.

9 **"It is not true as far as this headquarters"**: AP, "Voluntary POW Exchange Issue Is Still Unsettled," *Oshkosh Northwestern*, Oshkosh, Wisc., February 27, 1952, www.newspapers.com /image/476882851/.

9 **"Allied officers said Red charges"**: AP, "Voluntary POW Exchange Issue Is Still Unsettled."

9 **"This is an abnormally heavy dose"**: AP, "U.N. Says Red Fake Conceals Plague Peril," *Oakland Tribune*, Oakland Calif., February 27, 1952, www.newspapers.com/image /245474428.

9 **"when countless civilians in Chekiang"**: AP, "U.N. Says Red Fake Conceals Plague Peril".

9 **"this nonsense about germ warfare"**: NYT, "Acheson Belittles Foe's Germ Charge," March 5, 1952, 3.

9 **"Who will believe Acheson"**: "Outlaw Bacteriological Warfare—Punish the War Criminals!," *People's China*, April 1, 1952, massline.org/PeoplesChina/PC1952/PC1952 -07-OCR.pdf.

10 **Paul Ta-kuang Lin**: See "Paul T.K. Lin Papers," biographical note on the website of the Hong Kong University of Science and Technology, library.ust.hk/collections-resources /special-collections/lin/.

10 **studied at the University of Michigan and Harvard**: Paul T. K. Lin, with Eileen Chen Lin, *In the Eye of the China Storm: A Life Between East and West* (Montreal: McGill-Queen's University Press, 2011).

10 **"With the sneering cynicism"**: Lin Ta-kuang (Paul T. K. Lin), "The Case Against the U.S. Germ Warfare Criminals," *People's China*, April 1, 1952.

11 **One of the access-restricted documents**: Memo from Wilson to Grover, AFOAT BW-CW, RG 341, entry NM-15 199, 1951, box 1, file 471.6 BW Munitions, NA.

11 **probably Roscoe C. Wilson**: "Lieutenant General Roscoe C. Wilson," U.S. Air Force, www.af.mil/About-Us/Biographies/Display/Article/105188/lieutenant-general-roscoe -c-wilson/.

11 **"Accelerated, aggressive, if not drastic"**: "Memorandum for the Secretary of Defense" (draft of memo by Howard Bunker and Arthur Hoffman, for signature by Thomas Finletter, secretary of the Air Force), December 13, 1951, RG 341, entry NM-15 199, 1952, box 1, file BW-CW Folder #1, NA.

11 **"unconventional warfare and special operations"**: Psychological Operations Coordinating Committee, *Psychological Operations* (newsletter) 1, no. 3, January 1952, CREST, https://www .cia.gov/library/readingroom/docs/CIA-RDP80R01731R003400020053-9.pdf.

11 **believer in "thought bombs"**: Lloyd Norman, "Air Force Ready to Use 'Thought Bombs' on Foe," *Chicago Tribune*, January 14, 1952.

12 **"An investigation is being conducted"**: Army Biological Laboratories, Fourth Annual Report to the Committee on BW, Research and Development Board, 540801 DW, 1951, from Edward Hagerman's files.

March 11, 2019, Monday

14 **"knife thrust in the chest"**: Richard Valeriani, AP, "Castro Warns U.S. Not to Cut Sugar Purchases," *Post-Crescent*, Appleton, Wisc., June 24, 1960, www.newspapers.com/image /287406944/.

14 **Revolución, a Havana newspaper, claimed:** AP, "Cuban Fire Raid Charges Branded Absurd by U.S.," *Morning Call*, Allentown, Pa., January 14, 1960, www.newspapers.com/image /275131314/.

14 **former Hershey mill near Havana:** AP, "Cuba Links U.S. to Fire Bomb," *Spokane Chronicle*, Spokane, Wash., January 13, 1960, www.newspapers.com/image/565887672/.

14 **"Any implication that the United States":** AP, "Cuban Fire Raid Charges."

14 **"the full complicity":** AP, "Cubans Report 2 U.S. Fliers Killed on Fire-Bombing Raid," *Morning Call*, Allentown, Pa., February 19, 1960, www.newspapers.com/image /275085902/.

14 **Ray Treichler, one of the CIA's scientists:** CIA, "Chronology of Castro Assassination Plans," record no. 157-10004-10147, www.archives.gov/files/research/jfk/releases/2018 /157-10004-10147_1.pdf.

14 **It was time to "get tough":** Jack Pfeiffer, *Official History of the Bay of Pigs Operation*, vol. 3, CIA, 1979, nsarchive2.gwu.edu//NSAEBB/NSAEBB355/bop-vol3.pdf.

14 **"Approximately 300,000 tons of sugar":** Jack Hawkins, Record of the Paramilitary Action Against the Castro Government of Cuba, 17 March 1960–May 1961, CIA (1997 redaction), archive.org/details/RecordOfParamilitaryActionAgainstTheCastroGovernment OfCubaMarch171960-May1961; Hawkins, Record of the Paramilitary Action Against the Castro Government of Cuba (2012 redaction), https://www.cia.gov/library/readingroom /docs/CIA-RDP85-00664R000700150001-8.pdf.

15 **"These charges are totally false":** "Excerpts from Statements Made by Roa and Stevenson to U.N. Political Committee," NYT, April 18, 1961.

15 **Che Guevara sought out Kennedy adviser Richard Goodwin:** AP, "JFK Snubbed Cuba Peace Overture," *Ukiah Daily Journal*, Ukiah, Calif., April 29, 1996, www.newspapers.com /image/634257/.

15 **"He then went on to say":** Richard Goodwin to John F. Kennedy, Subject: Conversation with Commandante Ernesto Guevara of Cuba, August 22, 1961, FRUS, history.state.gov /historicaldocuments/frus1961-63v10/d257.

March 12, 2019, Tuesday

17 **his cryptonym was Typhoid:** Burton Hersh, *The Old Boys* (St. Petersburg, Fla.: Tree Farm Books, 1992); Evan Thomas, *The Very Best Men: Four Who Dared: The Early Years of the CIA* (New York: Simon & Schuster, 1995).

17 **danced the crab walk:** Thomas, *The Very Best Men*.

17 **code-named Aunt Jemima:** Adam Kline with Robyn Dexter, "Secret Weapons, Forgotten Sacrifices: Scientific R & D in World War II," *Prologue*, Spring 2016, NA, www.archives .gov/files/publications/prologue/2016/spring/osrd.pdf.

17 **"notably mild-mannered and conciliatory":** Ludwell Lee Montague, *General Walter Bedell Smith as Director of Central Intelligence, October 1950–February 1953*, vol. 3, CIA, Historical Staff, 1971.

17 **"OPC must, if it is effectively":** Frank Wisner to Marshall Chadwell, ca. June 1950, Records of the Advisory Committee on Human Radiation Experiments, NA.

18 **"subversion against hostile states":** "National Security Council Directive on Office of Special Projects," NSC 10/2, FRUS, Emergence of the Intelligence Establishment, Document 292, history.state.gov/historicaldocuments/frus1945-50Intel/d292.

March 13, 2019, Wednesday

21 **"a special agency program established":** Frank Wisner to Marshall Chadwell, ACHRE records, RG 220, entry A1 42100-H, container 143, NA.

21 **articles in the *Toronto Star* by reporter David Vienneau:** David Vienneau, "Ottawa Paid for '50s Brainwashing Experiments, Files Show," April 14, 1986; "No Secrets Hidden from CIA in 1950s, Former Official Says," April 14, 1986; "Ottawa Accused of Brainwashing Lies," April 15, 1986; "Ottawa Knew of Brainwashing," April 16, 1986;

"Colleague Says McGill Doctor Probably Unaware of CIA Role," April 17, 1986; "MP's Wife Fears She'll Die Before CIA Pays Restitution," April 20, 1986; *Toronto Star.*

22 **"small testing facility within CIA":** Project Coordinator to Deputy Director for Central Intelligence, "Project ⬜," ACHRE records, RG 220, entry A1 42100-H, container 143, NA.

22 **piece by Ted Gup in *The Washington Post*:** "The Smithsonian Secret: Why an Innocent Bird Study Went Straight to Biological Warfare Experts at Fort Detrick," *Washington Post Magazine*, May 12, 1985.

22 **One Smithsonian project, Operation Starbright:** Roy MacLeod, "'Strictly for the Birds': Science, the Military and the Smithsonian's Pacific Ocean Biological Survey Program, 1963–1970," *Journal of the History of Biology* 34 (2001).

22 **the role of "avian vectors":** MKULTRA Subproject 139, CIA, Internet Archive, archive .org/details/DOC_0000017398.

22 **his FOIA request was "awaiting processing":** Ted Gup, "The Smithsonian Secret," *Washington Post Magazine*, May 12, 1985.

23 **"Sabotage employment of biological weapons":** Haskins et al., "Report of the Ad Hoc Committee on Biological Warfare," July 11, 1949, President's Secretary's Files, Truman Library.

23 **His obituary in *The New York Times*:** Carla Baranauckas, "Caryl Haskins, 93, Ant Expert and Authority in Many Fields," NYT, October 13, 2001.

March 14, 2019, Thursday

24 **"The public business is the public's business":** "Availability of Information from Federal Departments and Agencies," Hearings, November 7, 1955, 84th Congress, 1st Session, Subcommittee of the Committee on Government Operations, catalog.hathitrust.org /Record/001142006.

25 **new, vehement campaign:** Horace S. Craig, Special Projects Staff, to Nelson Rockefeller, "Exposure in the United Nations of the International Communist Conspiracy," November 4, 1955, CREST, declassified 2002, https://www.cia.gov/library/readingroom/docs/CIA -RDP80-01446R000100170044-1.pdf.

25 **"promote illogical thinking and impulsiveness":** "Subproject 35 of Project MKULTRA," Technical Services Section, CIA, May 10, 1955, Internet Archive, archive.org/details/DOC _0000017432.

25 **Kissinger was executive director:** Geoffrey Taylor, "The Harvard Seminar," *Guardian*, July 7, 1955, www.newspapers.com/image/259438215/.

25 **Linebarger taught at the Johns Hopkins School:** "Red Challenge in Far East Will Be Topic," *Baltimore Sun*, April 21, 1953, www.newspapers.com/image/374830980/.

25 **"The world diplomatic front is a screen":** Paul Linebarger, Henry Kissinger, et al., "Psychological Aspects of United States Strategy," November 1955, CREST, declassified 2008, https://www.cia.gov/library/readingroom/docs/psych_aspects.pdf.

26 **"If you really study the whole subject":** "Availability of Information," Hearings, November 7, 1955.

27 **"Under project 465-20-001, insect strains":** Stephen Endicott and Edward Hagerman, *The United States and Biological Warfare* (Bloomington: Indiana University Press, 1998), 77. Also quoted in Jeffrey Lockwood, *Six-Legged Soldiers* (New York: Oxford University Press, 2009), 162.

27 **"Current work has been directed":** "Report of the Biological Department, Chemical Corps, to the Panel on Program of the Committee on Biological Warfare, Research and Development Board," Report Series No. 3 (Third Annual Report), October 1, 1949, Biological Department, Chemical Corps, Army Biological Laboratories, DPG Library, from Edward Hagerman's files.

27 **"More than 50 strains":** Chemical Corps Biological Laboratories, "Seventh Annual Report of the Chemical Corps Biological Laboratories," July 1, 1953, DTIC, primarysources

.brillonline.com/browse/weapons-of-mass-destruction/us-army-chemical-corps-report
-seventh-annual-report-chemical-corps-biological-laboratories-july-1-1953-top-secret
-dtic;wmdowmdo03061.

27 **"Where secrecy or mystery begins"**: Ted Gup, *Nation of Secrets* (New York: Doubleday, 2007).

27 **"The object in Cuba was not to put down"**: Taylor Branch and George Crile III, "The Kennedy Vendetta," *Harper's Magazine*, August 1975.

28 **"My idea is to stir things up"**: Arthur M. Schlesinger, Jr., *Robert Kennedy and His Times* (Boston: Houghton Mifflin, 1978), 476.

28 **It included Operation Bounty**: Jon Elliston, *Psywar on Cuba* (North Melbourne, Australia: Ocean Press, 2002), 83–86.

28 **"Entomological Warfare Target Analysis"**: Seán Murphy, Alastair Hay, and Steven Rose, *No Fire, No Thunder*, cited in Lockwood, *Six-Legged Soldiers*.

29 **These feasibility studies exist**: Louis C. Lamotte et al., "Yellow Fever Virus. Feasibility Study" and "Dengue Virus: A Feasibility Study," listed in TechRptsDPG_1950-1960.pdf, a database search record of technical reports at DPG and West Desert Technical Informational Center 1950–1960, www.governmentattic.org/10docs/TechRptsDPG_1950-1960.pdf.

29 **"He mentioned specifically the possibility of producing crop failures"**: Minutes of Meeting of the Special Group (Augmented) on Operation MONGOOSE, 6 September 1962, www.archives.gov/files/research/jfk/releases/docid-32105754.pdf. In 1951, Carter, working under Secretary of Defense Robert Lovett, had overseen the progress reports for Operation Baseless. Marshall Carter, Memorandum for Secretaries of the Army, the Navy, and the Air Force, "Report of the Secretary of Defense's Ad Hoc Committee on Chemical, Biological and Radiological Warfare, Implementing Actions and Progress," Office of the Secretary of Defense, December 10, 1951, RG 330, entry 199, box 275, CD 385 (Biological Warfare) 1951, NA.

29 **"There is a body of documents"**: John R. Tunheim and Thomas E. Samoluk, "Assassination Questions Remain," *Boston Herald*, November 21, 2013, www.bostonherald.com/2013 /11/21/assassination-questions-remain/.

29 **"There was lots of sugar being sent"**: Branch and Crile, "The Kennedy Vendetta."

29 **"world-renowned plant pathologist"**: "MKULTRA, Subproject 146," 3, Biological Branch, Technical Services Division, CIA, 1965, MKULTRA DOC_0000017406, archive.org/details/DOC_0000017406.

29 **"sugar cane crop vulnerabilities"**: "MKULTRA Briefing Book," CIA, January 1, 1976 (estimated), MKULTRA DOC_0000190090 archive.org/details/DOC_0000190090/.

29 **"maintain an offensive biological agent"**: "MKULTRA, Subproject 146," 5, 20, 28.

30 **"He will not continue his efforts"**: "MKULTRA, Subproject 146," 3.

30 **"sailing in a sea of difficulties"**: UPI, "Castro Admits Cuba Sailing on Rough Sea," *Orlando Sentinel*, March 18, 1980, www.newspapers.com/image/303123362/.

30 **"In the last two years"**: "Castro Blames U.S. for Plots, Plagues," *Miami News*, July 27, 1981, www.newspapers.com/image/302179770/.

30 **"totally without foundation"**: Bernard Gwertzman, NYT News Service, "Cuba Blames U.S. for Fever Outbreak," *Minneapolis Star Tribune*, September 8, 1981, www.newspapers .com/image/187774194/; "Epidemic in Cuba Sets Off Dispute with U.S.," NYT, September 6, 1981.

30 **Dean Fischer, a State Department spokesman**: AP, "U.S. Counters Castro's Charges About Epidemic," *Indianapolis Star*, July 28, 1981, www.newspapers.com/image/106355871/.

30 **"relieved of all restrictions"**: Dial Torgerson, "Castro Criticism of U.S. Is Strongest in Years," *Philadelphia Inquirer*, September 16, 1981, www.newspapers.com/image/173826084/.

30 **"Imperialism is using biological arms"**: "Fidel Castro Scores U.S. in IPU Speech," September 15, 1981, Foreign Broadcast Information Service, Castro Speech Database, Latin American Network Information Center, lanic.utexas.edu/project/castro/db/1981 /19810915.html.

31 **"Its intransigent refusal"**: Torgerson, "Castro Criticism of U.S. Is Strongest in Years."

31 **"unfair and often untruthful, certainly impolite"**: UPI, "Castro Blasts Reagan," *The Herald*, Crystal Lake, Ill., September 16, 1981, www.newspapers.com/image/185223136/.

March 15, 2019, Friday

32 **article by Nate Jones:** Nate Jones, "How to Ensure We Have a More Open, Accountable Government," *Washington Post*, March, 13, 2019, www.washingtonpost.com/outlook/2019 /03/13/how-ensure-we-have-more-open-accountable-government/.

32 **Jones, who works at the National Security Archive:** In November 2019, Jones became the FOIA director at *The Washington Post*.

33 **"yellow rain" controversy:** See Julian Robinson, Jeanne Guillemin, and Matthew Meselson, "Yellow Rain: The Story Collapses," *Foreign Policy* 68 (Autumn 1987); and Matthew Meselson and Julian Robinson, "The Yellow Rain Affair: Lessons from a Discredited Allegation," in Anne Clunan, Peter R. Lavoy, Susan B. Martin, eds., *Terrorism, War, or Disease?: Unraveling the Use of Biological Weapons* (Palo Alto, Calif: Stanford University Press, 2008), www.belfercenter.org/sites/default/files/legacy/files/Meselsonchapter.pdf.

34 **"wart hog disease":** William M. Creasy, "Presentation to the Secretary of Defense's Ad Hoc Committee on CEBAR," February 24, 1950, Chemical Corps, National Security Archive record no. 54874; also at Brill online, primarysources.brillonline.com/browse /weapons-of-mass-destruction/.

34 **"With at least the tacit backing":** Drew Fetherston and John Cummings, "Tacit CIA Backing Linked to Swine Fever in Cuba," *Los Angeles Times*, January 9, 1977, www .newspapers.com/image/383549772/.

34 **46,000 metric tons:** Virginia Hamill, "Cigar Factories in Cuba Closed," *Boston Globe*, March 16, 1980, www.newspapers.com/image/428199981.

34 **"You touch them and they turn to powder":** AP, "Blight Strikes Cuban Tobacco," *Journal Times*, Racine, Wisc., August 4, 1980, www.newspapers.com/image/342910731/.

34 **"in the interests of the United States":** Virginia Hamill, "Blight Snuffs Out Tobacco Crop and Cuts Jobs in Cuba," *Washington Post*, March 15, 1980, www.washingtonpost .com/archive/politics/1980/03/15/blight-snuffs-out-tobacco-crop-and-cuts-jobs-in-cuba /80298e9f-047b-49fe-8d1f-a178e31b5c40/.

35 **"The young plants display a severe wilt":** Paul J. Wuest, "Greenhouse Tests to Compare European and Beltsville Isolates of *Peronospora tabacina*," Crops Division, U.S. Army Biological Laboratories, February 1965, apps.dtic.mil/dtic/tr/fulltext/u2/457856.pdf.

35 **"Tobacco Growing and Economics of Tobacco":** Paul J. Wuest, "Tobacco Growing and Economics of Tobacco in Selected Countries of the World," Crops Division, U.S. Army Biological Laboratories, September 1965, apps.dtic.mil/dtic/tr/fulltext/u2/470690.pdf.

35 **"FOIA request for a list of technical reports:** U.S. Army Test and Evaluation Command, "Morisy FOIA FA -13-0036 dpg_1965," archive.org/details/713165-morisy-foia-fa-13-0036 -dpg_1965.

March 16, 2019, Saturday

38 **hecklers set off firecrackers:** Craig Swayze, "Endicott Denies Implicating Canada," *Windsor Star*, Windsor, Ontario, Canada, May 12, 1952, www.newspapers.com/image /500959310/.

38 **"As I listened to the testimony":** James G. Endicott, "I Accuse! Dr. James G. Endicott Describes Germ Warfare," *Peace Review* (Summer 1952).

40 **"It is easy to dismiss this book":** Sheldon Harris, review of Stephen Endicott and Edward Hagerman, *The United States and Biological Warfare: Secrets from the Early Cold War and Korea, Journal of American History* 87, no. 1 (June 2000), academic.oup.com/jah/article -abstract/87/1/285/717644.

40 **"The evidence Endicott and Hagerman present":** Ed Regis, "Wartime Lies?," *New York Times Book Review*, June 27, 1999.

40 **"Though some documents have been shredded"**: Stephen Endicott and Edward Hagerman, *The United States and Biological Warfare*, 142.

40 **"1951 Program Guidance Report"**: Committee on Biological Warfare, Research and Development Board, "1951 Program Guidance Report," December 5, 1950, RG 330, file CD 383.8 Biological Warfare, NA, declassified 1996, Edward Hagerman files.

41 **MIT-trained weaponeer William Webster:** Gerald Griffin, "Webster, New Defense Board Head, Puts Skill to Tough Scientific Tasks," *Baltimore Sun*, March 15, 1950, www.newspapers.com/image/370819695/.

41 **"Our outnumbered soldiers":** William L. White, "A Note on Wars," *Emporia Gazette*, Emporia, Kans., December 4, 1950, www.newspapers.com/image/10727063/.

41 **"The present international situation requires":** Committee on Biological Warfare, Research and Development Board, "1951 Program Guidance Report."

42 **"I was told to clear off"**: Peter Williams and David Wallace, *Unit 731: The Japanese Army's Secret of Secrets* (London: Hodder and Stoughton, 1989), 265–66.

March 17, 2019, Sunday

44 **"Vigil at Fort Detrick"**: Ronald W. May, "Into the Valley of Death: Vigil at Fort Detrick," editorial, *Gazette and Daily*, York, Pa., July 22, 1959, www.newspapers.com/image/64690634/.

44 **article earlier that year in *Harper's***: Jacquard H. Rothschild, "Germs and Gas: The Weapons Nobody Dares Talk About," *Harper's Magazine*, June 1959.

45 **the *Golden Rule***: Richard G. Hewlett and Jack M. Holl, *Atoms for Peace and War* (Berkeley and Los Angeles: University of California Press, 1989), 484; AP, "Will Sail to Test Area to Stop A-Bombs," *News Tribune*, Fort Pierce, Fla., February 10, 1958, www.newspapers.com/image/31977419/; "L. Bucks Man Plans Direct Plea to Reds," *Bristol Daily Courier*, Bristol, Pa., April 3, 1958, www.newspapers.com/image/48848881/.

45 **"We must turn back"**: Ronald W. May, "The Two Worlds of Fort Detrick, Maryland," *Gazette and Daily*, York, Pa., www.newspapers.com/image/64690762/.

45 **"The mute protest against germ warfare"**: AP, "Germ Warfare Protest Persists," *Courier News*, Bridgewater, N. J., January 12, 1960, www.newspapers.com/image/221806758/.

45 **A spinoff vigil began:** Donald Bremner, "Pickets at Edgewood to Protest Warfare," *Evening Sun*, Baltimore, Md., www.newspapers.com/image/367569891/.

45 **The Detrick vigilers ran a quarter-page ad:** Vigil at Fort Detrick advertisement, "More Humane?," *The News*, Frederick, Md., www.newspapers.com/image/8888269/.

45 **"We have both in hand and in research"**: "More Humane?," Vigil at Fort Detrick advertisement.

46 **It was one of the longest continuous:** AP, "Fort Detrick Vigil Ended," *Morning Herald*, Hagerstown, Md., March 31, 1961, www.newspapers.com/image/21313401/.

46 **Project Spice Rack:** "Protest Germ War Research," photo caption, *York Daily Record*, York, Pa., November 9, 1965, www.newspapers.com/image/553047975/. See also *Friends Journal*, May 15, 1967, www.friendsjournal.org/wp-content/uploads/emember/downloads/1967/HC12-50406.pdf.

46 **Harvard professors Matthew Meselson:** Rudy Abramson, "Scientists Petition for Chemical Weapons Ban," *Los Angeles Times*, September 20, 1966, www.newspapers.com/image/382311068/.

46 **Jean Mayer:** Jean Mayer, "Crop Destruction in Vietnam," *Science*, April 15, 1966, and "Starvation as a Weapon: Herbicides in Vietnam," *Scientist and Citizen*, August–September 1967.

46 **Victor Sidel:** "Germ Warfare Dangers Cited," *Boston Globe*, January 6, 1966, www.newspapers.com/image/433841953/. See also Jeanne Guillemin, *Biological Weapons* (New York: Columbia University Press, 2005).

46 **"to help out his crop failures"**: Drew Pearson, "New Leader's Thoughts," *Oneonta Star*, Oneonta, N.Y., January 20, 1961, www.newspapers.com/image/48101735/.

47 **"The inventory includes mosquitoes"**: Walter Schneir, "How Chemical Warfare Is Being Sold as 'Humane,'" *Gazette and Daily*, York, Pa., October 7, 1959, www.newspapers.com /image/64846312/.

47 **positioning a new, sleeker style of gas mask**: AP Wirephoto, "Latest Masks for Armed Forces and Civilians," *Ithaca Journal*, Ithaca, N.Y., January 20, 1959, www.newspapers.com /image/255335775/.

47 **"illustrate the effectiveness of some of the incapacitating chemicals"**: "Osmers Sees Dogs in Chemical Tests," *Herald-News*, Passaic, N.J., June 23, 1959, www.newspapers.com /image/525329380/.

47 **"Colonel Armitage and his staff put on an excellent show"**: C. P. Cabell to Marshall Stubbs, June 15, 1960, CREST, https://www.cia.gov/library/readingroom/docs/CIA -RDP80B01676R001200100022-6.pdf.

March 18, 2019, Monday

48 **named their son Matthew after Matthew Meselson**: Seymour Hersh, *Reporter: A Memoir* (New York: Knopf, 2018), chapter 6. For more on Meselson, see Jeanne McDermott, *The Killing Winds: The Menace of Biological Warfare* (New York: Harper, 1987).

48 **I found the piece**: Seymour M. Hersh, AP, "CBW: Gas, Germ Warfare and Its Possibilities," *Fort Lauderdale News*, April 9, 1967, www.newspapers.com/image/272088552/.

48 **Read before you write**: Eric Alterman, "The Ironies of Izzymania," *Mother Jones*, June 1988.

49 **"generously contributing to the image"**: Daniel S. Greenberg, "Certain Styles of Killing," *New York Times Book Review*, June 9, 1968.

49 **"Germ Warfare, for Alma Mater"**: Seymour Hersh, "Germ Warfare," *Ramparts*, December 1969, attachment to L. K. White, "Morning Meeting of 18 November 1969," CREST, https:// www.cia.gov/library/readingroom/docs/CIA-RDP80R01284A001800130047-3.pdf.

49 **"impair the effectiveness of an intelligence method"**: "Declassification Frequently Asked Questions," United States Department of Justice, www.justice.gov/open/declassification /declassification-faq.

49 **because we feel like it**: There's also exemption (b)(5), the "withhold it because you want to" exemption. Nate Jones, "The Next FOIA Fight: The B(5) 'Withhold It Because You Want To' Exemption," *Unredacted*, March 27, 2014, unredacted.com/2014/03/27/the-next-foia-fight -the-b5-withold-it-because-you-want-to-exemption/.

50 **"By 1947," she writes, "military planners"**: Dorothy Miller, "History of Air Force Participation in Biological Warfare Program, 1944–1951," Historical Study No. 194, Historical Office, Air Force Materiel Command, 1952, 64 EW-21060, 1.

51 **"In the absence of firm strategic guidance"**: Miller, "History of Air Force Participation in Biological Warfare Program, 1944-1951," 34–35.

March 19, 2019, Tuesday

54 **not in Lyme but in Wisconsin, in January 1969**: "The first described case in the US was reported from Wisconsin in 1970, before the disease was formally recognized." Anne Gatewood Hoen et al., "Phylogeography of *Borrelia burgdorferi* in the Eastern United States Reflects Multiple Independent Lyme Disease Emergence Events," *Proceedings of the National Academy of Sciences* 106, no. 35 (September 2009), https://www.ncbi.nlm.nih.gov/pmc /articles/PMC2727481/. Hoen et al. cite Rudolph J. Scrimenti, "Erythema Chronicum Migrans," *Archives of Dermatology* 102, no. 1 (July 1970). Scrimenti, a Milwaukee dermatologist, used antibiotics to cure a sick physician who'd been bitten by a tick while hunting for grouse in Wisconsin. Pamela Weintraub, *Cure Unknown: Inside the Lyme Epidemic*, revised edition (New York: Macmillan, 2013). Willy Burgdorfer et al. also cite Scrimenti's paper in "Lyme Disease—A Tick-Borne Spirochetosis?" *Science*, June 18, 1982, https://escholarship.org/content/qt9vj3t37b/qt9vj3t37b.pdf.

55 **research contract with Camp Detrick**: The contract, which began in 1953, was through Cornelius B. Philip, Willy Burgdorfer's supervisor. "Dr. Philip Is Named Director of

RML, World Center of Rickettsial Research," *NIH Record*, January 30, 1962, nihrecord
.nih.gov/sites/recordNIH/files/pdf/1962/NIH-Record-1962-01-30.pdf.

55 **"thousands and thousands and thousands" of them:** Willy Burgdorfer oral history,
Deirdre Boggs, interviewer, 2001, history.nih.gov/archives/downloads/wburgdorfer.pdf.

55 **watchmaker's forceps and eye-surgery scalpels:** Burgdorfer oral history.

55 **In a paper for *The Journal of Infectious Diseases*:** Willy Burgdorfer and Edgar G.
Pickens, "A Technique Employing Embryonated Chicken Eggs for the Infection of Argasid Ticks
with *Coxiella burnetii, Bacterium tularense, Leptospira icterohaemorrhagiae*, and Western
Equine Encephalitis Virus," *Journal of Infectious Diseases* 94, no. 1 (January–February 1954).

56 **"Passage of BW agents through various arthropods":** Chemical Corps Biological
Laboratories, "Seventh Annual Report of the Chemical Corps Biological Laboratories,"
July 1, 1953, DTIC, Brill online, primarysources.brillonline.com/browse/weapons-of-mass
-destruction/.

56 **Queensland, Australia, where cowboys:** "Q Fever and How It Acts," *Washington Missourian*,
Washington, Mo., March 19, 1953, www.newspapers.com/image/126309805/.

56 **"tank and bone house":** E. H. Derrick, "The Epidemiology of Q Fever," *Journal of Hygiene*
43, no. 5 (April 1944), www.jstor.org/stable/3860046.

57 **"It is suggested that inhalation of tick faeces":** Derrick, "The Epidemiology of Q Fever."

57 **He promptly fell ill:** Oscar Chaffee, "Q Fever Battle May Prove Boon to Stockmen," *Billings
Gazette*, Billings, Mont., June 26, 1960, www.newspapers.com/image/410220736/.

57 **found ways to modify the polio virus:** John Blake, "Pied Piper Wanted," *St. Joseph News-
Gazette*, St. Joseph, Mo., February 11, 1940, www.newspapers.com/image/558900595/;
Jamie Kugler, "Secrets of Building 7," *NIH Catalyst* 22, no. 5, September–October 2014, irp
.nih.gov/sites/default/files/catalyst/catalyst_v22i5_0.pdf.

57 **Q fever again:** "Dr. Armstrong himself was a 'Q' fever casualty during the pre-war
research period." UP, "U.S. Hunts Cure in Strange Malady," *Pittsburgh Press*, March 4,
1946, https://www.newspapers.com/image/149701834/.

57 **More than a dozen people:** "Rare Malady Kills One, 14 Others Seriously Ill," *Times-
Tribune*, Scranton, Pa., May 23, 1940, www.newspapers.com/image/533984706/.

57 **Asa Marcey, a sixty-year-old lab assistant:** Roger M. Cole, "Bacteriology and Mycology,"
in *NIH: An Account of Research in Its Laboratories and Clinics*, ed. Dewitt Stetten, Jr., and
W. T. Carrigan (Orlando, Fla.: Academic Press, 1984), 122, archive.org/details
/nihaccountofrese00stet/page/122; Michele Lyons, "Remembering IRP Scientists Who
Gave Their Lives for Their Work," *I Am Intramural Blog*, National Institutes of Health,
November 9, 2018, irp.nih.gov/blog/post/2018/11/remembering-irp-scientists-who-gave
-their-lives-for-their-work.

57 **In May 1942, he flew from Washington:** "Doctor, Now at Hamilton, Afflicted with
Tularemia," *Great Falls Tribune*, Great Falls, Mont., July 23, 1942, www.newspapers
.com/image/239789711/.

57 **He was laid up for months:** "Veteran Disease Fighter Stricken by Rabbit Fever," *York
Daily Record*, York, Pa., June 24, 1942, www.newspapers.com/image/553036383/; "Noted
Scientist Victim of Germ," *Semi-Weekly Spokesman-Review*, Spokane, Wash., July 21,
1942, www.newspapers.com/image/567715053/; AP, "Dr. Armstrong Moved to East,"
Semi-Weekly Spokesman-Review, Spokane, Wash., August 11, 1942, www.newspapers.com
/image/567671595/.

57 **"We started working on Q fever again":** AP, "Q Fever Hits 22 Workers in U.S. Health
Bureau," *Harrisburg Telegraph*, Harrisburg, Pa., February 28, 1946, www.newspapers.com
/image/43150527/.

57 **"This outbreak is most unfortunate":** UP, "New Outbreak of 'Q' Fever Is Reported,"
Daily Notes, Canonsburg, Pa., March 7, 1946, www.newspapers.com/image/53351565/.

58 **Two guinea pig populations:** Alexander D. Langmuir, "The Potentialities of Biological
Warfare Against Man: An Epidemiological Appraisal," *Public Health Reports* 66, no. 13
(March 30, 1951), www.jstor.org/stable/4587679.

58 **Q fever in Amarillo, Texas:** AP, "Mysterious Amarillo Malady Was 'Q Fever,'"*Pampa Daily News*, Pampa, Texas, May 9, 1946, www.newspapers.com/image/5872176/.

58 **Five meat inspectors:** "Chicago Cases Are Diagnosed as Q Fever," *Amarillo Globe-Times*, Amarillo, Texas, September 20, 1946, www.newspapers.com/image/29539024/.

58 **Building 7, with a superheated-grid:** Jamie Kugler, "Secrets of Building 7," *NIH Catalyst* 22, no. 5 (September–October 2014), irp.nih.gov/sites/default/files/catalyst/catalyst_v22i5_0.pdf.

58 **one researcher had died:** Kugler, "Secrets of Building 7."

58 **washed his sheets and towels:** Edward A. Beeman, "Q Fever: An Epidemiological Note, *Public Health Reports* 6, no. 3 (January 20, 1950), www.jstor.org/stable/4587216.

58 **"All who took part in the necropsy":** J. H. Whittick, "Necropsy Findings in a Case of Q Fever in Britain," *British Medical Journal*, April 29, 1950, 980, www.ncbi.nlm.nih.gov /pmc/articles/PMC2037478/.

58 **deserved intensified research:** The Research and Development Board called for "intensification of the program for the causative agents of Q fever, tularemia, and plague, so that they could be considered for end-item development." Committee on Biological Warfare, Research and Development Board, "1951 Program Guidance Report," December 5, 1950, RG 330, file CD 383.8 Biological Warfare, NA.

58 **Q fever tests at Dugway Proving Ground:** "The agents causing Q fever and psittacosis were tested at Dugway in 1951, again by Biological Laboratories personnel. From 1951 on, Dugway Proving Ground personnel have run BW trials on a continuing basis, testing agents and munitions developed in the Biological Laboratories. *B. suis, Brucella melitensis, B. tularense*, botulinum toxin and the virus of Q fever as well as simulants have been tested, utilizing the M114 bomb, the E61 bomb, the ADL and C generators, the E73 or feather bomb, and other devices." Chemical Corps Biological Laboratories, "Seventh Annual Report of the Chemical Corps Biological Laboratories," July 1, 1953, DTIC, Brill online, primarysources.brillonline.com/browse/weapons-of-mass-destruction/.

58 **In July 1955, a group of thirty:** David Snyder, "The Front Lines of Biowarfare," *Washington Post*, May 6, 2003. See Ed Regis, *The Biology of Doom: America's Secret Germ Warfare Project* (New York: Henry Holt, 1999) for more on Project Whitecoat.

58 **the jackrabbit population:** Brandon Davis, "The Desert Blooms as a Wasteland: An Environmental History of Utah's West Desert," MA thesis, Simon Fraser University, Summer 2007, summit.sfu.ca/item/8130.

March 20, 2019, Wednesday

60 **a fog of *Brucella* organisms:** The M-33 munition could also potentially hold anthrax or plague. "It is imperative that tests of Pestis in the M-33 in the 'Eight-ball' and at Dugway be conducted in the next ninety days," wrote Air Force general Howard Bunker on April 1, 1952. Howard Bunker, Memorandum to General Bullene, "Symposium on BW Agents," April 1, 1952, AFOAT BW-CW, RG 341, entry NM-15 199, 1952, file #6, box 2, NA. "Anthrax, a more potent agent, could be used as a fill for the M-33 bombs," Bunker wrote to General White in 1953. "Air Force Program for Biological and Chemical Weapons," April 22, 1953, RG 341, AFOAT BW-CW, entry NM-15 199, 1953, box 1, NA.

60 **"It consisted of placing 3,230 guinea pigs":** Joseph J. Clark for Milton A. Anderson, Chief, Offensive BW Section, AFOAT BW-CW, "Report of a Trip to Dugway 17–19 September 1952," September 23, 1952, RG 341, entry NM-15 199, box 4, NA.

61 **"The experimental animals are encased in rows":** Waldemar Kaempffert, "Tests Show How Airborne Germs Could Spread over Cities in Biological Warfare," NYT, April 22, 1951.

61 **Hooper Foundation for Medical Research:** Marion Lewis Meyer, "A Brief History of the George Williams Hooper Foundation for Medical Research," September 1983, University of California, San Francisco, calisphere.org/item/27718b00-ed58-4fab-b74b-78b36ec3ac4f/.

62 **"Usually the control died":** Edna Tartaul Daniel, "Medical Research and Public Health," Karl Meyer oral history, Bancroft Library, Regional Oral History Office, University of

California, Berkeley, conducted in 1961 and 1962, digitalassets.lib.berkeley.edu/roho /ucb/text/meyer_karl.pdf. "We were *the* plague organization in the United States," Meyer said.

62 **"human guinea pigs":** Al Ostrow, "San Quentin Prisoners Serve Society as Well as Time under Warden Duffy," *Dunkirk Evening Observer*, Dunkirk, N.Y., January 7, 1946, www .newspapers.com/image/56370815/.

62 **"Some prisoners were hospitalized":** AP, "Prisoners Volunteer for Vaccine Test," *Visalia Times-Delta*, May 26, 1945, www.newspapers.com/image/529702573/.

March 21, 2019, Thursday

64 **The contingency plan was published in full:** U.S. Senate, *Hearings Before the Select Committee to Study Government Operations with Respect to Intelligence Activities*, vol. 1, Unauthorized Storage of Toxic Agents, September 16–18, 1975, www.intelligence .senate.gov/sites/default/files/94intelligence_activities_I.pdf.

65 **The Summary Report was also released:** Philip Buchen, "Summary Report on CIA Investigation of MKNAOMI," JFK Assassination Records—2018 Additional Documents Release, record no. 178-10004-10087, www.archives.gov/research/jfk/release?page =1092&sort=asc&order=Agency.

65 **"From its outset the project":** CIA, "Summary Report on CIA Investigation of MKNAOMI," JFK Assassination Related Materials, 178-10004-10087, 17, www .archives.gov/files/research/jfk/releases/178-10004-10087.pdf.

65 **"A study on the vulnerability of subway systems":** U.S. Senate, "Unauthorized Storage of Toxic Agents," in *Hearings Before the Select Committee to Study Governmental Operations with Respect to Intelligence Activities*, vol. 1, 206.

66 **including how many ventilation chambers:** "Moscow Subway Construction," June 14, 1949, CREST, https://www.cia.gov/library/readingroom/docs/CIA-RDP82-00457R00 2800530011-5.pdf.

66 **how deep they were:** "Depth of Moscow Subway System," Central Intelligence Agency Information Report, May 8, 1950, CREST, https://www.cia.gov/library/readingroom/docs /CIA-RDP80-00926A002200040021-2.pdf.

66 **analysis of new subway construction in Budapest:** Directorate of Intelligence, CIA, "Resurgence of Subway Construction in the Communist Bloc," February 16, 1966, CREST, https://www.cia.gov/library/readingroom/docs/CIA-RDP79T01003A003100100001-5 .pdf.

66 **"Applications under the Freedom of Information Act":** Nicholas Horrock, "New Law Is Dislodging CIA's Secrets," NYT, May 14, 1975.

66 **UPI photo of an unsmiling Senator Frank Church:** Nicholas M. Horrock, "Colby Describes C.I.A. Poison Work," NYT, September 17, 1975.

66 **called a "nondiscirnable microbioinoculator":** U.S. Senate, "Unauthorized Storage of Toxic Agents," 17, 205. See https://babel.hathitrust.org/cgi/pt?id=uiug.30112119392220&. view=1up&seq=1.

66 **"would not appear in the autopsy":** U.S. Senate, "Unauthorized Storage of Toxic Agents," 17, 177.

66 **"Among plans being considered":** AP, "President Says He'll Revamp CIA," *Albany Democrat-Herald*, Albany, Ore., September 17, 1975, www.newspapers.com/image /440733452/.

March 22, 2019, Friday

69 **"Hundreds of thousands of men":** "Farmers' Roundup," *Columbus Telegram*, Columbus, Neb., April 6, 1944, www.newspapers.com/image/428830898/.

69 **"As easy as turning on a light switch":** Airosol, Inc., "Amazing Airosol DDT Atomizer," *Daily Oklahoman*, Oklahoma City, www.newspapers.com/image/449423818/.

69 **"In May 1943 the Munitions Branch":** Herbert Tanner, *Munitions for Biological Warfare*,

Special Report No. 44, Munitions Division, Chemical Warfare Service, DPG library, Edward Hagerman collection, 8.

70 **In 1943, on the advice of British bomb designers:** Tanner, *Munitions for Biological Warfare*, 13.

70 **about twenty-one inches long:** Rexmond Cochrane, *History of the Chemical Warfare Service in World War II: Biological Warfare Research in the United States* (hereafter Biological Warfare Research), Historical Section, Chemical Corps, November 1947, apps.dtic.mil /dtic/tr/fulltext/u2/b228585.pdf.

70 **"produce a cloud of 'N' affording 50% risk of death":** Tanner, *Munitions for Biological Warfare*, 13.

70 **"the Germans and Japanese would devote their greatest":** Cochrane, *Biological Warfare Research.*

71 **four Canadian germ men came down:** John Bryden, *Deadly Allies* (Toronto: McClelland & Stewart, 1989), 214.

71 **"yeast and ground alfalfa meal":** Cochrane, *Biological Warfare Research.* This phrase is almost cut off on the bottom of the page about insect vectors.

71 **late in the war, at the Suffield Experimental Station:** Bryden, *Deadly Allies*, 224–25.

March 23, 2019, Saturday

73 **"The matter must be handled with great secrecy":** Henry Stimson to President Roosevelt, April 29, 1942, quoted in Robert Harris and Jeremy Paxman, *A Higher Form of Killing* (New York: Random House, 2002), 97.

73 **"The town minded its own business":** Sidney Shallet, "The Deadliest War," *Collier's Magazine*, June 15, 1946. Quoted in "Camp Detrick Parent Research Center of New Type of Warfare," *The News*, Frederick, Maryland, June 7, 1946, www.newspapers.com/image /33889261/.

74 **glanders, tularemia, cutaneous anthrax:** Cochrane, *Biological Warfare Research*, 223.

74 **At its peak in 1945, 3,900 people:** Cochrane, *Biological Warfare Research.*

74 **"test tube animal":** Oram C. Woolpert, "Direct Bacteriological Experimentation on the Living Mammalian Fetus," *American Journal of Pathology* 12, no. 2 (1936), www.ncbi.nlm .nih.gov/pmc/articles/PMC1911059/pdf/amjpathol00363-0002.pdf.

74 **tuberculosis, diphtheria, and infantile paralysis:** AP, "Science Now Takes Guinea Pigs Unborn," *Indianapolis Star*, December 28, 1935, www.newspapers.com/image/105386231/.

74 **then infected them "intranasally":** H. E. Wilson, Samuel Saslaw, Charles A. Doan, Oram C. Woolpert, and John L. Schwab, "Reactions of Monkeys to Experimental Mixed Influenza and Streptococcus Infections," *Journal of Experimental Medicine*, January 31, 1947, www.ncbi.nlm.nih.gov/pmc/articles/PMC2135694/pdf/199.pdf.

75 **"casualty agent against troops":** Cochrane, *Biological Warfare Research.*

75 **"We think they've killed a lot of people":** Peter Williams and David Wallace, *Unit 731*. Also quoted in Daniel Barenblatt, *A Plague upon Humanity: The Secret Genocide of Axis Japan's Germ Warfare Operation* (New York: HarperCollins, 2004).

March 24, 2019, Sunday

77 **the list Rexmond Cochrane gives:** Rexmond Cochrane, *Biological Warfare Research*, 122.

77 **"to determine the effects":** Warren Moscow, "U.S. Pays $35 Each for Stray Dogs for Use in Atomic Research Work," NYT, December 28, 1951.

78 **"If you asked a man":** Moscow, "U.S. Pays $35 Each for Stray Dogs."

78 **"through health we can defeat the evil threat":** "Dean of Public Health Calls Fit Body Red Foe," *Harvard Crimson*, October 13, 1950, www.thecrimson.com/article/1950/10/13 /dean-of-public-health-calls-fit/.

79 **a particular colony shipped from the Philippines in 1925:** "Sleeping Sickness Fight Is Part of 35-Year Campaign," *St. Louis Post-Dispatch*, September 29, 1933, www.newspapers .com/image/138912436/. Joseph F. Siler sent the mosquitoes; see Goro Kuno, "Early

History of Laboratory Breeding of *Aedes Aegyptis*," *Journal of Medical Entomology* 47, no. 6 (November 2010).

79 **"the livestock population, as a target":** AP, "Cattle, Crops—Not Man—New Army Targets in Germ War Studies," *Evening Sun*, Baltimore, April 25, 1949, www.newspapers .com/image/367355239/.

81 **reportedly woke up screaming:** G. Pascal Zachary, *Endless Frontier: Vannevar Bush, Engineer of the American Century* (New York: Free Press, 1997), quoting Merle Tuve, Oral History, Albert Christman, interviewer, 1967, American Institute of Physics, www.aip.org /history-programs/niels-bohr-library/oral-histories/3894. According to the raw transcript, Tuve says: "For years after the war Van Bush would wake screaming in the night because of the—he burned Tokyo. The proximity fuze didn't bother him badly but—and even the atomic bomb didn't bother him as much as jellied gasoline. Oh, yes, we all suffer scars you know. . . ."

81 **Microbiologist Norman F. Conant:** "Guide to the Norman F. Conant Papers," Medical Center Archives, Duke University, archives.mc.duke.edu/xml?faids=collection-172 .xml#c01_8.

81 **highly virulent strains of Newcastle disease and fowl plague:** Cochrane, *Biological Warfare Research.*

81 **Stanley Lovell evaluated the military worth:** Cochrane, *Biological Warfare Research.*

81 **wire-rimmed dean of Harvard's Graduate School of Engineering:** "Prof. Fair Named New Master of Dunster House," *Boston Globe*, October 13, 1948, www.newspapers.com /image/433399918/.

81 **"Panel on BW Dissemination":** Ira F. Ferguson to Colonel Clark, "Meeting of the Panel on BW Dissemination," October 8, 1952, AFOAT BW-CW, RG 341, entry NM-15 199, 1952, box 4, NA.

82 **"He traveled widely":** Abel Wolman, "Gordon Maskew Fair," *Memorial Tributes: Volume 1* (Washington, D.C.: National Academies Press, 1979), www.nap.edu/read/578 /chapter/10.

82 **"continuously engaged in the Chemical Corps":** W. A. Perkins, F. X. Webster, S. W. Grinnell, Final Report No. 543-14, February 18, 1963, Aerosol Laboratory, Metronics Associates, Stanford Industrial Park, apps.dtic.mil/dtic/tr/fulltext/u2/418598.pdf.

82 **Dr. George Spendlove:** "Dr. George A. Spendlove," *American Fork Citizen*, American Fork, Utah, June 29, 1988, www.newspapers.com/image/286064090/.

82 **"Provided tests with N are conducted":** "Review of Field Data from Operation 'Airflow,'" September 26, 1953, Army Chemical Center, RG 175, Records of Chief Chemical Officer, entry 18, box 256.

83 **"The flight trials proved the feasibility":** Chemical Corps, Summary of Major Events and Problems, Fiscal year 1959, January 1960, Chemical Corps Historical Office, www .osti.gov/opennet/servlets/purl/16006843-5BAfk6/16006843.pdf=PA103.

83 **"it doesn't involve biological warfare at all":** Michael Sweeney, "Biological Warfare at Stanford," *Stanford Daily*, May 27, 1969, stanforddailyarchive.com/.

March 25, 2019, Monday

84 **"Citizens blamed everything from sewer gas":** "L.A. Smog Pays Call on San Franciscans," *Long Beach Independent*, Long Beach, Calif., September 22, 1950, www.newspapers.com /image/74189024/.

84 **"a combination of refinery, garbage, cooking":** "Storm Front Routs Heat Here," *Oakland Tribune*, September 22, 1950, www.newspapers.com/image/246241023/.

85 **"offensive possibilities of attacking a seaport city":** John S. McNulty, "Biological Warfare Trials at San Francisco, California, 20–27 September 1950," January 22, 1951, Chemical Corps Biological Laboratories, National Security Archive collection.

85 **stand-in for anthrax:** Rexmond Cochrane, *History of the Chemical Warfare Service in World War II: Biological Warfare Research in the United States*, Historical Section, Chemical Corps, November 1947, apps.dtic.mil/dtic/tr/fulltext/u2/b228585.pdf.

85 **nobody got sick:** Leonard A. Cole, *Clouds of Secrecy* (Lanham, Md.: Rowman & Littlefield, 1988), 93.

85 **"Inhalation of *Serratia marcescens*":** "Report of the Biological Department, Chemical Corps, to the Committee on Biological Warfare," October 1, 1949, DGP Library, Edward Hagerman's files.

86 **had invited Olson to join the team:** John Schwab, "Chronological Relationship with Dr. Frank R. Olson," CIA Documents Concerning the Death of Dr. Frank Olson, January 11, 1976, http://frankolsonproject.org/staging01/wp-content/uploads/2018/02/William_Colby -1975-documents.pdf.

86 **"I could only conduct such a test":** Cole, *Clouds of Secrecy*, 95.

March 26, 2019, Tuesday

89 **"smoke screen" tests:** "Smoke Screens to Be Tested in Minneapolis," *Minneapolis Star Tribune*, August 28, 1952, www.newspapers.com/image/183437490/. See also Leonard A. Cole, *Clouds of Secrecy* (Lanham, Md.: Rowman & Littlefield, 1988).

89 **Zinc cadmium sulfide dust was the simulant:** Marco A. Riojas, "Bioaerosol Dispersal Models and the In Silico Design of a Synthetic Strain of Bacillus Subtilis with Stringent Growth Regulation," dissertation, George Mason University, 2014, citeseerx.ist.psu.edu /viewdoc/download?doi=10.1.1.820.4736&rep=rep1&type=pdf. See also Edmund Crouch, "Appendix B: Summary of Doses and Concentrations of Zinc Cadmium Sulfide Particles from the Army's Dispersion Tests," in Edmund Crouch, *Toxicologic Assessment of the Army's Zinc Cadmium Sulfide Dispersion Tests*, prepared for the National Research Council, Subcommittee on Zinc Cadmium Sulfide (Washington, D. C.: National Academies Press, 1997), www.ncbi.nlm.nih.gov/books/NBK233498/.

89 **simulant for Kiev:** Marco A. Riojas, "Bioaerosol Dispersal Models." The cities of Minneapolis, St. Louis, and Winnipeg, Canada, writes Riojas, "were felt to be representative of the Soviet cities of Kiev, Leningrad, and Moscow."

89 **"ticking and purring":** Sterling Soderlind, "Mystery Boxes Tick, Purr, Say Nothing," *Minneapolis Star Tribune*, January 20, 1953, www.newspapers.com/image/183429162/.

89 **"They need changing every three hours":** Soderlind, "Mystery Boxes Tick, Purr, Say Nothing."

89 **"the penetrations of the aerosol cloud":** Cole, *Clouds of Secrecy*.

90 **elementary school and kindergarten:** "Public Schools Welcome New Kindergarten Crop," *Minneapolis Star Tribune*, April 19, 1953, www.newspapers.com/image/183729181/.

90 **simulant city for Leningrad:** Riojas, "Bioaerosol Dispersal Models."

90 **released from balloons:** "Army to Launch Balloons Here in Smoke Screen Test," *St. Louis Post Dispatch*, April 15, 1953, www.newspapers.com/image/139454022/.

90 **one of the Pruitt-Igoe residents:** CBS News, "Secret Cold War Tests in St. Louis Cause Worry," October 3, 2012, www.cbsnews.com/news/secret-cold-war-tests-in-st-louis-cause -worry/.

90 **"They were wearing masks":** Jack El-Hai, "Experimenting on the Innocent: The U.S. Army's Secret Chemical Testing in the 1950s & 1960s," *Wonders & Marvels*, 2014, www .wondersandmarvels.com/2014/06/experimenting-innocent-u-s-armys-secret-chemical -testing-1950s-1960s.html.

91 **"killing or damaging food crops":** Victor Bertrandias to Henry Arnold, May 29, 1945, Papers of Henry H. Arnold, box 114, folder 3, SAS 385, LC.

92 **"combustibility and firebreak analyses":** George C. McDonald to Luther Evans, February 17, 1948, Macleish-Evans Central File, Ref. 18-4 1948–1950, box 1014, Manuscript Division, Library of Congress. The documents quoted from here about Air Force programs at the Library of Congress can be found in the MacLeish-Evans Central File, boxes 1014, 1015, and 1017 (hereafter Macleish-Evans LC).

94 **"The project was completed":** C. P. Cabell to Luther Evans, December 14, 1948, MacLeish-Evans LC.

95 **"not really part of the Library program"**: Burton W. Adkinson to Luther Evans, "Report on My Conversation with the Acting Director of Intelligence, General Moore," January 3, 1950, MacLeish-Evans, box 1014.

95 **"Present plans call for converting"**: Luther Evans to C.P. Cabell, August 22, 1950, MacLeish-Evans, box 1014.

95 **"Library of Congress, at 153, Suffers"**: Paul Sampson, "Library of Congress, at 153, Suffers Acute Growing Pains," *The Washington Post*, April 19, 1953.

98 **nuclear targeting study from 1956:** Introduction to "Atomic Weapons Requirements Study for 1959," SM 129-56, June 15, 1956, National Security Archive, nsarchive2.gwu .edu/nukevault/ebb538-Cold-War-Nuclear-Target-List-Declassified-First-Ever /documents/section1.pdf.

98 **computer printout of several hundred pages:** "Complex List, with Weapons," in "Atomic Weapons Requirements Study for 1959," National Security Archive, nsarchive2.gwu.edu /nukevault/ebb538-Cold-War-Nuclear-Target-List-Declassified-First-Ever/documents /1st%20city%20list%20complete.pdf.

98 **Each target was accompanied by its corresponding number:** "Atomic Weapons Requirements Study for 1959," 16.

98 **"the most comprehensive and detailed":** William Burr, "U.S. Cold War Nuclear Target Lists Declassified for First Time," December 22, 2015, National Security Archive, nsarchive2.gwu.edu/nukevault/ebb538-Cold-War-Nuclear-Target-List-Declassified -First-Ever/.

98 **"population loss as the primary yardstick":** Maxwell Taylor to LeMay, Wheeler, McDonald, and Greene, "Review of the SIOP Guidance," June 5, 1964, CM-1407-64, National Security Archive, nsarchive2.gwu.edu//dc.html?doc=4775205-Document-02 -Joint-Chiefs-of-Staff-Chairman. William Burr discusses this document in "U.S. Nuclear War Plan Option Sought Destruction of China and Soviet Union as 'Viable' Societies," August 15, 2018, National Security Archive, nsarchive.gwu.edu/briefing-book/nuclear -vault/2018-08-15/us-nuclear-war-plan-option-sought-destruction-china-soviet-union -viable-societies.

March 27, 2019, Wednesday

102 **"Given all the illegal activities":** Amy Zegart, "Keeping Track of All the Redactions," *Washington Blog*, NYT, washington.blogs.nytimes.com/2007/06/26/entire-category-of -activities-still-classified/.

102 **he and the increasingly powerful Frank Wisner:** U.S. Senate, "Hearings Before the Select Committee to Study Governmental Operations with Respect to Intelligence Activities, Final Report, April 26, 1976, 108, ia800200.us.archive.org/21/items/finalreportofsel01unit /finalreportofsel01unit.pdf.

102 **"essentially a military operation":** Arthur Darling, "Hillenkoetter to Darling (Second Interview)," December 2, 1952, CREST, https://www.cia.gov/library/readingroom/docs /1952-12-02b.pdf.

103 **"Either obtain complete control of OPC":** Darling, "Hillenkoetter to Darling."

104 **"We should prepare a comprehensive summary":** Director's meeting, November 23, 1951, CREST, https://www.cia.gov/library/readingroom/docs/CIA-RDP80B01676R00 2300070071-4.pdf.

104 **"an acute security problem":** Deputies' meeting, June 19, 1952, CREST, https://www .cia.gov/library/readingroom/docs/CIA-RDP80B01676R002300100049-5.pdf. Wisner evidently assembled an early version of the Packet in December 1951 and showed it to a few people: "The 'Packet' of December 15, 1951, evidences the fact that CIA/OPC is principally engaged in developing a worldwide covert apparatus, including the establishment of facilities and the recruitment and training of personnel." The 10/5 Panel to the three members of the Psychological Strategy Board, "Interim Approval of the 'Packet' of December

15, 1951," file 091.411 Actions Taken on NSC 10/5, Psychological Strategy Board files, box 11, Truman Library.

March 28, 2019, Thursday

110 **"The purpose of the feather test"**: "Feathers as Carriers of Biological Warfare Agents: I. Cereal Rust Spores," Special Report No. 138, Special Operations Division, Biological Department, Chemical Corps, December 15, 1950, RG 330, entry 199, box 275, CD 385 (Biological Warfare), 1951, NA.

111 **"Project Purple"—so one document indicates**: "In addition to the oral presentation, the following films were shown: a. Pine Camp (Project Purple), Lt Horne, narrator. b. Carswell Vulnerability (Project Silver), Lt Horne, narrator. c. San Francisco Trials. Comdr. McNulty, narrator." Maj. George L. Neilsen, Memorandum for the Record, "Briefing on BW for SWC, 6 Sep 51," September 14, 1951, 350 Briefings, RG 341, AFOAT BW-CW, entry NM-15 199, 1951, box 2, NA.

111 **There were seventy thousand World War II leaflet-cluster bombs**: Dorothy Miller, "History of Air Force Participation in Biological Warfare Program, 1944–1951," 79–80.

111 **"performed meritorious service"**: "Commendation Ribbons for Detrick Officers," *The News*, Frederick, Md., April 24, 1951, www.newspapers.com/image/8437085/; and "Detrick Men Decorated," photo, *The News*, Frederick, Md., April 27, 1951, www.newspapers.com/image/8438811/.

111 **called Project Steelyard**: William R. Crook, Memorandum for the Record, "Project STEELYARD," October 19, 1951, AFOAT BW-CW, RG 341, entry NM-15 199, 1952, box 1, BW-CW Folder #1, NA.

111 **counterweighted steelyard scales**: Milt Salamon, "Catalog Worth Its Weight in Whatzits," October 18, 1995, *Florida Today*, Cocoa, Fla., www.newspapers.com/image/175148900/.

111 **"400 lbs of wheat rust (TX) and 1600 lbs of stem rust"**: "Information for Air Force Council Meeting Pertaining to Materiel and Services Branch," April 4, 1953, AFOAT BW-CW, RG 341, entry NM-15 199, 1953, box 1, NA.

111 **"plans now being formulated"**: William R. Crook, Memorandum for the Record, "Project STEELYARD."

112 **"Request immediate action to be taken"**: Cable to Commanding General, Wright Patterson Air Force Base, "Shipping instructions for Biological Warfare Munitions," September 19, 1951, RG 341, AFOAT BW-CW, entry NM-15 199, box 3, NA. Some components were shipped: In April 1952, according to another memo, there were eight hundred E-73 anticrop feather bombs "being modified at overseas Air Force bases at this time." William R. Crook, Memorandum for the Record, "Project STEELYARD."

112 **"The presently limited anticrop capability"**: James E. Totten, "Presentation to the Students and Faculty of the Air War College on Biological and Chemical Warfare," November 16, 1951, 19, Air Force Historical Research Agency, K239.716251-196.

112 **"Work is proceeding on anticrop operations in the Asiatic Theater"**: James E. Totten, "Report on Current Status of Air Force BW-CW Program," November 16, 1951, Air Force Historical Research Agency, K239.91625.196.

112 **"The anti-crop program is aimed at the bread basket"**: Claire E. Hutchin, Memorandum for the Secretary of Defense, "Subject: Chemical, Biological and Radiological Warfare," Tab D, p.13, RG 330, entry 199, box 275, CD 385 (Biological Warfare) 1951, NA.

113 **code-named GIBBETT**: "Under code name 'GIBBETT,' a 25-ton per day GB plant (40-ton maximum), is being built as a two-phase production facility," the memo says. "Target date for the completion of construction and phased-in production is June 1952. Quantity production of agent and filling of Air Force munitions are expected to be attained by September of 1952." Jonathan Tucker mentions GIBBETT in *War of Nerves: Chemical Warfare from World War I to Al-Qaeda* (New York: Pantheon, 2006), 128.

113 **"supervise covert operations"**: Stephen Endicott and Edward Hagerman, *The United States and Biological Warfare* (Bloomington: Indiana University Press, 1998), 120.

113 **"Additional BW requirements for the cluster adapter"**: Orrin Grover to Chief, Strategic Air Division and Chief, Aircraft and Armament Division, "Procurement of BW Munitions," October 22, 1951, RG 341, entry NM-15 199, 1952, box 1, NA. See also "Information for Air Force Council Meeting Pertaining to Materiel and Services Branch," April 4, 1953, RG 341, entry NM-15 199, box 1, 1953, NA.

113 **One alternate launching site**: "A total of 4,798 E73R1 clusters (hardware only) are on hand, 400 of these are prestocked at Lakenheath, England, and 400 at Wheelus, Tripoli. The remaining 3998 are stored at Eastern Chemical Depot, Md." "Information for Air Force Council Meeting Pertaining to Materiel and Services Branch," May 11, 1953, AFOAT BW/CW, RG 341, entry NM-15 199, box 1, 1953, NA.

113 **"If the attack is to be made"**: "The Pattern of Land Use in Relation to Target Grains in the USSR and the Probable Spread of Stem Rust on Cereal Grains," CIA/RR PR-23, February 18, 1953, declassified September 2, 1999, CREST, https://www.cia.gov /library/readingroom/docs/CIA-RDP79-01093A000300060002-8.pdf. The copyedited draft, dated October 1952, is at https://www.cia.gov/library/readingroom/docs/CIA -RDP79T01149A000300050001-8.pdf.

114 **"Hungary, once the granary of Central Europe"**: Richard O'Regan, AP, "Millions Starving Behind Iron Curtain," *Vancouver Sun*, Vancouver, B.C., July 8, 1953, www .newspapers.com/image/492382501/.

115 **wanted a "killer agent"**: James Totten, Memorandum for General Bunker, "Proposed Air Force Agenda for BW Inter-Service Coordinating Committee," May 5, 1952, AFOAT BW-CW, RG 341, entry NM-15 199, box 4, 1952, file 17, NA. Also: "The Air Force has an urgent need for a 'killer' agent for strategic operations." Howard Bunker, Memorandum for Colonel William G. Hipps, "Background and Functioning of BW-CW Inter-Service Coordinating Committee," October 31, 1952, AFOAT BW-CW, RG 341, entry NM-15 199, box 4, NA.

115 **"Captain Coggins stated that the Navy desired"**: Arthur Hoffman, Memorandum for the Record, "Conference with Captain Coggins on USAF Biological and Chemical Warfare Program," January 30, 1952, AFOAT BW-CW, RG 341, entry NM-15 199, box 4, NA.

115 **"Continuation of this project to include studies on man"**: Glenn E. Davis, Memorandum for the Record, "Conference at Naval Biological Laboratory," March 6, 1952, AFOAT BW-CW, RG 341, entry NM-15 199, box 4, 1952, NA.

116 **"get the Chinamen out of Korea"**: Barton Bernstein, "Truman's Secret Thoughts on Ending the Korean War," *Foreign Service Journal*, November 1980, www.afsa.org/sites/default/files /fsj-1980-11-november_0.pdf. This longhand note, kept secret until 1978, was discovered by historian Francis Loewenheim in 1980. "Truman, in 1952 Memos, Considered Nuclear Strike," NYT, August 3, 1980. Until recently it was posted in its entirety in color facsimile on the Truman Library website, along with all of Truman's diaristic notes; as of 2019 these facsimile notes are gone from the site.

March 29, 2019, Friday

118 **"Albania," Wisner wrote**: Frank Wisner, "Project BGFIEND Review for DCI," CIA, CREST, November 8, 1951, https://www.cia.gov/library/readingroom/docs/OBOPUS %20BG%20FIEND%20%20%20VOL.%202%20%28PROJECT%20OUTLINED %20REVIEWS%20TERMINATION%29_0034.pdf.

118 **"Our 'allies' wanted to make use"**: Stephen Dorril, *MI6: Inside the Covert World of Her Majesty's Secret Intelligence Service* (New York: Simon & Schuster, 2002), 401.

118 **"It seems to me that Guatemala"**: Richard H. Immerman, *The CIA in Guatemala: The Foreign Policy of Intervention* (Austin: University of Texas Press, 1982).

118 **would recommend "suitable indigenous"**: "Project Outline," August 23, 1950, CREST, https://www.cia.gov/library/readingroom/docs/DOC_0000915078.pdf. A "List of

Previously Released Guatemala Coup CIA Documents," with document numbers, is part of the Internet Archive, archive.org/stream/ListOfGuatemalaCoupCIADocuments /List of Guatemala Coup CIA Documents.

119 **"wished to offer the use"**: ⬭ to Deputy Director, Plans, November 5, 1951, CREST, https://www.cia.gov/library/readingroom/docs/DOC_0000915073.pdf.

119 **"HQ desires firm list"**: Cable from OPC/OSO to ⬭, January 26, 1952, CREST, https://www.cia.gov/library/readingroom/docs/DOC_0000135862.pdf.

119 **a weapons shipment**: Memorandum for General Smith, August 20, 1952, CREST, https://www.cia.gov/library/readingroom/docs/DOC_0000915023.pdf.

119 **"Subject: Guatemalan Communist Personnel"**: Memo, "Guatemalan Communist Personnel to Be Disposed of During Military Operations of Calligeris," September 18, 1952, CREST, https://www.cia.gov/library/readingroom/docs/DOC_0000135865.pdf.

120 **"In order to support"**: "Guatemalan Coffee Project," February 4, 1953 (per bibliographic record), or March 12, 1953, CREST, https://www.cia.gov/library/readingroom/docs/DOC _0000914953.pdf.

120 **"The objective of the FIBER program"**: Memorandum, "Operation FIBER," May 15, 1953, CREST, https://www.cia.gov/library/readingroom/docs/DOC_0000914886.pdf.

120 **"wetting down while in storage"**: "Guatemalan Coffee Project," https://www.cia.gov /library/readingroom/docs/DOC_0000914953.pdf.

121 **"When FIBER shipments are stopped"**: Memorandum for the Record, "Operation FIBER," May 15, 1953, CREST, https://www.cia.gov/library/readingroom/docs/DOC _0000914886.pdf.

122 **"Ship sabotage of Guatemalan coffee"**: "Guatemalan Coffee Study (W/Attachment)," June 2, 1953, CREST, https://www.cia.gov/library/readingroom/docs/DOC_0000914881.pdf.

122 **"'Black Bug' in Coffee Shipments"**: "RQM/OIS Support of PBSUCCESS," June 3, 1954, CREST, https://www.cia.gov/library/readingroom/docs/DOC_0000920237.pdf.

122 **"The operation as laid on"**: "RQM/OIS Support of PBSUCCESS," June 3, 1954, CREST, https://www.cia.gov/library/readingroom/docs/DOC_0000920237.pdf.

123 **"I now consider my involvement"**: Philip Roettinger, "For a CIA Man, It's 1954 Again," *Los Angeles Times*, March 16, 1986, www.latimes.com/archives/la-xpm-1986-03-16 -op-26822-story.html. Also in CREST, https://www.cia.gov/library/readingroom/docs /CIA-RDP91-00587R000100040022-5.pdf

123 **"Guatemala has suffered"**: Stephen Schlesinger and Stephen Kinzer, *Bitter Fruit* (Cambridge, Mass.: Harvard College, David Rockefeller Center for Latin American Studies, 2005), 250.

124 **Nancy Kegan Smith**: Philip Shenon, "Stinging Sandy Berger," *Washingtonian*, April 1, 2008, www.washingtonian.com/2008/04/01/stinging-sandy-berger/.

124 **"Okay, I know this is odd"**: U.S. House of Representatives, Committee on Oversight and Government Reform, "Sandy Berger's Theft of Classified Documents," January 9, 2007, fas.org/irp/congress/2007_rpt/berger.pdf.

125 **"gravely, gravely serious"**: David Paul Kuhn, "Partisan Spat over Berger Leak," CBSnews .com, July 21, 2004, www.cbsnews.com/news/partisan-spat-over-berger-leak/.

125 **"Political and Psychological Warfare 1947–1950"**: Policy Planning Staff/Council Subject Files 1947–1962, RG 59, General Records of the Department of State, Political and Psychological Warfare 1947–1950, entry A1-558B, boxes 28–29, NA.

129 **"I wish to assure you"**: James Forrestal to Robert Lovett, Acting Secretary of State, October 13, 1948, Policy Planning Staff/Council Subject Files 1947–1962, RG 59, General Records of the Department of State, Political and Psychological Warfare 1947–1950, entry A1-558B, box 28, NA.

129 **Kennan produced a paper**: George Kennan, "U.S. Propaganda to China: Allocation of Responsibilities Between Overt and Covert Operations," October 25, 1949, Policy Planning Staff/Council Subject Files 1947–1962, RG 59, General Records of the Department of State, Political and Psychological Warfare 1947–1950, entry A1-558B, box 29, NA.

March 30, 2019, Saturday

131 **"the sending to European ports"**: Policy Planning Staff, meeting minutes, December 7, 1948, Political and Psychological Warfare 1947–1950, RG 59, entry A1-558B, box 29, NA.

132 **"activities designed to influence the attitudes"**: Paul Nitze, Memorandum for Mr. Webb on Psychological Warfare, August 3, 1951, Political and Psychological Warfare 1951–1953, RG 59, entry A1-558B, box 29, NA.

132 **helped build the giant test sphere:** Chemical Corps Biological Laboratories, "Seventh Annual Report of the Chemical Corps Biological Laboratories," July 1, 1953, DTIC, 111–12, Brill online, primarysources.brillonline.com/browse/weapons-of-mass-destruction/. The Ralph M. Parsons Company had so much steady work from Camp Detrick that it opened a "Facilities Operation Division" with administrative headquarters in the Vindobona Hotel in nearby Braddock Heights, Maryland. "Camp Detrick News," January 3, 1955, *The News*, Frederick, Md., www.newspapers.com/image/16181447/. Later they moved to the Odd Fellows home in downtown Frederick, with additional space in an old cigar factory. In October 1953, a Parsons employee at Detrick, Ralph Elbert, twenty-four years old, died suddenly of "pneumonia and poliomyelitis" in the Camp Detrick infirmary. "Inquire into Elbert Death," *The News*, October 20, 1953, www.newspapers.com/image/; and "Report Polio, Pneumonia Cause of Worker's Death," *The News*, November 10, 1953, www.newspapers.com/image/7515895/. Parsons employed 450 people in 1955, when their Detrick contract ended. "90 Day Extension for Parsons Company to End Detrick Work," September 1, 1955, *The News*, www.newspapers.com/image/16695075/.

133 **"Upon release it will sink to the bottom"**: Chemical Corps Biological Laboratories, "Seventh Annual Report of the Chemical Corps Biological Laboratories."

133 **"wagon wheel" configuration:** Chemical Corps Biological Laboratories, "Seventh Annual Report of the Chemical Corps Biological Laboratories," 63. Using the XB-14B torpedo, Operation Whitehorse dispersed *Bacillus globigii*, *Serratia marcescens*, and (with the help of the Stanford Aerosol Laboratory) zinc cadmium sulfide particles off the Florida coast. National Research Council, *Toxicologic Assessment of the Army's Zinc Cadmium Sulfide Dispersion Tests* (Washington, D.C.: National Academies Press, 1997), appendix B, https://www.nap.edu/read/5739/chapter/13.

133 **in Operation Moby Dick:** National Research Council, *Toxicologic Assessment of the Army's Zinc Cadmium Sulfide Dispersion Tests*, appendix B, https://www.nap.edu/read/5739/chapter/13.

133 **"It is better to generate the cloud"**: James E. Fasolas, lecture, July 17, 1952, AFOAT BW-CW, RG 341, entry NM-15 199, box 4, file #15, NA. The original has "namely a man" in parentheses; I replaced the paragraph symbols with dashes in the transcript to make it clear that the phrase is from Fasolas's lecture and isn't my own explanatory interjection.

133 **"The Military Air Transport (MATS) has been assigned"**: Milton Anderson, Memorandum for Colonel Clark, "Status of Balloon Delivery System for BW Munitions," November 6, 1952, RG 341, entry NM-15 199, box 4, NA.

134 **His father made turbines:** "Fasolas" obituary, *Delaware County Daily Times*, Chester, Pa., December 27, 1969, www.newspapers.com/image/22402028/.

134 **he was listed as a potential attendee:** Howard Bunker, Memorandum to General Bullene, "Symposium on BW Agents," April 1, 1952, AFOAT BW-CW, RG 341, entry NM-15 199, 1952, box 2.

134 **began making stained-glass windows:** Peggy May, "Leaded Glass Renaissance Described by FWB Artisan," *Playground Daily News*, Fort Walton Beach, Fla., July 26, 1974, www.newspapers.com/image/54295633/.

134 **"Because of his knowledge of orientals"**: "James Elmer Totten," *Assembly*, 34 no. 4 (March 1981), 129.

135 **"As an amateur breeder"**: C. Roy Adair, "Edgar Cecil Tullis," *Phytopathology* 67, no. 6 (June 1977), www.apsnet.org/publications/phytopathology/backissues/Documents/1977Articles /phyto67n06_715.pdf.

March 31, 2019, Sunday

136 **"He wore a plaid sports coat"**: Michael Daley, "The Day the Subway Got Dusted," *New York Daily News*, February 22, 1998, www.nydailynews.com/archives/news/day-subway -dusted-article-1.794791.

137 **"the puzzlement of the poisons"**: U.S. Senate, Hearings Before the Select Committee to Study Government Operations with Respect to Intelligence Activities, vol. 1, Unauthorized Storage of Toxic Agents, September 16–18, 1975, 139, www.intelligence.senate.gov/sites /default/files/94intelligence_activities_I.pdf.

137 **He'd grown up on a Wisconsin dairy farm:** Jeremy Pearce, "Edward J. Schantz, Pioneering Researcher of Toxins, Including Botox, Dies at 96," NYT, May 4, 2005.

137 **Edward Schantz studied the remains:** "Testimony Given in Cow Deaths," *The News*, Frederick, Md., September 12, 1951, www.newspapers.com/image/8500086/.

138 **He was married to Anna Mae Burke Senseney:** "Charles Senseney," *Frederick News-Post*, Frederick, Md., June 2, 2007, www.legacy.com/obituaries/fredericknewspost/obituary.aspx?n =charles-senseney&pid=168463391&fhid=9952.

138 **one of Dudley Glick's six casket bearers:** "Dr. Glick Honored at Services," *The News*, Frederick, Md., December 4, 1964, www.newspapers.com/image/8990356/.

138 **"apparent heart attack"**: "Dr. Dudley Glick, 59, Army Bacteriologist," *Baltimore Evening Sun*, December 3, 1964, www.newspapers.com/image/372490124/.

138 **biological research and development victim:** Robert J. Peel, "How Detrick Named Its Streets," *Frederick News-Post*, Frederick, Md., www.fredericknewspost.com/archives /how-detrick-named-its-streets/article_e15f3c78-11e4-5113-bc11-085669716a64.html.

138 **two of the six casket bearers:** "Funerals," *The News*, Frederick, Md., March 28, 1951, www.newspapers.com/image/8424042/.

139 **"after a long illness"**: AP, "Walter Irving Nevius," NYT, March 26, 1951, www.newspapers .com/image/8422916/.

139 **"Both Dr. Olson and Dr. Stubbs came to Frederick"**: "Camp Detrick News," *The News*, Frederick, Md., April 21, 1953, www.newspapers.com/image/7500841/.

139 **worked on something blacked out in 1951:** Classified Database Search, "List of Technical Reports at Dugway Proving Ground (DPG) or West Desert Technical Information Center (WDTIC) at Dugway Proving Ground, 1950–1960," www.governmentattic.org/10docs /TechRptsDPG_1950-1960.pdf.

139 **"Pennsylvania Turnpike Test"**: Classified Database Search, "List of Technical Reports at Dugway Proving Ground (DPG) or West Desert Technical Information Center (WDTIC) at Dugway Proving Ground, 1961–1965," www.governmentattic.org/10docs/TechRptsDPG _1961-1965.pdf.

139 **tickets to the World Series:** "Fort Detrick News," *The News*, Frederick, Md., October 9, 1964, www.newspapers.com/image/8958745/.

139 **met Jack Dempsey:** "Fort Detrick," *The News*, Frederick, Md., July 1, 1966,

139 **walked the Freedom Trail:** "Fort Detrick," *The News*, Frederick, Md., August 10, 1966.

139 **drove a Plymouth Commando Fury:** "Fort Detrick News," *The News*, Frederick, Md., November 25, 1966.

139 **Frank Olson's well-attended funeral:** "Funerals," *The News*, Frederick, Md., December 4, 1953, www.newspapers.com/image/7517777/.

139 **"I don't want to say it"**: Egmont Koch and Michael Wech, *Code Name: Artichoke*, film transcript, web.archive.org/web/20100114170656/http://www.frankolsonproject.org /Articulations/Script-CodeNameArtichoke.html. Quoted in Hank Albarelli, *A Terrible*

Mistake: The Murder of Frank Olson and the CIA's Secret Cold War Experiments (Walterville, Ore.: Trine Day, 2009).

139 **"Frank was a talker"**: Scott Shane, "A Father Lost," *Baltimore Sun*, August 1, 2004, www .newspapers.com/image/248352705/.

139 **"The most efficient accident"**: CIA, "A Study of Assassination," undated, National Security Archive, nsarchive2.gwu.edu/NSAEBB/NSAEBB4/docs/doc02.pdf; transcription, nsarchive2.gwu.edu/NSAEBB/NSAEBB4/.

April 1, 2019, Monday

142 **"Striving to pry out"**: Raymond H. Anderson, "Izvestia Charges U.S. Scientists Spy," NYT, May 15, 1966.

142 **sent to Europe by the Tolstoy Foundation**: "Paul T. Lutov Dies," *Washington Post*, April 30, 1978.

142 **most active parishioners was Boris Pash**: Marilyn Swezey, "History of St. Nicolas Cathedral," St. Nicholas Cathedral, www.stnicholasdc.org/parishhistory.

142 **reputed arranger of assassinations**: Evan Thomas, *The Very Best Men*, 85. Pash told *The New York Times* that he was not involved in assassination planning at CIA; the assertion by E. Howard Hunt at a Senate committee hearing was "insidious and completely false," he said. "Retired Colonel Denies Heading C.I.A. Unit for Assassinations," NYT, January 8, 1976.

142 **"take up the individual Bolshevik rulers"**: Christopher Simpson, *Blowback* (New York: Open Road, 2014), quoting Sig Mickelson, *America's Other Voice: The Story of Radio Free Europe and Radio Liberty* (New York: Praeger, 1983), 40.

143 **"means and measures by which the legal systems"**: Annual Report of the Librarian of Congress for the Fiscal Year Ending June 30, 1950 (Washington, D.C.: Government Printing Office, 1951), 75, babel.hathitrust.org/cgi/pt?id=uc1.b3330774&view=1up&seq=81.

143 **"The Time Has Come to Settle"**: Israel Gutman, *Encyclopedia of the Holocaust* (New York: Macmillan, 1995). See also Timothy Snyder, *Bloodlands* (New York: Basic Books, 2010), 192.

144 **"accelerate our techniques of bomb damage assessment"**: All quoted Library of Congress correspondence in this chapter is from the MacLeish-Evans Central File, boxes 1014, 1015, and 1017, LC.

145 **"The study would evolve upon the premise"**: MacLeish-Evans, LC.

145 **assessed the efficacy of Japanese bombing raids**: Lynn Eden, *Whole World on Fire: Organizations, Knowledge, and Nuclear Weapons Devastation* (Ithaca, N.Y.: Cornell University Press, 2004), 155.

146 **"impossible to determine the fire area"**: Physical Vulnerability Division, Deputy Director for Targets, United States Air Force, "Fire Spread in Urban Areas," September 30, 1955, archive.org/details/DTIC_AD0094651.

April 2, 2019, Tuesday

149 **"Then you take the taped copy"**: "Sanitizing Documents," August 15, 1975, CREST, https://www.cia.gov/library/readingroom/docs/CIA-RDP82-00357R000200110017-4.pdf.

149 **"portions intended for redaction"**: "Sanitizing of Documents for Release Under FOIA," May 12, 1986, CREST, https://www.cia.gov/library/readingroom/docs/CIA -RDP87-00058R000400070013-1.pdf.

149 **name in the document is Lee Strickland**: "Lee S. Strickland," College of Information Studies, University of Maryland, February 1, 2007, web.archive.org/web/20070202233559 /http://www.clis.umd.edu/news_events/lee-strickland.shtml.

149 **"We first encountered him"**: Steven Aftergood, "Lee S. Strickland, Former CIA Officer," *Secrecy News*, Federation of American Scientists, February 6, 2007, fas.org/blogs/secrecy /2007/02/lee_s_strickland_former_cia_of/.

150 **FOIA lawsuit filed by Aftergood**: Steven Aftergood, "FAS Sues CIA for Intelligence Budget Disclosure," *Secrecy News*, Federation of American Scientists, May 19, 1997, fas .org/sgp/foia/ciafoia.html.

150 **"This move was opposed"**: Steven Aftergood, "FAS Wins Lawsuit Against CIA on Intelligence Budget Disclosure," *Secrecy News*, Federation of American Scientists, October 1997, fas.org/sgp/foia/victory.html.

150 **"We will continue to protect from disclosure"**: Steven Aftergood, "FAS Wins Lawsuit."

150 **"CIA's sustained refusal"**: Steven Aftergood, "Supplemental Complaint for Injunctive Relief Under the Freedom of Information Act," *Secrecy News*, Federation of American Scientists, October 17, 2002, fas.org/sgp/foia/1947intb.html.

150 **"It is ironic"**: Scott Shane, "Official Reveals Budget for U.S. Intelligence," NYT, November 8, 2005.

151 **"of a highly confidential nature"**: Tom Knudson, "Hog Cholera Bomb in '50s Tied to Iowa," *Des Moines Register*, July 18, 1982, www.newspapers.com/image/129066080/.

151 **discoverer of equine encephalitis in the brains of children**: Vlado A. Getting, "Equine Encephalomyelitis in Massachusetts," *New England Journal of Medicine* 224, no. 24 (June 12, 1941), www.nejm.org/doi/pdf/10.1056/NEJM194106122242401.

151 **scans of the material on hog cholera**: Tom Knudsen Papers, MS 399, Special Collections Department, Iowa State University Library.

152 **Each container was made of kraft paper**: "Field Evaluation Study of Desiccated Agent on Carrier for an Antianimal Biological Warfare Munition (Operation Green)," Special Report No. 159, Chemical Corps Biological Laboratories, March 12, 1952, 26, Tom Knudson Papers, MS-399, box 1, Iowa State University Library.

153 **"with the exception of two"**: "Field Evaluation Study of Desiccated Agent," 34.

153 **A campaign of sabotage**: AP, "Vast Anti-Red Sabotage Reported in East Germany," *Daily Press*, Newport News, Va., July 19, 1954, www.newspapers.com/image/231103354/.

153 **"covertly stimulate strikes"**: "Summary of PSB D-45, June 22, 1953, 'Interim U.S. Psychological Plan for Exploitation of Unrest in Satellite Europe,'" June 23, 1953, CREST, https://www.cia.gov/library/readingroom/docs/CIA-RDP80-01065A000300100040-0 .pdf. Another strategy paper said that American covert capabilities, despite weaknesses, "should be able to contribute effectively to maintaining and extending the existing unrest." Psychological Strategy Board, "Interim U.S. Strategy Plan for Exploitation of Unrest in Satellite Europe (NSC Action 817-e)," June 22, 1953, CREST, https://www.cia.gov/library /readingroom/docs/CIA-RDP80R01731R003200140004-2.pdf.

154 **after the CIA-abetted**: Scott Lucas, *Freedom's War: The US Crusade Against the Soviet Union* (New York: NYU Press), 181.

154 **"largely spontaneous," Berlin riots**: "Probable Developments in East Germany Through 1955," CREST, https:// www.cia.gov/library/readingroom/docs/DOC_0000269326 .pdf; quoted in Ronald Landa, "Almost Successful Recipe: The United States and European Unrest Prior to the 1954 Hungarian Revolution," National Security Archive, declassified with major redactions in 2016, nsarchive2.gwu.edu//dc.html?doc=3473778-Document -01-Almost-Successful-Recipe-The-United; John Prados, "CIA Tries to Roll Back History of Eisenhower's Rollback Doctrine," *Unredacted*, National Security Archive, May 4, 2017, unredacted.com/2017/05/04/cia-tries-to-roll-back-history-of-eisenhowers-rollback -doctrine/.

154 **"mercenaries and criminal elements"**: AP, "Russia Rejects U.S. Food Offer for East Reich as Propaganda," *St. Louis Post-Dispatch*, July 12, 1953, www.newspapers.com/image /139461180/.

154 **"Nine persons had been tried"**: AP, "Vast Anti-Red Sabotage Reported."

154 **"not inconsiderable problem"**: "Hog Cholera in East Germany," May 19, 1954, CREST, https://www.cia.gov/library/readingroom/docs/CIA-RDP80-00810A004200510005-4 .pdf. The report was at pains to stress that hog cholera was a disease of animals, not humans: "The hog cholera harassing East Germany is not communicable to human beings."

154 **"During the last six months"**: "Arrest of DDR Veterinarians in Hog Cholera Epidemic," December 23, 1954, CREST, https://www.cia.gov/library/readingroom/docs/CIA-RDP80 -00810A005200380006-0.pdf.

154 **"I assume that our objective"**: James Conant to John Foster Dulles, August 8, 1953, FRUS, history.state.gov/historicaldocuments/frus1952-54v07p2/d743.

155 **"His face is gaunt"**: S. J. Woolf, "Chief of Staff on the Science Front," NYT, January 23, 1944.

155 **"The subject of so-called bacteriological warfare"**: Vannevar Bush to Dr. Lewis Weed, quoted in John Bryden, *Deadly Allies* (Toronto: McClelland & Stewart, 1989), 93.

155 **"development or improvement of weapons"**: Vannevar Bush, "Joint Research and Development Board Rules of Organization and Procedure," October 7, 1946, CREST, https://www.cia.gov/library/readingroom/docs/Joint_R%26D_Board_Rules_of _Organization_and_Procedure_7_Oct_1946.PDF.

156 **"Biological warfare has potentialities"**: Department of Defense, "Report on the Appraisal of the Technical Aspects of Biological Warfare," August 26, 1947, Top Secret, NARA, primarysources.brillonline.com/browse/weapons-of-mass-destruction.

157 **"For quite a while"**: Vannevar Bush, *Pieces of the Action* (New York: William Morrow, 1970), 303.

157 **"Special BW Operations"**: Department of Defense, Research and Development Board, Committee on Biological Warfare, "Special BW Operations," October 5, 1948, primarysources .brillonline.com/browse/weapons-of-mass-destruction.

April 3, 2019, Wednesday

160 **"strange and unusual disease"**: Hal Gold, *Unit 731 Testimony: Japan's Wartime Human Experimentation Program* (Singapore: Yenbooks, 1996), 71.

160 **"I had to participate in the experiments"**: Peter Williams and David Wallace, *Unit 731* (London: Hodder and Stoughton, 1989), 40.

160 **they were "holding back"**: Sheldon H. Harris, *Factories of Death: Japanese Biological Warfare, 1932–1945, and the American Cover-up* (New York: Routledge, 2002), 264.

161 **who was in charge of the interrogation program:** Jeanne Guillemin, *Biological Weapons* (New York: Columbia University Press, 2005), 35.

161 **promise of immunity:** Harris, *Factories of Death*, 297.

161 **"Ishii states that if guaranteed immunity"**: C. S. Myers, cable message C-52423 to War Department and Alden Waitt (JWC 243/14), May 6, 1947, Reference Collection, Japanese Biological Warfare in WWII, box 1 of 2, reference room, NA. See also the spreadsheet of Japanese War Crimes (JWC) documents in William F. Cunliffe, Select Documents on Japanese War Crimes and Japanese Biological Warfare, 1934–2006, www.archives.gov /files/iwg/japanese-war-crimes/select-documents.pdf. This 1947 cable from MacArthur's office to Washington was first quoted by John W. Powell, "Japan's Germ Warfare: The US Coverup of a War Crime," in *Bulletin of Concerned Asian Scholars* 12, no. 4 (October–December 1980), and John W. Powell, "A Hidden Chapter in History," *Bulletin of the Atomic Scientists*, October 1981.

161 **"I consider it vital"**: Harris, *Factories of Death*, 298.

161 **"The utmost secrecy is essential"**: Harris, *Factories of Death*, 285.

161 **worked at a mine:** "Fell Is Promoted by Buick Company," *News Journal,* Wilmington, Del., January 5, 1932, www.newspapers.com/image/161399254/.

161 **patented a hay-fever drug:** "Chemist's Patent Aims Control over Hay Fever," *Miami News*, April 1, 1945, www.newspapers.com/image/298675139/.

161 **"approximately 8,000 slides"**: Norbert H. Fell to Chief, Chemical Corps (Alden Waitt), "Brief Summary of New Information About Japanese B.W. Activities," June 20, 1947, Select Documents on Japanese War Crimes and Japanese Biological Warfare, JWC 123, IWG Reference Collection (two boxes of photocopied documents in the reference room compiled by William Cunliffe), NA.

162 **"Baron von Willoughby"**: Eiji Takemae, *The Allied Occupation of Japan* (New York: Continuum, 2003), 161.

162 **"direct payments, payments in kind"**: Christopher Reed, "The United States and the

Japanese Mengele: Payoffs and Amnesty for Unit 731," *Asia-Pacific Journal* 4, no. 8 (August 14, 2006), apjjf.org/-Christopher-Reed/2177/article.pdf.

162 **"Both men were extremely cooperative":** Edwin V. Hill and Joseph Victor, "Songo: Epidemic Hemorrhagic Fever," November 13, 1947, in "Summary Report on B.W. Investigations," JWC 35, Select Documents on Japanese War Crimes and Japanese Biological Warfare, IWG Reference Collection, RG 9999, entry ZZ-106, stack 230, row 86, compartment 45, shelf 01, NA.

163 **"A 10% emulsion of infected squirrel brain":** "Typhus" (interview with Masaji Kitano), and Kitano, "On a New Preparation of Typhus Vaccine," Hill and Victor, "Summary Report," Select Documents, JWC 35, NA.

163 **Genji Sakuyama said he infected:** "Typhus" (interview with Genji Sakuyama), Hill and Victor, "Summary Report," Select Documents, JWC 35, NA.

163 **Dr. Takahashi told them:** Hill and Victor, "Summary Report," "Aerosols," in "Summary Report on B.W. Investigations," December 12, 1947, Select Documents on Japanese War Crimes, JWC 35, NA.

163 **"It was believed that western Oregon":** Hill and Victor, "Summary Report," "Plant Agents," Select Documents, JWC 35, NA.

163 **Three days later the man:** Hill and Victor, "Summary Report," "Shiga Dysentery," Select Documents, JWC 35, NA.

163 **The disease was very contagious:** Hill and Victor, "Summary Report," "Paratyphoid," Select Documents, JWC 35, NA.

164 **"No question of immunity":** Hill and Victor, "Summary Report," Select Documents, JWC 35, NA.

April 4, 2019, Thursday

165 **who'd won an award:** "Detrick Men Decorated," photo, *The News*, Frederick, Md., April 27, 1951, www.newspapers.com/image/8438811/.

165 **for his work on the feather bomb:** "Feathers as Carriers of Biological Warfare Agents: I. Cereal Rust Spores," Special Report No. 138, Special Operations Division, Biological Department, Chemical Corps, December 15, 1950, RG 330, entry 199, box 275, CD 385 (Biological Warfare) 1951, NA. "Captain Glenn E. Davis, Captain George Nielsen, Major Horace A. Templeton, and Lt. Raymond E. Horne, Air Force Field Office, Camp Detrick, Maryland, aided materially in locating and preparing the test area and in conducting these trials."

166 **"In keeping with BASELESS":** Cable AFOAT 52526 from Lt. Col. Baker to seven Air Force commands, October 9, 1951, RG 341, entry NM-15 199, 1951, box 2, file 343 BW Training, NA.

166 **"If protoplasm and poison can assist":** Major Glenn E. Davis, "Presentation to the Students and Faculty of the Air War College on Biological and Chemical Warfare," lecture, November 8, 1951, call number K239.716251-196, Air Force Historical Research Agency.

166 **male typist in 1953:** Benjamin J. Wilson, James E. Ogg, and Eugene M. Hamory, "Summation of Screening Investigations of *Actinobacillus Mallei* and *Pseudomonas Pseudomallei*," Chemical Corps Biological Laboratories, November 1959, 33, DTIC 314193, https://apps.dtic.mil/dtic/tr/fulltext/u2/314193.pdf.

167 **died in an accident:** "Camp Detrick News," *The News*, Frederick, Md., December 3, 1954, newspaperarchive.com/news-dec-03-1954-p-11/; and "Shot from Plane, Pilot Is Killed," *Baltimore Sun*, November 27, 1954, www.newspapers.com/image/374852520/.

April 8, 2019, Monday

169 **"The phenomenon reported is something real":** Nathan Twining to Commanding General, Army Air Forces, "Opinion Concerning 'Flying Disks,'" September 23, 1947, files .ncas.org/condon/text/appndx-r.htm.

170 **"Russia's fingers are in the fire"**: International News Service wire story, "General Says Korea Preliminary to 'Bout,'" *Galveston Daily News*, August 26, 1950, www.newspapers.com/image/22395495/.

170 **"The Joint Chiefs of Staff have agreed"**: Nathan F. Twining, Memo to Deputy Chiefs of Staff, "Biological and Chemical Warfare," October 20, 1950, Air Force, Plans, RG 341, entry 335, box 581, NA. Also in AFOAT BW-CW, RG 341, entry NM-15 199, 1952, box 1, BW-CW Folder #1, NA.

170 **changed to Project Respondent:** "The code word RESPONDENT (CONFIDENTIAL) has been substituted for the code word BASELESS (CONFIDENTIAL) due to a suspected compromise." HQ USAF AFCAG-25, file 373 Projects, RG 341, entry NM-15 199, box 2, NA. See also Howard Bunker, "Proposed Military Characteristics for Units Required to Support the BW Program under Project 'Respondent,'" May 12, 1952, AFOAT BW-CW, entry NM-15 199, 1952, box 2, file #1, NA.

171 **"General Doolittle, without doubt"**: "The James H. Doolittle Library," University of Texas at Dallas, web.archive.org/web/20120715002255/http://www.utdallas.edu/library/uniquecoll/speccoll/hac/doolittle/jdlttl.html.

171 **"General Doolittle has expressed his desire"**: Howard Bunker to General C. P. Cabell, Director of Intelligence, "BW Briefing," August 10, 1951, AFOAT BW-CW, RG 341, entry NM-15 199, box 1, file 334 Boards and Committees, NA.

172 **another proponent of biological warfare:** "In July 1948 a report made to Major General E. E. Partridge, Director, Training and Requirements at Headquarters, USAF, stated that lack of sufficient recognition in high USAF levels of the potentialities of BW had resulted in inadequate USAF participation in the program." Dorothy Miller, "History of Air Force Participation in Biological Warfare Program, 1944–1951," 32.

172 **"From everything I've heard today"**: James Doolittle, "Transcript of General Doolittle's Remarks Prior to His Departure from the Symposium," April 17, 1952, RG 341, entry NM-15 199, box 2, NA.

173 **"It is now clear that we are facing"**: James Doolittle et al., "Report on the Covert Activities of the Central Intelligence Agency," September 30, 1954, CREST, https://www.cia.gov/library/readingroom/docs/DOC_0000627859.pdf (blacked-out version), and https://www.cia.gov/library/readingroom/docs/CIA-RDP86B00269R000100040001-5.pdf (whited-out version). See also Tim Weiner, *Legacy of Ashes* (New York: Doubleday, 2007), 125.

173 **served on the boards of directors of mining companies:** James S. Allen, *Atomic Imperialism: The State, Monopoly, and the Bomb* (New York: International Publishers, 1952), 101, ia802802.us.archive.org/9/items/allen_atomic/allen_atomic.pdf.

173 **assistant secretary of commerce for air:** "Investment Firm Formed: William A. M. Burden Plans to Handle Own Capital," NYT, July 19, 1949.

174 **"This was an immensely interesting"**: William A. M. Burden, "Reminiscences of William A. M. Burden: Oral History, 1968," John Luter, interviewer, Columbia University.

174 **is interested in agents and munitions:** Memo for Colonel Totten, "Possible Inspection of Detrick and Edgewood by Secretary Finletter," October 31, 1951, RG 341, entry NM-15 199, box 2, file 333.1 BW Inspections, NA.

175 **meeting with the British prime minister, Winston Churchill:** Arthur E. Hoffman, memo for the record, "Informal Briefing of Mr. Burden on BW-CW Agents," October 11, 1951, RG 341, entry NM-15 199, BW/CW Gen. Dec. Files, box 1, file 350, NA.

175 **He is opposed to any sort of "retaliation only" restriction:** W. M. Canterbury, memorandum for record, "BW Policy," December 12, 1951, RG 341, entry NM-15 199, box 1, file 381, NA.

175 **"What is being done about the policy"**: William Burden to Arthur Hoffman, November 26, 1951, RG 341, entry NM-15 199, 1951, box 1.

175 **"informal conversation between Mr. Burden"**: Arthur Hoffman to General Bunker, "Proposals by Mr. Burden's Office," October 16, 1951, RG 341, entry NM-15 199, 1951, box 2.

175 **"The present center at Dugway is unsatisfactory":** William A. M. Burden, memo for General Bunker, "Notes on Important Points in Department of Defense, and Especially Air Force, BW Program," RG 341, entry NM-15 199, box 1, file 381, NA.

175 **"Might it be helpful to have General Doolittle":** Doolittle and Burden are given as two "high level individuals" available for biological warfare projects in August 1952. Burdsall Miller, "Indoctrination for New Officers Assigned to the Division," August 6, 1952, AFOAT BW-CW, RG 341, entry NM-15 199, 1952, box 4.

175 **another "lifelong friend":** Burden, "Reminiscences of William A. M. Burden."

176 **funding, and co-opting, of leftist:** Frances Stonor Saunders, *The Cultural Cold War*, second edition (New York: The New Press, 2013).

176 **source of most of the world's available supply of uranium:** Stephen Kinzer, *The Brothers: John Foster Dulles, Allen Dulles, and Their Secret World War* (New York: Times Books, 2013). American Metal Climax was formed by the 1957 merger of American Metal with Climax Molybdenum, which had a mining and processing subsidiary in Colorado, Climax Uranium. Robert S. Allen, ia802802.us.archive.org/9/items/allen_atomic/allen_atomic.pdf, 160. "American Metal, Climax Moly in Consolidation," *Los Angeles Times*, November 8, 1957, www.newspapers.com/image/381297703/. The Hiroshima bomb used Congolese uranium.

176 **President Eisenhower came to agree:** Martin Kettle, "President 'Ordered Murder' of Congo Leader," *Guardian*, August 10, 2000, www.theguardian.com/world/2000/aug/10/martinkettle.

176 **"something—I can no longer recall the word":** George Lardner, Jr., "Did Ike Authorize a Murder?" *Washington Post*, August 8, 2000.

April 9, 2019, Tuesday

178 **"four solid gold buttons":** Earle Partridge Diary, November 16, 1950, Air Force Historical Research Agency.

179 **"You, and your boys":** Partridge Diary, December 21, 1950.

179 **"positive clandestine intelligence mission":** John P. Dickey, "Intelligence Operations in the Korean War," *Studies in Intelligence* 44, no. 2 (2000) CREST, https://www.cia.gov/library/readingroom/docs/DOC_0000872714.pdf.

179 **talking about A. Clifford Cohen:** "Notes About Authors," *Journal of the American Statistical Association* 55, no. 289 (March 1960), www.jstor.org/stable/2282188.

180 **"Typhus and smallpox are endemic":** Partridge Diary, March 6, 1951.

181 **"The primary source of written material":** Blaine Harden, *King of Spies: The Dark Reign of America's Spymaster in Korea* (New York: Viking, 2017).

182 **"I've witnessed many executions":** Donald Nichols, *How Many Times Can I Die* (n.p.: D. Nichols, 1981),142. Thanks to Blaine Harden for sending a PDF copy of this exceedingly scarce book.

182 **"Many other concepts are floating":** Nichols, *How Many Times Can I Die*, 124.

183 **recipient of a Legion of Merit:** Clayton Fritchey, "And Now, a CIA Spy in the Cold?," *Boston Globe*, October 5, 1966, www.newspapers.com/image/433833591/.

183 **"Basically I was told to choose a site":** Joseph Goulden, *Korea: The Untold Story of the War* (New York: Times Books, 1982), 466.

183 **"We never asked for military orders":** Goulden, *Korea*, 471.

183 **special "chemical section":** Stephen C. Mercado, review of *Ban Shigeo, Rikugun Noborito Kenkyujo no Shinjitsu* [The Truth About the Army Noborito Research Institute], in *Studies in Intelligence* 46, no. 4 (2002), https://www.cia.gov/library/center-for-the-study-of-intelligence/csi-publications/csi-studies/studies/vol46no4/article11.html.

184 **"a 'belt' across the peninsula":** Goulden, *Korea*, 468.

184 **"intestinal fever and malaria":** "Tofte Recovering in Tokyo Hospital," January 26, 1951, *Globe-Gazette*, Mason City, Iowa, www.newspapers.com/image/38169863/.

184 **"get ready for the big showdown":** "Says Russ Could Erase Optimism in a Hurry," March 27, 1951, *Globe Gazette*, Mason City, Iowa, www.newspapers.com/image/38192176/.

184 **"the size of a Manhattan phone book"**: Goulden, *Korea*, 471.

184 **Tofte worked as Frank Wisner's personal aide**: Ruth Montgomery, "Sad Plight of a Hero," March 31, 1967, *Grand Prairie Daily News*, Grand Prairie, Texas, www.newspapers.com /image/15166739/.

184 **he fell out with the CIA**: AP, "CIA Says It Will Fire Hans Tofte," September 15, 1966, *Globe Gazette*, Mason City, Iowa, www.newspapers.com/image/391294639/.

184 **"silly cloak and dagger raid"**: E.A.N., "Straws," June 22, 1961, *Globe-Gazette*, Mason City, Iowa, www.newspapers.com/image/39168337/.

185 **"including a 130-carat half-moon sapphire"**: Morton Mintz, "Tofte Case Blew Covers," *Washington Post*, jfk.hood.edu/Collection/Weisberg%20Subject%20Index%20Files/C%20 Disk/CIA%20General/Item%20006.pdf. See also Julian Morrison, "CIA Prepares to Suspend One of Its Super-Sleuths," *Washington Daily News*, August 4, 1966, CREST, https:// www.cia.gov/library/readingroom/docs/CIA-RDP75-00001R000400390049-9.pdf.

185 **Among the papers**: AP, "Bay of Pigs Information 'Embarrassing' for CIA," *Brownwood Bulletin*, Brownwood, Texas, www.newspapers.com/image/6425099/,

185 **Tofte sued Helms and the CIA**: AP, "Ex-Agent Files Suit," *Abilene Reporter-News*, Abilene, Texas, www.newspapers.com/image/45278553/.

185 **Helms later admitted**: AP, "CIA Chief Reported to Admit Error in Search of Home," *York Daily Record*, York, Pa., March 1, 1967, www.newspapers.com/image/553455968/.

185 **"Without the C.I.A.'s covert action"**: Hans V. Tofte, "What the CIA Accomplished in Iran," letter, NYT, December 20, 1978.

April 10, 2019, Wednesday

186 **"The feathers used for this test were washed"**: "Feathers as Carriers of Biological Warfare Agents: I. Cereal Rust Spores," Special Report No. 138, Special Operations Division, Biological Department, Chemical Corps, December 15, 1950, RG 330, entry 199, box 275, CD 385 (Biological Warfare) 1951, NA.

189 **"On March 5 the enemy artillery"**: U.S. Department of State, "The Bacteriological Warfare Campaign," Appendix B to "The Soviet Hate America Campaign," Soviet Affairs Note No. 140, November 28, 1952, 47 (hereafter "Soviet Hate America Campaign"). Held at U.S. Army Heritage and Education Center, Carlisle Barracks, Pa., HM263 .S68 1952.

189 **"covert or sabotage operations"**: Dorothy Miller, "History of Air Force Participation in Biological Warfare Program, 1944–1951," 53.

189 **"BW weapons are uniquely suited"**: National Security Council, "Unconventional Weapons," January 26, 1950, Harry S. Truman Library, in Weapons of Mass Destruction, primarysources.brillonline.com.

189 **"With the exception of limited covert"**: Mark A. Ryan, *Chinese Attitudes Toward Nuclear Weapons: China and Korea During the Korean War* (Armonk, N.Y.: M. E. Sharpe, 1989), 241.

190 **"Some of the other delivery ways"**: "Biological Warfare: A Lecture Prepared by the Evaluation Staff of the Air War College," March 1, 1951, AFHRA K239.716251-185, 11.

190 **"Biological warfare is half in, half out"**: Hanson Baldwin, "There Is No Military Miracle in Sight," NYT, October 14, 1951.

191 **"Two false regions of infection were simulated"**: Kathryn Weathersby, "Deceiving the Deceivers: Moscow, Pyongyang, and the Allegations of Bacteriological Weapons Use in Korea," *Cold War International History Project*, Bulletin no. 11, Winter 1998, www .wilsoncenter.org/sites/default/files/CWIHP_Bulletin_11.pdf. Weathersby's article was accompanied by a paper by Milton Leitenberg, "New Russian Evidence on the Korean War Biological Warfare Allegations: Background and Analysis." Endicott and Hagerman replied to Weathersby's finds: Stephen Endicott and Edward Hagerman, "Twelve Newly Released Soviet-era 'Documents' and Allegations of U. S. Germ Warfare During the Korean War," www.yorku.ca/sendicot/12SovietDocuments.htm. See also Stephen S. Rosenfeld, "The 'BW' Myth Debunked," *Washington Post*, July 25, 2000. Leitenberg,

well-intentioned but cranky, who when I interviewed him was fiercely critical of Endicott and Hagerman (he then wrote me that he refused to be quoted unless he had a chance to review what he'd said), contends that the Communist germ-warfare charges are altogether false, based entirely on fabricated evidence. He summarizes his conclusions in "False Allegations of U.S. Biological Weapons Use During the Korean War," in Anne Clunan, Peter R. Lavoy, Susan B. Martin, eds., *Terrorism, War, or Disease?: Unraveling the Use of Biological Weapons* (Palo Alto, Calif.: Stanford University Press, 2008).

191 **"stirred up some life in the BW counterattack":** Director's meeting, March 11, 1952, CREST, https://www.cia.gov/library/readingroom/docs/1952-03-11.pdf.

191 **"produce two or three sentences":** Director's meeting, March 13, 1952, CREST, https://www.cia.gov/library/readingroom/docs/1952-03-13.pdf.

192 **"fire our big gun":** Director's meeting, March 19, 1952, CREST, https://www.cia.gov/library/readingroom/docs/CIA-RDP80B01676R002300090030-7.pdf.

192 **"mass extermination of civilian populations":** UP, "Russia, Before UN, Accuses U.S. of Germ Warfare," *The Times*, San Mateo, Calif., www.newspapers.com/image/51696014/.

192 **the time was not "propitious":** "Russian Tells U.N. U.S. Uses Germ War; Angry Denial Made," NYT, March 15, 1952.

192 **"We don't intend to let him":** UP, "United States May Demand Check by UN on Reds' Germ War Charge," *Corvallis Gazette*, Corvallis, Ore., March 15, 1952, www.newspapers.com/image/384006331/.

192 **"new low of falsehood and fantasy":** "Falsehood and Fantasy," NYT, March 16, 1952.

192 **"As the Roman tyrant Nero demonstrated":** Ivan H. Peterman, "Soviets Use U.N. to Push 'Germ' Hoax," *Philadelphia Inquirer,* March 18, 1952, www.newspapers.com/image/178112975/.

193 **"The New Song of the Flea":** "Soviet Hate America Campaign," 33–34.

193 **editors were friendly with the CIA:** The Director's Log records a call from Donald Robinson, a writer for *The Saturday Evening Post,* to Admiral Hillenkoetter, CIA director, in April 1949, relaying a message from a *Post* editor: "Passed on message for Director from Stuart Rose, one of the editors of *The Saturday Evening Post,* to the effect that he would be willing to undertake temporary assignments in behalf of CIA on intelligence missions abroad, using his entree as a newspaper correspondent as cover." Director's Log, April 8, 1949, CREST, https://www.cia.gov/library/readingroom/docs/1949-01-03.pdf.

193 **"The effect of the fraudulent germ-warfare scare":** Betty Milton Gaskill, "Russia's New Hate-America Campaign," *Saturday Evening Post,* August 9, 1952, archive.org/details/the-saturday-evening-post-1952-08-09/page/n25.

194 **"Neither at the present time":** Eddy Gilmore, AP, "Soviet Double-Talk Aimed at Americans," *The Morning Herald,* Hagerstown, Md., August 2, 1952, www.newspapers.com/image/21011747/. Eddy Gilmore was a Pulitzer Prize–winning AP reporter; he was married to a Russian ballerina. See also "Has Somebody Floundered?," *Star-Gazette,* Elmira, N.Y., August 19, 1952, www.newspapers.com/image/279104863/.

194 **"whipping up propaganda":** Gilmore, "Soviet Double-Talk Aimed at Americans."

195 **"big germ-warfare lie":** *Life,* April 14, 1952.

196 **consulted for the War Department on Project Y:** Gerard J. Fitzgerald, "René Dubos in the Library with a Candlestick," George Washington University, *Recent Science Newsletter* 2, no. 2 (Fall 2000), and Gerard J. Fitzgerald, "From Prevention to Infection: Intramural Aerobiology, Biomedical Technology, and the Origins of Biological Warfare Research in the United States, 1910–1955," dissertation, Carnegie Mellon, 2003, 12–13, 232.

196 **"There is not one scintilla of truth'":** AP, "Ridgway Hints Crisis in Korea Truce Talks," March 11, 1952, *San Francisco Examiner,* www.newspapers.com/image/458904292/.

196 **"completely in accord with the deliberate":** AP, "Ridgway Urges Nation to Be Patient During Truce Negotiations," *Cincinnati Enquirer,* March 24, 1952, www.newspapers.com/image/103261085/.

196 **"The baseless charges"**: International News Service, "Red Screening Deal Part of Ransom for Dodd," *Palladium-Item*, Richmond, Ind., May 12, 1952, www.newspapers.com/image /249806156/.

197 **"In the whole black record of false propaganda"**: "Text of Gen. Ridgway's Report to Congress on Korea and Japan," NYT, May 23, 1952.

197 **"The Kremlin bombards the world"**: Harry Truman, *Public Papers of the Presidents of the United States: Harry S. Truman, 1952–1953*, 378.

April 11, 2019, Thursday

198 **"flat, indignant denial"**: Memorandum for the Record, 29 November 1954 (MORI No. 144130), Center for the Study of Intelligence, https://www.cia.gov/library/center-for-the -study-of-intelligence/csi-publications/books-and-monographs/on-the-front-lines-of-the -cold-war-documents-on-the-intelligence-war-in-berlin-1946-to-1961/5-3.pdf.

199 **"The bomb was exploded"**: *Materials on the Trial of Former Servicemen of the Japanese Army Charged with Manufacturing and Employing Bacteriological Weapons* (Moscow: Foreign Languages Publishing House, 1950), archive.org/details/MaterialsOnTheTrialOfFormer Servicemen.

200 **"deliberately protecting" Ishii, Kitano**: AP, "U.S. Will Use Germs, Russ Claims," *The News*, Frederick, Md., December 29, 1949, www.newspapers.com/image/8924590/.

April 12, 2019, Friday

202 **On December 26, 1949, Nishi Toshihide**: *Materials on the Trial of Former Servicemen of the Japanese Army*, archive.org/details/MaterialsOnTheTrialOfFormerServicemen.

204 **"Headquarters added that the Japanese"**: AP, "Reds Say Japs Confess Using GIs in Germ Test," *Philadelphia Inquirer*, December 27, 1949, www.newspapers.com/image/173792873/.

205 **"developing brand new unprecedented devices"**: UP, "U.S. Building New, Fearful Weapons," *Wilmington Morning News*, Wilmington, Delaware, March 18, 1950, www .newspapers.com/image/155535475/.

April 13, 2019, Saturday

206 **serialized in several big newspapers**: Those papers included *The Boston Globe* and the *St. Louis Post Dispatch*.

206 **"Wise and Ross trace the development"**: John Berry, "Complex of Intrigue," *Hartford Courant*, July 19, 1964, www.newspapers.com/image/367781792/.

206 **"This book is an education"**: "Courier Book Shelf," *Pittsburgh Courier*, September 5, 1964, www.newspapers.com/image/38651087/.

206 ***The New York Times* obituary**: Katherine Q. Seelye, "David Wise, Journalist Who Exposed C.I.A. Activity, Dies at 88," NYT, October 9, 2018.

207 **"lessen the book's impact"**: Barbara Gamarekian, "Novel Sneaks Peek at Spying Game," NYT, December 1, 1983.

207 **"The discrediting and dissolution"**: Jenkin Lloyd Jones, "CIA Not Likely to Run Wild," *Cincinnati Enquirer*, July 26, 1964, www.newspapers.com/image/104375063/.

207 **Jones's "most interesting"**: Allen Dulles to Jenkin Lloyd Jones, August 15, 1958, CREST, https://www.cia.gov/library/readingroom/docs/CIA-RDP80B01676R003800100010-1 .pdf.

207 **They sued the CIA**: Nick Cullather, *Secret History*, second edition (Palo Alto, Calif.: Stanford University Press, 1999), 122.

208 **"The majority of the cases occurred north"**: D. Carleton Gajdusek, "Hemorrhagic Fevers in Asia: A Problem in Medical Ecology," *Geographical Review* 46, no. 1 (January 1956), www.jstor.org/stable/211960.

208 **"The epidemic area extends"**: Joseph E. Smadel, "Epidemic Hemorrhagic Fever," *American Journal of Public Health* 43 (October 1953), ajph.aphapublications.org/doi/pdf /10.2105/AJPH.43.10.1327.

208 **in touch with Songo scientist Kitano Masaji:** See note 22 of Smadel, "Epidemic Hemorrhagic Fever," which cites "personal communication" with Kitano and Kasahara as authority for the following statement: "Both the Russian and Japanese workers demonstrated that the disease could be transmitted from man to man by inoculation of body fluids obtained during the first few days of the febrile illness."

208 **known to American Army doctors for months:** Joseph McNinch, "Far East Command Conference on Epidemic Hemorrhagic Fever: Introduction," *Annals of Internal Medicine* 38, no. 1 (January 1, 1953), annals.org/aim/article-abstract/675182/far-east-command-conference -epidemic-hemorrhagic-fever-introduction.

209 **"United Nations troops in Korea":** UP, "Atlanta's Colonel Bartlett Connects Bite of Mite to Disease Attacking Troops," *Atlanta Constitution*, November 9, 1951, www.newspapers .com/image/398120013/.

209 **"A mysterious new disease":** AP, "Mysterious New Disease Hits United Nations Troops in Korea," *Moberly Monitor-Index*, Moberly, Mo., November 8, 1951, www.newspapers.com /image/19634905/.

209 **"after the name of the river":** AP, "U.N. Soldiers Hit by Strange Fever," *Gazette and Daily*, York, Pa., November 9, 1951, www.newspapers.com/image/351654935/.

209 **"The censor declined to pass":** AP, "Mystery Germ Strikes Allied Korean Troops," *Wisconsin State Journal*, Madison, Wisc., November 9, 1951, www.newspapers.com/image /400545600/.

209 **"There was no suggestion in any dispatches":** AP, "Mystery Malady Strikes Down Troops in Korea," *Altoona Tribune*, Altoona, Pa., November 9, 1951, www.newspapers .com/image/58023216/.

209 **"tame enough to take food":** R. Andrew, "Epidemic Haemorrhagic Fever: 40 Cases From Korea," *British Medical Journal* 1, no. 4819 (May 16, 1953): 1063–68, www.jstor.org/stable /pdf/20311248.pdf.

211 **"There was no history of hemorrhagic fever":** Thomas Kennedy, "I Got Sick in the Korean War," Veterans for Peace, https://www.veteransforpeace.org/files/9414/2349/6876 /Tom.Kennedy.Memoir.pdf.

211 **"I should be back":** Jack Elbon, *West Virginian Survives in Korea* (n.p.: Jack Elbon Books, 2017).

211 **"I was one of the first victims":** Jack Elbon, "UNCMAC 3/12-53 Munsan-Ni," August 30, 2003, Korean War Project, www.koreanwar.org/html/units/8102au.htm.

212 **"The facts available appear to encourage":** Hal Gold, *Unit 731 Testimony*, 126.

April 14, 2019, Sunday

214 **"The advantages of arthropods":** "Summary of Major Events and Problems, Fiscal Year 1959," U.S. Army Chemical Corps Historical Office, January 1960, 101, www.osti.gov /opennet/servlets/purl/16006843-5BAfk6/16006843.pdf=PA103.

214 **"Yellow fever has never occurred":** "Summary of Major Events and Problems, Fiscal Year 1959," 102.

215 **Jenkins and colleagues published a paper:** G. W. Wharton, Dale W. Jenkins, James M. Brennan, Henry S. Fuller, Glen M. Kohls, C. B. Philip, "The Terminology and Classification of Trombiculid Mites (Acarina: Trombiculidae)," *Journal of Parasitology* 37, no. 1 (19510201): 13–31, www.jstor.org/stable/3273518.

215 **There's a picture of him:** Nicholas J. Kramis (photographer), Tsutsugamushi Research, Montana Memory Project, mtmemory.org/digital/collection/p16013coll2/id/314/.

216 **"42 Stricken, 15 Dead":** Headline in the *Ottawa Journal*, April 22, 1949, www.newspapers .com/image/48792116/.

216 **how to grow vast quantities:** Cornelius B. Philip, "Tsutsugamushi Disease (Scrub Typhus) in World War II," *Journal of Parasitology* 34, no. 3 (June 1948), 172, www.jstor.org/stable /3273264.

216 **how to induce egg-laying in female mosquitoes:** Herbert T. Dalmat, "Induced Oviposition

of Simulium Flies by Exposure to CO2," *Public Health Reports* 65, no. 16 (April 21, 1950): 546n., www.jstor.org/stable/4587316.

217 **"In 1951 and 1952, the Communists loudly"**: Dale W. Jenkins, "Defense Against Insect-Disseminated Biological Warfare Agents," *Military Medicine* 128 (February 1963): 116, academic.oup.com/milmed/article-abstract/128/2/116/4920135.

218 **On a YouTube channel:** "1952 Chinese Film—US Bacteriological Warfare in Korea and Northeast China (Part 1)," Real Military Flix, YouTube video, 10:25 www.youtube.com /watch?v=b2qAvzXLF5Q.

218 **"Notes on Some Chiggers":** E. W. Jameson, Jr., and Seiichi Toshioka, "Notes on Some Chiggers (Acarina: Trombiculidae) from Southern Korea," *Pacific Science* 8 (January 1954), pdfs.semanticscholar.org/d251/2de672eada82b07738f9a177f8b2587c1ed3.pdf. "The work was initiated while the senior author was associated with the 406th Medical General Laboratory and the Far East Medical Research Unit in Japan during the period January–October 1952."

219 **"great care has to be taken":** Sakaki Ryohei, "Bacteriological Warfare" (abridged translation), Sunday *Mainichi*, January 27, 1952, Appendix Q, in Joseph Needham et al., "Report of the International Scientific Commission of the Facts Concerning Bacterial Warfare in Korea and China," 1952, nrs.harvard.edu/urn-3:FHCL:9976297?n=1 283.

219 **Joseph Needham, the British scientist:** See Simon Winchester, *The Man Who Loved China: The Fantastic Story of the Eccentric Scientist Who Unlocked the Mysteries of the Middle Kingdom* (New York: Harper, 2008), which discusses Needham's role in the germ-warfare controversy.

219 **all of it beautifully photographed:** "Report of the International Scientific Commission of the Facts Concerning Bacterial Warfare in Korea and China," 1952.

219 **More recently, Jeff Kaye:** Needham et al., "Report of the International Scientific Commission," assets.documentcloud.org/documents/4334133/ISC-Full-Report-Pub-Copy .pdf. See Jeffrey S. Kaye, "Revealed: The Long-Suppressed Official Report on US Biowarfare in North Korea," *Medium*, February 20, 2018, medium.com/insurge-intelligence/the-long -suppressed-korean-war-report-on-u-s-use-of-biological-weapons-released-at-last -20d83f5cee54.

222 **"something to really bitch about":** Ed Evanhoe, *Darkmoon: Eighth Army Special Operations During the Korean War* (Annapolis, Md.: Naval Institute Press, 1995, cited in Mark R. Jacobson, "'Minds Then Hearts': U.S. Political and Psychological Warfare During the Korean War," thesis, Ohio State University, 2005, media.leeds.ac.uk/papers/vp010457 .html. "The soldiers caught large frogs," writes Jacobson, "painted them bright red and placed them into cages designed for dropping carrier pigeons to partisans. As part of regular CCRAK missions about one hundred frogs dropped into the Chinnamp'o-P'yongyang area." CCRAK stands for Covert, Clandestine, and Related Activities, Korea, or Combined Command Reconnaissance Activities, Korea; see "The Secret War in Korea," 1964, CREST, https://www.cia.gov/library/readingroom/docs/DOC_0001459071.pdf.

222 **"very peculiar" locations:** Needham et al., "Report of the International Scientific Commission," 169.

222 **they fed them with dried yeast pellets:** Louis J. Lipovsky and Stewart C. Schell, "Collembola as Food for Chiggers," *Journal of Parasitology* 37, no. 3 (June 1951) (research funded by the Office of Naval Research); and Lipovsky, "Observations on the Food Habits of Postlarval Chiggers" (also funded by the Office of Naval Research, and published "while the author was engaged in chigger investigations in Korea"), DTIC, apps.dtic.mil /dtic/tr/fulltext/u2/015790.pdf. See also Elizabeth B. Jackson et al., "Occurrence of *Rickettsia Tsutsugamushi* in Korean Rodents and Chiggers," *American Journal of Hygiene* 66 (1957), 311. "A colony of small springtails, *Sinella curviseta* Brooks, was kept in this container to provide eggs as food for the nonparasitic nymphal and adult chiggers."

223 **"highly satisfactory" chigger food:** Lipovsky, in "Collembola as Food for Chiggers," writes that "some spider eggs (Agelinidae and Lycosidae) were found highly satisfactory

for this purpose." Lycosidae is the taxonomic name of the wolf spider family. Wolf spiders are discussed in "Report of the International Scientific Commission," 160–62.

223 **"found in large numbers"**: "Report of the International Scientific Commission," 162.

April 15, 2019, Monday

226 **"This has been tried and it works"**: Daily Log, Hillenkoetter, May 2, 1950, CREST, https://www.cia.gov/library/readingroom/docs/1950-05-01.pdf.

April 16, 2019, Tuesday

227 **function as "penetration agents"**: "REDBIRD/Summary of Projects for ⬚," June 30, 1951, CREST, https://www.cia.gov/library/readingroom/docs/AESAURUS%20A ENOBLE%20%20%20VOL.%201_0005.pdf.

227 **"covert resistance nets"**: To ZACACTUS, "Transmittal of CARCASS Protocol and Report," CREST https://www.cia.gov/library/readingroom/docs/AESAURUS%20 AENOBLE%20%20%20VOL.%201_0012.pdf. "Caboche" is French for blockhead, presumed source of the Allies' pejorative word for Germans in World War I, "the Boche."

227 **called Project AEROSOL**: Memo to Chief of Station, Karlsruhe from Chief, Foreign Division S, "AEROSOL/Implementation of Project Carcass," August 21, 1951, CREST, https://www.cia.gov/library/readingroom/docs/AESAURUS%20AENOBLE %20%20%20VOL.%201_0006.pdf. Also "REDSOX/AEROSOL/CARCASS—Revised Operational Plan," February 28, 1952, CREST, https://www.cia.gov/library/readingroom /docs/AESAURUS%20AENOBLE%20%20%20VOL.%201_0020.pdf.

227 **"dissemination of propaganda, encouragement of defection"**: "REDBIRD/Summary of Projects for ⬚," June 30, 1951, CREST, https://www.cia.gov/library/readingroom /docs/AESAURUS%20AENOBLE%20%20%20VOL.%201_0005.pdf.

228 **Nazi War Crimes Disclosure Act of 1998**: See Executive Order 13110, "Nazi War Criminal Records Interagency Working Group," fas.org/sgp/clinton/eo13110.html.

228 **"The Albanian project at this time"**: "History of OPC," November 1954, CREST, https://www.cia.gov/library/readingroom/docs/OBOPUS%20BGFIEND%20%20 %20VOL.%2013%20%20%28BGFIEND%20OPERATIONS%29_0055.pdf.

228 **"a coordinated program of political"**: "BGFIEND Status Report," January 9, 1951, CREST, https://www.cia.gov/library/readingroom/docs/OBOPUS%20BGFIEND%20 %20%20VOL.%205_0013.pdf

228 **"Its maximum objective was the overthrow"**: "Project BGFIEND Review for DCI," November 8, 1951, CREST, https://www.cia.gov/library/readingroom/docs/OBOPUS %20BG%20FIEND%20%20%20VOL.%202%20(PROJECT%20OUTLINED %20REVIEWS%20TERMINATION)_0034.pdf.

228 **"black propaganda"**: "Extract from Report of Operations for the Quarter Ended 30 June 1951," CREST, https://www.cia.gov/library/readingroom/docs/OBOPUS%20BGFIEND %20%20%20VOL.%2017%20%20(BGFIEND%20OPERATIONS)_0048.pdf.

228 **Sometimes the leaflet drops were "deceptive"**: "Extract from Report of Operations," CREST.

228 **or "diversionary," meant to distract**: "Albania: General Developments," September 1953, CREST, https://www.cia.gov/library/readingroom/docs/OBOPUS%20BGFIEND%20 %20%20VOL.%2026%20%20(BGFIEND%20OPERATIONS)_0030.pdf.

228 **"Leaflets were dropped"**: "Apple Tree Team Resupply and Leaflet Drop 5/6," September 10, 1952, CREST, https://www.cia.gov/library/readingroom/docs/OBOPUS%20BGFIEND %20%20%20VOL.%206_0010.pdf.

228 **"intense guerrilla training"**: "BGFIEND Status Report," January 9, 1951, CREST.

228 **"The apparent ease with which security forces"**: "Project BGFIEND Review for DCI," November 8, 1951.

228 **"All these 13 spies"**: AP, "Albania Says Spies Are Killed by Forces," October 24, 1951, www.newspapers.com/image/80370003/.

229 **"From a purely cold-blooded point of view"**: Memo from Frank Wisner (DDP) to

Kilbourne Johnston (ADPC), "Pros and Cons of Proposal to Detach Albania from the Soviet Orbit," June 4, 1952, CREST, https://www.cia.gov/library/readingroom/docs /OBOPUS%20BG%20FIEND%20%20%20VOL.%201%20(COUNTRY%20 PLAN%20ALBANIA)_0027.pdf. Quoted in Albert Lulushi, *Operation Valuable Fiend*, 2014, https://play.google.com/books/reader?id=gXvoBAAAQBAJ&pg=GBS.PT314.

230 **"Skillet should not"**: Cable for Skillet from Whiting (Frank Wisner), Re: DIR 45998, April 10, 1954, CREST, https://www.cia.gov/library/readingroom/docs/DOC_0000923798 .pdf.

230 **recipient of the Distinguished Service Cross**: "Kilbourne Johnston," Hall of Valor Project, valor.militarytimes.com/hero/31528.

230 **"the use of cereal rusts as biological"**: Mr. Johnson, Air Targets Division, to AFOAT BW-CW, "Transmittal of Report," January 14, 1952, RG 341, entry NM-15 199, box 3. NA. "Mr. Johnson" has the same phone number, 76425, as Kilbourne Johnston. The report was "prepared under Central Intelligence Agency contract to the ⊏══⊐. The report deals directly with the use of cereal rusts as biological warfare agents in the USSR."

230 **"Soviet Vulnerability to CW-BW"**: Director of Intelligence to AFOAT BW-CW, "Request for Mr. K.T. Johnson," November 1, 1951, RG 341, entry NM-15 199, 1951, box 2, file 290 Civilian Personnel, NA.

230 **"with special attention to hog cholera"**: R. P. Todd to AFOAT BW-CW, "Request for Presentation on Biological and Chemical Warfare," August 5,1952, RG 341, entry NM-15 199, box 3, NA.

230 **Kilbourne Johnston was in the Far East**: Director's meeting, March 11, 1952, CREST, https://www.cia.gov/library/readingroom/docs/1952-03-11.pdf.

231 **The summary report that someone in Johnston's party**: "(Sanitized) Report on CIA Installations in the Far East," March 14, 1952, CREST, https://www.cia.gov/library /readingroom/docs/CIA-RDP80B01676R004000130005-1.pdf.

231 **still sick in August**: "In connection with the Chief, Planning and Program Coordination, the Director noted that Gen. Balmer should be considered as a possible replacement for Col. Johnston in the event Col. Johnston's health prevented him from returning to duty. Mr. Wisner noted that ⊏══⊐ was acting for Col. Johnston." Deputies meeting, August 12, 1952, CREST, https://www.cia.gov/library/readingroom/docs/1952-08-12.pdf.

231 **headed a lithography company**: "Champion Unit Picks New Vice President," *Asheville Citizen-Times*, Asheville, N.C., May 6, 1952, www.newspapers.com/image/196238704/.

231 **He died in 1972 in Santa Cruz**: "Col. Kilbourne Johnston Dies, Rites Wednesday," *Santa Cruz Sentinel*, January 14, 1972, www.newspapers.com/image/61240156/.

231 **"General Ridgway was in accord"**: Director's meeting, January 14, 1952, CREST, https://www.cia.gov/library/readingroom/docs/1952-01-14b.pdf.

April 17, 2019, Wednesday

234 **"Is the agency covering up"**: Bruce Falconer, "Inside the CIA's (Sort of) Secret Document Stash," *Mother Jones*, April 3, 2009, www.motherjones.com/politics/2009/04/cias-open -secrets/.

234 **"locally-produced scandal sheet"**: Name-redacted letter attached to a copy of "Searching for Bill Walton," *Mother Jones*, September–October 1978, CREST, https://www.cia.gov /library/readingroom/docs/CIA-RDP91-00901R000100230081-6.pdf.

235 **"I know I've done something"**: AP, "Ex-AOL Worker Who Stole E-mail List Sentenced," August 17, 2005, www.nbcnews.com/id/8985989/ns/technology_and_science-security/t /ex-aol-worker-who-stole-e-mail-list-sentenced/.

235 **Peter Kornbluh, for instance**: "CIA FOIA Processing Notes for 5 Oldest Requests," MuckRock.com, www.muckrock.com/foi/united-states-of-america-10/cia-foia-processing -notes-for-5-oldest-requests-135/#file-11847.

235 **"Complaints received by the CIA"**: "Complaints Received by the CIA about Its Employee Cafeterias," MuckRock, www.muckrock.com/foi/united-states-of-america-10/complaints

-received-by-the-cia-about-its-employee-cafeterias-231/. See also JPat Brown, "CIA Cafeteria Complaints Document the 2012 'Jazz Salad Incident,'" MuckRock, www.muckrock .com/news/archives/2014/jul/14/doc-note-cia-cafeteria-complaints/.

236 **"I hereby request the following records"**: Jason Smathers to CIA, July 1, 2011, www .muckrock.com/foi/united-states-of-america-10/crest-database-cia-670/.

236 **"We have determined that the requested material must be denied"**: Susan Viscuso, Information and Privacy Coordinator, to Jason Smathers, F-2011-01751, August 17, 2011, www.muckrock.com/foi/united-states-of-america-10/crest-database-cia-670/#file -3266.

236 **"The Central Intelligence Agency has a track record"**: Michael Morisy, "Why We're Suing the CIA," June 11, 2014, www.muckrock.com/news/archives/2014/jun/11/why-were -suing-cia/.

236 **"As of this writing"**: Michael Morisy, "Freedom of Information Request, CREST Records," June 4, 2014, *MuckRock v. Central Intelligence Agency*, Civil action no. 1:14-CV -00997 (KBJ), document 14-11.

237 **unreasonable and unduly burdensome**: "Declaration of Martha M. Lutz," January 16, 2015, *MuckRock, LLC v. Central Intelligence Agency*, Civil action no. 1:14-CV-00997 (KBJ), document 14-3, Pacer.gov, 36.

237 **It would take someone twenty-eight years**: Kel McClanahan, "Our Three-Year Saga to Release 13 Million Pages of CIA Secrets," MuckRock, www.muckrock.com/news /archives/2017/jan/19/three-year-saga-behind-CIA-release/; and "Declaration of Martha M. Lutz," *MuckRock v. CIA*, 35.

237 **found by "hostile adversaries"**: "Declaration of Martha M. Lutz," January 16, 2015.

237 **"extremely unique" nature**: "Declaration of Martha M. Lutz," February 13, 2015, *MuckRock v. CIA*, document 15-1, Pacer.gov, 11.

237 **"CIA has intentionally decided"**: Josh Gerstein, "CIA Needs Just 6 Years to Release Data, Not 28," *Politico* blog, February 14, 2015, www.politico.com/blogs/under-the-radar /2015/02/cia-needs-just-6-years-to-release-data-not-28-202603.

238 **In December 2010, Scudder submitted three FOIA**: *Jeffrey Scudder v. Central Intelligence Agency*, Civil action no. 12-807, Case 1:12-cv-00807-RBW, Document 9, June 11, 2013, legaltimes.typepad.com/files/cia-electronic.pdf.

240 **"Moving these documents online"**: "CIA Posts More than 12 Million Pages of CREST Records Online," January 17, 2017, https://www.cia.gov/news-information/press-releases -statements/2017-press-releases-statements/cia-posts-more-than-12-million-pages-of -crest-records-online.html.

240 **501st Communications Reconnaissance Group**: Michael E. Bigelow, "A Short History of Army Intelligence," Federation of American Scientists, fas.org/irp/agency/army/short .pdf.

240 **"An unidentified Chinese Communist unit"**: Suede report, March 6, 1952, CREST, https://www.cia.gov/library/readingroom/docs/1952-03-06a.pdf.

241 **"The spies are putting poison"**: Suede report, February 19, 1952, CREST, https://www .cia.gov/library/readingroom/docs/1952-02-19a-A.pdf.

241 **"A North Korean battalion commander"**: Suede report, February 29, 1952, CREST, https://www.cia.gov/library/readingroom/docs/1952-02-29a.pdf.

242 **"Another message from a Chinese Communist artillery"**: Suede report, March 9, 1952, CREST, https://www.cia.gov/library/readingroom/docs/1952-03-09.pdf. A CIA intelligence analyst, reviewing this intercepted enemy intelligence, is determined to attribute the Chinese charges to propaganda: "These messages provide further evidence that there is no serious epidemic within these units. The continued and unprecedented coverage given the BW theme in Communist broadcasts, moreover, supports the view that propaganda motives are behind the charges of UN use of BW in Korea."

242 **"The seriousness with which the enemy"**: Suede report, March 4, 1952, CREST, https:// www.cia.gov/library/readingroom/docs/1952-03-04a.pdf.

242 **"A Chinese Communist artillery unit"**: Suede report, March 9, 1952.

242 **"A North Korean east coast defense unit"**: Suede report, March 4, 1952.

242 **"*Enemy units still reporting BW agents*"**: Suede report, April 2, 1952, CREST, https://www
.cia.gov/library/readingroom/docs/1952-04-02-A.pdf. The parentheses are in the original.

April 18, 2019, Thursday

244 **"Small bombs were desired"**: Herbert Tanner, *Munitions for Biological Warfare*, Special
Report No. 44, Munitions Division, Chemical Warfare Service, DPG library, Edward
Hagerman collection, 76.

245 **spray a solution of VKA**: Cochrane, *Biological Warfare Research*.

245 **"Advocates of bombing the rice paddies"**: "Bomb the Paddies," *Rocky Mount Telegram*,
Rocky Mount, N.C., www.newspapers.com/image/375080091/.

245 **"Special measures might be taken"**: Ernest Lindley, "Japan Being Shattered," *Des Moines
Register*, June 5, 1945, www.newspapers.com/image/128680552/.

245 **"While the naval blockade is being enforced"**: "Suzuki and His Extraordinary Cabinet
Sessions," *Montana Standard*, Butte, Mont., June 2, 1945, www.newspapers.com/image
/349690610/.

245 **"Is it possible to drop chemicals"**: "What Kind of War," *San Bernardino Daily Sun*, San
Bernardino, California, July 6, 1945, www.newspapers.com/image/49443222/.

245 **"I have heard the War Department experts"**: C. L. Chennault to Curtis Lemay, July 9,
1945, box B-11, file III I A (7), Special Official Correspondence with General Officers,
Curtis LeMay Papers, LC.

246 **"the feasibility of sabotaging"**: Donald Summers, "Conference Pertaining to Diseases of
Cereal," April 4, 1945, OSS records, entry 210, box 92, NA.

246 **"crop-dusting" of rice paddies**: "2 Flyers Now Home Tell of Hits on Japs," March 12,
1945, *St. Louis Post-Dispatch*, www.newspapers.com/image/138426404/. The situation in
Bougainville was "completely in hand," said Brigadier General Ray Owens, commander
of the 13th Air Force in the Pacific, in July 1945. "The minute the Japs come in, they start
gardens," Owens explained. "On Bougainville our planes are spraying the Jap gardens with
Diesel oil." "General Owens Says Yanks Beat Schedule," *Spokane Chronicle*, Spokane, Wash.,
June 19, 1944, www.newspapers.com/image/563650148/.

246 **"Then they shot tracer bullets"**: *Nevada State Journal*, Reno, Nev., May 5, 1945, www
.newspapers.com/image/78790350/.

246 **"many Japanese in the northern Palaus"**: Robert Trumbull, "Fliers Starve Foe on Palau
Islands," NYT, August 8, 1945, timesmachine.nytimes.com/timesmachine/1945/08/08
/88274867.pdf.

247 **"Let them starve to death slowly"**: U.S. Navy, "Minutes of Press Conference Held by
Admiral Halsey," February 19, 1945, Minnesota Historical Society, www2.mnhs.org
/library/findaids/00202/pdfa/00202-00084-1.pdf. The United Press account of the press
conference is a paraphrase: "As for the by-passed Japs, he said the Navy intended to let
them starve to death, slowly and painfully." Frederick C. Othman, "Admiral Halsey Does
His Best in Interview; Calls Japs Rats," *News-Herald*, Franklin, Pa., February 21, 1945,
www.newspapers.com/image/56862950/.

247 **"while the world awaited"**: AP, "B-29s Drop 6,000 Tons on 6 Points," *Courier-Journal*,
Louisville, Ky., August 15, 1945, www.newspapers.com/image/107138813/.

247 **"As a climax"**: Jerome Bernard Cohen, *The Japanese War Economy, 1937–1945* (London:
Oxford University Press, 1949), 367.

247 **"A leading Jap financier"**: UP, "New Nip Cabinet Repeals Curbs on Free Speech," *Los
Angeles Times*, October 13, 1945, www.newspapers.com/image/380750579/.

248 **"We had dispatched to the Marianas"**: Hanson Baldwin, *Power and Politics* (Claremont,
Calif., Claremont College, 1950), 58.

248 **"We had not only the A-bomb"**: Robert Lovett, *Reminiscences of Robert Abercrombie
Lovett*, oral history, Donald F. Shaughnessy, interviewer, 1959, Columbia University.

248 **approved the use of "plant BW"**: Jeffrey Kaye, "Secret Report: US Military Approved Offensive Use of Biological Warfare on Enemy Agriculture in World War 2," medium .com/@jeff_kaye/secret-report-us-military-approved-offensive-use-of-biological-warfare-on -enemy-agriculture-in-26b658ae04c9

249 **"a matter that I asked"**: Jacob Darwin Hamblin, *Arming Mother Nature: The Birth of Catastrophic Environmentalism* (New York: Oxford University Press, 2013), 26.

249 **"A North Korean message of 22 February"**: Suede report, February 29, 1952, CREST, https://www.cia.gov/library/readingroom/docs/1952-02-29a.pdf.

249 **"A North Korean coastal security unit"**: Suede report, March 7, 1952, CREST, https://www.cia.gov/library/readingroom/docs/1952-03-07a.pdf.

April 19, 2019, Friday

251 **"The release of the redacted Mueller report today"**: "Redactions: The Declassified File," *Unredacted*, April 18, 2019, nsarchive.gwu.edu/briefing-book/foia/2019-04-18 /redactions-declassified-file.

252 **planned to "destroy records"**: JPat Brown, "While at the CIA, William Barr Drafted Letters Calling for an End to the Agency's Moratorium on Destroying Records," MuckRock, April 16, 2019, www.muckrock.com/news/archives/2019/apr/16/cia-barr-crest/.

253 **"I do not believe the tools"**: Senate Select Committee on Intelligence, Committee Study of the Central Intelligence Agency's Detention and Interrogation Program, December 9, 2014, 166, fas.org/irp/congress/2014_rpt/ssci-rdi.pdf.

April 22, 2019, Monday

255 **And one is by Kati Marton**: Kati Marton, *The Polk Conspiracy: Murder and Coverup in the Case of CBS News Correspondent George Polk* (New York: Open Road Media, 2014).

256 **"kill CBS correspondent George Polk"**: Journal, Office of Legislative Counsel, March 28, 1978, CREST, https://www.cia.gov/library/readingroom/docs/CIA-RDP80-00941 A000600010004-5.pdf.

257 **"Over my stated objections"**: Memorandum for the Record, MKULTRA, January 17, 1957, CREST, https://www.cia.gov/library/readingroom/docs/DOC_0005444811.pdf.

257 **"It was a conscious decision"**: "An Interview with Richard Helms," *Studies in Intelligence* 44, no. 4, CREST, https://www.cia.gov/library/center-for-the-study-of-intelligence/kent -csi/vol44no4/html/v44i4a07p_0021.htm.

258 **"On Saturday the 10th of December"**: Memorandum for the Record, "Burning of Files for Chemical Branch," December 13, 1960, CREST, https://www.cia.gov/library/readingroom /docs/CIA-RDP78-03642A001700010036-3.pdf.

259 **The Intellofax System:** "The Intellofax System," draft, ca. 1973, CREST, https://www .cia.gov/library/readingroom/docs/CIA-RDP84-00951R000300100001-9.pdf.

259 **"On opening the metal cans"**: Memorandum for Chief, CIA Archives and Records Center, "Evidence of Rust in Microfilm Storage Cans," August 11, 1972, CREST, https:// www.cia.gov/library/readingroom/docs/CIA-RDP75-00163R000100050001-2.pdf.

259 **"It was at this point"**: Paul Wolf, "Colombian 'Magnicidio' Remains a Mystery After 60 Years," *Counterpunch*, April 9, 2008, www.counterpunch.org/2008/04/09/colombian-quot -magnicidio-quot-remains-a-mystery-after-60-years/.

260 **beat him with shoeshine boxes:** Anthony R. Carrozza, *William F. Pawley: The Extraordinary Life of the Adventurer, Entrepreneur, and Diplomat Who Cofounded the Flying Tigers* (Lincoln, Neb.: Potomac Books, 2012); Mac R. Johnson, "Violence, Anarchy Unchecked in Bogota," *Oakland Tribune* (article originally written for the *New York Herald Tribune*), April 10, 1948, www.newspapers.com/image/205483108/.

260 **kicked him to death:** UP, "Colombia Liberal Shot, Wounded; Assailant Kicked to Death by Mob," *Camden Evening Courier*, Camden, N.J., April 9, 1948, www.newspapers.com /image/.

260 **They dragged his broken corpse:** Johnson, "Violence, Anarchy Unchecked in Bogota."

260 **"Armed individuals and bands"**: The Ambassador in Colombia (Beaulac) to the Acting
      Secretary of State, April 9, 1948, FRUS, 1948, *The Western Hemisphere*, vol. IX,
      document 22, history.state.gov/historicaldocuments/frus1948v09/d22.

260 **"They killed our leader, Gaitán!"**: Johnson, "Violence, Anarchy Unchecked in Bogota."

260 **"It was explained"**: "Coup Denied Here," NYT, April 10, 1948, timesmachine.nytimes
      .com/timesmachine/1948/04/10/106929245.pdf.

261 **"Fortunately Secretary Marshall drove by"**:. Carrozza, *William F. Pawley*.

261 **"a person apparently of Communist affiliation"**: "Killing Spurs Riot," NYT, April 10,
      1948, timesmachine.nytimes.com/timesmachine/1948/04/10/106929249.pdf.

261 served in Castro's army: AP, "American Cleared of Killing Cuban," *Palladium-Item*,
      Richmond, Ind., April 26, 1959, www.newspapers.com/image/249807344/.

261 Gaitán's daughter, Gloria, believed: Gloria Gaitán, "Gaitán and the U.S. Head to
      Head," in Rebeca Toledo, et al., eds., *War in Colombia: Made in U.S.A.* (New York:
      International Action Center, 2003).

April 23, 2019, Tuesday

262 **"If you saw a mob of wild-eyed anarchists"**: Elvin C. Stakman, "Destroy the Common
      Barberry," pamphlet, Farmer's Bulletin no. 1058, U.S. Department of Agriculture, 1919,
      University of North Texas Digital Library, digital.library.unt.edu/ark:/67531/metadc85897/.

263 **More than 400 million barberry bushes**: United States Dept of Agriculture, "A Situation
      Report: Race 15B, Stem Rust of Wheat," ARS 22.10, December 1954, archive.org/details
      /situationreportr10unit.

263 **"And yet we've got to think"**: The Reminiscences of Elvin C. Stakman, Pauline Madow,
      interviewer, Columbia University Oral History Office, 1971, vol. 8, p. 96, umedia.lib.umn
      .edu/item/p16022coll342:3203/p16022coll342:3122.

263 worst wheat-rust epidemic in American history: "Stem Rust Invasion Is Declared the
      Worst in United States History," *Calgary Daily Herald*, Alberta, Canada, September 28,
      1935, www.newspapers.com/image/481360627/. See also Alan P. Roelfs, "Estimated
      Losses Caused by Rust in Small Grain Cereals in the United States, 1918–1976," U.S.
      Department of Agriculture, March 1978, 3.

263 160 million bushels were lost: Jack Rodney Harlan, *The Living Fields: Our Agricultural
      Heritage* (Cambridge: Cambridge University Press, 1998), 38.

264 they chose race 56: Simon Whitby, *Biological Warfare Against Crops* (New York: Palgrave
      Macmillan, 2001), 256.

264 who celebrated Robigalia: James G. Horsfall, "Impact of Introduced Pests on Man," in
      Exotic Plant Pests and North American Agriculture, ed. Charles L. Wilson and Charles L.
      Graham (Cambridge, Mass.: Academic Press, 1983), 2.

264 a feast and dog sacrifice: Frank Gardner Moore, *The Roman's World* (New York: Columbia
      University Press, 1936), 122.

264 in the summer the pustules are red: Stakman, "Destroy the Common Barberry."

264 **"A single rust pustule"**: USDA, "A Situation Report."

264 stored them in glass jars: "Information for Air Force Council Meeting Pertaining to
      Materiel and Services Branch," May 11, 1953, AFOAT BW-CW, RG 341, entry NM-15
      199, box 1, 1953, NA.

264 **"Rust spores can be produced"**: "Report of the Biological Department, Chemical Corps, to
      the Committee on Biological Warfare," October 1, 1949, DGP Library, Edward Hagerman's
      files.

265 **"a complicated vacuum cleaner"**: James E. Fasolas, Lecture, June 17, 1952, AFOAT
      BW-CW, RG 341, entry NM-15 199, box 4, NA.

265 **"Precautions against contamination"**: J. B. Rowell, "Controlled Infection by *Puccinia
      graminis* f. sp. *tritici* Under Artificial Conditions," in *The Cereal Rusts: Origins,
      Specificity, Structure, and Physiology*, ed. William Bushnell (Cambridge, Mass.: Academic
      Press, 1984), 297.

265 **Greenhouse space was "critically inadequate"**: "Report of the Biological Department, Chemical Corps, to the Committee on Biological Warfare," October 1, 1949, DGP Library, Edward Hagerman's files.

265 **"In 1949, Detrick worked on developing"**: U.S. Army Corps of Engineers, St. Louis District, "Archives Search Report: Operational History for Potential Environmental Releases," Fort Detrick, June 16, 2014, commons.wikimedia.org/wiki/File:Ft_Detrick _Area_B_ECON310.pdf.

265 **"Two races of stem rust"**: "New Rusts Threaten State Wheat, Oats," *St. Cloud Times*, St. Cloud, Minn., www.newspapers.com/image/224776111/.

266 **"Race 15B, which had lurked"**: USDA, "A Situation Report."

266 **Race 15B "astounded everyone"**: E. C. Stakman and H. A. Rodenhiser, "Race 15B of Wheat Stem Rust—What It Is and What It Means," in *Advances in Agronomy*, vol. 10, ed. A. G. Norman (Cambridge, Mass.: Academic Press, 1958). Norman, who left Detrick in 1952, taught botany at the University of Michigan and directed the University of Michigan Botanical Gardens. In 1962, he became the university's vice president of research. In 1974 he headed an investigation into the health effects of Agent Orange, a substance he had helped to develop: The investigatory panel determined that there were no demonstrable adverse health effects. Albert J. Mauroni, *America's Struggle with Chemical-Biological Warfare* (Westport, Conn.: Greenwood, 2000), 266.

266 **"All of a sudden it was everywhere"**: Norman Borlaug, "Comments from APS Award of Distinction Honoree," *Phytopathology News* 41, no. 10 (October 2007), www.apsnet.org /members/community/phytopathologynews/Issues/2007_10.pdf.

266 **"Durum wheat, used for making spaghetti"**: "Race 15B," *Time*, March 5, 1951.

266 **"It was too dangerous"**: John B. Rowell, "Cereal Rust Laboratory," in *Aurora Sporealis, 75th Anniversary Edition*, Department of Plant Pathology, University of Minnesota, June 1983, conservancy.umn.edu/bitstream/handle/11299/5921/AuroraSporealis_specialissue _1983.pdf.

266 **"three locations in Wisconsin"**: Arthur E Hoffman, "Field Trip to Project 'SIRLOIN,'" January 28, 1952, AFOAT BW-CW, RG 341, entry NM-15 199, box 4, file 17, NA.

266 **"Like balloons," said the Minnesota Agricultural Experiment Station**: Otto Lugger, "The Black Rust or Summer Rust," in Annual Report of the Agricultural Experiment Station of the University of Minnesota, Fiscal Year July 1, 1898, to June 30, 1899, 536.

267 **"On the recommendation of the Crops Panel"**: Memorandum for Record, "Visit to Bureau of Plant Industry, Beltsville, Md., 24 June 1953," June 30, 1953, RG 341, entry NM-15 199, box 4.

267 **"When you're starving, you can't fight"**: Eliot Kleinberg, "Veteran Recalls Secret Weapon Work at Boca Airfield," *Palm Beach Post*, Palm Beach, Fla., July 7, 2002, www .newspapers.com/image/134250212/.

268 **"a massive cloud of wheat rust spores"**: "Special Weapons," c. 1969, NSA record no. 42855, Edward Hagerman files.

268 **"Yield was reduced from 62 bushels"**: Roland F. Line, Clyde E. Peet, and Charles H. Kingsolver, "Stem Rust Infection and Development in Artificially Inoculated Fields of Wheat at Hays, Kansas, and Its Effect on Yield, 1960 to 1965," August 1, 1968, Fort Detrick Technical Manuscript 468, DTIC, apps.dtic.mil/dtic/tr/fulltext/u2/843597.pdf.

268 **chief of the Biological Branch:** I think the chief of the Biological Branch in 1967 was Ray Treichler—the signature on the memo is whited out—but it may possibly have been Nathan Gordon. The CIA's Biological Branch was folded back into the Chemical Branch in 1969, after Nixon's decision to end offensive biowar research. See James N. Roethe, "Interview with M. David Boston," April 24, 1975, JFK records no. 157-10014-10218, NA; see also "Unauthorized Storage of Toxic Agents," U.S. Senate, Hearings Before the Select Committee to Study Governmental Operations with Respect to Intelligence Activities, September 16–18, 1975, 54, www.intelligence.senate.gov/sites/default/files/94intelligence _activities_I.pdf.

268 **"Three methods and systems for carrying out"**: Memorandum for Chief, TSD, "MKNAOMI: Funding, Objectives, and Accomplishments," October 13, 1967, in U.S. Senate, Hearings Before the Select Committee to Study Governmental Operations with Respect to Intelligence Activities, vol. 1, Unauthorized Storage of Toxic Agents, September 16–18, 1975, 205, www.intelligence.senate.gov/sites/default/files/94intelligence_activities _I.pdf.

268 **Charles "King" Kingsolver, former saxophonist:** "Charles Huston Kingsolver, August 31, 1914–June 23, 2013," Keeny & Basford P.A. Funeral Home, Frederick, Maryland, www .keeneybasford.com/obituary/5822382.

269 **The three methods:** Steve Goldstein, "A Deadly Crop of Economic Weapons," *Philadelphia Inquirer*, September 13, 1999, https://www.newspapers.com/image/179171910/.

April 24, 2019, Wednesday

271 **Tibetan "resistance fighters":** "The DCI [Allen Dulles] requested approval for the continuation of the program to supply arms and ammunition to the resistance elements so far identified and to those which are expected to be contacted in the future." Gordon Gray, "Discussion with the President on Tibet," February 4, 1960, Eisenhower Library, declassified 2013, https://www.eisenhowerlibrary.gov/sites/default/files/research/online -documents/declassified/fy-2014/088-017.pdf. A redacted version of this memo, with the mention of arms and ammunition removed, appears in FRUS, https://history.state.gov /historicaldocuments/frus1958-60v19/d400.

271 **Eisenhower instructed NASA:** AP, "Jet Unarmed Says U.S.; Pilot Unconscious," *Boston Globe*, May 5, 1960, https://www.newspapers.com/image/433427624/. See also Michael Beschloss, *Mayday: Eisenhower, Khruschev, and the U-2 Affair* (New York: Open Road, 2016), and Evan Thomas, *Ike's Bluff: President Eisenhower's Secret Battle to Save the World* (New York: Little, Brown, 2012).

271 **"Our assumption is that the man":** AP, "Spy Incident Chronology," *Daily Press*, Newport News, Va., May 17, 1960, https://www.newspapers.com/image/232222164/.

271 **NASA, covering for the CIA:** NYT, "Text of the U.S. Statement on Plane," May 6, 1960.

271 **Powers said, according to Khruschev:** NYT, "Confession Cited," May 8, 1960.

271 **"Ike, Nikita Clash":** *Nashville Banner*, Nashville, Tenn., May 16, 1960, https://www .newspapers.com/image/603234944/.

271 **"Pessimism Grows," said *The New York Times*:** Robert C. Doty, "Summit Talks Open Today; President in Paris Trades Snubs with Khruschev," NYT, May 16, 1960.

271 **"If I had to do it all over again":** David Wise, *The Politics of Lying: Government Deception, Secrecy, and Power* (New York: Random House, 1973), 33–35.

272 **"Existing decontamination facilities":** U.S. House of Representatives, Committee on Armed Services, Hearings on H.R. 4766, July 13–22, 1949, hdl.handle.net/2027/umn .31951p004923310.

272 **fancy bathroom and kitchenette:** Drew Pearson, "Washington Merry-Go-Round," *Gazette and Daily*, York, Pa., March 25, 1949, www.newspapers.com/image/377296231/, and Pearson, "Washington Merry-Go-Round," *St. Louis Star and Times*, August 1, 1949, www .newspapers.com/image/204732083/.

272 **fired for influence peddling:** Walter H. Waggoner, "Gen. Waitt Is Out, Feldman Restored After 5% Inquiry," NYT, September 11, 1949.

273 **"This amount of tularemia and brucellosis":** Biological Department, Chemical Corps, "Report of the Biological Department, Chemical Corps to the Panel on Program of the Committee on Biological Warfare, Research and Development Board," October 1, 1949, from Edward Hagerman's files.

273 **"it was found that each step":** Arnold G. Wedum, "Safety Program at Camp Detrick, 1944–1953," Chemical Corps Biological Laboratories, July 1953, archive.org/details /DTIC_AD0310671.

274 **"We're doing a job not only for the United States":** "$300,000 Is Paid Monthly at

Detrick," *The News*, Frederick, Md., October 11, 1950, www.newspapers.com/image /8893923/.

274 **His hand held a gun:** "Colonel Kills Self," *Wilmington News-Journal*, Wilmington, Ohio, November 14, 1950, www.newspapers.com/image/60898859/.

274 **"during study of the foaming process":** Wedum, "Safety Program at Camp Detrick."

274 **"Death was due to acute bronchial pneumonia":** "William A. Boyles," *The News*, Frederick, Md., www.newspapers.com/image/8533421/.

274 **anthrax was found in the main hallway:** Wedum, "Safety Program at Camp Detrick."

274 **shot himself in the forehead:** Ed Regis, *The Biology of Doom: America's Secret Germ Warfare Project* (New York: Henry Holt, 1999), 226.

274 **bitten by an animal:** Norman Covert, *Cutting Edge: A History of Fort Detrick, Maryland, 1943–1993* (Fort Detrick: Public Affairs Office, 1993), https://archive.org/details /cuttingedgeahist00fort/page/41.

274 **"I watched him die":** AP, "Army Never Told Widow Disease Killed Husband," *Courier News*, Bridgewater, N.J., September 22, 1975, www.newspapers.com/image/223016105/.

274 **"The aquifer underneath the Fort Detrick":** Office of Solid Waste and Emergency Response, "Support Document for the Revised National Priorities List: Final Rule—Fort Detrick Area B Ground Water," April 2009, Environmental Protection Agency, www .fightingforfrederick.org/media_kit/EPA%20Report%20April%202009.pdf.

April 25, 2019, Thursday

275 **three-foot-high, self-immolating:** "WWII D-Day Paradummys—WW2 Ruperts Fake Parachutists," Forces War Records, www.forces-war-records.co.uk/blog/2013/10/04/old -wwii-d-day-paradummy-found-residing-in-garden-shed.

275 **"The importance of cloaking":** Jerome C. Dunbar, "Operational: Cover and Deception," CREST, https://www.cia.gov/library/readingroom/docs/DOC_0000916154.pdf.

276 **Somoza, who was photographed peering:** International Roundphoto, *Marysville Journal-Tribune*, May 22, 1954, www.newspapers.com/image/4300321/.

276 **"very serious business":** AP, "Soviet-Made Arms Found in Nicaragua," *Times-Tribune*, Scranton, Pa., May 7, 1954, /www.newspapers.com/image/531429070/.

276 **"traitors whom we should kill":** PBSUCCESS: *The Sherwood Tapes*, 170, CREST, https:// www.cia.gov/library/readingroom/docs/DOC_0000135031.pdf.

276 **"Like a coward, you killed by iron":** PBSUCCESS: *The Sherwood Tapes*, 31. The Spanish is: "Como cobarde mataste a hierro, / Tambien a hierro debes morir. / Van a matarte, tal como un perro, / Y el mero dia ya va venir." I've changed the English translation slightly to preserve a sense of the rhyme. "The broadcasts of SHERWOOD contained programs designed to make Communist leaders and groups shake in their boots," said David Atlee Phillips afterward. Debriefing Reports for PBSUCCESS, September 1, 1954, https://www.cia.gov /library/readingroom/docs/DOC_0000935207.pdf.

276 **"From the first day of broadcasting":** Debriefing Reports for PBSUCCESS, September 1, 1954.

277 **"THE EMPLOYMENT OF▭":** "Joint Chiefs of Staff Decision on J.C.S. 1927/3," September 28, 1949, JCS 1927/3, JCS Subject Series Papers, RG 319, entry 33, box 311.

277 **"Authority was granted to continue initial preparations":** "Report by the Joint Strategic Plans Committee to the Joint Chiefs of Staff on the Employment of ▭ Support of U.S. Military Position and Policy," September 12, 1949, JCS 1927/3, JCS Subject Series Papers, RG 319, entry 33, box 311, p.85.

277 **in favor of a commando raid:** Burton Hersh, *The Old Boys,* ch. 13, quoting from an interview with Charles Saltzman of the Department of State.

277 **to "indicate firmness":** "Report by the Joint Strategic Plans Committee to the Joint Chiefs of Staff on the Employment of ▭ Support of U.S. Military Position and Policy," September 12, 1949, 85.

277 **"unproductive and wasteful in nature":** Joint Chiefs of Staff, Appendix to JCS 1927/3,

88. See also Thaddeus Holt, *The Deceivers: Allied Military Deception in the Second World War* (New York: Simon and Schuster, 2010), 801.

280 **"cover and deception" folders:** RG 319, entry NM-3 101-A, Records of the Office of the Assistant Chief of Staff, G-3, Operations, Cover and Deception Folders 88–93, NA.

281 **letter from Frank Wisner to Colonel Ivan Yeaton:** "Scientific Steering Committee," September 13, 1949, ACHRE records, RG 220, entry A1 42100-H, container 143, NA.

281 **a set of minutes for the first-ever meeting:** Memorandum for the Record, "Scientific Steering Committee," October 3, 1949, ACHRE records, RG 220, entry A1 42100-H, container 143, NA.

283 **"The United States has not been":** "Rockets for Our Next War," *Daily Notes*, Canonsburg, Pa., October 25, 1949, www.newspapers.com/image/268676067/.

283 **"Screaming and thundering":** "Missiles with Speeds of 6,000 Miles Per Hour to Be Tested by U.S. Air Force," *Dixon Daily Telegraph*, Dixon, Ill., November 18, 1949, www.newspapers.com/image/21599765/.

283 **"And there's the weird":** The *Liberty* article is quoted in "Death by Remote Control: 6000 MPH Guided Missile So Deadly as to Ban Itself," *Capital Journal*, Salem, Ore., November 21, 1949, www.newspapers.com/image/94705137/.

283 **"so lethal, so total, that fear":** "Missiles with Speeds of 6,000 Miles Per Hour to Be Tested by U.S. Air Force."

284 **"armed forces special weapons project":** AP, "Military Hints at Work on New Secret Weapons," *Boston Globe*, January 31, 1950, www.newspapers.com/image/433341149/.

284 **"new wave of war hysteria":** Harrison E. Salisbury, "Soviet Holds U.S. Can't Frighten It," NYT, February 10, 1950, timesmachine.nytimes.com/timesmachine/1950/02/10/89717609.pdf.

284 **"Not only did the U.S. disinformation program":** Raymond L. Garthoff, "Polyakov's Run," *Bulletin of the Atomic Scientists*, September/October 2000, journals.sagepub.com/doi/pdf/10.2968/056005011. See also David Wise, *Cassidy's Run* (New York: Random House, 2000).

April 26, 2019, Friday

287 **"The CIA's record of responding":** *Congressional Record*, House, September 17, 1984, CREST, https://www.cia.gov/library/readingroom/docs/CIA-RDP92B01283R0001000 70002-7.pdf.

288 **a cluster of 1,030:** Louis F. Fieser, *The Scientific Method* (New York: Reinhold Publishing, 1964), 131, library.sciencemadness.org/library/books/the_scientific_method.pdf. Fieser uses "vector" in reference to bats on 132.

288 **"Dear Van, I am most appreciative":** Earl Stevenson to Vannevar Bush, November 23, 1949, Vannevar Bush papers, box 109, Library of Congress.

289 **"The United States must not arbitrarily deny":** "Report of the Secretary of Defense's Ad Hoc Committee on Chemical, Biological and Radiological Warfare" (Stevenson Report), June 30, 1950, Reference Collection, "Japanese Biological Warfare in WWII," research room, NA. Online at Brill Primary Sources, primarysources.brillonline.com/browse/weapons-of-mass-destruction/dod-report-report-of-the-secretary-of-defenses-ad-hoc-committee-on-chemical-biological-and-radiological-warfare-june-30-1950-top-secret-nara;wmdowmdo02012.

289 **"virulent biological organisms in quantity":** Stevenson Report, 17.

290 **declassified with redactions in 1987:** The 1987 version, a copy of which is in the Reference Collection, Japanese Biological Warfare in WWII, at the National Archives, has a number of large chunks removed; the blank space is stamped "SANITIZED COPY / SENSITIVE INFORMATION DELETED."

290 **"The outbreak of war in Korea":** "Summary History of the Chemical Corps, 25 June 1950–8 September 1951," October 30, 1951, Historical Office, Office Chief Chemical Officer, rockymountainarsenalarchive.files.wordpress.com/2011/07/chem-corps_june1950 sept1951.pdf.

April 27, 2019, Saturday

292 **"the bacteria bomb classified as mosquito"**: Suede report, March 17, 1952, CREST, https://www.cia.gov/library/readingroom/docs/1952-03-17a.pdf.

292 **"Communist dispatches reported today medical teams"**: Henry R. Lieberman, "Chinese Reds Send Doctors to Korea," NYT, March 11, 1952.

293 **"Frankly," says O'Neal, "I was, I think"**: "1952 Chinese Film—US Bacteriological Warfare in Korea and Northeast China (Part 4)," Real Military Flix, YouTube video, 11:49, https://www.youtube.com/watch?v=l-dTYJoMylk. A partial transcript appeared in *Time*, November 9, 1953.

294 **"I did sign a confession relating"**: "Germ Warfare: Forged Evidence," *Time*, November 9, 1953.

295 **"It wasn't a method of physical torture"**: AP, "Tell Red Torture in Germ War 'Confessions,'" *Chicago Tribune*, September 24, 1953, www.newspapers.com/image/370723012/.

295 **"Toward the end of January 1952"**: "Transcript of Deposition by Colonel Frank H. Schwable," in Raymond B. Lech, *Broken Soldiers* (Champaign-Urbana: University of Illinois Press, 2000), Appendix C; "Deposition by Colonel Frank H. Schwable," *People's China*, March 16, 1953, massline.org/PeoplesChina/PC1953/PC1953-06-MissingP15-18-OCR .pdf. See also Raymond B. Lech, *Tortured into Fake Confession: The Dishonouring of Korean War Prisoner Frank H. Schwable, USMC* (Jefferson, N.C.: McFarland, 2011).

296 **a "bogus confession"**: International News Service, Raymond Wilcove, "Colonel Faces Probe on Germ War Tales," *Pittsburgh Sun-Telegraph*, January 24, 1954, www.newspapers .com/image/524033738/.

April 29, 2019, Monday

299 **"Without the FOIA the information"**: Robert Stinnett, *Day of Deceit: The Truth About FDR and Pearl Harbor* (New York: Simon and Schuster, 2001).

299 **"Robert Stinnett is hardly the first"**: Robert B. Stinnett and Stephen Budiansky, "The Truth About Pearl Harbor: A Debate," January 30, 2003, www.independent.org/issues /article.asp?id=445.

300 **"The Communist conspiracy is a definite"**: Harry S. Truman, *Public Papers of the Presidents of the United States, 1952–53*, 251.

300 **"We've crushed the Communist conspiracy"**: Truman, *Public Papers*, 266.

300 **"We moved in and stopped"**: Truman, *Public Papers*, 268.

300 **"Skillfully and systematically, the FBI"**: Truman, *Public Papers*, 296.

301 **"I think one man is just as good as another"**: Harry S. Truman to Bess Wallace, June 22, 1911, formerly available in transcript and facsimile on the Truman Library website, now scrubbed. Quoted in Richard Lawrence Miller, *Truman: The Rise to Power* (New York: McGraw-Hill, 1986), 84.

301 **"this —— kike town"**: Truman to Bess Truman, March 25, 1918, formerly available in transcript and facsimile on the Truman Library website; the letter is included in Harry Truman, *Dear Bess: The Letters from Harry Truman to Bess Truman, 1910–1959* (Columbia, Miss.: repr., 1998), 254.

301 **"The Jews, I find"**: Truman Diary, July 21, 1947, formerly available in transcript and facsimile on the Truman Library website. See "Truman Wrote of '48 Offer to Eisenhower," NYT, July 11, 2003; and Toby Harnden, "Truman Library Reveals Scorn 'For Cruel Jews,'" *The Telegraph*, July 12, 2003, www.telegraph.co.uk/news/worldnews/middleeast /israel/1435930/Truman-diary-reveals-scorn-for-cruel-Jews.html.

301 **"Ordinarily, Negro voters would be out"**: Drew Pearson, "Truman's Outbursts Leak Out," *Capital Times*, Madison, Wisc., March 8, 1948, www.newspapers.com/image /521610498/.

301 **"He walked right out on the arm rest"**: Truman to Bess Truman, September 15, 1940, formerly available in transcript and facsimile on the Truman Library website; quoted in Miller, *Truman*, 325.

301 **"I never had any thought when I set up the CIA"**: Harry Truman, syndicated by the North American Newspaper Alliance, "Truman Says CIA Was Diverted from Its Original Assignment," *Green Bay Press-Gazette*, Green Bay, Wisc., www.newspapers.com/image /189307104/.

301 **"He wanted us to try to develop some plan"**: Thomas Laird, *Into Tibet: The CIA's First Atomic Spy and His Secret Expedition to Lhasa* (New York: Grove Press, 2003), citing Robert M. Blum: *Drawing the Line: The Origin of American Containment Policy in East Asia* (New York: Norton, 1982), 163 and n14, 253, which refers to a memo of Webb's conversation with Truman, "Development of Possible Plan in Connection with Mohammedan and Buddhist Population Along Southern Coast at the U.S.S.R.," October 31, 1949, RG 59, Records of the Executive Secretariat, NA.

302 **"Interestingly," Kaufman writes, "the CIA's director"**: Victor Kaufman, "Trouble in the Golden Triangle: The United States, Taiwan and the 93rd Nationalist Division," *China Quarterly* 166, June 2001, www.jstor.org/stable/3451165.

302 **"Mr. Wisner stated that OPC was in a position"**: Memorandum for Record, "Meeting Held in Office of H. Freeman Matthews," July 31, 1951, CREST, https://www.cia.gov /library/readingroom/docs/OBOPUS%20BGFIEND%20%20VOL.%2017%20 %20%28BGFIEND%20OPERATIONS%29_0082.pdf.

303 **"responsibility and authority of the Director"**: "Actions Taken by the National Security Council on Scope and Pace of Covert Operations," document 90, FRUS, The Intelligence Community, 1950–1955, history.state.gov/historicaldocuments/frus1950-55Intel/d90.

303 **"expanded guerrilla activities"**: The redacted phrase is: "authorizes the conduct of expanded guerrilla activities in China." See Michael Warner, ed., *The CIA Under Harry Truman, Part III—The Smith Years* (Honolulu: University Press of the Pacific, 1994), 439, https://www.cia .gov/library/center-for-the-study-of-intelligence/csi-publications/books-and -monographs/the-cia-under-harry-truman/pdfs/Part%20III%20-%20The%20Smith %20Years.pdf.

303 **"Most interesting possibility presents"**: Cable from Frankfurt to Policy Coordination, June 3, 1950, Nazi War Crimes Disclosure Act Collection, CREST, https://www.cia.gov /library/readingroom/docs/LCPROWL%20%20%20%20VOL.%204_0023.pdf.

304 **"Proposal regarded favorably"**: Cable from Policy Coordination to Frankfurt, June 6, 1950, CREST, https://www.cia.gov/library/readingroom/docs/LCPROWL%20%20%20 %20VOL.%204_0024.pdf.

304 **ZRCANDY—Marshall Plan**: Cable, Frankfurt to Washington, KMPRUDE, June 9, 1950, CREST, https://www.cia.gov/library/readingroom/docs/LCPROWL%20%20%20 %20VOL.%204_0025.pdf. See also "Extracted from: LCPROWL (Dated 24 January 1951)," CREST, https://www.cia.gov/library/readingroom/docs/LCPROWL%20%20 %20%20VOL.%201_0044.pdf, where it says: "Funds are ostensibly from private and industrial anti-Communist donors and organization dues," and "ZRCANDY funds have been approved for Phases 2 and 3."

304 **paramilitary and sabotage teams**: Memo for Deputy Director (Plans), "History of LCPROWL Project," CREST, https://www.cia.gov/library/readingroom/docs/LCPROWL %20%20%20%20VOL.%201_0026.pdf.

304 **"In the light of recent developments in Korea"**: "Proposal Presented to OPC Project Review Board," August 28, 1950, "LCPROWL—Proposed Activation of Guerrilla Warfare and Sabotage Training in Germany," CREST, https://www.cia.gov/library/readingroom /docs/LCPROWL VOL. 1_0042.pdf.

304 **KMMANLY, a project to neutralize**: Badis Ben Redjeb, "Project KMMANLY: U.S. Intelligence and the Subversion of Media in Post-War Germany," *International Journal of Humanities and Cultural Studies* 2, no. 4 (March 2016), www.ijhcs.com/index.php/ijhcs /article/view/191/201.

304 **"A hangman's noose and death sentence"**: Memorandum for Deputy Director (Plans), "Fighting Group Against Inhumanity—Current Psychological Attack Against East German

Communists," March 26, 1952, CREST, https://www.cia.gov/library/readingroom/docs
/DTLINEN-KGU%20%20%20VOL.%201_0036.pdf.

305 **Operation Earthenware:** "Project Outline, DTLINEN," October 27, 1954, CREST,
https://www.cia.gov/library/readingroom/docs/DTLINEN-KGU%20%20%20VOL
.%201_0064.pdf.

305 **"several poison-pen campaigns directed":** Memorandum for Deputy Director (Plans),
"Fighting Group Against Inhumanity—Current Psychological Attack Against East German
Communists."

305 **Nazi War Crimes Disclosures Act of 1998:** "Nazi War Crimes Disclosure Act," October
8, 1998, NA, www.archives.gov/about/laws/nazi-war-crimes.html; "Nazi War Criminal
Records Interagency Working Group," January 11, 1999, Federation of American Scientists,
fas.org/sgp/clinton/eo13110.html.

305 **"A Secret Organization Unearthed":** "Coverage of the Partisan Affair in the German
Press," October 1952, LCPROWL records, CREST, https://www.cia.gov/library
/readingroom/docs/LCPROWL%20%20%20VOL.%201_0033.pdf.

305 **"All measures taken must be stern":** "Coverage of the Partisan Affair in the German Press."

306 **"The CIA can neither confirm nor deny":** Kathryn Dyer, letter to Daniele Ganser,
December 28, 2000.

306 **"Arrangements will be made for its consideration":** Kathryn Dyer, CIA, Reference no.
F-2000-02528, February 7, 2001.

306 **"Although Ganser's sourcing is largely secondary":** Hayden B. Peake, "The Intelligence
Officer's Bookshelf," *Studies in Intelligence* 49, no. 3 (2005), https://www.cia.gov/library
/center-for-the-study-of-intelligence/csi-publications/csi-studies/studies/vol49no3
/html_files/Bookshelf_11.htm.

April 30, 2019, Tuesday

308 **Linebarger gave a talk on psychiatric warfare:** "Calmness Called Free World Hope,"
Newport Mercury, Newport, R.I., January 25, 1952, www.newspapers.com/image/16375368/.

308 **black or gray "poker-faced propaganda":** Lt. Gerald L. Geiger, "Project ESSEX,"
April 3, 1952, USAF Psychological Warfare Division, Psychological Strategy Board
Files, box 33, Truman Library. Geiger explained that he'd named his project "Essex"
after "Psykewar—Experimental," or S-X. His paper was circulated for comment within
the Psychological Strategy Board.

309 **"Nerve War Against Individuals":** To Guatemala from Lincoln, "Instruction 'Nerve
War Against Individuals,'" June 9, 1954, https://www.cia.gov/library/readingroom/docs
/DOC_0000135892.pdf.

310 **"sending death notices":** Lincoln to Acting Chief of Station, Guatemala City, "Tactical
Instructions (Part II)," May 26, 1954, CREST, https://www.cia.gov/library/readingroom
/docs/DOC_0000135891.pdf

310 **cryptonym for Albert Haney:** John Prados, *Safe for Democracy: The Secret Wars of the CIA*
(Chicago: Ivan R. Dee, 2006), 110.

310 **death-notice operation, "right now":** Lincoln to Chief of Station, Guatemala,
"KUGOWN, Death Notices," April 28, 1954, CREST, https://www.cia.gov/library
/readingroom/docs/DOC_0000916117.pdf. "KUGOWN" is the code word for CIA's
psychological and paramilitary operations staff.

311 **"Request forward soonest":** Cable to Director from Guatemala City, May 14, 1954,
CREST, https://www.cia.gov/library/readingroom/docs/DOC_0000135902.pdf.

May 2, 2019, Thursday

313 **B. F. Skinner's pigeon-bomb project:** Joseph Stromberg, "B.F. Skinner's Pigeon-Guided
Rocket," *Smithsonian Magazine*, August 18, 2011, www.smithsonianmag.com/smithsonian
-institution/bf-skinners-pigeon-guided-rocket-53443995/.

313 **Skinner "Air Crib":** Nick Joyce and Cathy Faye, "Skinner Air Crib," September 1, 2010,

Association for Psychological Science, www.psychologicalscience.org/observer/skinner
-air-crib.

314 **"The current experiment in penetrating"**: Drew Pearson, "Washington Merry-Go-Round," *Intelligencer Journal*, Lancaster, Pa., August 17, 1951, www.newspapers.com /image/558090196/.

314 **"the regime is weakening"**: Herbert A. Freidman, "Free Europe Press Cold War Leaflets," www.psywarrior.com/RadioFreeEurope.html.

314 **"For some time there has existed"**: AFOAT BW-CW to Commanding General, Air Research and Development Command (Earle E. Partridge), "Balloon Delivery of BW Munitions," file 471.6 BW Agents, RG 341, entry NM-15 199, 1951, box 2, NA. This memo gives two contract numbers for General Mills's balloon bomb work: 4-04-14-011 and 4-04-14-012.

315 **"This munition is expressly designed"**: Ralph E. Stine, "Status Report No. 53-1, Biological Bomb for Balloon Delivery," May 15, 1953, Munitions Division, Chemical Corps Biological Laboratories, in "Three Technical Reports released by US Army Dugway Proving Ground, 1953-1966," www.governmentattic.org/3docs/3DugwayReports_1953-1966.pdf.

315 **1300th ARC Squadron (Special)**: Michael E. Haas, *Apollo's Warriors* (Collingdale, Pa.: Diane Publishing, 1998), 106–7.

315 **2,400 E-77 anticrop test balloons**: "Tests have been conducted on 2,400 balloons launched from five (5) sites," wrote Lieutenant Colonel Van E. Neal, chief of the Tactics and Techniques Section of the Plans and Operations Branch of the BW-CW Division. "The 1300 ARC Squadron has been charged with the responsibility of operating the Balloon-Delivery System under its present state of development." Van E. Neal, Memorandum for the Record, "Staff Visit to ARDC," April 27, 1953, File 333 Inspections, RG 341, entry NM-15 199, 1953, box 4, NA. Colonel Neal and Colonel Retzer went on a field trip to Minnesota and other places and paid a visit to E-77 balloon launching sites. Three launching sites were named: one at Tillamook, Oregon, one at Vernalis, California, and one at Edwards Air Force Base in California. File 333 Inspections, RG 341, entry NM-15 199, 1953, box 4, NA.

316 **the launching sites included**: Van E. Neal, Memorandum for the Record, "Field Trip," May 5, 1953, File 333 Inspections, RG 341, entry NM-15 199, 1953, box 4, NA. Colonel Neal and Colonel Retzer had a talk with a "Mr. Hackeynackey" of General Mills.

316 **a naval air station in Vernalis, California**: "In the 1950's, the Air Force used the airfield to launch 300-ft. diameter balloons that carried electronic equipment for experiments in the stratosphere," writes M. L. Shettle, in "Naval Auxiliary Air Station, Vernalis," www .militarymuseum.org/NAASVernalis.html. There is no mention of the anticrop balloons. See also "Vernalis Naval Auxiliary Air Station," Stratospheric Balloon Bases in the World, stratocat.com.ar/bases/66e.htm.

316 **naval air station in Tillamook, Oregon**: High-altitude Moby-Dick balloons also rose from Tillamook in 1953, and one "animal capsule." See "Tillamook Auxiliary Naval Air Station," Stratospheric Balloon Bases in the World, stratocat.com.ar/bases/63e.htm.

316 **"harass and weaken the Soviet administration"**: "Project Outline," October 27, 1954, CREST, https://www.cia.gov/library/readingroom/docs/DTLINEN-KGU%20%20%20 VOL.%201_0064.pdf.

316 **"confusion operations" continued**: "DTLINEN Project Renewal Request," June 26, 1957, CREST, https://www.cia.gov/library/readingroom/docs/DTLINEN-KGU%20%20 %20VOL.%202_0007.pdf.

316 **"ridicule, confuse, and undermine"**: "Project Outline," October 27, 1954.

316 **"These operations appear to be the most infuriating"**: "DTLINEN Project Renewal Request," June 26, 1957.

316 **"inclined to be devious"**: "Unconventional Warfare," January 2, 1951, Vannevar Bush papers, box 139, Library of Congress.

May 3, 2019, Friday

320 **but it was paid for a different way:** "Summary of Major Events and Problems, United States Army Chemical Corps, Fiscal Year 1959," January 1960, www.osti.gov/opennet /servlets/purl/16006843-5BAfk6/16006843.pdf.

320 **"An ability to induce famine by antifood warfare":** Simon Whitby, *Biological Warfare Against Crops* (New York: Palgrave, 2002), 175.

320 **"Dear Stak,"** Minarik wrote: Charles Minarik to Elvin Stakman, October 9, 1958, Stakman papers, box 8, folder 22, University of Minnesota Libraries, umedia.lib.umn .edu/item/p16022coll342:49589.

320 **"molds that deteriorate grain":** John Cookson and Judith Nottingham, *A Survey of Chemical and Biological Warfare* (New York and London: Monthly Review Press, 1969).

320 **"the use of chemicals to attack the rice":** Maxwell Taylor to Kennedy, November 3, 1961, Vietnam, vol. 1, 1961, FRUS, history.state.gov/historicaldocuments/frus1961-63v01/d210.

321 **"The President has approved":** McGeorge Bundy, "Defoliant Operations in Vietnam," November 30, 1961, The Pentagon Papers, www.fold3.com/image/271155296.

321 **"The most effective way to hurt":** Dean Rusk to Kennedy, "Viet-Nam: Project for Crop Destruction," August 23, 1962, document 270, Vietnam, vol. 2, 1962, FRUS, history .state.gov/historicaldocuments/frus1961-63v02/d270.

321 **"the percentage of days favorable":** Thomas H. Barksdale and Marian W. Jones, "Rice Blast Epiphytology," June 1965, Army Biological Laboratories, apps.dtic.mil/dtic/tr/fulltext/u2 /362021.pdf.

321 **"The advent of modern biological and chemical agents":** Dunlap and Associates, with Paul Linebarger, "Analysis of Strategic Anti Crop Weapons Systems," June 29, 1962, Chemical Corps Biological Laboratories, www.dtic.mil/dtic/tr/fulltext/u2/334517.pdf.

322 **"The need still exists to get herbicides":** Vesta Z. Mattie, "Proceedings of the First Defoliation Conference, July 29–30, 1963," January 1964, U.S. Army Biological Laboratories, apps.dtic.mil/dtic/tr/fulltext/u2/427874.pdf.

322 **"our present starvation tactics in Vietnam":** Richard Dudman, *St. Louis Post-Dispatch*, March 31, 1963, www.newspapers.com/image/142117974/.

323 **"diseases of rice which, if used in Southeast Asia":** "Student Sees 'Complicity in Genocide' in University's Germ Warfare Research," *Gazette and Daily*, York, Pa., November 9, 1965, www.newspapers.com/image/383302718/.

323 **"The more I learned":** Helen Alexander, "Letters," *The News*, Frederick, Md., May 18, 1968, www.newspapers.com/image/8867207/.

323 **"Would you care to comment":** Telegram, Bunker to Secretary of State, "Cambodian Herbicide Operation," September 7, 1971, CREST, https://www.cia.gov/library/readingroom /docs/197116.pdf.

324 **"According to research conducted":** "Rusty Cheerios and the CIA," *Daily Beacon*, University of Tennessee, October 9, 1979, CREST, https://www.cia.gov/library /readingroom/docs/CIA-RDP88-01315R000400410008-8.pdf.

324 **"From 1948 on, American intelligence activities":** David Truong, "Running Drugs and Secret Wars," *Counterspy* 28 (Summer 1987), CREST, https://www.cia.gov/library /readingroom/docs/CIA-RDP90-00845R000100170001-8.pdf.

324 **"baseless criticism designed to undermine confidence":** Laurence Stern, "The Poppies and the Pushers," review of Alfred W. McCoy, *The Politics of Heroin in Southeast Asia*, *Washington Post Book World*, September 17, 1972, CREST, https://www.cia.gov/library /readingroom/docs/CIA-RDP84-00499R000100040001-1.pdf.

May 4, 2019, Saturday

326 **"Although the number of isolates":** Le Dinh Don et al., "Population Structure of the Rice Blast Pathogen in Vietnam," *Annals of the Phytopathological Society of Japan* 65, 1999.

327 **"Justice Minister Stuart Garson said"**: "Treason Charge Still Possible," *Times Colonist*, Victoria, B.C., May 13, 1952, www.newspapers.com/image/506835305/.

May 5, 2019, Sunday

329 **"a document kept under wraps"**: Norman Polmar and Thomas B. Allen, "The Most Deadly Plan," *Proceedings* 124, no. 1, U.S. Naval Institute, January 1998.

329 **Somebody later inserted the handwritten word "Retaliatory"**: Jeanne Guillemin, *Hidden Atrocities* (New York: Columbia University Press, 2017), fn 31 to chapter 2.

329 **an initial "gas blitz"**: Polmar and Allen, "The Most Deadly Plan."

330 **"You Can Cook Them Better"**: Lead Sunday editorial, "You Can Cook Them Better with Gas," *Chicago Tribune*, March 11, 1945, www.newspapers.com/image/371115943/.

331 **"It would help here"**: Lodge to Rusk and McNamara, June 5, 1964, document 198, FRUS 1964–68, vol. 1, Vietnam, history.state.gov/historicaldocuments/frus1964-68v01/d198.

331 **"The war is in a new phase"**: Henry Cabot Lodge, letter to Clark Clifford, August 30, 1965, Lodge Papers II, Massachusetts Historical Society.

333 **Dr. Charles Geschickter, a cancer researcher**: "Subproject 35 of Project MKULTRA," Technical Services Section, CIA, May 10, 1955, archive.org/details/DOC_0000017432.

333 **"benign and malignant diseases of the breast"**: "Pathologist to Speak at 'Carbondale Night,'" *Times-Tribune*, Scranton, Pa., April 29, 1949, www.newspapers.com/image/534806846/.

333 **"absolutely false and inaccurate"**: AP, "CIA Gave Millions for Research," *Decatur Herald*, www.newspapers.com/image/77534065/.

333 **experimented with knockout drugs on advanced cancer patients**: U.S. Senate, Subcommittee on Health and Scientific Research, "Human Drug Testing by the CIA, 1977," Hearings, September 20 and 21, 1977, 86, babel.hathitrust.org/cgi/pt?id=mdp .39015013739365&view=1up&seq=90.

333 **a "perfect concussion"**: Select Committee on Intelligence, Project MKULTRA, The CIA's Program of Research in Behavioral Modification, 1977.

333 **"carefully controlled impacts deliberately delivered"**: "Non-penetrating Impact as an Agent for Personnel Incapacitation," January 31, 1972, MKULTRA documents, Black Vault, documents2.theblackvault.com/documents/cia/behavioral/C00022037 .pdf.

333 **produce a "calibrated blackjack"**: "Non-penetrating Impact as an Agent for Personnel Incapacitation," 3.

334 **"It is felt that the ⬜ proposal"**: Memorandum for ⬜, "Animal Programs," December 19, 1967, MKULTRA documents, Black Vault, documents2.theblackvault .com/documents/cia/behavioral/C00021906.pdf.

334 **"This project which has also been underway"**: Memorandum for ⬜, May 27, 1965, MKULTRA documents, Black Vault, documents2.theblackvault.com/documents/cia /behavioral/C00021864.pdf.

335 **"We are negotiating with a contractor"**: Memorandum for ⬜, May 27, 1965.

335 *What kind of animals?*: Neither "cold-blooded" nor "warm-blooded" fit the space. The CIA did however pay a contractor to investigate the use of electrical brain stimulation on unspecified cold-blooded animals: "Some of the uses proposed for these particular animals," according to the MKULTRA file for Subproject 142, "would involve possible delivery systems for BW/CW agents or for direct executive action type operations as distinguished from eavesdropping application of ⬜." See "Project MKULTRA, Subproject No. 142," May 22, 1962, archive.org/details/DOC_0000017402/page/n18; also John Marks, *The Search for the "Manchurian Candidate"* (New York: W. W. Norton, 1979), 210.

335 **"shock-induced fighting response"**: "Studies of Screening of Chemical Compounds for Detection of Behavioral Effects," March 4, 1968, MKULTRA, documents2.theblackvault .com/documents/cia/behavioral/C00021828.pdf.

May 6, 2019, Monday

337 **the CIA and the Air Force secretly reclassified:** Matthew Aid, "Declassification in Reverse," February 21, 2006, National Security Archive, nsarchive2.gwu.edu/NSAEBB /NSAEBB179/, and "Secret Agreement Reveals Covert Program to Hide Reclassification from Public," April 11, 2006, National Security Archive, nsarchive2.gwu.edu/news /20060411/index.htm.

337 **"As a group we applaud":** www.governmentattic.org/6docs/CIA-comments_1994-2005u .pdf.

May 7, 2019, Tuesday

340 **"Make economy scream":** Peter Kornbluh, *The Pinochet File* (New York: The New Press, 2016).

340 **"throw them right back on their haunches":** Henry Cabot Lodge to C. D. Jackson, March 9, 1953, Lodge Papers II, Massachusetts Historical Society.

340 **"press releases, movies, statements of denunciation":** Henry Cabot Lodge to C. D. Jackson, March 28, 1953, Lodge Papers II, Massachusetts Historical Society.

340 **"It is of the utmost importance for us to counter":** Henry Cabot Lodge to C. D. Jackson, March 12, 1953, Lodge Papers II, Massachusetts Historical Society.

341 **"review evidence on Commie 'brain-washing' activities":** Staff Meeting, "Brain-Washing," March 11, 1953, Psychological Strategy Board Central Files, box 29, PSB 702.5, Eisenhower Library.

341 **"pitched in an extremely low key":** Meeting minutes, "State Department Exploitation of Communist BW Charges," July 6, 1953, Psychological Strategy Board Central Files, box 29, PSB 702.5, Eisenhower Library.

341 **including *The New York Times*'s Arthur Krock:** Arthur Krock, "Allen W. Dulles Describes 'Warfare for the Brain,'" NYT, April 16, 1953.

341 **"the perversion of the minds of selected individuals":** Allen Dulles, "Brain Warfare," April 10, 1953, CREST, https://www.cia.gov/library/readingroom/docs/CIA-RDP80R0 1731R001700030015-9.pdf.

341 **"The North Korean radio resumed":** "Reds Resume 'Germ War,'" NYT, March 21, 1953

342 **"It couldn't be just 'hate America'":** C. D. Jackson to Eisenhower, April 21, 1953, Jackson Papers, box 50, Eisenhower Library.

342 **The returning POWs were carefully vetted:** Robert H. Beezer, "Trip Report," May 1, 1953–May 5, 1953, PSB 383.6, PSB Central Files, box 26, Eisenhower Library.

342 **the hard-core collaborators, thought to be security risks:** Robert T. Stevens to Secretary of Defense, "Report of Special Ad Hoc Committee for Korean Captured U.S. Personnel," June 10, 1953, file PSB 383.6, PSB Central Files, box 26, Eisenhower Library.

343 **surrounded by military police with machine guns:** Memorandum for the Record, Horace Craig, "Returned POWs at Valley Forge General Hospital," May 12, 1953, C. D. Jackson file, Lodge Papers II, Massachusetts Historical Society.

343 **"Communist Dupes Destined for High Level Psychiatric":** Robert H. Beezer, "Trip Report."

343 **"considered irreclaimable and constituting security risks":** Stevens to Secretary of Defense, "Report of Special Ad Hoc Committee for Korean Captured U.S. Personnel."

343 **"Among this group there was no evidence":** Henry H. Rogers et al., to Assistant Chief of Staff, G-1, "Report of Special Ad Hoc Committee for Korean Captured U.S. Personnel," May 8, 1953, file PSB 383.6, PSB Central Files, box 26, Eisenhower Library.

344 **"National Operations Plan":** Operations Coordinating Board, "National Operations Plan to Exploit Communist Bacteriological Warfare Hoax, Mistreatment of Prisoners of War, and Other Atrocities Perpetrated by Communist Forces during the Korean War," October 14, 1953, PSB 383.6 Prisoners of War, PSB Central Files series, box 26, Eisenhower Library.

344 **hoping to put out a documentary film:** "Comments on Preparing a BW Documentary Film," undated, PSB 729.2 Biological Warfare Propaganda, PSB Central Files, box 29, Eisenhower Library.

344 **"mind-murder," or "menticide":** Psychological Strategy Board, "Proposal," undated, PSB 702.5, PSB Central Files, box 29, Eisenhower Library.

344 **"a major 'quickie' paper-back book":** Ralph Block to Charles R. Norberg, "Requirements for Projected Coordinated Campaign on Communist Treatment of UNC POWs," October 7, 1953, PSB 383.6 Prisoners of War, PSB Central Files series, box 26, Eisenhower Library.

344 **"Every man has his breaking point":** See the clip in Phil Tinline, *Every Man Has His Breaking Point*, documentary, at 2:23, Hidden Persuaders, Birkbeck College, www.bbk.ac.uk/hiddenpersuaders/documentaries/every-man-breaking-point-reagan-brainwashing-movies/.

344 **"It is not a pretty story":** Charles W. Mayo, "The Role of Forced Confessions in the Communist 'Germ Warfare' Campaign," *Department of State Bulletin*, November 9, 1953; "Torture Methods in Korea Detailed," NYT, October 27, 1953.

344 **"The statement was a good example":** Lodge to C. D. Jackson, October 27, 1953, PSB 729.2, PSB Central Files, box 29, Eisenhower Library.

345 **"an insidiously planned conspiracy":** Philip J. Corso, "Chinese Communist Aggression, Barbarism and Criminal Activities," September 11, 1953, File PSB 383.6, PSB Central Files, box 26, Eisenhower Library.

345 **"extra-terrestrial biological entities":** John Hockenberry, interview of Philip Corso, *Dateline*, June 24, 1997. See also Corso's bestseller, *The Day After Roswell* (New York: Pocket Books, 1997).

345 **writer of United Nations speeches:** *Princeton Alumni Weekly*, "Wallace Irwin, Jr. 40' *48," March 17, 2010, paw.princeton.edu/memorial/wallace-irwin-jr-'40-48.

May 8, 2019, Wednesday

347 **"Improvement in anthrax strains":** Herbert Friedlander, Memorandum for Record, "Status of Anthrax," RG 341 entry NM-15 199, 1952, box 4, NA.

347 **"A new world's record for hand-launched":** "Model Glider, Hand-Launched by Boy, 16, Sets New Record of 2 Minutes 58 Seconds," NYT, October 31, 1938, 17.

348 **served as a bomber navigator in the war:** "With Our Fighters," *Brooklyn Daily Eagle*, March 15, 1944, www.newspapers.com/image/52692455/.

348 **"research into those offensive aspects":** Jonathan B. Tucker, "A Farewell to Germs: The U.S. Renunciation of Biological and Toxin Warfare, 1969–70," *International Security* 27, no. 1 (Summer 2002).

348 **Mrs. Crymble had provided the FBI:** "The Movement for a New Society," FBI file 62-116464, JFK release, www.archives.gov/files/research/jfk/releases/docid-32989700.pdf

349 **A military police vehicle ran over the tree:** Patrick Gilbert, "14 Protesters Arrested at Edgewood Arsenal," *Evening Sun*, Baltimore, July 10, 1970, www.newspapers.com/image/372038783/.

350 **arrested at Edgewood Arsenal:** Edna Goldberg, "2 Arrested in Edgewood Protest," *Baltimore Sun*, July 14, 1970, www.newspapers.com/image/377304543/.

350 **began destroying its biological weapons stockpile:** Tucker, "A Farewell to Germs."

350 **"harvested by Air Force personnel":** Jim Knipp, "'Buried Treasure' at Rocky Mountain Arsenal," 1998 CPEO Military List Archive, www.cpeo.org/lists/military/1998/msg00302.html. See also "TX Anticrop Agent & Project 112," Rocky Mountain Arsenal Archive, rockymountainarsenalarchive.wordpress.com/category/project-112/.

350 **"Nixon Says Ft. Detrick to Be Top Cancer":** *Baltimore Sun*, October 18, 1971, www.newspapers.com/image/372096432.

350 **"Where we have previously had scientists":** Samuel Lopez, "Echoes from the Past: A

New Institution for Cancer Research is Born," NCI at Frederick, May 1, 2019, ncifrederick.cancer.gov/about/theposter/content/echoes-past-new-institution-cancer-research-born.

May 9, 2019, Thursday

352 **"hit back" propaganda poster:** To Chief, Western Hemisphere Division, from Chief of Station, Guatemala, "ESSENCE Activities," January 13, 1954, PBSUCCESS files, CREST, https://www.cia.gov/library/readingroom/docs/DOC_0000923950.pdf.

352 **"Supply has 8 new government sterile 22 cal":** TO SLINC, ATTN: CADICK, January 10, 1954, CREST, https://www.cia.gov/library/readingroom/docs/DOC_0000136397.pdf.

352 **about certain teams: "K teams":** "Contact Report," January 13, 1954, CREST, https://www.cia.gov/library/readingroom/docs/DOC_0000135889.pdf.

353 **Allen Dulles said, "⬚⬚⬚":** Deputies' meeting, January 22, 1954, CREST, https://www.cia.gov/library/readingroom/docs/CIA-RDP80B01676R002300150056-2.pdf.

353 **Guatemala's press office issued its five-thousand-word:** Jules Dubois, "Guatemala Cabinet Charges Plot to Overthrow President," *Chicago Tribune*, January 30, 1954, www.newspapers.com/image/371221412/.

353 **"government of the north":** "Guatemala Says Neighbors and U.S. Plot an Invasion," NYT, January 30, 1954; AP, "Charge Made by Guatemala," *Florence Morning News*, Florence, S.C., January 30, 1954, www.newspapers.com/image/67145448/.

353 **"Super saboteurs and assassins":** Blanche Wiesen Cook, *The Declassified Eisenhower* (New York: Penguin, 1984), 249–50.

353 **a United Fruit employee named Colonel Studer:** Reuters, "Plot to Unseat Arbenz Alleged," *Semi-Weekly Spokesman Review*, Spokane, Wash., January 30, 1954, www.newspapers.com/image/568406871/;

353 **"ridiculous and untrue":** AP, "U.S. Charged with Approving Plot to Overthrow Regime in Guatemala," *Newport Daily News*, January 29, 1954, www.newspapers.com/image/59279662/; "U.S. Accused by Guatemala," *Des Moines Register*, January 30, 1954, www.newspapers.com/image/127799288/; Cook, *Declassified Eisenhower*, 250–51. Cook identifies Bedell Smith as the author of the press release denying the charges.

353 **"Those people are just seeing monkeys":** "Plot Link to U.S.," *Kansas City Times*, January 30, 1954, www.newspapers.com/image/51144531/.

353 **"White paper has effectively exposed":** Cable to Director from Lincoln, January 30, 1954, CREST, https://www.cia.gov/library/readingroom/docs/DOC_0000923907.pdf.

354 **"increasingly mendacious propaganda campaign":** AP, "U.S Denies Charges, Claims Counter-Plot by Guatemala," *Democrat and Chronicle*, Rochester, N.Y., January 31, 1954, www.newspapers.com/image/135522822/.

354 **"a Communist inspired provocation":** Cable from J. C. King, February 9, 1954, CREST, https://www.cia.gov/library/readingroom/docs/DOC_0000136855.pdf.

354 **"fabrications and forgeries":** Memorandum for CWH, "Counter-Attack Against Further Guatemalan Revelations of CIA Plans Against Guatemala," February 10, 1954, https://www.cia.gov/library/readingroom/docs/DOC_0000913557.pdf.

354 **two "assassination specialists":** "Conference Held at Lincoln 10 A.M. 13 February 1954," CREST, https://www.cia.gov/library/readingroom/docs/DOC_0000135886.pdf. See also Gerald K. Haines, "CIA and Guatemala Assassination Proposals 1952–1954," June 1995, CREST, https://www.cia.gov/library/readingroom/docs/DOC_0000135796.pdf; and Kate Doyle and Peter Kornbluh, eds., "CIA and Assassinations: The Guatemala 1954 Documents," National Security Archive, nsarchive2.gwu.edu/NSAEBB/NSAEBB4/.

355 **"assault on the freedom and independence of the people":** AP, "U.S. Blamed by Russia for Guatemalan Revolt," *Dayton Daily News*, June 20, 1954, www.newspapers.com/image/402205121/.

355 **A P-47 plane crashed in Mexico:** AP, "Guatemala Reported Readying 'Taxi Army' to Battle Invaders," *Morning News*, Wilmington, Del., June 21, 1954, www.newspapers.com

/image/155528101/; and AP, "Guatemalan Cease-Fire Voted in UN," *Miami News*, June 21, 1954, www.newspapers.com/image/298678762/.

355 **"hotly" denied the charges:** AP, "Guatemalan Cease-Fire Voted in UN."

355 **"The situation," Lodge said, "does not involve":** AP, "Guatemalan Rebels Claim Gains; Russia Demands Action by U.N.," *Burlington Free Press*, Burlington, Vt., June 21, 1954, www.newspapers.com/image/199582597/.

May 13, 2019, Monday

356 **"To report this book":** Annie Jacobsen, *Operation Paperclip: The Secret Intelligence Program that Brought Nazi Scientists to America* (New York: Little, Brown, 2014).

357 **"That monkey survived the flight":** Mae Mills Link, "Space Medicine in Project Mercury," 1965, history.nasa.gov/SP-4003/toc.htm.

357 **Four of five monkeys:** AP, Frank Carey, "Mice, Monkeys Survive Rocket Ride into Space," *Evening Independent*, Massilon, Ohio, March 19, 1952, www.newspapers.com /image/11881357/.

357 **bred potato beetles and dropped them from airplanes:** Erhard Geissler, Lajos G. Gazsó, and Ernst Buder, *Conversion of Former BTW Facilities* (New York: Springer, 2012); Ute Deichmann, *Biologists Under Hitler* (Cambridge, Mass.: Harvard University Press, 1996); and Jeffrey Lockwood, *Six-Legged Soldiers* (New York: Oxford University Press, 2009).

358 **"When membranes are hurt":** Jacobsen, *Operation Paperclip*.

358 **unspecified "special matter":** Jacobsen, *Operation Paperclip*.

358 **"The Americans are supplying to German bacteriologists":** "U.S. Department of State, "The Bacteriological Warfare Campaign," Appendix B to "The Soviet Hate America Campaign," Soviet Affairs Note No. 140, November 28, 1952, 9–10. Held at U.S. Army Heritage and Education Center, Carlisle Barracks, Pennsylvania, HM263 .S68 1952, 3.

358 **"large amounts of potato bugs":** UP, "German Reds See Potato Bug War," May 26, 1950, www.newspapers.com/image/19050358/; and UP, "Eisler Makes 'Em Bug-Eyed," *New York Daily News*, May 26, 1950, www.newspapers.com/image/449973641/.

358 **This was a new twist:** "Difficulty Not Expected," *Times*, London, May 26, 1950, 6, www .thetimes.co.uk/archive/article/1950-05-26/6/2.html.

358 **"Potato bugs were found":** AP, "Charges West Has Sprayed E. Reich with Potato Bugs," *Jacksonville Journal*, May 26, 1950, www.newspapers.com/image/48433576/?terms =%22potato+bug%22+germany.

358 **"new crime of the Americans":** AP, "Potato Bug Plots Angers Germans, Russians Claim," *Albuquerque Journal*, May 29, 1950, www.newspapers.com/image/158223190/.

359 **"Today they are dropping":** Drew Middleton, "Communists Call for West's Ouster From All Germany," NYT, May 28, 1950.

359 **With it was a report by an East German commission:** AP, "Soviets Claim U.S. Drops 'Potato Bugs,'" *Ogden Standard-Examiner*, Ogden, Utah, July 2, 1950, www.newspapers .com/image/31021120/.

359 **"Russian Note Insists U.S. Hurled Spud Bugs":** AP, *Rochester Democrat and Chronicle*, Rochester, N.Y., July 2, 1950, www.newspapers.com/image/136010658/.

359 **"In the present world situation":** UP, "Soviet Potato Bug Case Gets Strong Case of Diplomatic DDT," *Waco News-Tribune*, Waco, Texas, July 7, 1950, www.newspapers.com /image/47932175/.

359 **"an act of war and no longer cold war":** Donald J. Gonzales, "Believe Red's Potato Bug Story Cloaks Sinister Plot," *Sandusky Register*, July 7, 1950, www.newspapers.com/image /4945781/.

359 **"The embassy," the statement said, "ventures to suggest":** UP, "No Bugs on Payroll, U.S. Assures Czechs," *Daily News*, N.Y., July 7, 1950, www.newspapers.com/image/450141195/; Ellis Briggs, *Farewell to Foggy Bottom: The Recollections of a Career Diplomat* (Philadelphia: McKay, 1964).

May 16, 2019, Thursday

362 **As Bruce Cumings wrote years ago:** "By 1952 just about everything in northern and central Korea was completely leveled. What was left of the population lived in caves." Bruce Cumings, *North Korea: Another Country* (New York: New Press, 2011), 27.

363 **"I doubt that ever in the history of the world":** "Relief Handicaps in Korea Stressed," NYT, May 22, 1951.

364 **now classified as one of the hantaviruses:** Colleen B. Jonsson et al., "A Global Perspective on Hantavirus Ecology, Epidemiology, and Disease," *Clinical Microbiology Reviews* (April 2010), www.ncbi.nlm.nih.gov/pmc/articles/PMC2863364/.

364 **"The State Department used ridicule in combatting":** "Briefing, 7 March 1952: Propaganda Campaign in Korea—BW," CIA Office of Current Intelligence, archive.org/details /07March1952PropagandaCampaigninKoreaBW.

364 **"short-range crash training":** James E. Totten, "Presentation to the Students and Faculty of the Air War College on Biological and Chemical Warfare," November 16, 1951, Air Force Historical Research Agency, 10. There are many mentions of the crash training program in the AFOAT BW-CW papers, e.g., Burdsall Miller, "Indoctrination of New Officers Assigned to the Program," August 9, 1952, AFOAT BW-CW, RG 341, entry NM-15 199, box 4, NA.

365 **encephalitis of "extreme virulence":** Joseph Needham et al., "Report of the International Scientific Commission Concerning Bacterial Warfare in Korea and China," 1952, 482.

366 **"We had already dispatched men (including myself)":** Wu Zhili, "The Bacteriological War of 1952 Is a False Alarm," Wilson Center, digitalarchive.wilsoncenter.org/document/123080.

366 **The insects were real:** One Suede intercept says: "A North Korean unit on coastal security in eastern Korea reported to Naval Defense Headquarters near Wonsan on 2 March that although on the 28th insects were again dropped at Paekyang, Sinpung, and Innam, 'no one has been infected yet.'" Suede report, March 7, 1952, CREST, https://www.cia.gov /library/readingroom/docs/1952-03-07a.pdf.

367 **"pushed through and approved":** The Plan Takeoff correspondence and drafts are currently in box 31, file 387.4, Psychological Strategy Board Files, Harry Truman Library. File 387.4 has several folders, some about Takeoff and some about a related plan, Hummer. See the finding aid for the Psychological Strategy Board files: www.trumanlibrary.gov /library/truman-papers/harry-s-truman-papers-staff-member-and-office-files-psychological -strategy.

368 **"Exploitation of Psychological Possibilities of Covertly-Claimed Radiological":** 384.7 Korea—File #2 [1 of 2], Psychological Strategy Board Files, box 31, Truman Library.

369 **"Atomic Death Belt Urged for Korea":** NYT, April 17, 1951.

May 18, 2019, Saturday

371 **Frank Wisner had the first of several breakdowns:** The stages of Wisner's collapse are chronicled in three classic works: Thomas Powers, *The Man Who Kept the Secrets: Richard Helms and the CIA* (New York: Pocket Books, 1979); Burton Hersh, *The Old Boys*, and Evan Thomas, *The Very Best Men.*

371 **"That's when he first went nuts":** Christopher Simpson, *Blowback*, quoting from an interview with Braden.

371 **"oriental fulminating hepatitis":** Thomas, *The Very Best Men*, ch. 10, n17. In a January 1957 letter to Joe Alsop Wisner called his disease "fulminating viral hepatitis."

371 **two high-level doctors:** Hersh, *The Old Boys*, ch. 21.

371 **Dr. Irving Brick:** Gilbert A. Lewthwaite, "Reagan to Undergo Minor Operation for Removal of Polyp," *Baltimore Sun*, July 11, 1985, www.newspapers.com/image/377778129/.

371 **Dr. Joseph E. Smadel:** Joseph E. Smadel, "Epidemic Hemorrhagic Fever," *American Journal of Public Health* 43 (October 1953), ajph.aphapublications.org/doi/pdf/10.2105

/AJPH.43.10.1327. Smadel was also an expert on plague, tsutsugamushi disease, and Rocky Mountain spotted fever.

371 **"the rather unusual character":** Quoted in Hersh, *The Old Boys*, ch. 21.

372 **on orders from President Eisenhower:** Tim Weiner, *Legacy of Ashes* (New York: Doubleday, 2007) 170.

372 **hectoring his secretary:** Thomas, *The Very Best Men*.

372 **"Frank Wisner has had a very hard time":** Allen Dulles to William Jackson, December 7, 1958, CREST, https://www.cia.gov/library/readingroom/docs/DOC_0000481706.pdf.

372 **"In view of his protracted illness":** Allen Dulles, "Announcement of Assignments to Key Positions," December 5, 1958, CREST, https://www.cia.gov/library/readingroom/docs/CIA-RDP33-02415A000400120004-9.pdf.

372 **several differently redacted versions:** Allen Dulles, "Announcement of Assignments," CREST, https://www.cia.gov/library/readingroom/docs/CIA-RDP61-00549R0002000 30031-7.pdf, https://www.cia.gov/library/readingroom/docs/CIA-RDP83-00764R000 600050027-3.pdf, and https://www.cia.gov/library/readingroom/docs/CIA-RDP83-00764 R000600040032-8.pdf.

373 **"Persons having the deepest and most legitimate insights":** Frank Wisner, "On 'The Craft of Intelligence,' " *Studies in Intelligence*, CREST, https://www.cia.gov/library/readingroom /docs/CIA-RDP84-00161R000100170006-6.pdf.

373 **a bad book with a fraudulent premise:** Frank Wisner to Thomas Braden, March 9, 1965, Frank Wisner papers, University of Virginia Library.

374 **"practiced hands in the underworld crimes":** James E. Jackson, "One Head Less," *New Times*, November 7, 1965, CREST https://www.cia.gov/library/readingroom/docs/CIA -RDP75-00001R000200520011-7.pdf.

374 **"There has passed the greatest":** "Frank G. Wisner," *Oceanside Blade-Tribune*, November 3, 1965, CREST, https://www.cia.gov/library/readingroom/docs/CIA-RDP75-00001R000 200520016-2.pdf.

Index

Girl Talk

CASSIDY STORM